Keep ENL 2017

THE ENGLISH TEACHER'S HANDBOOK

THE ENGLISH TEACHER'S HANDBOOK

■

Ideas and Resources for Teaching English

Stephen N. Judy
MICHIGAN STATE UNIVERSITY

Susan J. Judy
CENTRAL MICHIGAN UNIVERSITY

WINTHROP PUBLISHERS, INC. ■ CAMBRIDGE, MASSACHUSETTS

Library of Congress Cataloging in Publication Data

Judy, Stephen N
The English teacher's handbook.

Bibliography: p. 369
Includes index.
1. English philology—Study and teaching.
I. Judy, Susan J., joint author. II. Title.
PE65.J8 807 78–27365
ISBN 0-87626-243-4
ISBN 0-87626-242-6 pbk.

Cover, illustrations, and text design by Susan Marsh

17 Dunster Street, Cambridge, Massachusetts 02138

 Printed in the United States of America.

10 9 8 7 6 5 4 3 2 1

For Stephen and Emily
and their English teachers

CONTENTS

SECTION B
TEACHING COMPOSITION

SECTION C
LANGUAGE STUDY

PREFACE

Many of the materials in this book have their origin in a publication called *The Inkwell,* a monthly newsletter for English teachers, which we published over a two-year period. We had sensed in our university classes and at professional meetings a strong interest in practical, how-to-do-it materials for teachers, and found in *The Inkwell* a way of getting teaching ideas into the hands of a number of English and language arts teachers. At the suggestion of our friends and readers, however, we decided to condense and reorganize the materials into the present book form.

The reader will note that several of the sections of the book were originally drafted (for use in *The Inkwell*) by other authors. For their willingness to let us use their work in this book we want to thank Betsy B. Kaufman (Queens College), Pamela Waterbury (Washington, D.C.), Maggie Parish (University of North Carolina at Wilmington), and Ted Hipple (University of Florida). Their work has been blended with our own, however, and we take all responsibility for the accuracy and validity of the ideas in the book. We also wish to thank the people who read and critiqued early drafts of the manuscript for their careful, thoughtful, and detailed commentary: Carol Kuykendall (Houston Public Schools), Sy Yesner (Minneapolis Public Schools), Dan Kirby (University of Georgia), Patrick Courts (State University of New York at Fredonia), and Charles R. Kline, Jr. (University of Texas). In addition, we want to acknowledge that a great many of the ideas in the book were gleaned from our students at Northwestern University, Michigan State University, Central Michigan University, and the University of British Columbia, and from participants in our workshops at meetings and conferences in many states.

Finally, we want to give special thanks to Paul O'Connell, John Covell, and the staff at Winthrop Publishers, first, for their enthusiasm for the project from the very beginning, and second, for the dispatch and skill with which they have managed our manuscript.

THE ENGLISH TEACHER'S HANDBOOK

INTRODUCTION

Contemporary English Teaching: Some Basic Premises

We teach in dramatic, exciting, and controversial times. The past two decades have seen extraordinary changes in the schools and in the teaching of English. You merely need to think back to as recently as the 1960s, to your own schooling, perhaps, or to your early years of teaching to recall when:

- a survey revealed that *Silas Marner* was required reading in 75 percent of this nation's high schools;
- paperback books were a novelty in English classes, and the "important" question being asked by administrators was, "Will paperbacks hold up as well as hardbound books in the classroom?"
- *Catcher in the Rye* was thought a dirty book;
- the only electives in the English program were "supplementary" courses like *Journalism* or *Yearbook,* and the only "choice" offered to students was whether they wanted to enter the college preparatory or the business track; and
- the movies shown in English classes were grainy, black-and-white affairs with titles like *Using Lively Adverbs* or *The Life and Writing of Stephen Vincent Benét.*

So things have changed—and for the better. The use of media, paperback books, elective courses and thematic units, and alternative kinds of language study have made English classes vastly more interesting and productive than they were two decades ago. "English," which used to mean little more than grammar, the history of literature, and an occasional five-hundred-word theme, has burst out of its traditional boundaries, so that today young people read contemporary literature as well as classic, compose in speech and media as well as writing, and become immersed in the study of language in society rather than arranging words in artificially constructed sentence diagrams.

With these changes have evolved new roles for teachers. English teaching was once a matter of simply following the course outline or textbook in sequences that were obvious, if dull: "The sentence" always followed "parts of speech"; "organizing a composition" followed "paragraphs"; early-twentieth-century "modern" literature followed "realism and naturalism." Teaching methodology consisted largely of something called "lecture-discussion," with the teacher talking most of the time, either telling the students what they were supposed to know or quizzing them on whether they knew it. At regular intervals, the good teacher stuffed 150 compositions into a briefcase or shopping bag and trundled home to spend weekends or evenings penciling in critical comments, most of which were ignored by the students.

Now English teachers talk less, and their students talk more. The rows of seats have been broken down for many class activities, and young people talk as much to each other as to the teacher. Reading and writing programs are frequently individualized, so that literary eras no longer follow one another in strict chronology, and original writing flows from the students' experiences rather than from the dictates of the composition book. Teachers used to be preachers; now they are good listeners, too, hearing students' concerns, their ideas, their insights.

This kind of teaching is unquestionably exciting. It allows a teacher constantly to take a fresh approach with his or her courses—teaching new literature and new media, looking for alternate directions in composition, finding out fascinating things about students.

But contemporary English teaching is also terribly demanding, for it creates a drain on material resources, on the teacher's energy, originality, and creativity. While English teachers once could anticipate teaching the same courses and books over and over again (stories about teachers who had memorized the text are no exaggeration), today's teacher is constantly reading new texts, surveying fresh paperbacks, and planning original courses and units.

Yet along with the breadth of English—which, we think, makes it an exciting, vibrant subject to teach—comes what seems the singular intent of school systems to create unteachable settings for English teachers. For example, despite the fact that the student load assigned to teachers has been under attack for fifty years, the size of English teachers' classes has not diminished at all in this century; in economically troubled times, it has actually increased. English/language arts teachers regularly have to face 150 or more students, five days a week, 180 days a year. ("Why don't you teach more writing?" asks the same critical administrator who will, next September, calmly add two students to the load of every English teacher because of "fiscal constraints" that do not allow him to replace a retiring teacher.)

The schools cling to a number of, at best, cumbersome and, at worst, obsolete structures and traditions that make teaching difficult: bell schedules; alphabet grades; the bureaucracy of tardy slips, admits, attendance dossiers, field trip permissions; and PA announcements in the middle of a class period. In many schools, "innovative" or creative teaching is viewed with suspicion. Janitors complain that the movable desks aren't kept in straight rows (just as if they were bolted down); principals observe, "All this self-expression is well and good, but just plain composition would suffice"; parents puzzle over the new ways and, seeking safety, lament the disappearance of what they recall as "the good old days."

In such a setting, it becomes easy for teachers literally to burn out. After a brief fling with contemporary teaching techniques, many retreat in the direction of the tradition—to the grammar book or anthology—"spicing up" their lessons with an occasional film or creative writing assignment, but essentially teaching from a conservative base. Alternatively, they quit; they go back to school for a law or business degree. Or they stay in the profession and simply become pessimists, unhappy with their teaching, their students, and themselves.

Yet a great many English teachers not only survive, but thrive, despite the difficult settings and complex times in which they find themselves. One sees and hears them at teacher conventions, faculty meetings, PTA sessions. We think they represent a majority of English teachers in this day and age. Without them, contemporary English would disappear from the schools.

It is in support of these teachers that this book has been prepared. Whether you are an undergraduate in a methods course getting ready for your first formal teaching assignment or someone who has been out in the field for a decade or two, we feel you need all the help you can get. Faced with an enormous teaching load, conflicting demands, yet still wanting to do new and interesting things in your classes, you need ideas and resources to supplement your own. *The English Teacher's Handbook* supplies them. Its principal function is to serve as an idea book, to offer suggestions to add to your lessons.

A great many of the teaching ideas presented here grow directly from our own teaching experiences, which include urban and suburban schools; private and public schools; and preschool, elementary, middle-school, junior-high, senior-high, and college students. Other ideas have been gleaned from experienced teachers who have participated in our university classes and workshops at professional meetings. The ideas are thus "classroom tested," and we feel confident that you will find them useful and practical.

At the same time, we feel it important to enter two cautionary notes:

1. The teaching ideas presented here are meant to be catalysts to your own thinking, not surefire gimmicks. Adapt them to your needs, to your students, to your classes. Don't simply pull an idea from page 175 or 222 and expect it to work without modification. Further, don't pick ideas just because they are unusual or because they have shock value. Students can be tricked, manipulated, and "gimmicked" only so many times before the novelty wears off.

2. Don't use this book as a "cookbook." The ideas in the book are not "recipes," and the book is intended to supplement your course planning, not to replace it. Don't make your teaching a smorgasbord of ideas picked at random from here and there. Thus, we begin the book with an intensive section on course planning, and we urge you to use the book to plan the broad dimensions of your course and curriculum before selecting individual activities.

We have also been highly selective in choosing the ideas presented here. We don't have much respect for so-called eclectic teaching, which praises any idea that "seems to work" without regard for pedagogical or philosophical consistency. The ideas we recommend show internal consistency; we have not included techniques that superficially seem to work but lack a sound rationale. Thus, we won't present ideas on "101 Novel Approaches to the Book Report!" (we think that "genre" is not a particularly effective way of helping students enjoy literature), but we will explain *many* ways of helping students extend their responses to literature in writing (and speaking and media work). We won't show you ways of "Making Grammar Fun!" (we think such techniques frequently sugarcoat the teaching of terminology that doesn't help students write or speak better anyway), but we will show you many ways of exploring language use and misuse in school and society, including an exploration of contemporary approaches to teaching English syntax. We will not present techniques on teaching "The Five-Paragraph Theme" (which, as someone remarked, is a "pedagogical device," not an art form), but we will suggest dozens of ways of engaging students in writing well-organized expository prose.

Underlying all of our discussions is the belief that *teachers* are at the heart of solving classroom teaching problems. We do not believe that change can be imposed from the outside. Growth in teaching evolves from within, from teachers who are willing to explore and experiment with new ideas and techniques and possibilities. *The English Teacher's Handbook* is designed to aid and enrich that kind of teaching.

Some Basic Premises

We want to describe our basic beliefs, premises, and postulates about teaching contemporary English. This is a credo of sorts, but certainly not dogma, for English teaching is too unsettled a field for anyone—textbook author or teacher—to offer inflexible fiats about what *should* or *must* happen in English classrooms. In presenting our premises, however, we want to show you some of the principles upon which teaching ideas for later sections were based. Ideas or strategies selected for the book had to be consistent with and enhance these seven basic premises:

1. Reading, writing, listening, and speaking are learned by doing, not principally by studying abstractions or doing exercises. More and more it seems clear to us that English is a learn-by-doing skill, that the most important role of the teacher is not telling students about language, but getting them to use it. To this end, the *Handbook* is aimed at helping teachers develop a *language-centered classroom,* a place where students are engaged constantly in using language: using a rich variety of materials, reading and writing and speaking in many modes of discourse.

If you are a propaganda analyst, however, you will have noted the waffle words, "not principally," in our premise. We do not claim that language is learned without teacher intervention, and it seems to us that some direct discussion of language skills is important. However, decades of research into language learning demonstrate persuasively that such study must be peripheral to actual language use.

2. English/language arts classes should expose students to as many different language forms and genres as possible. In recent years there has been increasing discussion of "survival English" for career preparation, with a corresponding devaluing of any "nonessential" language forms (especially poetry). We think such an emphasis is extremely narrow and, in the long range, incapacitating to people who find themselves indoctrinated into a limited range of language skills. While we don't claim that writing poetry will get students good jobs or that learning to critique television programs will land one a job with NBC or *TV Guide,* we feel strongly that the English program should allow students to experience a variety of reading and writing forms and genres: creative writing as well as expository, popular literature as well as classic. English teachers must extend the dimensions of literacy, not restrict them.

3. Creativity is not synonymous with chaos. In the heyday of student-centered education in the 1970s, a great many people talked about the need to emphasize creativity in English. Yet many critics seemed to muddle this concept with their own vague dislike of "permissivism" and attacked contemporary English for refusing to teach "discipline"—both the discipline of language and literature and the discipline of classroom behavior. In fact, to suggest that language use is creative merely emphasizes that students must learn to assimilate their experiences and ideas and write and talk about them in original, independent, "creative" ways. Students need not, in fact, write poems to write creatively; a good piece of reportage or research can be highly creative. Similarly, creative expression, if it is to reach its audience, must be disciplined and controlled. We refuse, in short, to accept the traditional dichotomies that separate writing into creative and an unspecified opposite, conceptions that stereotype the creative person as somehow "different"—unruly, undisciplined, and otherworldly. In fact, we'll go a step further and present a related premise: *Every student in every class is creative,* which simply means that every student you ever teach has the potential to deal sensibly and imaginatively with his or her experiences through the medium of language. It is the job of the English teacher to foster that creativity.

4. *Correctness does not stifle self-expression.* We agree with those who argue that "good" English is far less important than the content of what a student reads, writes, or speaks. We also agree that the schools have spent far too much time attempting to regularize the dialects of speakers of nonstandard English. But we think it would be extreme to dismiss correctness altogether or to tell children that it "doesn't matter." It obviously *does,* and the schools cannot ignore it. If correctness is not made an end in itself, is not seen as the most important part of the learning experience, if students are not misled about the nature of correctness, and if correctness is made a natural part of writing for audiences, it need not destroy student self-expression and, in fact, can actually enhance the student's abilities to share ideas successfully.

5. *Popular literature is not incompatible with the classics; media studies are not incompatible with literary work.* Some teachers seem to fear that allowing popular materials—adolescent novels, best-sellers, TV programs—into the English class is debasing and points the way to the death of the classics. We feel that such is not the case and that arbitrary debates on the merits of different genres and forms is either harmful or pointless. The plays of William Shakespeare, for example, will survive quite nicely without the interference of English teachers claiming that thirteen-to-seventeen-year-olds "must" read them to be "properly educated." At the same time, generations of thirteen-to-seventeen-year-olds have shown that they are quite capable of enjoying Shakespearean plays when those plays are dramatized or filmed rather than locked within the pages of a textbook. A balanced English program will include classic as well as contemporary literature and will draw naturally on a wide range of forms and media.

6. *English must integrate its diverse components: literature, reading, composing, speaking, listening, film, video, grammar, semantics, and so forth.* Integrated Eng-

lish is not easy to achieve. In fact, it's simpler in many respects to isolate the parts, teaching something called "literature" on Tuesdays or Thursdays and doing "composition" on Fridays. But this fragments literacy. Although this book may seem to imply breaking down English by its division into subsections—"Literature and Reading," "Teaching Composition," "Language Study," and "Multimedia English"—we want to emphasize that such divisions are for convenience only. Within each section, we will show the ways activities can be reintegrated. In a good contemporary English class, these components will flow naturally into one another.

7. The teaching and learning of English is a natural, pleasurable, invigorating experience. We're distressed by the way English has, in some schools, become a hated or feared subject, usually because of overemphasis on correctness and traditional literature. Using language is, above all, a delightful experience, and that delight is shared equally by the babbling two-year-old, the punning nine-year-old, the jiving high-school student, and the joking adult. Reading, when not bogged down with enormous critical compendia or those annoying "comprehension questions," is an enriching experience. Writing, when freed from an obsessive concern for correctness, is a comfortable, engaging activity for most young people and adults. To capitalize on this natural pleasure in language, one need not create an English classroom that is a "circus" or reduce all language activity to fun and games. Nevertheless, "fun" is an important word and crops up frequently in our discussions, whether it be the "fun" of writing jokes and riddles or the serious fun of preparing a persuasive essay on a cause in which one believes. Two popular books, *The Joy of Cooking* and *The Joy of Sex,* were "how to" books that combined discussion of naturally pleasurable activities with techniques and resources for making that pleasure greater. Perhaps we should have titled this book *The Joy of Teaching English.*

PART ONE

Curriculum Planning and Course Design

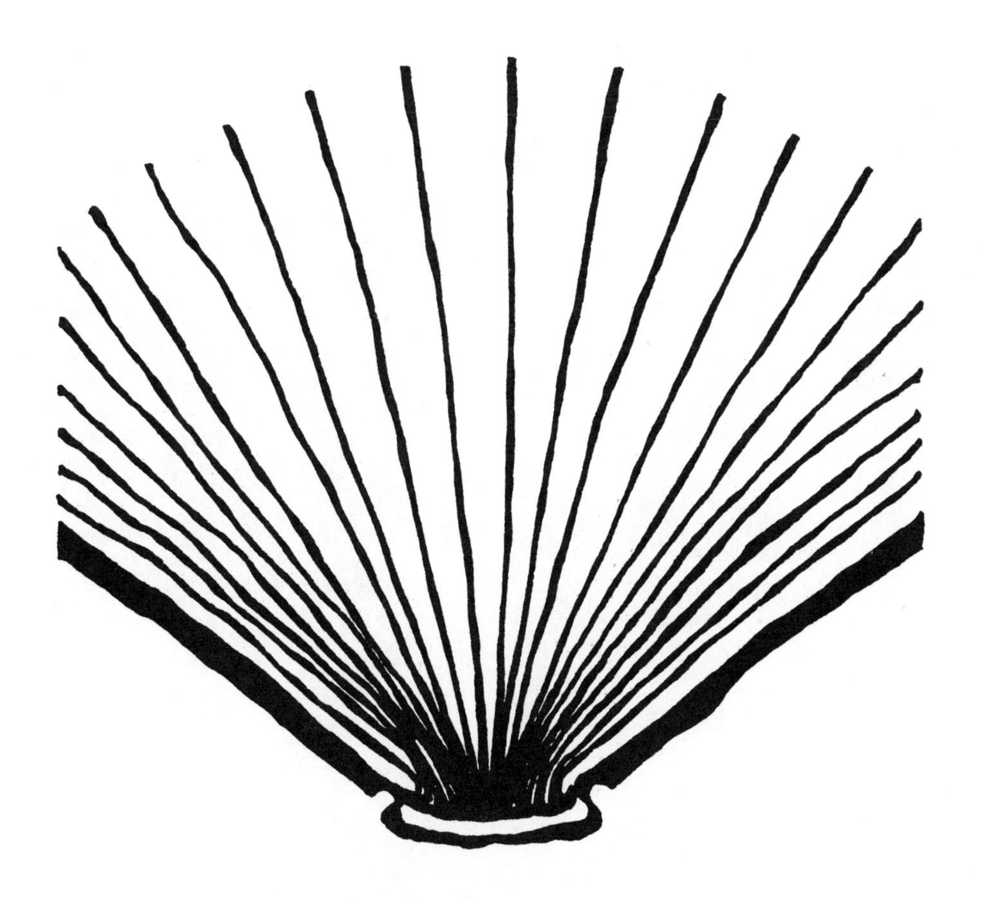

CHAPTER 1

Course Planning and Design

IT has been remarked that educators have a "course-giving mentality": As soon as they learn something new, they figure out how to give a *course* in it. Be that as it may, the course—whether a three-week minicourse, nine-week elective, ten-week quarter course, fourteen-week trimester, sixteen-week semester, year-long course, evening offering, or even a set of lessons on how to stroke a tennis ball—is the heart of our educational system. While most of us would probably prefer an arrangement that would let us teach individual children one-to-one in natural settings as Rousseau recommended—sitting on a log in the forest describing the function of insect colonies or sitting in a well-stocked study to read and talk about books—the economics of education make working with larger groups of children in places with centralized resources necessary. So the course system has evolved, with class size determined to a great extent by whatever "pupil load" the administration thinks a teacher can handle.

A lot of disadvantages are built into this system. For one, a group of twenty-five to thirty-five students is simply too large for easily managed discussion. Research shows that when teachers attempt to break down the lecture system and "discuss" with the whole class, the class is still likely to become teacher dominated. Thus, teachers spend lots of energy evolving strategies for individualized and small-group work, pushing their classroom back in the direction of Rousseau's tutorial. Similarly, teaching large clumps of children forces teachers to consider mass evaluation techniques, since one-to-one evaluation may become unduly time consuming. From this grows a reliance on tests (particularly short-answer tests) and ultimately on grading, where the teacher must assess a course-worth of performance with a single, arbitrary symbol: *A, 2.5, 95.*

Nevertheless, the course seems here to stay, and from grade five or six on, most children find themselves within a course structure. What surprises us is how little attention is paid to the planning and design of courses. Far too many courses, we think, simply "happen," evolving willy-nilly as a term or semester wears along, with structure dictated by whatever textbook or collection of paperbacks the teacher (or adoption committee) happened to select months or years ago.

School pressures also militate against thorough course development. Many school districts, for example, are unwilling to supply anything like a reasonable amount of time for planning. Thus, teachers are paid just one extra day to come in after Labor Day to plan and organize for the year or given a week of planning time in August, one frequently interrupted by staff meetings or discussions of bookroom inventory. Similarly, the daily planning period—one forty-five-minute time bloc per day—is quickly consumed by the paperwork of school life: tardy slips, admits, notes to parents, and so on. Finally, teacher course loads—for most English teachers, three or more preparations and 150 or more students—make long-range planning extraordinarily difficult. Getting through the day consumes all of one's time and energy, and it's difficult to think ahead till Monday, much less plan for events four or ten weeks down the road.

Nevertheless, we believe that few teachers want to have their teaching lives dictated by either textbook or happenstance, and we're convinced that with more advanced planning, teachers can retain control of their classes and, much more important, considerably enrich the dimensions of their instruction.

What Makes a Good Course?

Before planning a course, it is useful to think about criteria for excellence. Think back through the myriad courses you have taken in your career. (If you're an experienced teacher, think back as well to the most successful courses you've taught.) Probably the first thing that comes to mind is the instructor and his or her teaching style. As Leslie Fiedler has remarked, each of us may have just one basic course to teach: *ourselves.* Yet without ignoring that individual teaching styles and talents differ, and without implying that the flamboyant teacher (or even the most memorable) is necessarily the best, it seems clear that other factors enter in. For example:

1. A good course is on a topic that somehow intrigues or piques curiosity or meets a directly felt need in the student. In other words, the course must *interest* the student. The evolution of elective programs in the secondary schools was a great boon to students and teachers, because the rich variety of choices and materials offered increased the likelihood that a student could find a course that met his or her needs or attracted interest. Yet even in the most rigid systems, teachers have some latitude in selecting course aims and materials, so that whether you are teaching an elective course of your own choosing, or a set course like Comp. I or English Literature, you can seek out materials and issues of interest to your students (and yourself). This leads directly to a corollary:

1'. A good course is on a topic that intrigues or piques the curiosity and draws on the skills and knowledges of the teacher. In other words, it helps a lot if you're interested in the course, too. It's quite possible for a teacher to shape instruction around his or her special interests without sacrificing the needs of the students. (A list of some of the many exciting units and topical courses presently offered in American high schools is presented in figure 1.)

2. A good course offers a rich variety of materials for study. We hope that the age of the textbook is waning. During the past two decades, English teachers have learned that their courses need not be dictated by a single book. Instead of adopting class or school sets, many schools are choosing individualized paperbacks, buying a variety of inexpensive materials. Furthermore, the entrance of media studies into English opens up many more possibilities for the use of films, tapes, slides, and other audio and visual materials.

3. A good course has clear direction. Another side benefit of the elective movement was to help teachers gain a sense of direction in their teaching. When English courses were labeled simply English I, II, III, and IV, it was difficult for teachers to "get a handle" on what was to be taught. Literature, language, and composition units frequently were intermingled without rhyme or reason. The experience of electives has shown us that focused courses—whether on theme, literary genre, or even basic skills (writing, reading)—are more effective than directionless general courses.

4. A good course makes its aims and expectations clear. We've all suffered through courses where a teacher or professor never made it clear "what he wanted," where we spent more time figuring out what we were s'posed to do than actually doing it. Some critics of education have argued, further, that vagueness in courses often results from instructors who quite simply don't know what they are doing. We don't think that the writing of long lists of behavioral objectives is an answer to the problem, but a good course must make its aims and directions clear to its students. (In the process of making those aims explicit, most teachers find that their own performance improves as well.)

5. A good course has a payoff for the individual student. This is not to say that every course must be "practical" or must teach demonstrable new skills like paragraph writing or omelet cooking. Students must however, *make connections*

SOME TOPICS FOR UNITS AND ELECTIVES

Contemporary Fiction
Detectives and Sleuths
Science Fiction
Contemporary Poetry
American Studies
The Magazine
Minority Literatures:
  Black
  Chicano
  Oriental-American
  Jewish-American
  American Indian
  Eskimo
  White Ethnic Minorities
Folklore
Fantasy Literature
Adventure and Romance
Children's Literature
Media Literature
Conflict
Coming of Age
Man and Nature
Frontiers
Dreams and Visions
Bridges
Literature of Rebellion
Sports Literature
Poetry for People Who Hate Poetry
The Poet's View of Himself
French Writers
Existential Literature
Literature of East and West
Survival
Decision Making
Sin
The Quality of Mercy
Cities
Politics and Literature
The Shocker in Literature
Human Relations
Young Adults and the Law
Humor

Satire
Modern Literature
Legend/Myth/Fable
World Literature
Canadian Studies
Nonfiction
Women in Literature
Literature of Social Criticism
Literature and Film
Michigan (or other state) Literature
The Bible in Literature
War and Peace
Definitions of Humankind
The American Revolution
1930s (or 1940s or 1950s)
The American Dream
Utopias
Classical Literature for Today
Hero/Antihero
Impossible Dreams
The Psychological Novel
Speeches Heard Round the World
Perspective and Literature
Mother Russia
Philosophy in a Low Key
Might and Right
Brave New World
Alienation
Visions and Impossible Dreams
Water
Crisis in the Environment
Literature to Understand Oneself
Literature to Understand Others
Literature to Understand Literature
Comic Literature
Supernatural Literature

The Sea
Contemporary Problems
The Devil in Literature
Dreams and Nightmares
Twain and Vonnegut
Death: The Last Taboo
Gods and Goddesses
Thinking About Things (Objects)
American Ethnic Studies
Nobel Prize Literature
Hangups
Literature from Prison
Women's Lib-erature
People in Crisis
Working
A Child's World
American Nonfiction
Doublespeak
Fiction and Social Reform
Renewal Through Nature
It'll Never Happen
Technical Communication
The Language of Law
Alienation
Career Planning
Escape Routes
Growing Up in America
Hindu Religious Literature
Myths of Modern Man
Nonverbal Communication
Old Testament Literature
Shop Talk
The Mystery Thriller
Studies in Scarlet
From Pandora to Nora: Women in Literature
Rags and Riches in Literature
The Harlem Renaissance
Career Education
American Drama

Source: This list was gleaned from numerous course catalogs and from course descriptions appearing in The English Journal.

FIGURE 1

with the subject matter; they must find ways of relating it to their lives—whether the inner life of the mind or the outer life of the "real" world. A corollary, then, is that:

5′. A good course lets the student set some of his or her own goals. While few teachers want to turn course planning over to the students altogether, a good course will provide ways for the students to talk or write about their needs and evolve ways of meeting those needs through individualized learning.

6. A good course lets students know where they stand. Grading, as we have suggested, is an inadequate form of evaluation, a necessary evil, perhaps, but one that creates many more problems than it solves. Among those problems is that we often tend to forget about alternative methods of assessment. In the quest for grades, students become teacher-dependent, and despite having received an "A" or "D" on the midterm, they never seem to know just where they stand. A good course finds other ways of telling people how well they are fulfilling the assigned tasks. As a corollary, we need to add:

6′. A good course lets the teacher know where he or she stands. In designing a course you need to build in feedback sources for *yourself,* to monitor the progress of the course, to know whether to continue on a tack, alter it slightly, or come about onto a new heading altogether.

In many ways, the criteria we suggest add up to one thing:

7. A good course is organized. The instructor has a sense of direction and purpose, conveys that to the students, and systematically (and imaginatively) goes about achieving the course aims.

With those criteria in mind, we present a six-stage outline for planning units and courses. It is a scheme we have used with both experienced and inexperienced teachers, and the courses it leads to seem substantial. The stages are:

1. Describing the Student Population.
2. Setting Out Course Aims and Objectives.
3. Selecting Materials.
4. Designing Course Activities.
5. Creating Sequence and Structure.
6. Evaluation and Followup.

We'll take these in order.*

* We are indebted to Robert Beck, Swett High School, Crockett, California, for the genesis of this idea. At the 1974 Secondary Section Conference of the National Council of Teachers of English, Bob presented a workshop called "How to Create a World Famous Elective" based on a similar process. With his permission we have adapted the scheme for use in our own classes and workshops.

DESCRIBING THE STUDENT POPULATION

Whenever you begin a new course you are facing a group of unknowns—young people you've probably never met or spoken to—whose interests, concerns, and abilities are largely a mystery. A good deal of misdirection in teaching results from the fact that the teacher never takes time to think or find out about the students sitting in those seats.

Often, describing the students you will teach must be done a priori; you must plan your course in August, and you won't meet the class until September. Nevertheless, it is important to take time to write down a description of the students you expect:

1. What ages/grades will your course include?

2. Will students be grouped, tracked, or otherwise segregated by abilities?

3. What do you know about the likes, dislikes, and interests of these kids? Do you expect bubble-gum-chewing teeny-boppers or big-time high-school sophisticates? Are your pupils newcomers to the school or veterans? Will they be sports fans, music freaks, or so engrossed in members of the opposite sex that they have no time for anything else?

4. What do you know about the reading, writing, speaking, and listening abilities and interests of these students? What kinds of writing can you expect? What do they like to read? Are they more likely to be reading *Nancy Drew* or *Gone With the Wind? Spiderman Comics* or *A Clockwork Orange?* (Be careful not to *under*estimate their reading/writing abilities. Most young people can read and write on topics of their own choice far better than teachers think.)

5. Do school records supply any information of interest? We suggest proceeding with *great* caution here, for in our experience, school records tend to be a mixed bag of information and misinformation. Standardized tests are often a poor indicator of a student's specific abilities, and grades and teacher comments seem to reflect behavior much more than they do academic achievement. Nevertheless, in learning about the students you will teach, a quick, critical review of the files might be in order. Naturally one wants to be cautious about overgeneralizing, pigeonholing, or stereotyping children before one ever meets them.

Spending time describing the population can be helpful in focusing your course, even if your description turns out to be as short as the one in figure 2, penned by a high-school teacher anticipating the students he would be teaching in an introductory high-school freshman composition course.

Of course, you will also want to revise your description of the population as soon as you meet the students. Later in this chapter we present some strategies

I expect this to be the most heterogeneous group I've ever taught. We don't group by abilities, and the students in this course will not be prescreened in any way. Thus, I expect I will have some very good writers and some young people who have never had much experience composing at all. Ditto with their reading skills, which will range all over the lot. This will be their first year at —— H.S., so they will be both intimidated and, like so many first-year students, boisterous, especially the boys. My course will define "High School English" for them, so I want it to be diverse enough to meet their needs and general enough to attract their interest. At the same time, it will be important to make certain they have the skills of English necessary to carry them through the next four years.

FIGURE 2

for learning about the specific individual needs, interests, and concerns of your students.

SETTING OUT COURSE AIMS AND OBJECTIVES

The writing of goals and objectives is described in considerably more detail in chapter 7, "Accountability and Assessment." At this point, we'll note that a good statement of objectives should answer a very simple question: *Why should anybody take this course?* In answering that question, you will be dealing with such issues as: Why will students profit from taking it? What is so important about it that someone should spend ten or twenty or forty weeks of his or her life following your outline? Objectives can be written in behavioral terms ("The students will read, write, discuss, etc. . . ."); as teacher goals ("I will attempt to . . ."); class activities (reading, writing, discussions, etc.); or essay form ("This course is designed to . . ."). One of the most difficult (and most useful) forms of objective writing is to write a letter to the students themselves, explaining what they will be doing in your class and why. With that audience in mind, your objectives will be precise and specific—you *know* that kids won't accept any gobbledygook. Of course, in many schools you will also need to incorporate school or districtwide objectives. But this gives you an opportunity to enrich those common objectives by showing precisely how they fit into the broader aims of your course.

SELECTING MATERIALS

Brainstorm for materials. This is something you *can* do in June or August and *should* do long before the students walk in the door. Although you may be using a prescribed text or anthology, rack your brain to come up with the title or name of every resource that might possibly be used in the course, including:

novels
nonfiction
magazines
articles
poems
plays
short stories
films
public radio
free and inexpensive materials
recorded literature
recorded music
painting
sculpture
interdisciplinary materials (from science, math, history)
filmstrips
television programs
information sources
speakers and consultants

Spend half an afternoon browsing in a paperback bookstore looking for new titles and a half day in the public library. Turn your course title over to the school librarian and ask for a list of the resources available within the school itself. With this procedure you will very quickly come up with a list of dozens of titles that can be of help to you in your course.

When you have generated this list, skim through it, coding the selections, using a symbol system such as this:

W = Appropriate for use with the *Whole Class*
S = Best with *Small Groups* of students
I = Suitable for *Individualized Study.*

From your *W*s will probably evolve the class book list, the four or ten books that you want to teach to the class as a whole. The *W*s will also include such common class activities as film viewing, speakers, and so on. But the *S*s and *I*s are equally important, for through them individualization can take place.

Some questions to ask about your materials list:

- Do the selections represent many different genres, or just one or two?
- Are ethnic and other minorities adequately represented?
- Have you been able to include the works of foreign as well as American writers?
- Are any classical works appropriate?
- Have you found materials from the popular culture?
- Do the materials allow for various levels of reading ability?
- Are reading materials diverse enough to allow students with different interests to find something they will enjoy?
- Are there nonfiction as well as fiction materials?

DESIGNING COURSE ACTIVITIES

You have a set of objectives. You have a list of materials. Now brainstorm for the substance of your course, linking objectives and materials by developing the actual reading/writing/speaking activities for your students. You might develop a list of as many as one hundred different activities. As before, code the activities according to appropriateness for whole class (*W*), small groups (*S*) or individual work (*I*). A checklist of considerations:

- What writing assignments are appropriate to this course?
- In what ways can the reading selections stimulate writing in this course?
- Have you provided for a variety of ways for students to respond to literature?
- Are your assignments such that students can seek out reading material and project work appropriate to their ability levels?
- How might this course evoke writing for some other audience than the teacher?
- How can students furnish writing topics for the class?
- Can students locate some of their own reading materials?

- What forms of independent writing are appropriate?
- What kinds of speaking/listening activities are appropriate?
- Can you draw on the media—film, video, and recordings—to extend the dimensions of your activities?
- Do the activities help kids read materials successfully?
- How can you use drama in the course through improvisation, readers' theater, play acting?
- Can students move outside the school for field trips, speakers, movie viewing, etc.?
- List topics for debates and panel discussions.
- List ideas for creative writing.
- List ideas for media composition.

CREATING SEQUENCE AND STRUCTURE

This is the hard part: how to get from here to there, from A to Z, from beginning to end, from objective to fulfillment. Structuring the course is perhaps the most difficult activity, for there are no set patterns to follow. It's your course, with your materials and your students. Each teacher has a different "rhythm" of teaching: Some like to follow a project from beginning to end without interruption, while others like to break up the activities into bits and pieces. Nevertheless, as you consider the ten or twenty or forty weeks available, you may want to build in the following kinds of movement or flow:

- from whole class activities to individualized
- from teacher-directed activities to student project work
- from common class readings to individualized
- from easy tasks to more difficult or complex
- from where the students are to where they want to be.

Of course, any structure you design prior to the course is tentative—a rough scenario, not a blueprint to be followed in detail. Although some teachers feel that the typing out a syllabus or course outline is unduly restrictive, in all of our courses we give out what we call a "Tentative Plan," so that the students have a sense of where the course is going.

At the very least, you'll probably want to block out flexible phases or units for your course, perhaps like those in figure 3 for the sixteen-week ninth-grade course described earlier.

UNIT 1. (2 weeks) Getting acquainted. Using interest inventories to learn about students. Reading of short stories to whole class. Reacting to several short films. Students begin writing journals.

UNIT 2. (4 weeks) Personal writing. Students extend journal entries into personal narratives about their experiences. Some small-group work editing and revising stories. Common class reading of literature about adolescence.

UNIT 3. (4 weeks) Public writing. Students review public writing forms and write for "real" audiences in school and around town: essays, letters to the editor, submissions to school newspaper. Reading materials focus on popular newspapers and magazines in small-group work.

UNIT 4. (4 weeks) Individual projects. Students select one area for in-depth reading and writing, drawing on their earlier expressions of interest. Individualized reading from classroom library. Students also block out reading activities in conference with the teacher.

UNIT 5. (2 weeks) Students come back together for presentation and evaluation of final projects.

FIGURE 3

EVALUATION AND FOLLOW-UP

This topic is also described in detail in chapter 5, "Alphabet Soup," and it is sufficient to say that evaluation is far more than grading. A number of alternative forms of evaluation exist, including conferences, contracts, and so on. Any evaluation scheme, however, needs to take into account the objectives of the course (either as originally written or as revised in process), conveying systematically to the students a sense of their own progress and providing a means for the teacher to evaluate his or her own success in meeting objectives for the course. Further, it is important to stress the obvious: It's no fair changing evaluation schemes in midcourse or evaluating on criteria that have never been made explicit to the students.

Follow-up is also an important part of the closing phases of a course. Students take English courses within the context of the school curriculum. Yours is probably not the first course they have taken; nor is it likely to be the last. At the end of a course, the teacher is in a unique position to assess a student's strengths or weaknesses and to advise him or her about future work that might be interesting, fruitful, or necessary to success in school or elsewhere. A good course, in short, ends with the question "What next?"

(The process of course planning is summarized in figure 4.)

A Short Guide to Lesson Planning

The six-step procedure described above will help you create your syllabus, a master plan for the course or unit, but will not supply you with the details of day-to-day teaching. The term *lesson plan* is anathema for many teachers, principally because lesson plans often serve the needs of principals, supervisors, or methods instructors far more than they do the classroom teacher. The traditional lesson plan was a kind of script, written in advance by the teacher, listing a sequence of questions and some "suggested" answers:

Question: What is the symbolic significance of the forest in Robert Frost's "Stopping by Woods on a Snowy Evening?"

Suggested answers: Death, the unknown, weariness with life.

Armed with this document, the teacher charged into class:

Question: What is the symbolic significance of the forest in Robert Frost's "Stopping by Woods on a Snowy Evening?"

AN OUTLINE FOR COURSE AND UNIT PLANNING

1. Describing the Student Population. Write down your description of what you think the students will be like. Assess their concerns and interests, their ability with language. Consider how you want to affect their learning through your teaching.

2. Setting Out Objectives. Describe what you propose to have happen in the course. What will the students learn, do, talk about, read, write, etc.? Whenever possible, describe objectives in terms of the language students will actually produce to prove that they have "mastered" the material.

3. Brainstorm for Materials. List everything you can possibly think of that might be of use in the course—all forms, modes, and media. Identify those materials best used with the whole class, small groups, or for individual study.

4. List Course Activities. Brainstorm for reading/writing/listening/speaking activities appropriate to the course, including in-school and out-of-school projects. Again, indicate which are appropriate for whole-class, small-group, or individual studies.

5. Sequence and Structure. Divvy up your activities and readings in an ordered, sensible pattern to provide for growth, structure, and flow in the course.

6. Assessment and Follow-up. Develop assessment procedures for the course, not just grading schemes, which evaluate student growth in the broad sense and provide an assessment of your own teaching. Include provisions for follow-up work or counselling that allows the students to extend the work beyond the boundaries of your course.

FIGURE 4

ʼ forgot my book.

ı didn't read it.

ıt 3: (*sotto voce*): That's where he got laid last summer.

ɔtudent 4: The woods?

Student 5: Nothing.

Student 6: Possibly death, the unknown, or the poet's weariness with life. Student 6 goes on for a Ph.D. in English at Yale, while the rest of the kids get D's for not being able to follow the teacher's script.

Obviously, one doesn't want to waste time writing a detailed plan that will never be followed by students *or* teacher. Yet some lesson planning is essential, and the guide shown in figure 5 allows the teacher to get his or her ideas and materials written in a convenient form. You'll note that it parallels, in most divisions, our outline for course planning so that sketching out lessons becomes, in effect, a more detailed variation of describing your course.

We suggest that you mimeograph or ditto a batch of blank forms (modified as needed) early in the year for your own planning and start a notebook for your various classes. (A sample is given in figure 6.) Lesson planning of this kind is relatively painless, and it has distinct advantages:

1. It provides a useful reference tool for your future teaching. While few teachers want to do the same course year after year, it's helpful to see where you've been, to learn from your mistakes.

2. It presents an invaluable day-to-day record for your teaching competence. In this age of accountability, it is enormously practical to be able to show administrators and parents on a day-to-day basis exactly what you've been doing. The form provided here, if kept faithfully, offers a dated, documented statement of your aims, your methods, your assessment procedures.

Interest Inventories
(Letting the Student Population Describe Itself)

Once a course is underway, the first thing the teacher will want to do is revise and sharpen that description of the student population, altering the general expectations of August to meet the realities of September and replacing generic terms—kids, students, ninth-graders—with names: Larry, Sam, Emily, Margaret, Jack. Much of this information can be supplied directly by the students themselves. Instead of assigning the traditional theme, "My Summer Vacation,"

A SHORT FORM FOR LESSON PLANNING

1. Objectives.
   In two to three sentences, describe the major objectives of the lesson: what the kids will read, talk about, write, say, think about, or do. Avoid vague phrases like "understand" and "appreciate" and focus whenever possible on the language that the students will actually produce.

2. Materials.
   List the basic resources involved in the lesson: texts, records, films, speakers (even paste, pencils, scissors, and glue). Where appropriate, attach a copy of materials being used for future reference.

3. Procedures.
   Outline what you plan to do in as much detail as is required for clarity and for your own understanding, but don't lock yourself into a script that the students won't follow. Thus . . . indicate how you plan to open the class (don't try to wing it); spell out how you plan to run the session; list possible questions; list an alternative strategy or two in case the main plan fails; include some sort of wrap-up or concluding moment.

4. Evaluation and Extension.
   Like courses, lessons take place in context. A good (or even unsuccessful) lesson leads to another. In this section note down how you propose to assess the lesson (not necessarily grade it), and where you plan to go next.

5. In Retrospect.
   Leave this blank at first. After you have finished your lesson, spend just a minute or two writing up your own reactions. How did it go? How should it be done differently? If you were to teach it again tomorrow, how would you change it?

FIGURE 5

WOODY ALLEN J. H. S.

Course Title: English 7

Day/Date: Monday, December 10

Lesson Title: Describing Feelings

Teacher: Greenway

1. Objectives.

By helping the students become aware of their physical and emotional responses to things they touch (and which touch them back), I will provide material for writing. The student papers should demonstrate use of good sensory details.

2. Materials.

Materials are hidden in a box: old spaghetti, a box of miniature marshmallows, a piece of satin, a cactus.

3. Procedures.

Lead-in:

Explain that the students will have a chance to feel, then talk and write about some "strange" and "weird" objects. Build up the mystery!

FIGURE 6

Development:

1. Blindfold students and let them feel objects one at a time. Don't let them guess what the object is. Simply describe: how it feels; how the student feels.
2. Then show the contents of box.
3. Give imaginary writing assignments: "You are alone in the forest on a dark, stormy night. What do you feel? What do you touch? How does this make you feel?"

Wrap-up:

Read or have kids read papers to class. Encourage them to comment on rich sensory details.

4. Evaluation and Extension.

As above, evaluate through class discussion. Follow-up: Let kids write a page of sensory impressions in their journals.

5. In retrospect.

Don't use cactus! Otherwise, it went very well. Kids giggled a lot, but wrote some excellent descriptive pieces. Do this again.

EXPERIENCE PORTFOLIO

Read over the following activities/subjects/experiences and respond to each by writing in the appropriate letter(s):

(A) Haven't the faintest idea about this one
(B) Yeah, I could fill you in a little
(C) You're getting warm – I know quite a bit
(D) This is really down my alley
(E) I'd like to know more about this area

( ) 1. dirt-biking
( ) 2. cameras & photography
( ) 3. scuba diving
( ) 4. Kung Fu
( ) 5. needlepoint
( ) 6. Transcendental Meditation
( ) 7. rock hounding
( ) 8. sewing
( ) 9. horses
( ) 10. boating
( ) 11. candle-making
( ) 12. gymnastics
( ) 13. writing
( ) 14. macramé
( ) 15. sky-gliding
( ) 16. ceramics
( ) 17. car engines
( ) 18. chemistry
( ) 19. singing
( ) 20. playing a musical instrument (type:_________)
( ) 21. rocketry
( ) 22. homemade ice cream
( ) 23. cooking
( ) 24. flying
( ) 25. traveling
( ) 26. backpacking
( ) 27. life saving
( ) 28. fly-tying
( ) 29. clamming
( ) 30. canoeing
( ) 31. rock climbing
( ) 32. embroidery or crewel
( ) 33. wood carving
( ) 34. carpentry
( ) 35. electronics
( ) 36. deep sea fishing
( ) 37. poetry
( ) 38. pop music
( ) 39. deep sea diving
( ) 40. hunting
( ) 41. leatherwork
( ) 42. camping
( ) 43. pen & ink drawing
( ) 44. horse racing
( ) 45. sign language
( ) 46. rodeos
( ) 47. lobstering
( ) 48. pinball machines
( ) 49. gumball machines
( ) 50. ice fishing
( ) 51. stamps
( ) 52. skating
( ) 53. coins
( ) 54. antiques
( ) 55. pastels
( ) 56. haircutting
( ) 57. foraging
( ) 58. bowling
( ) 59. ski-mobiling

FIGURE 7

( ) 60. sailing
( ) 61. track & field
( ) 62. swimming
( ) 63. skateboards
( ) 64. astronomy
( ) 65. astrology
( ) 66. models-constructing
( ) 67. modelling (clothes)
( ) 68. collecting mushrooms
( ) 69. paper plane construction
( ) 70. judo
( ) 71. wild flowers
( ) 72. acting
( ) 73. acupuncture
( ) 74. softball
( ) 75. water colors
( ) 76. chess
( ) 77. taffy pulls
( ) 78. maple syruping
( ) 79. diving
( ) 80. railroads
( ) 81. trapping
( ) 82. Disney World
( ) 83. national parks
( ) 84. origami
( ) 85. weaving
( ) 86. oil painting
( ) 87. Parcheesi
( ) 88. Majong
( ) 89. movie-making
( ) 90. impersonations
( ) 91. batiking
( ) 92. caterpillars & insects
( ) 93. kite flying
( ) 94. frisbee throwing
( ) 95. indoor plants
( ) 96. kite construction
( ) 97. silversmithing
( ) 98. script writing
( ) 99. karate
( ) 100. falconry
( ) 101. gerbils
( ) 102. kazoos
( ) 103. bobsledding
( ) 104. soccer
( ) 105. lacrosse
( ) 106. surfing
( ) 107. backgammon
( ) 108. squash (game)
( ) 109. tropical fish
( ) 110. trivia
( ) 111. jug & bottle bands
( ) 112. ballet
( ) 113. puppetry
( ) 114. knitting or crocheting
( ) 115. Monopoly
( ) 116. football
( ) 117. baseball
( ) 118. skiing
( ) 119. ski-jumping
( ) 120. animal training

( ) 121. Areas or subjects in which I excel that have been left off the list: ______

( ) 122. Something I've done that no one in the class has ever done:

______

Source: Johanna Sweet, "An Experience Portfolio," The English Journal 66 (September 1976): 51.

INTEREST INVENTORY

1. What kinds of shows do you like to watch on television?
2. What kinds of programs do you like to listen to on the radio?
3. What kinds of motion pictures do you like to see?
4. What hobbies do you have or would you like to have?
5. What sports do you like to participate in or see?
6. What kind of work do you do (or have you done)?
7. What kind of work would you like to do?
8. If you could be anyone for a day, what person would you like to be?
9. If you could travel anywhere, what places would you like to visit?
10. If you would like to live in the past or future, what period of time would you like to live in?
11. What animals would you like to raise or see or know more about?
12. What problems or subjects would you like to understand better or know more about?

ACTIVITIES INVENTORY

These are activities you can do during class when you complete assignments. Check the ones you would like to do. Then double-check three you would like to do most:

1. Sit by yourself and do nothing.
2. Talk to your friends quietly.
3. Do homework for a different class.
4. Work out in the gym.
5. Practice in the music room.
6. Write stories, poems, or letters.
7. Play checkers or chess.
8. Play games, like Scrabble, Monopoly.
9. Play sports games.
10. Draw or paint.
11. Learn a hobby or craft.
12. Work as an aide in the office or as a teacher's aide.

INVENTORY OF PROBLEMS AND GOALS

A. Which of these are problems for you in this class? Check them.
   1. Do you have trouble understanding what you are reading?
   2. Do you have trouble figuring out what you are supposed to do with a reading assignment?
   3. Do you have trouble understanding many of the words in the reading assignment?
   4. Do you have trouble paying attention to what you are reading?
   5. Do you have trouble completing assignments on time?
   6. Do you feel that you spend too much time on

FIGURE 8

the reading for the amount of pages you finish?

7. Do you seldom like what you are reading?
8. Do you have trouble finding the section in a book you are supposed to read?
9. Do you have trouble finding books or magazines you would like to read in the library?
10. Do you have trouble remembering important information or ideas for tests?
11. When there is a discussion about the reading, do you have trouble following it?
12. Are you reluctant to participate in discussions?
13. Do you have trouble relating the lecture to the reading?
14. When you have to write about what you have read, do you have trouble getting started?
15. When you write, do you have trouble spelling many of the words?

B. Which one would you like to work on as a goal for the next two weeks? Double check that.

READING INTERESTS INVENTORY

Rate these types of reading. Put an A before the ones you read a lot. Put a B before the ones you sometimes read. Put a C before the ones you never read (or hardly ever read).

1. News stories
2. Sports stories
3. Editorials
4. Comic strips
5. Advice columns
6. Reviews of books, theater, films and T.V.
7. Society pages
8. Ads
9. Comic books
10. Sports magazines
11. News magazines
12. Movie magazines
13. Science magazines
14. "Mechanical" magazines
15. "Social" magazines
16. Biographies
17. Autobiographies
18. How-to-do books
19. Religious books
20. Science fiction
21. Short stories
22. Novels
23. Poems
24. Plays
25. Essays

Source: Walter Lamberg, "Helping Reluctant Readers Help Themselves: Interest Inventories," The English Journal 66 (November 1977): 42-43.

A PERSONAL LITERACY HISTORY

What is the all-time best book you ever read? Why did you like it so much? How many times did you read it?

What is the worst book you ever read? Did you finish it? Who or what made you read it?

Who taught you to read? How much can you remember about learning to read? What's the first book you can recall reading?

Did your parents read to you much when you were a child? What fairy stories or children's rhymes can you recall by heart from childhood?

What's your favorite reading now? What magazines or newspapers do you look at regularly?

What would you rather do? List your preferences in order:

A. Read a book
B. Watch a TV documentary
C. See a play
D. Talk with friends
E. Read a textbook
F. Read poetry
G. Go to a sporting event
H. Listen to music
I. Play music
J. See a film

Where do you like to read? In your room? In the library? Someplace else?

When you are given a writing assignment, do you approach it with:
A. a sense of joy and vigor?
B. a feeling of awe and inadequacy?
C. a conviction that you will fail?
D. a feeling that you can do it OK?
E. a sharpened pencil?

Do you write fast or slowly?

What do you think are your major strengths as a writer?

What weaknesses do you feel you have in writing?

What's the most interesting composition assignment you ever received?

What is the worst assignment you can recall having? What made it so terrible?

Do you think that TV and telephones make writing and reading out of date? Why or why not?

FIGURE 9

which ostensibly helps teachers learn about students and their language abilities, we suggest trying a sequence of interest inventories: short questionnaires that not only tell you about your students but generate lists of ideas to supplement your own descriptions of course materials and activities. For example:

Johanna Sweet uses something she calls an "Experience Portfolio" to discover student interests. It asks students to indicate their interest in and knowledge of a range of fascinating subjects from dirt-biking to animal training (figure 7).

Walter Lamberg has created a series of inventories to help students describe their interests and relate those interests to their reading skills (figure 8). Students first write about their outside-of-school interests, and then they describe the kinds of activities in which they like to engage (which helps the teacher gain a feeling for whether the students are interested in academics or not, more concerned with active or quiet activities). Finally they are asked to assess their problems and goals in reading, and to describe the kinds of reading they like to do.

We have assessed students' reading/writing interests with what we call a personal literacy history, which asks the students to recall early episodes with reading and writing, something that can give you insight into their previous bouts with reading and writing, both at home and in school (figure 9).

Obviously, you wouldn't want to administer all of these inventories to any single class. They probably should be supplemented with some initial writing activities (journals seem a useful activity here) and with some informal reading and discussion of literary works and/or magazine articles. But time spent on this information-gathering stage is well spent. It lets you know if your initial judgment of the class was remotely accurate and, even more important, helps the teacher get to know the students on a one-to-one basis from the start.

CHAPTER 2

Individualizing: One to One

There is little disagreement among teachers about the value of individualizing instruction to meet the needs and interests of students. But when it comes to implementing a program or setting up a classroom designed to be responsive to different interests, learning styles and preferences, language abilities, reading levels, ways of interacting, attitudes toward school, and needs for structure and freedom, the overwhelmed teacher often prefers a less effective—but also less chaotic—"shotgun" approach, teaching a little bit of everything, hoping that everyone will get something he or she needs or can use.

Individualizing, however, is possible, if teachers are aware in advance of the kinds of adjustments necessary. Consider the following adaptations that need to occur when individualizing your classroom:

The role of the teacher is widely varied. Sometimes the teacher is at the center of the classroom, providing instruction or directions for a project in which the whole class is involved. At other times, the teacher acts as a resource person, moving from student to student, from group to group, helping students make decisions about how they want to approach their projects or seek answers to their own questions. The teacher also acts as a resource person in helping students locate materials. For many teachers, this means going beyond a narrow range of literature and knowing a few texts very well to provide information about many more materials. Often this means making suggestions for literature or resource material without the security of the "tried-and-true" success. The role of teachers also changes, for they must be constantly alert to techniques and approaches to involve many different kinds of students. Which students need limited choices and structured activities? Which students function best in small groups? Which students function successfully with maximum choice and self-direction? What methods are helpful in getting students to become independent, to make choices on their own? What forms of evaluation seem most appropriate for different kinds of people?

The roles of students change. They take increased responsibility for what they learn and how they will learn it. This is often a problem for students in early stages of individualization. They are accustomed to being given specific assignments or projects with immovable due dates and absolute standards of measurement. They don't know what is important to learn, because they haven't been encouraged to think about it; and they have seldom had much practice in asking questions and in pursuing answers to those questions. When thrown into a situation in which they are to make decisions about what to do, they often choose to do *nothing.* This is less the fault of the students, however, than a result of the structure of their past learning situations. It is the teacher's job to broaden the options gradually, deciding *with* the students what activities and materials are appropriate. For some students the move to autonomy is very slow, but it is the students' responsibility, as well as the teachers'.

The individualized classroom requires new ways of assessing students' progress and keeping records. Just as setting goals and objectives for projects or units is based on mutual agreement between student and teacher, evaluation and assessment should be mutually decided. Both contracts and student-teacher conferences allow the students to discuss their own goals and the progress they have made in achieving their goals. Evaluation, then, becomes not a mere tabulation of numbers, but an analysis of growth and learning, with students and teachers sharing their perceptions. (See also chapter 5, "Alphabet Soup," and chapter 7, "Accountability and Assessment.")

Individualization requires a reorganization of materials. When you decide to individualize instruction, it's a good idea to begin clipping articles, short stories, news reports, feature articles, editorials, comics, puzzles, and recipes from magazines and newspapers to make available to students working on various units and projects. Look for such things as old newspapers and magazines; unused anthologies of American literature, world literature, and poetry; single-copy paperbacks (not just English, but social studies, science, music, as well); multiple copies of books that might have once been class sets. Go on a scavenger hunt from classroom to classroom, asking teachers for "loose ends" in their rooms that they don't use. (See chapter 3, "Beachcombing.")

Individualizing your classroom often requires some physical rearrangement of the classroom. The individualized classroom needs to be flexible. Sometimes everyone will be together for a presentation for the entire class; sometimes the class will be working in small groups; other times students will be working alone. It helps, then, to have movable desks or small tables for six to eight students. If your classroom is large enough, it can be separated into various areas, with a reading area in one corner, resource books and handbooks for revision and editing writing in another area, graphics and publication materials in a third, media materials (filmstrips, tape recorders) in a fourth. Even with limited space, however, it is possible to provide students with some flexibility by partitioning a small area with bookshelves or folding dividers for kids working on individualized projects or independent readings.

Some First Steps

One of the most important things to remember when you have decided that you want to individualize your classes is that it takes time. Don't try to do all of your classes at once and don't be discouraged when your early attempts to reach the unreachable student fail or when some kids sit around doing nothing during the first week of an independent project. The following first steps might help individualize your classroom:

- Set up one corner in your classroom to be used by students when they have completed their regular classwork. Stock it with magazines, current newspapers, a paperback book rack, a file of crossword puzzles or word games, index cards with creative writing ideas, attractive paper and felt pens. Try to keep track of what students use from that corner and let them make suggestions for additional language activities.
- Make every Friday free-reading or free-writing day. Allow students to read anything they want (except homework for other classes). Or let them spend the hour writing anything they wish, with the option of showing it to you.
- Use free-reading/writing days as conferences days; talk with students individually about their favorite assignments, books, or projects; give them help with reading and writing assignments; discuss what they might like to do in future work; share assessments about class activities and the student's progress.
- Spend two hours a week clipping from magazines, newspapers, and (if you can get away with it) old texts. Consider taking some anthologies apart for inclusion in individualized packets. Develop broad categories for cataloguing your "finds."

➨ Locate another teacher in your school who would like to develop some individualized units. Work together in preparing materials for use in your classes. Better yet, initiate plans for an in-service day to be used for materials development. Collect materials individually and use the meeting to develop activities and projects that can be used in various units.

➨ Try involving the uninvolved, unmotivated student by designing a program especially for him or her with the student's help. Spend some time with two or three "underachievers" or "nonattenders" to develop some activities that they really want to do.

➨ If you are accustomed to having the whole class doing the same thing, take out one week in which you divide the class into small groups and give them week-long projects to be presented to the whole class at the end of the week.

➨ Gradually expand the number of options of assignments over a period of three or four weeks. Note which students have trouble getting started and provide those students with more specific directions for a time.

➨ Set up a workshop corner in the room. Have students bring in materials (articles, stories, poems from magazines or newspapers) that they would like to contribute to one of your units. Let them add writing assignments or projects to go along with their contributions. Add all student-done work to your individualized units.

➨ Prepare a survey to assess student interests and needs. Ask what they like to read, what they watch on TV, what movies they have seen and liked, what their favorite courses are, what their outside interests and hobbies are, what they hate, where they've been, what they've seen, what they want to do with their lives, what they would like to accomplish in your class. Use the results to prepare assignments and projects. And draw on the expertise of students in your classes as one of your important resources. (See chapter 1, "Course Planning and Design.")

➨ Begin a records folder for each student; have him or her keep assignments, evaluations, project ideas, lists of accomplishments, and a chart of skills development so that you have quick access to his performance and progress for yourself, the student, administrator, and parents.

➨ Have a pillow party. Spend two or three days of your class making classroom furniture: big pillows for reading; sets of shelves for various kinds of reference books and games; decorated bins to collect new materials.

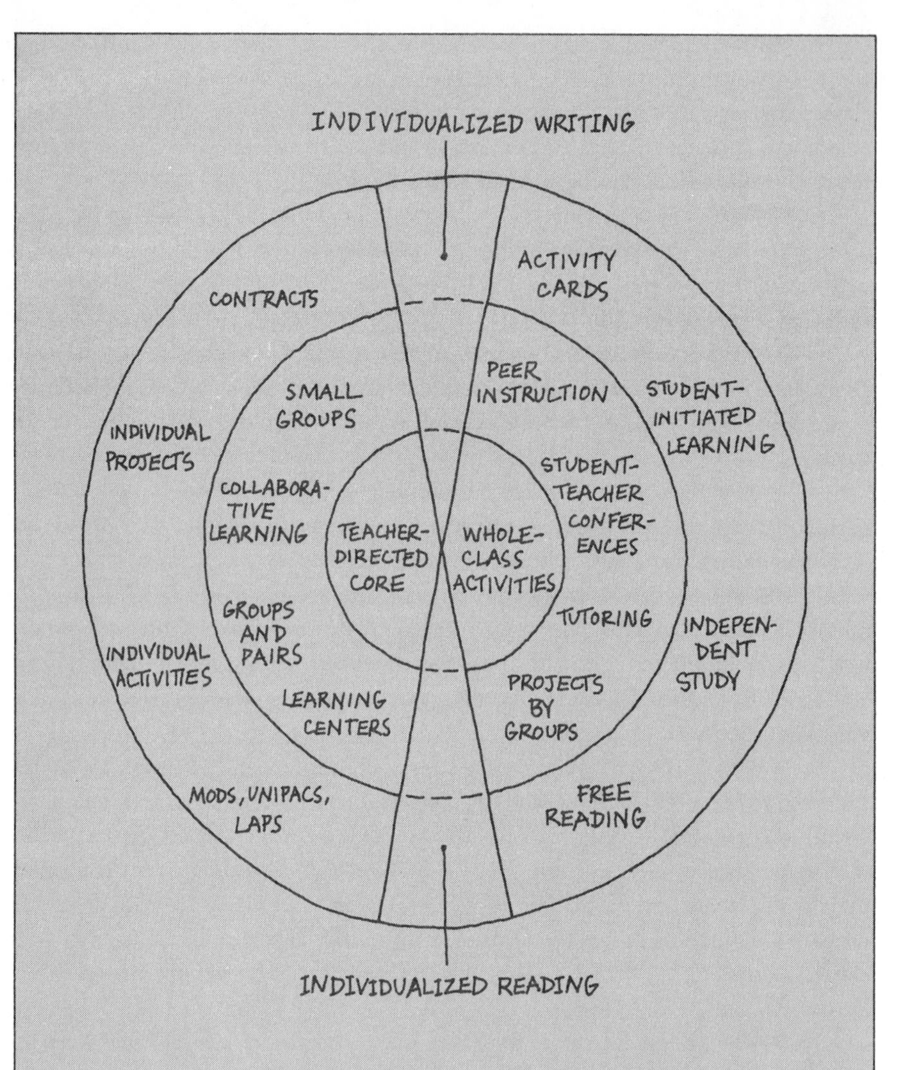

Source: Freely adapted from Ken Styles and Gray Cavanagh, "How to Design a Multi-level Course of Study to Bring About Quality Learning," The English Journal 64 (February 1975): 73-75; and Margaret Rinkel, "A Kaleidoscopic View of Individualization," The English Journal 64 (October 1975): 27-39.

FIGURE 1 AN INDIVIDUALIZED LEARNING MODEL

A Catalogue of Techniques for Individualizing English

The ideas, techniques, and programs described below have been or are being tried in a number of schools in many different forms and combinations. Each has strengths and weaknesses, advantages and drawbacks. Some will work in your school, with or without modification; others won't. We recommend that you pick and choose from the list, shaping and adapting to meet your needs. (See figure 1 for a model of individualized learning activities and structures.) Using this list, too, you can begin introducing strategies one at a time, increasing the degree of individualization as approaches prove successful.

THE PROJECT METHOD

This technique dates back to the 1920s, when progressive education was experimenting with new approaches. The class (or a group of students) selects a "project" and individualization comes about through differentiated roles for each student. Sybil Marshall in *An Experiment in Education* (Cambridge: Cambridge University Press, 1973), describes a group of primary-school children who wrote a history of their British town, each child "specializing" in a particular period, information source, or writing task. Junior-high kids in Morrice, Michigan, compiled a *Bicentennial Cookbook* featuring recipes contributed by the governors and spouses of forty-nine states. Eliot Wigginton's *Foxfire* magazine is a good example of the project method, and it can even be adapted to city living. (See Deborah Insel, "Foxfire in the City," *The English Journal* 74 [September 1975].) Projects don't necessarily have to carry students outside the classroom; they can be based entirely on books and media resources available in the school. For an outstanding discussion of the project method and a list of detailed "topics," see Geoffrey Summerfield, *Topics in English* (London: Batsford, 1965).

TEACHERLESS TEACHING

In many individualized learning programs, the "teacher" plays the role of administrator, while students and others teach and learn from each other. Some possibilities:

Cross-age teaching. Many schools have been experimenting with using lay teachers, tutors, and helpers. Second-grade children read books to kindergartners. Tenth-grade students read to elderly convalescents. Junior-high students put on a puppet show for fourth-graders. College education students teach senior-high writing. Parent aides teach children at all levels. Children at many levels teach adult learners. The "teachers," it has been discovered, gain as much or more from the experience as the people they are helping.

Each one teach one (*peer tutoring*). Equals can learn an astonishing amount from each other. Peer tutoring frequently turns out to be not the sharing of ignorance, but a sharing of growth. Let kids tutor each other in reading, writing, literature. Perhaps the most important prerequisite here is developing what Herbert Thelen (University of Chicago) has identified as "the caring relationship." Daniel Fader (University of Michigan) similarly talks about children taking responsibility for each other, which is catalyzed in collaborative learning situations where students are both tutor and tutee.

Tutoring programs boost self-esteem for all participants. Training is required, but it is not as complicated or difficult as it might seem. An excellent handbook on peer-teaching programs is *Children Teach Children,* by Alan Gartner, Mary Kohler, and Frank Riessman (New York: Harper & Row, 1971). Consider the following ways of establishing peer teaching in your school or classroom:

Student assistants. Using students as teacher aides is an exciting concept, provided the teacher makes "aiding" a positive learning experience, not just a chore. At Thunderbird Elementary School in Vancouver, Canada, teams of aides help the librarian put together collections of reading materials for in-class libraries that are rotated on a twice-monthly basis. Student aides can help in the preparation of material, selection of reading materials, and "prereading" books that the teacher doesn't have time to read. In Grand Rapids, Michigan, some fourth-grade children set up a tape-recorded book review service, so that children interested in books can listen to a taped commentary by a peer before making a selection.

Small group teaching and tutoring. Let the class poetry experts teach poetry to others. Let good writers conduct a symposium on writing the essay or short story. Use group presentations frequently, not as the *end* of a project, but as the *beginning* of an individualized class experience. Following the peer-tutoring notion, let small groups develop expertise and teach each other.

Teacherless classes. Get a copy of Peter Elbow's *Writing Without Teachers* (New York: Oxford, 1974) and consider the possibility of doing a "teacherless" writing class, where a group of students teach each other writing by the simple formula of having each member of the group write once a week and respond to the writing of others on a weekly basis. Again, training is required to make such a program work, but Elbow gives some workable strategies.

Synergy. "Synergy Schools" operate on a sharing basis; people teach whatever skills they have to anybody who wants to learn them. Set up a "skills-sharing" school-within-a-classroom. You can have students share a broad range of skills (football, weaving, guitar) and induce a lot of "languaging," or you can have the students share language skills exclusively, including reading and writing, favorite novels, speaking and debating skills, panels.

ACTIVITY CENTERS

In activity centers, materials do the work of structuring for you (or allow you to structure beforehand and leave the scene). Accumulate materials—commercial or homemade—and prepare an instructional poster describing legitimate activities for the center. (Like most individualized activities, using centers requires a monitoring system that allows students and teacher to keep a record of what is accomplished. Consider an activities checklist or experience portfolio for each student.) Some possibilities for activity centers include:

- reading (free or guided)
- responding (discussion of literature)
- writing (a place well equipped for writing, with comfortable furniture and lots of writing utensils)
- editing/copyreading (for "polishing" papers, complete with proofreading advice)
- graphics (for production of books, magazines, posters, slides, transparencies)
- listening (recorded literature)
- language games ("Scrabble," crosswords, codes and ciphers, word play)

Ideally, if you move into activity centers you will have your own classroom, a place where you leave things on display permanently. But if you don't have that arrangement, you can still create portable or semiportable activity kits. Get some large cardboard boxes (twenty-seven-inch television boxes); put the materials on the inside; write instructions on the outside. Activity kits can be used for a period, then stored in the closet.

CLUBS

Remember the fascination when you were a kid of starting up your own club? A secret society? A group of blood brothers or blood sisters? A cowboys and Indians club? A space exploration society? Clubs are really quite effective as self-structuring, individualized learning devices. Instead of having clubs function outside of school time, establish a series of clubs within your class: The Creative Writing Club, The Cinema Society (which gets films for the whole class), the Magazine Association (magazine readers), the *Underground Press* (class newsletter), the Author's Club (readers), the (insert name of favorite author) Club.

SIMULATIONS AND GAMES

Simulations and games also involve a kind of self-structuring, where students create and work out roles for themselves and thus become their own assignment makers. *Simulations* simply model "the real thing"; you can do simulations of newspaper and magazine production, an ideal society, problems in society today, trials, conferences, or radio and television production. Encourage interested students to write about insights gained in simulations or to read further about a subject in which they become interested.

Games can involve simulation or not, but use the aspect of competition to engage the players in self-structuring roles. The *Psychology Today* simulation games, "Man vs. Woman," "Black vs. White," "Problems of Society," are particularly useful in English classes as a way of getting students started on projects. Check your local bookstore for games that might work in your classroom.

ACTIVITY OR JOB CARDS

Activity cards are an especially useful way of initiating an individualized program. You can begin by preparing just a few cards; then, as your supply increases and students have learned how to use them, increase the number, diversity, and sophistication. In essence, an activity card contains: a task or an assignment and instructions on how to accomplish it (or where to find out how). You can construct activity cards for:

- writing assignments
- "solo" projects

- individual novels
- groups of poems
- individual poets
- literary themes
- writing skills
- reading skills.

Activity cards can be self-contained (one complete activity per card), or you can create sequences of cards (a series of cards for one novel, a series of cards for a sequence of novels, five cards on how to complete an informal writing project, five sequential writing projects).

MODS, LAPS, PIKS, UNIPACS, AND COMPS

These acronymns* cluster around a single basic concept: a self-instructional "kit," or package of materials. The common components generally include: a description of goals or planned activities (what you will learn from this packet); instructional materials (readings, activity cards, assignments, projects, advice); and measurement of "exit skills" (what you can do when you've finished). For a detailed description of the development of such materials, see the close-up section, "Individualized Learning: Theory into Practice" in the October 1975 issue of *The English Journal.*

INDEPENDENT STUDY

Independent study is one of the most traditional forms of individualized learning, one often overlooked in the schools. A problem with independent study is that students don't know how to handle it at first. We'd like to see schools offer instruction in independent study at all levels. It seems feasible to put, say, 10 percent of the freshman class on short-term independent projects at any given time for an initial experience under close supervision. As the students become

* Answer key for the acronyms: MODS are *modular* units, each of which takes up one component of a program; LAPS, *L*earning *A*ctivity *P*ackets; and PIKS are *P*ersonalized *I*nstruction *K*its. UNIPACS are MODS, PIKS, or LAPS based around a single objective or concept. COMPS are competency-based LAPS, MODS, PIKS, or UNIPACS with an emphasis on having the student demonstrate (show competency) in the final study. (For a detailed description of the preparation of Activity Cards and LAPS, see chapter 3, "Beachcombing.")

more skilled and more mature, the amount of independent study time can be increased, so that seniors might spend, say, 50 percent of their time pursuing independent projects. Even if a schoolwide program isn't possible, you can teach students how to pursue independent study in as short a period as a semester.

INDIVIDUALIZED READING

This is also a traditional approach, but so fundamental to an individualized program that perhaps we should have put it first in our list. If you can get an individualized reading program going, you can buy time for yourself to introduce other individualized activities: time to get small groups of students started in activity centers; time to meet with tutors; time to oversee independent study; time to monitor kids' progress through LAPS, MODS, PIKS, and PODS; time to guide students in the use of activity cards; time to supervise clubs.

CHAPTER 3

Beachcombing: Teacher-Constructed Materials

IF the budget won't stand it, do it yourself. In an era when school financing is becoming tighter, teachers are finding it increasingly difficult to obtain the materials they need to conduct a broadly based literacy program. Though paperbacks are available in reasonable quantity for some classrooms, few teachers have enough materials to sustain their courses through a term or a year at a truly satisfactory level. Further, in the wake of the back-to-basics movement in this country, many school systems effected a return to the traditional hardbound anthology, much to the dismay of the English staff. Under these circumstances, *beachcombing*—putting together a program based on free and inexpensive materials—has considerable appeal.

Though the range and quality of commercial texts has increased immeasurably during the past few years, most commercial materials are aimed at a mass market of teachers and students. Even the most innovative materials are frequently geared to a mythical, strongly conservative adoption committee. The publishers feel a need to play it safe to obtain wide-scale adoptions. Your own teacher-constructed materials can be designed to meet directly the needs and interests of your own students, within the context of your own school and community. The range and depth of materials you can provide for students is considerably richer than most commercial packages.

Teacher-built materials also have considerable motivational appeal for young people. Kids recognize when a teacher cares enough about them to take time for special preparations, and they appreciate it. Many teachers we know report that simply because materials are homemade, their students respond positively. One might think that kids would resent homemade stuff, but this doesn't seem to be the case, at least for teacher-made materials that are attractive and well designed.

Finally, teacher-made materials *are* economical, a point not lost on school administrators. For half the amount a school might spend on a class set of grammar books or literature anthologies, a teacher can prepare a staggering amount of individualized material. Departments that go on a beachcombing kick frequently find themselves presented as models of economy to other members of the faculty.

Sources of Free and Inexpensive Material

For ten dollars in stamps and stationery, you can initiate a flow of free materials to your classroom that may quickly inundate you. The sources of low-cost print and nonprint materials available to English teachers are numerous, and we have listed many in Appendix F, "It's Free." Paperback bookstores carry a variety of publications that list sources: these range from *1001 Things You Can Get Free* to an intriguing *Catalog of Catalogs.* One teacher we know taught the form of the business letter by having her students write away for quantities of free things: catalogues, pamphlets, circulars, sample kits, posters, advertising packets, bibliographies, films, promotional materials, and the like.

The United States government also offers a wealth of materials, print and nonprint, which you will find useful. Look up our list of the sundry bureaus and departments, and then write (or have your students write) for materials on such diverse topics as air and water pollution, American Indians, drugs, nutrition, family care and planning, plumbing, and parks and recreation.

Local resources are also abundant and even obvious. Beachcombing is sometimes less a matter of knowing *what* you'll find than knowing *where* to look. Thus, in any community you will find valuable resources at garage and sidewalk sales; in university, state, and community film libraries; in drugstores and surplus stores; in specialized museums and libraries; in political and legal and medical offices. Again, set your students to the task.

Although conditions and generosity vary from city to city, English teachers have generally had good success in obtaining contributions of books and magazines from bookstores and paperback distributors, following the model in Fader's *Hooked on Books* (New York: Berkeley Medallion, 1976). Such "giveaways" are in the best interest of the bookstores, for the stores gain positive publicity and help create a reading interest in young people—their next generation of customers.

New potentially helpful resources are the parent and citizen watchdog groups being created around the country. Instead of fighting such committees,

English teachers might form alliances with them, engaging groups in the task of coming up with more materials for English classes and seeing that budgets include enough money for literacy materials. Federal and state reading programs also have resources for materials acquisition that can be directed toward English programs.

Individualized Materials for the English Program

Although do-it-yourself materials involve a fair amount of work, getting started is not unduly complicated or expensive. Our do-it-yourself workshop is stocked with some basic tools and art supplies: scissors, paper cutter, razor blades, an artist's mat knife, rubber cement, white glue, felt-tip pens (in a variety of sizes and colors), stencils, dry transfer or rub-on lettering, crayons, poster paint, construction paper, poster board, and bond or mimeograph paper in different colors. If your school has a dry-mounting press or equipment for laminating materials in plastic, your workshop will be even more complete.

Once you have assembled your materials—magazines, anthologies, paperbacks, pamphlets—the basic pattern for constructing materials consists of choosing an item—poem, play, photograph, whatever—mounting it on poster board or construction paper, and adding whatever instructions are needed. (More detailed "recipes" follow in the next section.) Even if you don't feel you have much artistic talent, you can use brightly colored art supplies to create an attractive set of materials.

Using Homemade Materials in the English Program

Few teachers can produce enough materials in a summer or a term to move to the exclusive use of homemade materials from the start. Most will want to create an expanding collection of activity cards for use on an individual basis during free time or workshop periods. As both teacher and students became more accustomed to making and using these materials, the range, sophistication, and complexity can be increased (see figure 1).

FIGURE 1 "HOMEMADE" TEACHING MATERIALS

Activity card made of a file folder

Homemade instructional poster

Here are some suggestions for basic do-it-yourself materials in the three major language arts areas:

IN WRITING

Writing idea cards. These cards provide a useful way of individualizing writing assignments and helping students who have "nothing to say." Clip a poem and mount it, suggesting ways for students to respond in writing. Offer ideas for writing short stories, essays, playlets, television scripts. List ideas for creating advertising, commercials, or propaganda. Paste down a photograph and invite the students to write a reaction or a description. Let students write new lyrics to old songs or parody the lyrics of new songs. The possibilities are endless. Many teachers like to include a model of the writing they want to elicit—preferably a model written by a student—on the back of the writing idea card.

In an evening or two you can develop a score of top-quality writing cards; in the course of a summer, you can produce a hundred or more. In September, simply place some cards (not your whole supply) at a convenient spot in the room and invite the students to browse, to select a card, and to write. Some teachers use these cards as a journal-starter; others try a contract system and ask the students to write from a given number of cards during the term; still others find that the writing activity cards are exciting enough that students will write on their own. Replenish the supply of cards from time to time to produce a fresh supply of writing ideas. Invite students to create their own idea cards as well.

The writing skills center. The writing skills center (see chapter 14, "Teaching the Basics") is a place where kids can get prompt, efficient help with matters of proofreading and correctness. Although commercial skills centers are available (at $80 to $100), the teacher can easily create a proofreading self-help center using the concept of activity cards. A good handbook contains most of the information one needs to obtain a reasonable degree of correctness in every area from spelling and usage to footnote form. Drawing on such a source, you can prepare a series of cards or file folders that make help readily available in a form more palatable and portable than the conventional language arts text.

How-to-write-it cards or folders. These are also a useful addition to the writing program. A good many teachers have come to feel that providing students with instruction in writing form or structure prior to actual writing, whether essay or sonnet, is not especially productive, because it drives the writer to shape his or her thoughts and ideas into a restrictive structure. Further, research in psycholinguistics seems to support the idea that "form" is something that evolves *from* the specific content with which the writer is engaged. Still, there are times, particularly when the class is working on an individualized basis, that students need advice on structure. At that time, they will find "How-to-Write-It" cards helpful. Prepare cards on "How to Write an Essay" (including some information about form and structure and the conventions of the contemporary essay) or "How to Write a Poem" (with information on basic poetic structures, styles, and the like). Other forms or genres for which materials can be prepared include stories, plays, biography and autobiography, films, newspaper stories, reminiscences, and letters.

IN LITERATURE

Do-it-yourself reading materials are possible in almost endless permutations. An obvious extension of the free reading approach is to offer students a rich variety of *short* works: poems, stories, one-act plays, essays, editorials, and the like. To prepare such materials, get out your razor blades and start clipping from newspapers, circulars, advertisements, obsolete language arts anthologies, little magazines, big magazines. . . . When you are knee deep in literature that you think the kids will enjoy reading, start sorting, looking for obvious categories. Depending on the kinds of literature and the kinds of student interests you perceive, you may find some of the following useful in developing and structuring your materials:

➡ *Bin files.* The simplest and most direct approach—one borrowed directly from librarians—is simply to use boxes or envelopes (bins) to file related materials. A list of topics or categories provided to the class may be all that is needed to start students reading in an area of their choice.

➡ *Thematic packets.* A more literary approach is to organize materials along themes—Love, Hate, Courage, Frontiers, Coming of Age, Identity—themes calculated to appeal to the reading interests and personal needs of young people. Thematic packets can also contain a bibliography of related full-length works of fiction and nonfiction. Thematic packets are enhanced by including a series of related or complementary writing activities.

➡ *Special-interest packs.* The interests of young people are endless. In any given class you might find kids excited about yoga, track and field, women's rights, astronomy, carpentry, deserts, stamps and coins, photography, or backpacking. Develop as many special-interest packs as your class can pursue. Or let students develop packets as a final project or independent study. (Suggestion: If your school or community is concerned about career education, developing a set of interest packs on careers may be one way of fulfilling your obligation to teach about careers without turning your class into a version of the Job Corps.)

Genre groupings. Some students like to read plays—or poems, or mysteries, or science fiction, or motorcycle tales, or teen romances, or. . . . Create a series of bin files on these and other genres. A good spin-off project from a genre grouping is to have the students create their own materials in the same vein, their own plays or poems or mysteries or motorcycle stories or. . . .

Bard cards. The Centre for Internationalising English produces some inexpensive "bard cards"—postcards containing a poem plus a bit of information about the poet. Make your own set of bard cards, with perhaps two or three poems by a particular poet on one side and a bibliography and biographical note on the reverse. These cards are a useful way of helping students get to know authors and their works without the pain of formal biographical study. (If you ever played the card game "Authors" as a child, you can probably still remember the drawings of those authors and the titles required to fill out one of their "books.")

Novel teasers. Pull two or three exciting, unusual, or intriguing (but representative) passages from a novel and paste them on a card, along with information about where the book can be located.

IN LANGUAGE

Language studies—especially studies *other* than grammar—provide a useful area for development of imaginative, teacher-built materials:

Game cards. These are a natural. Any paperback bookstore contains books and magazines with hundreds of interesting language games: crosswords, diacrostics, word searches, anagrams, riddles, tongue twisters, etc. Acquire a variety of these materials and cut and paste to create activity cards. Most teachers who try this are astonished by the number of students attracted to these kinds of games.

Dialect puzzlers. A number of contemporary textbooks contain useful information on regional dialect differences. What do you call the kitchen utensil in which fried foods are prepared? How do you pronounce the beer that claims to have "gusto"? What do you call the part of the house beneath the first floor? Adapt such materials to provide miniresearch projects, where students can explore each others' dialects. This is an especially useful way of helping students develop an awareness of dialect differences without creating a sense of self-consciousness or snobbery.

Doublespeakers. Paste up examples of the most outrageous examples of public doublespeak you can find. On the reverse of an activity card, write a "translation" or place an "answer key" in an envelope glued to the back. Or give students "straight" English sentences and let them explore ways of translating them into doublespeak.

Sales hype. Collect newspaper and magazine advertisements and create activity cards which encourage students to explore truth in advertising.

Other Forms of Do-It-Yourself Materials

POSTERS

Everybody reads posters, nonreaders included. If you really want students to read something, don't assign it—*post it.* Not only will your kids read it, a good proportion of the school population will as well.

Poetry posters. Similar in conception to the bard cards described earlier, poetry posters include six short poems by an individual poet, plus biographical notes and sample discussion questions.

Fiction posters. A friend of ours posts his unpublished novel, chapter by chapter, and leaves a blank sheet of paper for comments. Try this with published novels (a chapter a week), long stories, or student writing.

Book review posters. Feature brief reviews of new books. The librarian may help you in preparing these. (Also look for announcements of the annual displays prepared by the Children's Book Council. These inexpensive materials are useful in promoting reading.)

How-to-do-it posters. Provide practical information on media projects, library use, proofreading, writing an essay or short story, or any of a dozen other skills.

LEARNING ACTIVITY PACKETS

The term LAP has been applied to a wide variety of teacher-constructed learning materials, ranging from skill-learning packets to independent reading guides. For our purposes, a LAP can best be described as a sequenced set of materials designed to reach a specific concept or skill. We've seen LAPs built on such topics as writing haiku, making a film or slide tape, editing one's own writing, recognizing parts of speech, and constructing a learning activity packet (a LAP on LAPs). The packets we've seen also vary widely in quality; some develop ideas with freshness and originality, while others seem to be little more than traditional textbook material in a loose-leaf form.

In general, LAPs have the following common characteristics:

1. *A statement of goals, aims, or objectives* (*not* invariably in behavioral terminology). The objectives section makes it clear to the student what he is going to learn or what he will be able to do upon completion of the packet.

2. *Some preliminary "diagnostic" material* (an optional feature). It is often useful to assess the student's interest in, or previous experience with, the area or to gauge his familiarity with the concept to be taught. It is important to emphasize that this section need *not* be a test (though many LAPs begin with a brief pretest). It might consist of an informal questionnaire or interest inventory, on the basis of which the student is channeled into the resources of the packet.

3. *Teaching materials.* This section, of course, determines the success or failure of the LAP, as well as its overall quality and appeal to students. The best and most interesting LAPs contain a rich variety of activities and options—usually *un*like those found in conventional textbooks—which treat the skill or concept imaginatively. LAPs also need to include material that guides the student through the activities. This can be as structured as a programmed text (usually appropriate for teaching simple skills) or as flexible as a broad set of directions (more appropriate for complex skills or multiple concepts).

4. *Evaluation and follow-up.* This may be a test, but need not be. Many LAPs include instructions for self-assessment and self-evaluation, thus giving students practice in determining their own success or failure at various learning tasks. In any event, it is important for the student to have some sense at the end of the program of whether or not he has accomplished the task or learned the skill in question.

BROADSHEETS

These are self-contained leaflets or folders with several literary selections, some discussion questions or project topics, and references to longer works. They are more complex than activity cards because of the diversity of materials they present. Unfortunately, the best illustration of broadsheets is a difficult-to-obtain series written by Peter Abbs and published in Great Britain by Heinemann. Abbs's broadsheets are attractively illustrated, contain high-interest literature, and ask response-oriented, open-ended questions. His topics include such diverse themes as "Living Men, Dead Animals," "Modern Advertising," "Nonsense Poetry," "Old Age," "The End of the World," "Rhythm and Rhyme," "Images," "Onomatopoeia," "The Future," and "Growing Up." You can make your own set of broadsheets using file folders or large sheets of construction paper to create four-page leaflets on a host of subjects.

JACKDAWS

The jackdaw is another British creation, a loose-leaf collection of materials with an emphasis on "facsimile" documents and primary historical sources. A jackdaw can contain newspaper clippings, notes, letters and memos, tapes of radio broadcasts, magazine articles, advertisements, plus related literary selections. While jackdaws often have a history or social studies emphasis (a result of their reliance on primary sources), they are extremely useful in English classes, particularly those with an interdisciplinary focus. Jackdaws also offer an imaginative approach to the old bugbear of the "term paper" by providing a controlled set of materials that can be used for creative research. (A commercial set of jackdaws has been prepared by Grossman Publishers, Inc. English-related jackdaws in their series include "The Young Shakespeare," "Wordsworth," "Charles Dickens," "The Brontës," "The Development of Writing," and "Caxton and the Early Printers." The historical focus of jackdaws shows through in this list, but teachers need not limit themselves to biographical or historical materials in creating their own jackdaws.) Let your students explore, research, and write about such topics as "Cities," "Noise," "The Literature of the Thirties," "Rock Poetry," "The History of the Cinema," "Jazz," "Floods," "Education," "Careers," "Dialects," or "Dramatics." Small jackdaws (containing fifteen or twenty source items) can sustain individual or small-group study for several days or a week; larger jackdaws can provide work for an entire class for days, weeks, or (quite literally) an entire term.

MAGAZINES

Though some claim students don't read as much as they used to, magazine reading seems to retain its appeal for secondary-school students. A teacher we know had students create their own magazines on special-interest topics—from fashion to automotive repair. Each magazine contained editorial matter, feature stories, columns, fiction, advertisements, and special features prepared by the students. Magazines can be duplicated for the entire class or prepared as one-of-a-kind publications. Random House has produced a teaching kit called "The Mag Bag" that you might find a useful resource. "The Mag Bag" includes sample copies of a variety of commercial magazines, a magazine explaining how to write and edit a magazine, and a series of activity cards useful for small-group work on aspects of magazine production.

ANTHOLOGIES

A few years ago, Aspen Communications published *The Comp Box,* by Ray Kytle (reissued by Random House, 1975). It consists of loose-leaf reprints of a number of magazine articles, arranged thematically, and the gimmick of the "text" was that college freshmen were to put together their own anthology or contemporary magazine. The idea has obvious extensions to the secondary school. Why not let your students create a series of topical anthologies based on their own experiences with literature? After a class unit or at the close of an elective, let students prepare anthologies on "Science Fiction" or "Black Poetry" or "Folklore," including essays and articles, book reviews, and even quizzes or project ideas. The next time you teach the unit or course, consider using the students' anthologies in lieu of (more expensive) common texts.

BOOKS

The "language experience" approach to reading, widely practiced at the elementary-school level, deserves a great deal of credit for popularizing "book making" in the schools. Language experience makes children's own writing the "stuff" of the reading program, and it builds in provisions for young children to dictate stories and poems to older children or adults, eventually leading to student-written books from which the kids learn to read.

In many schools where language experience is used, bound copies of the children's books are placed in the library, where they are catalogued along with the "regular" books. This provides the young author-reader with the enormous satisfaction of seeing his or her book shelved and having his name listed in the school's card catalog. (In elementary schools where this is done, one frequently sees children looking up their own books—just checking and smiling.)

In schools where funds are limited (and in schools where funds are *not* limited), book making has great appeal, and it promotes both the reading and writing programs. Students can make books on any conceivable subject, from Zen to the art of motorcycle maintenance. They can make cookbooks and dictionaries. They can bind anthologies of poems, stories, and essays, their own or those selected from other sources. (We have had particularly good luck with a book called *The Book of Myself,* a hand-bound collection of the student's best, most personal writing.)

Much of the intrinsic appeal in book making comes in the process of binding the book itself. A number of "recipes" for preparing and binding books are in circulation. (See figure 2.) The best single reference we've found is *How to Make Your Own Books,* by Harvey Weiss (New York: Crowell, 1974). Weiss reviews such matters as finding interesting papers for text and covers, cutting and folding paper to create signatures, as well as procedures for binding an attractive variety of books, including journals and diaries, flip books (or flip movies), albums, accordian-folded books, scrolls, and novelty books with cut-outs, paste-ups, and see-throughs.

To supplement the bookmaking process, we also suggest that the teacher bring in some rudimentary printing supplies, including typewriter, rubber lettering stamps, stick-on lettering, and the like. (In some communities, students have gained access to letterpress equipment and had the excitement of handsetting the type for their own publication, a process recommended only for shorter works, not novels or essays.)

MEDIA PROJECTS

Given the appeal of media, the teacher can bolster his or her supply of materials by consciously planning to use kids' media projects as a class resource. (See chapter 24, "Media in the Classroom.") Students can make films or slide-tapes treating the work of an individual poet or the poetry of a period; they can prepare taped radio documentaries on literature, current events, and even the writing

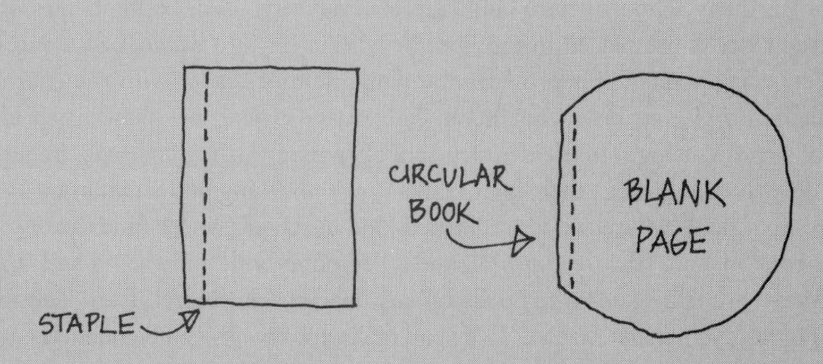

1. After completing your book, add one blank page at the front and back and staple along the left side. (Books can be almost any size or shape.)

2. Cut two pieces of stiff cardboard roughly ½" larger in all dimensions than your page size. (Set aside the book for a bit.)

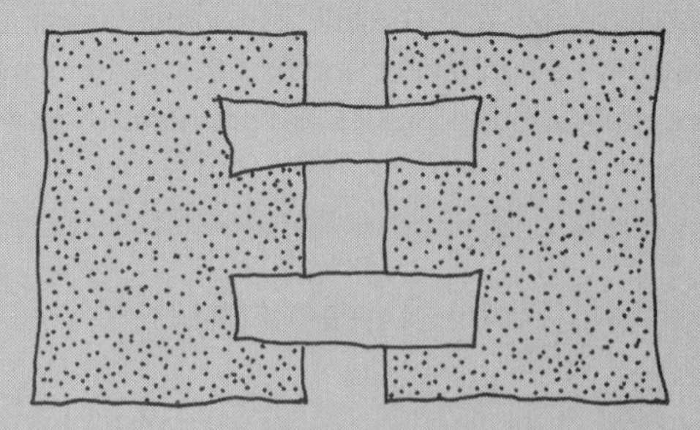

3. Tape the two cardboard covers together with cloth or strapping tape, leaving approximately ½" (more for large books).

FIGURE 2

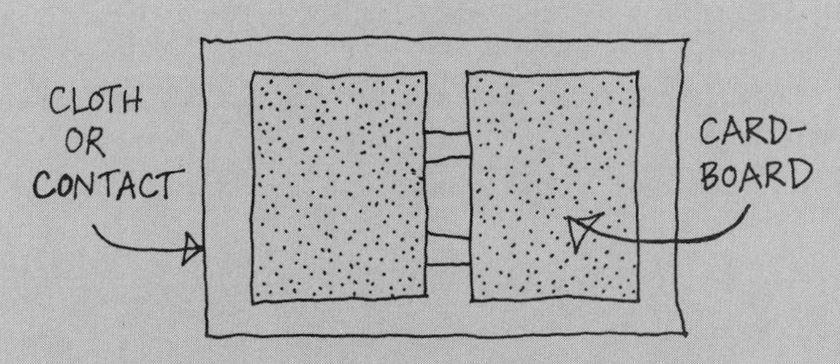

4. Cut a piece of fabric or contact paper approximately ¾" larger in all dimensions than your taped covers.

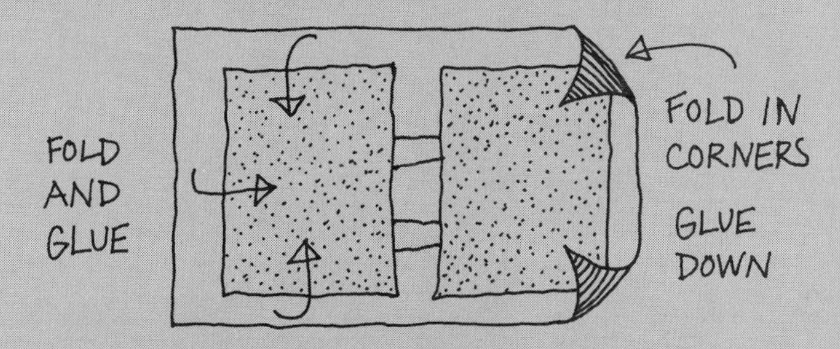

5. Using white glue for cloth or natural "stickum" for contact, "miter" the corners, and glue the covers to the cloth or contact.

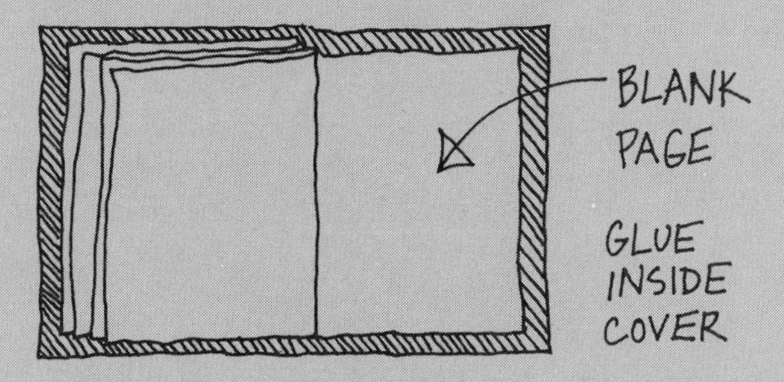

6. Insert the text in the covers and glue the blank front and back pages to the cardboard.

process; they can videotape scenes from literary works, one-act plays, and "interviews" with authors; they can tape-record dramatic and readers' theater presentations. By incorporating media projects in this way, you not only enhance your supply of materials, you bring media out of the realm of "novelty" and into the mainstream of English.

CHAPTER 4

Outsiders In: Using Paraprofessionals and Aides

The use of teacher aides, interns, and paraprofessionals has increased dramatically in the past decade and a half. In the early sixties, federally funded lay reader programs brought aides into the schools. Later in the decade, programs like Head Start featured low student-teacher ratios with the use of volunteers. Still later, colleges and universities became interested in volunteer and field experience programs to increase the number of aides available to teachers.

Unfortunately, sophistication in the *use* of aides had not developed as rapidly as the availability of people who want to help, and in many schools, paraprofessional programs have floundered, creating bad feelings among teachers, administrators, and the volunteers or aides.

There seem to be three principal sources of the discontent:

1. Frequently the time aides spend in the schools is disjointed. The aide comes in only once or twice each week, and teachers find it difficult to integrate him or her into regular class activities. As a result, the aide is assigned whatever task of the moment the teacher has on hand and feels frustrated.

2. Too often teachers have used aides strictly for trivial projects: filing papers and correcting exams—tasks that are the emotional equivalent of dusting the erasers. While aides should be willing to participate in routine classroom items, they ought to have a crack at exciting and original things as well.

3. Planning time is not available. The aide shows up at 9:00 A.M. for a 9:05 class; the teacher is harassed trying to make last-minute plans; no planning takes place and the aide feels unwanted and unused.

Interestingly enough, one area of concern that proves *not* to be much of a problem is the amount of formal training the aide has received. Whether or not the aide has a degree in English (or even any training beyond high school) does not seriously hamper a program if (and it's a big *if*) the teacher and aide are able to work together closely.

While there are no easy solutions to these problems, we want to share a way of proceeding that has worked with success for us. It consists of a long list of projects that we have found appropriate for teacher aides of varying degrees of skill and sophistication. It is based on our belief that aide programs work best if the teacher views the helper not as someone to take over dull aspects of the class, but as a person whose time can be used to *enrich* the class offerings.

To use the checklist:

1. Duplicate the list, adding additional projects that seem appropriate for your class.

2. Have your aide look through the list, checking off projects that he or she feels qualified to lead and is interested in doing.

3. Go through the list yourself, checking off the priority items for your class.

4. Compare lists and negotiate a set of activities for, say, the next nine weeks, that fit your aide's pattern of attendance.

Planning Checklist for Teacher Aides*

( ) Interview students about their writing interests and their concerns about writing. Prepare a report or profile for the teacher.

( ) Help the English department prepare a schoolwide survey of writing in English (and other) classes. How often do teachers ask students to write? What kinds of writing are demanded? What are teachers doing to give young people the skills required for those projects?

( ) Leaf through a collection of writing books and pluck out all of the writing assignments that look interesting and exciting. Put them on index cards for the teacher.

( ) Check out the room environment. In what ways is it (or isn't it) conducive to learning? Prepare a list of ways of improving the environment.

( ) Make a survey of the learning resources available in the school or district. Check for AV equipment, learning centers, and resource centers. Look into local and state libraries and the services of the sundry government bureaus.

( ) Help the teacher prepare a list of recommended acquisitions for the

* We wish to thank Karen Rottink for her assistance in developing an early draft of this checklist, which has been tested in the English education program at Michigan State University.

school library. (Check first with the librarian to learn the procedure.) Do the same with film and media resources.

( ) Review free reading books for the class, checking (among other things) for language or scenes that might be objectionable to some members of the community.

( ) Visit a paperback bookstore and prepare a list of new titles that might be useful in the English class.

( ) Take a group of students on a pilgrimage to a paperback store.

( ) Assist a group of students in setting up a book review service for free reading paperbacks and other materials.

( ) Begin a series of readings from literature for interested students in the class. Announce titles a week or so in advance so that students and the teacher can plan.

( ) Do the same with a series of recorded readings or dramatizations from literature.

( ) Work with small groups of students helping them learn how to edit their own writing.

( ) Assist a small group in preparing a dramatic presentation for the rest of the class.

( ) Set up the mechanism for an in-class newspaper or magazine, including procedures for preparing and editing copy and actual production of the paper, whether by ditto, mimeo, or offset printing.

( ) Form a poetry club or help establish a place where the poetry addicts can read and write poems for their own pleasure.

( ) Do the same for future journalists.

( ) Organize a young writers workshop for a single class or a school. Locate area writers who are willing to talk with young people about writing and get them to conduct a workshop.

( ) Check your state council for the arts to see if it has a poets in the schools program. Help the teacher plan and organize the visit of a poet.

( ) Write the drama department of a nearby university to see if it can present plays for the school where you are working.

( ) Media projects are always time consuming and present a supervision problem for teachers. Learn a bit about media production yourself and help small groups of students in the preparation of films, photo essays, slide tapes, radio broadcasts, and the like.

( ) Help students set up a paperback bookstore for the entire school. See your local paperback distributor for help.

( ) Organize a used paperback drive within the community.

( ) Help the teacher in the preparation of homemade materials: activity cards, resource packets, free reading libraries, and the like.

( ) Provide help for "slow" readers. You don't have to have special training in reading to help a kid get through his or her homework assignment successfully.

( ) Make a survey of student reading interests for use in preparing a class library.

( ) Gather materials on a theme selected for study by the class: "Self-Discovery," "Science Fiction," "Poetry of the Thirties." Search out print and nonprint materials: books, poems, films, recordings. Work with the teacher in organizing a series of lessons on a theme.

( ) With other aides, organize and establish a tutoring center, where kids can come at any time of the school day for help with reading and writing problems.

( ) Contact the local chamber of commerce and/or service clubs to obtain a list of community members who are willing to speak on various topics.

( ) Arrange for community business leaders to talk with students about the literacy demands of their business or industry.

( ) Serve as liaison between the English department and the Parent Teacher Organization, drawing on your knowledge of the school as a way of informing parents.

( ) Lead small discussion groups as part of regular English lessons.

( ) If your interest runs along this line, take over the class for a session . . . or two . . . or several. Work closely with the teacher to supplement his or her plans for the class.

And so forth. . . . We hope this series of ideas gives you some indication of the exciting range of activities that teacher aides can conduct. Presumably the teacher can double or triple the list with activities directly related to an American Studies, Creative Writing, Mythology, or Folklore class.

But What If You Don't Have Any Aides?

Some sources of free and inexpensive people:

Parents interested in education. Parents are increasingly concerned about the teaching of literacy in the schools. "Why are the SAT scores in decline?"

"Whatever happened to the three R's?" Instead of fighting such groups, ask for their help. Contact the PTO and actively solicit their assistance. Advertise for parent aides through articles in the local newspaper. Try to develop in parents a sense of responsibility for what's happening in your school. Also, give credit and praise *lavishly* for parents who participate.

University methods courses. University instructors are increasingly eager to find teachers who want to provide their students with a field experience. Call up the English or education department if a university is nearby and ask to talk with the "methods" instructor.

University volunteer programs. Look into the various volunteer groups on most college campuses. You may wind up with "nonspecialists," but on the other hand, you might find it very useful to have a chemistry or biology major working with those of your students who have a science interest.

Young people. Many schools have experimented with peer instruction—seniors tutoring sophomores, high-school students tutoring in the junior high, junior-high young people working with elementary students. In one school we've visited, a "prize" for the successfully reading first-grader is the right to visit and read to the (nonreading) kindergartners. Obviously not all students can function well in this arrangement (either as tutors or students). Nevertheless, in the situations where students have the basic aptitudes, peer instruction is remarkably successful.

Senior citizens. Perhaps the most wasted resource of this nation is its retirees, many of whom would be delighted to be invited to work with young people. Check with retirement communities and senior citizen groups in the search for aides.

CHAPTER 5

Alphabet Soup: A Stock of Grading Alternatives

Teachers are often afflicted by the "end-of-the-term blues," not just because they have papers and projects stacked up to read, but also because they must then assign a final grade. Students must be sorted and categorized so that they can fit into their place in the unyielding ABC system, and teachers who have worked to make their classrooms a productive place for seeking and questioning must, to some extent, undercut their acceptance of students by pigeonholing them. The problem is expressing the complexity of a student's growth through an abstract symbol. Should the teacher grade on interest and involvement? Cooperation? Growth? Competency? Work output? Effort? And what emphasis is put on each of these? What does one do about the student who comes in with little interest and great difficulty with language, but works hard during the term, even though he cannot deal with the same work that the rest of the class is doing? And what about the composition student who writes creative and imaginative stories but can't spell or punctuate? Or the student who is very competent in reading and writing but produces uninvolved work and grows very little during the course? Finally, how do the grades we give to students affect the way they think of themselves—as readers and writers, as learners, as human beings?

No one is completely satisfied with the grading system as it is, and there is plenty of evidence to support the case that grading has negative effects. Writing in *The English Journal* [74 (March 1975)], Maran Doggett catalogues the disadvantages of the grading system and "The ABC Affair." He objects that grades deny the psychological principle of individual differences and individual rates of growth; preoccupy parents and students, so that emphasis is placed on what a student "gets" rather than how and what he or she learns; give the appearance of objectivity, but are variable and subjective; and often influence teachers toward narrow teaching—requiring memorization and rote learning—which can be graded more objectively. Grades are elitist, rather than democratic; grades encourage unhealthy competition between students and create student dependence on teachers; and finally, grades have negative emotional impact (p. 72).

Even though educators, psychologists, and learning theorists can present strong evidence against the practice of grading, the system is strongly entrenched in the educational establishment. Students and their parents, we are told, "need" grades; they "want to know where they stand," how they rank, what their position is in relation to others'. Some teachers require grades so that they can tell with a glance at the records what a student's academic history and standing has been. College officials and employers rely on grades to determine the suitability of a student for their institution or business. So the education mill continues to grind out products and give them rank ordering.

What is the response of the humanistic teacher who wants evaluation to be a part of the growing and learning process, yet finds grading harmful? What alternatives are there to the abstract and simplistic systems of evaluation most of us are now using?

The School and the Grading System

Schools and school systems occasionally have experimented with alternatives to the traditional ABC grading system with some success, and efforts toward such experimentation seem worthwhile, if only to raise questions about the importance and usefulness of grades. In *Wad 'Ja Get?* (New York: Hart Publishing, 1972), a book on alternatives to grading, Simon, Napier, and Kirschenbaum suggest that schools establish a task force to work on reform in grading. They state that teachers, parents, administrators, and board members need to collect and communicate valid information about the use and the abuse of grading to other teachers, community members, and people in decision-making positions in order to promote changes in the grading system. Such a committee, we think, might review several grading systems which offer alternatives to the traditional evaluation symbols. The following have been used with success in some schools:

➡ *Pass/fail; credit/no credit.* Variations on the Pass/Fail grading system are common. The *Pass/Fail* denotation on the student record does not provide detailed information to the student or the parents about the student's performance. However, it creates a deemphasis on class standing and weighting of evaluation items, so that the teacher is able to focus more on the whole student and his or her progress and growth. In the Pass/Fail grading system the teacher is able to set minimum standards—perhaps the equivalent of "C" level—for student achievement, and students falling below that level fail. The *Credit/No Credit* system provides the same sort of open-ended expectations, but failure is deemphasized, for students who do not meet minimum standards simply do not receive credit for the course.

➡ *Pass/question; pass/incomplete.* These two schemes do not assume closure at the end of the course and emphasize the need to understand the task, the student's relationship to the task, what went wrong, and how that student might be successful. *Pass/Incomplete* courses give students the opportunity to complete the task successfully after the end of the marking period. The *Pass/Question* grade ("Question" simply means that the teacher questions the thoroughness or acceptability of the student's work) places emphasis on the complexity of the learning process, so that if a student is not able to be successful in a particular course, he is not penalized and a question of what went wrong is raised. Student inadequacy is not automatically assumed. Another variation, *Pass/Question and Describe,* takes the questioning of student performance even further by actually having written evaluations of students accompany grades of question.

Working within the Grading System

No matter what sort of official grading system one uses, the need to provide students (and their parents) a full and accurate, evaluation of growth and performance is necessary. Moreover, any really useful evaluation (any evaluation that is truly part of the learning process) requires that a student have a clear sense of the basis for evaluation and ideally some opportunity to participate in the evaluation.

➡ In "Putting the Hidden Curriculum of Grading to Work" (*The English Journal* 74 [March 1975]: 83), Kenneth Lewis provides one model of grading that takes into consideration and makes explicit some of the qualities often implicit when teachers give grades (figure 1). Lewis distributes his list of standards at the beginning of the term and allows students to discuss them and suggest modifications. Their discussion brings everyone's values out in the open and allows the students to fully understand the expectations placed on them.

The following forms of evaluation also allow both teachers and students to make explicit their values in grading. They may be used throughout the course to describe ongoing progress as well as at the end.

GRADING STANDARDS

QUALITY OF WORK – written, oral reports, etc. (This is in comparison with a high and demanding standard I carry around in my head – not in comparison with anyone else in this class.)

Excellent – consistently meeting or even exceeding the high standards I hold . . . . A
Good – accurate but not top-notch, or inconsistent work . . . . . . B
Mediocre – barely meeting assignments – so-so quality C
Poor – low quality . . . . D

EFFORT

Always work to best of your ability – every activity, be it writing or oral work was accomplished with pride and a determination to do your best . . . . A
Making a good effort – good but not consistently giving your "all" . . . . B
So-so effort – or extremely inconsistent effort – you didn't consistently care much or try very hard C
Little effort – only a flicker of response – not trying or caring, only filling a space up . . . . D

CLASS PARTICIPATION, COOPERATION, ATTITUDE

Significant contribution – forwarding all group activities – positive, open attitude – constant and spontaneous effort to make this class (this partnership of teacher and students to learn) work . . . . A
Some contribution – working for the class sometimes – "proper" attitude . . . . B
Answers when obliged to – neutral attitude – irregular cooperation C
Filling a space – little cooperation – indifferent – even hostile – gets in the way of the class . . . . D

INDIVIDUAL IMPROVEMENT (within the limitations of my ability as a teacher and the structure of this class – obviously you should not be penalized if I or the class do not aid your honest and deliberate efforts at improvement)

Marked and growing . . . . A
Signs of progress, responding to class or individual stimulation . . . B
No progress C

Source: Kenneth Lewis, "Putting the Hidden Curriculum of Grading to Work," The English Journal 74 (March 1975): 83.

FIGURE 1

Written evaluation (*or twenty-six-letter grading*). Written evaluations simply mean making clear all of the qualities and variables you took into consideration when giving a grade. In a written evaluation, everything you take into consideration should be explained. (Of course, we assume that these things are explained at the outset of a course, as well.) Did the student work to capacity? Did he or she use all the resources available? Did the student show care in the preparation of the assignment? Did the student respond to ongoing evaluation of his work? Written evaluations also give the teacher the opportunity to talk about things that might not be reflected in a grade. What are the student's strong points as a writer/speaker/listener/reader? What areas cause the student problems and what specific things might he or she do to work on weaknesses? What further directions of study are appropriate for the student?

Self-evaluation. Often, both teachers and students balk at the idea of student self-evaluation. It is believed traditionally that the teacher's expertise makes him the best judge. While it is true that teachers have been trained to be perceptive about language performance, we think that the need for self-appraisal and self-understanding in the form of self-evaluation is a crucial part of growth. In a three-part self-evaluation, the student may do the following:

1. *Describe.* Describe the project and the work you did. What was the purpose? What did you wish to accomplish with it? What books did you read? What other reading resources and materials did you consult? What people resources did you use? Media resources? What form is the final project? What other forms or ways of presentation did you consider? How much time was involved in the preparation of the project? What pitfalls and problems did you have to overcome in doing the project? What satisfactions did you find?

2. *Assess.* Did the project turn out as you wanted it to? What parts are you most satisfied with? Which are least satisfactory? How would you do it differently if you were to do it again? What problems did you have?

3. *Predict.* How do you expect your audience to respond to your project? Where do you want to go from here? What reading and writing would you like to do next? What related project would you like to pursue? What is the most helpful or valuable thing you learned while doing this assignment? How could you improve your efforts in this area?

Student and teacher evaluation. Rather than sending an evaluation into the void, an evaluation shared by the student and teacher allows the two to compare perceptions and opinions. The ideal is for student and teacher to have an evaluation conference, but it is also possible for students and teachers to share opinions in written form, with student or teacher responding to the initial evaluation of the other.

Experience portfolio. An experience portfolio is simply a folder of all the student's work done throughout the semester. In addition to written papers, the portfolio may contain records of students' oral presentations, small-group work, dramatic participation, etc. Student self-evaluations and teacher feedback are kept in the folder as a quick reference to the work the student has done and to the teacher's response to that work. Peer evaluations of papers and presentations may also be a part of an experience portfolio.

Performance checklist. The performance checklist provides both teacher and student with a clear sense of the expectations for the course or unit. The checklist can be a very specific list of class activities, such as "Read *The Pigman* and write a character sketch of a character from the novel"; "Read three newspaper editorials and write a newspaper editorial"; or "Lead a small group discussion on doublespeak." Or the checklist can list skills and abilities the student has developed during the term.

Again, student and teacher are aware at a glance what the student is accomplishing. Student or teacher evaluation can also accompany the form to indicate quality as well as quantity of work done.

Giving the Grade

Even when you are able to develop an evaluation system that you feel provides both you and the students with a clear sense of the students' growth and performance, there still comes, for most of us, the time when we must distill all that we know about a student's language abilities, grasp of ideas and concepts, public performance, investment and enthusiasm into a grade. A pure averaging of grades never seems adequate, and the teacher who has abandoned grades for a fuller form of evaluation throughout the term finds the final giving of a grade difficult. Consider some of the following, alone or in combination:

Self-grading. If students have been given the responsibility of evaluating themselves throughout the term, it seems sensible (and fair) that they also have a part of that responsibility when it comes to giving a grade. Students who are mature and who have developed the habit of looking at their work critically handle self-grading very well and, in our experience, are all too likely to give themselves grades lower than what the teacher might give (contrary to the belief that they will all give themselves an A).

Recommended grades. Rather than give the responsibility of grading solely over to the student, recommended grades again give the student the opportunity to tell the teacher what grade the student thinks best reflects the work he or she has done (with supporting documentation). The teacher takes the student's evaluation into consideration when giving the grade.

► *Matched grades.* The student and the teacher prepare evaluations and give grades separately. The two grades are averaged.

► *Conference grading.* Recommended grades and matched grades in which the teacher uses the student's self-evaluation can probably be handled fairly, if the teacher and student have the opportunity to discuss one another's grade when there is a difference of opinion. Grades don't have to be settled on before the conference, however. Teacher and student can use the conference to discuss a grade on which they could both agree.

The above grading systems, of course, require the student's taking over a great deal of responsibility for his learning and for developing an awareness of his own goals and his growth and progress toward those goals. This also means that the teacher must give over to the students what has often been assumed to be the teacher's area of responsibility. When using these grading systems, then, it's important that the teacher be honestly willing to share these roles of goal setter/evaluator. It is a destructive breach of trust to pretend to encourage that sort of sharing and then, when grading time comes around, to ignore or diminish the importance of the student's evaluations.

Several other grading systems provide for students a clear sense of what's expected of them, place the responsibility of the grade on the learners, yet allow the teacher to set the standards for grades.

► *Minimum plus.* In this system, the teacher sets the minimum standards for a passing grade, and additional work done in the course or unit improves the grade. For example, to get a C in a writing course, a student may have to do a minimum number of papers, say five in a nine-week unit. To get a B or an A, the student fulfills requirements that the teacher sets in advance. For a B, the student may have three additional papers, write an extended paper on a new area of exploration, or make a how-to tape for the composition library; for an A, the student may, in addition, polish and publish two papers for sharing with the class through readings, bulletin boards, or class publication. Or the student may have to be responsible for serving as a consultant in the editing corner for a certain period of time.

► *Point system.* The point system operates on the same notion as the minimum plus system, but point values are attached to projects and tasks that, when summed up, determine the grade the student gets for his work in the course. Successful completion of the basic projects in the course—a certain number of assigned projects—will give a student a C or Pass. Additional projects or assignments are given points according to their value and sophistication. In a literature course, for example, students may receive ten points for every book they read accompanied by a response card or brief paper. If the teacher would like ten books to be a minimum number of books read, 100 points is set as the number needed for C. To get a B, the student must accumulate 150 points, and for an A, 200 points. The teacher then designs projects worth various points from which the student may choose: 50 points for a film based on a poem or story; 20 points for an improvisation of a scene from a novel; 30 points for producing a play; 10 points for a poem poster; 30 points for an oral presentation.

When using individual or group projects for students to fulfill course requirements, it is important to have a detailed scheduling system with deadlines and due dates in order to avoid the last-minute crush of students trying to garner points in the last week of class. It's also important to have a good bookkeeping system to keep track of the assignments students have done and the points earned.

Performance mastery by levels. This approach provides teachers with a means of describing quality and sophistication of work. The teacher describes various levels of performance (for example, mastery of writing "modes"), knowledge (extent of information about authors, books, genres, etc.), or skills (ability to use library and resource materials, write bibliographies and footnotes, write a variety of sentence types or paragraph organizations, etc.). Because using language is so complex, description of performance mastery requires the teacher to describe fully what success in the use of language is. Alternatively, performance mastery levels can be used to itemize the picky little things you usually see described in behavioral objectives.

Blanket-grading. For some teachers, grading and evaluating student performance is a contradiction to what they see as their more important role: nurturing the growth of thought and feeling. For those teachers, the blanket grade provides an out from the grading dilemma. They simply tell students at the beginning of the course that everyone in the course will get the same grade (usually an A or B). Then the worries and pressures of fulfilling requirements to get a particular grade are gone, and teacher and students can concentrate on the business of reading and writing, of exploring their language, their world, and themselves in personally satisfying ways. The question of fairness ("I did more, I should get more") loses significance in light of attention to personal goals and growth.

Managing Individualized Grading: The Contract

The contract provides students the opportunity to set their own goals and their own standards of achievement. In addition, it provides the teacher a means of individualizing evaluation of students and managing a multiplicity of class projects.

Simply, the contract is an agreement between the student and teacher about what the student wishes to accomplish in a particular class and the grade he or she should receive for fulfilling these goals. Components of the contract include:

1. Description of area of study. Within the limits of a particular course, students decide the areas they are most interested in and would like to pursue in more detail. In a course on American Humor, for example, the student may decide to research and describe humor in records, humor in music, or humor in comic books and cartoons.

2. Objectives. The student then develops a list of objectives related to his or her subject. If he or she decides to explore humor in comic books, for example, the list of objectives might look like this: to discover when and how the comic book began; to learn about the categories of humorous comic books; to discover who reads funny books and what they find humorous; and to try to make projections into the future of comics. The list of objectives also includes projects the student will complete: a class presentation, a media show, a formal paper, a survey form and interview summary, etc.

3. Evaluation criteria. These may be established in terms of amount of time the student devotes to the work, the volume of work completed, and/or the quality of the work done. The minimum plus system, the point system, and the mastery level system may all be used with the contract. Most important is that the student will determine in advance his own standards of achievement and the grade that he or she will earn in meeting those standards.

4. The "plan of attack." From a list of project ideas and resources provided by the teacher and extended by the student, the students develop their plan of attack for fulfilling the objectives they have set. What reading resources are available related to their subject? Magazines? Newspapers? Fiction and nonfiction? To whom might they talk? Are there community organizations that might have information? Can government agencies supply information? What businesses might send materials? Are there television shows or movies that could provide insight into their subject?

After students have decided the resources they want to use, they need to set up a schedule for accomplishing their objectives. Which items have priority?

If they are going to write letters, they will want to do that early. Interviews also need advance planning. A *calendar* or *checklist* can be included with the students' project files to help them and you to see what they have accomplished and what they have yet to do.

In addition to each student's list of activities and deadlines, the teacher can create a master list with dates for student performances, presentations, and progress reports to be given to the whole class. A list of whole-class activities gives students an idea of when they need to take out time from their own work and shows them what there is to look forward to.

In addition to having a schedule and checklist, students should have the opportunity to meet and talk with the teacher to provide a progress report and to receive help and guidance with their work. With students involved in individualized projects, you are free to spend a great deal of time helping students locate resources, make contacts, find forms for their ideas, and get through writing blocks and energy lags.

5. Student self-evaluation. The students' sense of their own progress and growth is especially important when using a contract in which the student sets his own goals. Self-evaluation should be a continuing part of the class rather than something done just at the end, with the student providing assessments of where he or she is in accomplishing his or her goals. A formal evaluation should occur at the end.

6. Teacher evaluation. Students need feedback about how they are doing and how they are being perceived by others. The teacher's evaluation should not be a surprise at the end, but should be an ongoing part of the course.

7. Implications for future work. Part of the evaluation system should include a look beyond the course for both the teacher and the student. As a result of this work, what future work would the student like to do? Have new areas aroused his or her interest? What reading and writing would the student like to try next? For the teacher: Are there new resources the students have discovered that you can offer in subsequent courses? Did the students encounter problems that you can smooth over in the future? What other activities might students do in a contract course? Did students have problems with defining areas of study, evaluation, or objectives? How can you make that easier? Did you provide too much guidance? Too little?

Evaluation, for both student and teacher, should be an ongoing process and clearly connected to the goals and aims that both teacher and student understand.

CHAPTER 6

The English Department: Aims and Priorities

English departments have a strange power base. They don't collect dues like the YMCA or a professional group; they don't have a great deal to say about who belongs or who doesn't like a fraternity or a sorority; and they aren't formed by a group of people just for purposes of doing something interesting like bowling or playing bridge. Though English departments usually have some sort of constitutional or democratic procedures blocked out and frequently elect their own leadership, the real "president" of the English department is someone outside its membership—the principal. In this respect, it's sad to say, an English department most resembles a school newspaper, which appears to be autonomous, yet has all of its decisions reviewed and inspected by an outside authority with veto power.

Even so, a well-organized, smoothly functioning English department can accomplish an extraordinary amount and make teaching life easier for all its members. Yet surprisingly few English departments run well. The general lack of good organization is indicated by numerous surveys that show that in many schools the English department hasn't ever written down a rationale for itself. In such a situation, the department is reduced to little more than a records-keeping center; it has no other philosophical or pedagogical raison d'etre.

A Community of Teachers

The metaphor that we think most satisfactorily describes a good English department is that of a *community*—a group of people who work (and sometimes play) together, who are united in a common concern (teaching literacy as well as it can possibly be taught), functioning under a common set of liberties and constraints (freedom to write the curriculum, but hampered by this year's minuscule supplies budget). A community of teachers will grant freedom to its members to teach as they wish, to teach as best they can, yet it will also discuss common concerns and seek solutions to problems.

The department-as-community needs to spend time discussing basic issues and fundamental questions to help discover its own nature and the skills of its members. Whether or not your department members can agree on the answers, spend some time in department meetings on such questions as:

■ What is our subject (call it English, language arts, humanities, communication arts, or whatever)? What (if anything) do young people need to know about English these days? How do people use language in society?

■ Is there any role for English teachers beyond the teaching of "fundamentals?"

■ Should English be a required subject? What would happen to our department if it were no longer required?

■ What are we doing right? And . . . to the contrary?

■ What are our unique strengths as teachers? How can we draw on those strengths as a group? Have a department meeting where you talk candidly about your teaching skills: "This I do well . . . this, not so well." Take responsibility for sharing one of your strengths with someone else.

■ What are our priorities? What issues, problems, or topics must concern us most deeply? What action can we take to solve those problems?

In far too many schools, departments get together so infrequently that they are little more than collections of individuals who happen to teach in the same building. Some projects for the departmental *community:*

► Have a session called "This Works (for Me)." Price of admission: a dittoed or mimeographed handout describing one teaching technique that works (for you).

► Create a "Free Ditto Exchange" and make the sharing of teaching ideas a tradition in the department. You may have trouble overcoming past bad experiences with this one, since many teachers jealously guard their ideas for fear that someone will "steal" them. To help solve that, set up ground rules about the use and misuse of other people's ideas. Also make it policy that when you use someone's idea you write him or her a note acknowledging it.

► In schools where departments simply *can't* function, perhaps owing to poor leadership or irreconcilable teaching styles, seek alternative ways of developing a sense of community and cohesiveness within the faculty. For instance, you might be able to establish a school-within-a-school or an experimental program taught by the people who *can* work together successfully.

- Fight for control of your departmental budget. Ask the administrator or the department head to give small grants for the purchase of materials by individual teachers, rather than forcing teachers to go through the process of schoolwide adoptions.
- To stir up an inactive department, start writing proposals for pilot programs. Make the department respond to your ideas. If the department is not the problem, try the same technique with the principal.
- Hold a joint meeting with the history and/or social studies departments to consider possible multidisciplinary courses. Use such courses as a way of breaking down conventional curricular or administrative structures.
- Try a teacher exchange between school buildings or even school districts for a week or two. This brings in fresh ideas and costs nothing.
- Initiate the same kind of exchange with a nearby college or university. Have the college supply an instructor for your course while you work with the prospective teachers.
- Try to obtain released time and adequate compensation for your department head. It is difficult for any department to function successfully when its leader has to teach four or five courses like everyone else.
- Give polls and surveys to students, teachers, parents, and other concerned people about their wishes and dreams for the schools. Put the computers to work analyzing their answers instead of processing standardized test scores.
- Keep administrators informed about departmental activities. One technique that seems to work well involves asking the administration's advice on solving a curriculum or teaching problem. That way, the administrators have a direct stake in the success (or failure) of the department.
- Take a counsellor to lunch and talk about what you are doing in your classes.
- Have a "Problems and Pleasures" session where you talk over the things in your teaching that give you greatest pleasure, along with things that present problems. It is a great deal easier to talk about failings if you describe them yourself rather than waiting for someone else to do it, and it may be that your problem is someone else's pleasure.
- Hold an articulation meeting for the junior-high/middle-school and senior-high faculties—but don't hold the meeting until both groups have worked out their individual rationales and can talk articulately about what they

are trying to accomplish. Ground rule: Neither group is to attack the other. Senior-high teachers are not allowed to criticize the preparation of incoming freshmen. Junior-high/middle-school people must restrain their comments about what happens to kids when they are "thrown into the high-school jungle."

Meet with the librarian or media resource person to discuss energizing the school's resources. Make the library a functioning extension of the English program, not just a place to send bright kids or troublemakers, or the location of once-a-year lectures on the use of the card catalogue and the mysteries of the Dewey Decimal System.

Setting Instructional Priorities

Perhaps at no other time in educational history has the stating of priorities mattered so much for teachers. We are besieged on all sides with complaints about the quality of our work; yet with the financial squeeze continuing, we have fewer and fewer resources available.

We can't do everything at once; human energies and financial resources won't permit it. But we can plan—as individuals, as departments, even as entire schools—to establish and order our priorities and concerns so that changes come about systematically, rather than willy-nilly. In figure 1 you will find an inventory that can be used by your department to assess your priorities for teaching and to come up with an informal rank ordering of projects that need attention.* It consists of a set of statements describing possible techniques, approaches, and methods for teaching English. Some of these practices center on teaching conditions (class size, for example); others focus on aims for teaching literature, writing, and language. In combination, the items pretty well cover the spectrum of English, but we have left blank spaces to indicate that you can add additional items.

PRIORITIES

Stage I: Rank Priorities

Go through the list and, after careful consideration, indicate on the scale of zero to five whether the item is high (5) or low (0) priority or something in

* We are indebted to M. Robert Graham, Oakland Schools, Pontiac, Michigan, for suggesting this general idea to us.

1. All departments in the school take responsibility for teaching the reading and writing skills needed for their content area.
   0 1 2 3 4 5
2. Resource libraries of books and media materials are a part of every English classroom.
   0 1 2 3 4 5
3. Letter grades are replaced by other forms of assessment and evaluation.
   0 1 2 3 4 5
4. The teaching of "oracy"—speaking and listening—is given attention along with "literacy" (reading and writing).
   0 1 2 3 4 5
5. Literature by and about minorities is included in literature and reading courses.
   0 1 2 3 4 5
6. Students must pass an examination in written English and mechanics as a prerequisite to graduation.
   0 1 2 3 4 5
7. Literature courses explore topical subjects or themes; such as "The Family," "War and Peace," "The Cities."
   0 1 2 3 4 5
8. Grade-level minimum objectives have been established by the English department.
   0 1 2 3 4 5
9. English course loads are reduced.
   0 1 2 3 4 5
10. Students are involved in free and/or guided individual reading programs.
    0 1 2 3 4 5
11. Creative dramatics and role playing are incorporated in English classes.
    0 1 2 3 4 5
12. Student writing is considered part of the "literature" of the English courses.
    0 1 2 3 4 5
13. Theme readers are provided to aid English teachers in the assessment of essays.
    0 1 2 3 4 5
14. Students explore their own experiences and concerns through personal and creative writing.
    0 1 2 3 4 5
15. Literary instruction includes such critical principles as the nature of form, style, versification, biographical backgrounds, and

FIGURE 1 WHAT'S FUNDAMENTAL?

literary content.

0 1 2 3 4 5

16. Teachers allow students to use the dialect of their regional, racial, ethnic, or social background.

    0 1 2 3 4 5

17. Literature study gives students an understanding of their cultural heritage through British, American, and world literature.

    0 1 2 3 4 5

18. The school system as we know it is dissolved and replaced by a network of community and alternative schools.

    0 1 2 3 4 5

19. The materials of popular culture – films, recordings, radio and TV, magazines – are included in the English course.

    0 1 2 3 4 5

20. Students must read within two years of grade level in order to be promoted.

    0 1 2 3 4 5

21. The "basics" of mechanics and usage are a concern of teachers in all English courses.

    0 1 2 3 4 5

22. Media composition – making films, tapes, slide shows – is included as a component in English courses.

    0 1 2 3 4 5

23. Students who are speakers of nonstandard dialects are encouraged to become bidialectal (using standard English as a "second language").

    0 1 2 3 4 5

24. Teachers are free to develop their own course objectives and to select their own reading materials.

    0 1 2 3 4 5

25. Students read a basic core of "clasic" literature in the secondary English program.

    0 1 2 3 4 5

26. Composition courses teach the writing forms commonly used in college and university courses.

    0 1 2 3 4 5

27. Course syllabi and reading materials are evolved through a departmentwide process.

    0 1 2 3 4 5

28. The English department has an established book selection and censorship policy.

    0 1 2 3 4 5

29. Students serve as critics and editors of their own writing.

    0 1 2 3 4 5

30. Curriculum offerings are clustered and/or required rather than presented as a completely free and open array of courses.
0 1 2 3 4 5

31. Instruction in "basics" takes place in specialized courses and laboratories staffed by specialists.
0 1 2 3 4 5

32. Teachers are provided with released time and inservice time for development and evaluation of courses.
0 1 2 3 4 5

33. English departments and teachers meet to discuss articulation at appropriate levels (school-college, high school-junior high, secondary-elementary).
0 1 2 3 4 5

34. Writing instruction teaches the basic forms of practical communication; such as applications, letters, forms.
0 1 2 3 4 5

35. Students receive regular course-selection guidance from English teachers and/or counsellors.
0 1 2 3 4 5

36. Literature study asks students to bring their personal values and experiences to their reading.
0 1 2 3 4 5

37. English courses include the materials of history, art, philosophy, psychology, and music.
0 1 2 3 4 5

38. English projects, activities, and assignments are made on an individual basis.
0 1 2 3 4 5

39. Composition instruction includes the principles of structure, style, form, unity, coherence, and organization.
0 1 2 3 4 5

40. English courses cross interdisciplinary lines to include the materials of science, mathematics, and the practical arts (for instance, architecture).
0 1 2 3 4 5

41. ______________________________
____
____
0 1 2 3 4 5

42. ______________________________
____
____
0 1 2 3 4 5

FIGURE 1 (CONT.)

between in terms of your teaching. This is an "idealized" listing. Don't worry about whether something is possible or practical. If you think it is *important,* rank it high. Indicate your score by circling the appropriate number:

0 1 2 3 (4) 5

Then sum up the scores on a master list and discuss. Order priorities from high scores to low. This will provide you a sequenced list of *Quintessentials,* the changes or program components that you and your department members see as most important.

Stage II: Describe Realities

Go through the list a second time, this time ranking items in terms of how commonly they are practiced or how frequently this happens in your school or classroom. If you do something very regularly, rank it (5); if you do it infrequently, give it a (1); if you do not do it at all, give it a (0); and so on. Mark the appropriate number by drawing an × through it:

Again, sum your scores to create a list of *Realities,* a profile of English as it is being taught in your school. Discuss the list.

Stage III: Examine Discrepancies

Whether you're working alone or in a group, subtract your *Reality* scores (the ×-scores) for your *Quintessentials* (the circled scores). This will give you an indication of the *Discrepancy* between what you see as important and what you (and your colleagues) are actually doing at the moment. For example, in the illustration: 4 (priority score) − 1 (reality score) = 3 (discrepancy).

INTERPRETING SCORES

A *negative score* indicates that what you are doing (reality) *is not* in keeping with your own, self-proclaimed priorities; that is, you are spending time doing things that you don't think are particularly important. The message here is that you should discuss *why* so that you can cease burning energy where it is not needed.

A *low* or *zero score* indicates that your priorities and realities mesh pretty well. In that case, there's little point in spending more energy here, either. But don't be complacent. It's conceivable that both your priorities *and* your energies are being misdirected.

High positive scores indicate the areas where you and your colleagues would most like to change your teaching. On the basis of that list, you can begin to make plans for department or inservice meetings.

Thus, if you come up with a high positive score for, say, item number 2, "Resource libraries of books and media materials are part of every English classroom," you may want to plan a series of meetings with the library staff or launch a new paperback reading program. If your high score is on number 12, "Student writing is considered part of the 'literature' of the English course," you will want to direct your efforts toward integrating reading and writing activities.

Public Relations and the English Department

As communications specialists, English teachers have seldom done an adequate job of communicating with the public. We have, unfortunately, been successful in transmitting a fear of "bad English" to the public, and this increases the difficulty of working closely with parents. Too often the public is not adequately informed about our plans and hopes, with the result that parents learn about programs secondhand. When that happens, they often fail to get the full picture and are misinformed about what is happening: "The English department has just tossed out grammar. They'll let those kids say anything down there." "Did you hear they're teaching dirty and un-American books in a course called 'The American Dream'?" "There's a new course called 'Reading for Pleasure' at the junior high. Can you imagine? The kids just sit around reading, not learning anything!"

Once those anguished cries (unfair though they may be) reach the ears of the administration, the English department is in trouble, for no amount of rational explanation will allay fears based on hearsay. The English department, then, needs to develop a positive public relations program, informing parents and administrators (not conning them) about the aims and techniques of the program:

- Formulate and publicize a book-selection and censorship policy, one that explains how required and voluntary books are selected and "cleared" by the department. (The American Library Association, the National Council of Teachers of English, and the Speech Communication Association have developed materials that can be of assistance.) Involve community members in the project and elicit their support. Make certain your policy includes provisions for community members to have a say in the selection process (though obviously, as professionals, the English teachers should not surrender the right to select their own teaching materials).

➡ Publicize your program. Invite parents to come hear about the English curriculum. If they won't come, write a feature article about your department. Take photographs. Deposit the story with the editor of your local newspaper, who will probably be delighted to run ready-made copy.

➡ Use student publications to build good public relations. Parents love to see their kids' work in print, and nothing provides more dramatic proof of the success of your program than good student work. Don't let your department's publications be limited to the yearbook or a single literary magazine. Arrange for a flood of publications to come from English classes—dittoed, mimeographed, printed and hand-copied newsletters, fliers, posters, pamphlets, booklets, broadsheets, etc. Make it a goal to give every student in each class the opportunity to be published at least once each term. That's not as difficult as it sounds.

➡ Establish an informative newsletter, a page or so in length, which goes home with students and explains the nature of your plans and curriculum.

➡ Form a "Parents' Paperback Committee," a group of interested community members who are assigned the task of getting free and inexpensive materials for your department.

➡ Use parents as volunteers and tutors, especially in "remedial" programs. Give parents full credit (but only partial responsibility) for improving the quality of students' reading and writing. (See chapter 4, "Outsiders In.")

➡ Hold a public meeting on the use and abuse of standardized tests. Educate parents about the fallacies involved in interpreting test scores. Don't let your program be judged unfairly by inadequate data from state or national assessments or college entrance scores. (The National Council of Teachers of English has prepared an especially useful kit of materials on this topic: *The Use and Abuse of Standardized Tests—A First Aid Kit for the Walking Wounded.*)

➡ Develop an accountability system acceptable to your school district. One needn't be accountable solely on the basis of *behavioral* objectives and *standardized* tests. There are dozens of ways in which one can formulate objectives and assess whether or not students are learning. Explore some of the alternatives. (See Chapter 7, "Accountability and Assessment.")

Above all, be conscious of semantics in your public relations work, remembering that what the public hears is not always what you think you stated. For example, *don't* announce, "We're getting rid of grammar," since most parents will interpret that as meaning, "We are no longer concerned about the standards of 'good' English." Rather, talk about your new, broadly based language program that goes beyond matters of mere correctness into new areas of the social and practical uses of language. And show them how you are dealing with doublespeak and propaganda and advertising and mass media and dialects. Parents don't need to fear the "new English," but they do need to understand it.

CHAPTER 7

Accountability and Assessment

The accountability movement in this country is now over a decade old; in state after state and city after city, systems of objectives and tests have evolved and been implemented with the aim of improving instruction. Given the strength of this movement (by now almost a *tradition*), it seems appropriate to examine the accountability approach to education and English and to do a little assessing of our own. Has accountability worked? Is it producing the kinds of changes its promoters claimed it would?

Before continuing, however, we want to go on record as *not* opposing the concept of accountability in its broadest sense; we believe that teachers should be willing to state their aims and objectives clearly, directly, and publicly, and to take responsibility for their success or failure in meeting those objectives.

But it seems to us that a great many accountability systems distort the concept beyond recognition or become so entangled in mechanics as to lose sight of the original idea altogether. In many cases, listing objectives and testing students have been counterproductive, inhibiting growth in teaching rather than promoting it.

Indeed, the very term *accountability* is suspect, because of its connotations of blaming, of making teachers "answer for" their behavior. *Accountability* implies that someone out there has been getting away with something, that it's time for a day of reckoning. Accountability systems have often been linked (subtly, to be sure) to forms of intimidation: "If test scores don't go up, then heads are going to roll." Teaching children by intimidation has never worked very well, and we don't think that trying to intimidate teachers works any better.

But perhaps most important is to look at the track record of accountability programs. Have they worked? In state after state, in city after city, the answer seems to be "No" by almost any measure. Are parents happy with the reading and writing skills of their children? Demonstrably not. The public outcry is, if anything, louder than it was in the late sixties when accountability programs first came in. Are teachers able to use the results of accountability programs to better their own instruction? Most of the teachers we have worked with say, "No": The annual release of test scores does very little to contribute to instruction and simply destroys teacher morale.

We attribute the failure of most existing accountability programs to three major flaws:

1. The accountability movement has focused attention almost exclusively on so-called minimums of language arts instruction. The schools need English programs based solidly in reading and writing, not just on mastery of peripheral skills like grammar or dictionary use. If anything, emphasis on "minimum" skills has distracted teachers from teaching reading and writing and led to a concern for conventional rule study and drill.

2. Accountability programs have not been based on research into the real languaging needs and skills of young people. Most sets of objectives are simply reordering of age-old lists of grammatical skills. We don't know of *any* program that began by collecting writing samples or observing children reading before making pronouncements about what young people "ought" to know.

3. Programs have been overly concerned with the form of objectives rather than their substance, with the "testability" of goals rather than their content. "The medium is the message," and the "medium" of the standardized test is a limited one. Accountability programs have, in many cases, been dominated by the testing system; the "real" objectives of English become lost in the process.

This may seem a rather stern indictment of the accountability movement, so we want to reemphasize our initial note that accountability, in itself, is not a bad idea; in fact, it is potentially very useful. At the same time, we shudder to think of the millions of dollars and teacher hours spent in the development of ineffectual accountability programs. If that time and money had been put into, say, teacher institutes, teacher released time, and development and purchase of new materials, we think far better results might have been achieved.

Nevertheless, accountability is with us and shows few signs of going away. In this chapter, we discuss some of the alternative approaches to accountability which seem true to the concept and in keeping with what many English teachers want to accomplish. We suggest a three-part approach to accountability:

1. Telling what you plan to do.
2. Telling why you plan to do it.
3. Assessing whether or not you've done it.

Within each section we offer a variety of techniques and strategies, with the thought that you can "mix and match" these components to create a system that works for you (and your school, your school administration, your public).

Telling What You Want to Do

Writing in the April 1976 issue of *The English Journal* ("Learning Objectives and the Teaching of English"), John L. Wright noted correctly, "The objectives listed by many English educators . . . have not been very good objectives; in the first place, they have not been well thought through, and in the second place, they have lacked solid underpinning, both psychologically and philosophically." We'll add a third point: Objectives have been stated vaguely and inconsistently, so that they mask or confuse intentions rather than revealing them explicitly. As a profession, we have been guilty of at least one charge leveled by proponents of accountability programs: "What happens in your classrooms is too often a matter of chance." But there are *many* ways objectives can be stated explicitly. A good accountability program will allow teachers to select among different ways of stating objectives explicitly. Here are some ways:

Behavioral objectives. In one sense, all objectives, even vague ones, are "behavioral," for they deal with student or teacher behaviors. In a specialized sense, however, the "behavioral" or "performance" objective refers to a specific way of stating goals as developed by Robert Mager in *Preparing Instructional Objectives* (New York: Fearon, 1962). The form of behavioral objectives includes: stating the skill or concept to be mastered; specifying the level of mastery to be achieved; and describing the condition under which the skill will be demonstrated. Thus: "The student will master a twenty-five-item spelling list so that he or she can spell the words with ninety-percent accuracy on a dictation test."

The behavioral objective works pretty well for discrete skills and for concepts or knowledges that are easily described and directly observable. As critics have noted, however, this form of statement breaks down when skills become complex or move in the direction of the affective domain. Attempts at writing so-called humanistic behavioral objectives (objectives for the affective domain) have seldom been successful because they become evasive or become mere approximations of the desired behavior. Thus, when we get into the domain of literary appreciation, the humanistic behavioral objective is not very satisfactory:

"The student will demonstrate that he values literature by checking out on a voluntary basis at least ten books during a term." Or "The student will do a paper that reflects his or her own response to literature according to criteria established by student and teacher." Other ways of describing such objectives are more satisfactory, including . . .

➡ *S-V-O objectives.* Alan Purves describes a more flexible system of objectives in *How Porcupines Make Love* (Boston: Ginn/Xerox, 1972). He suggests visualizing objectives as simple, though specific, sentences consisting of a *S*ubject, *V*erb, and *O*bject. "The subject," he suggests, "is usually a student or a group of students," such as *Johnny, a student, Mary, my fourth-period class, everybody at B.O.H.S.* The verb tells what the subject is to do, usually through describing an observable action: *will recite, will read, will interpret, will express.* The object "usually has something to do with what the curriculum is all about": *a poem, Catch-22, the theme of the novel, an essay.*

Typical S-V-O objectives include: "Students will act out their version of a story." "That kid in the third row will describe a poem in his own words."

S-V-O objectives seem *specific*—"accountable," as it were—without being restrictive. (If this system appeals to you, you should probably read the entire chapter in *Porcupines* [pp. 183–99], which provides considerably more detail.)

➡ *Global descriptions plus skill descriptions.* Proponents of behavioral objectives have argued, rightly, that many of the terms English teachers use are too vague to be of any use: *appreciate, value, interpret, compose.* One way to solve the problem is to present, first, a global, admittedly rather vague, description of what you want and then to describe the skills that contribute to it. Thus, a global description might state the goal: "The student will learn how to write a good essay." That is initially not very helpful. What's a "good" essay? How will we know when the student has learned to write one? But if you then go on to describe some of the skills that contribute to the activity, your course of instruction becomes clearer. Thus, you might specify that to write a good essay the student will need to gather information, synthesize information to create a basic pattern, plan the essay, edit and revise the draft. Each of these skills could, of course, be broken down further; you could list *dozens* of additional subskills that fit under the categories of, say, *gathering information* or *editing a rough draft.* Again, this system allows you to specify your goals in as much detail as you (or your administrator) want. It also has the advantage of linking goals systematically: Instead of producing a mere "laundry list" of skills, you create clusters of related objectives, thus simplifying planning your instruction.

➡ *Contracts.* The contract method of teaching is described in chapter 5. We will simply note that writing contracts encourages both students and teacher to discuss objectives in detail, with specificity, so that both teacher and student will demonstrate accountability.

➡ *Task pack.* A task pack is a list of projects or activities that constitute "acceptable" work in a course. Thus, in a course on American Culture, students might be offered the options of reading and reporting on the Civil War, doing a slide-tape project on America in the twenties, and doing research on education in colonial New England. Projects can be described in as much or as little detail as the students or teacher desire. The complete list of projects constitutes a set of "goals" by simply describing the dimensions of the course.

➡ *Scenario.* Coupled with other kinds of objectives, you might enjoy writing a scenario for your course. If all goes the way you intend, what will the course look like? How will it evolve? What will the students be doing in the first several weeks? What will they do later? Naturally, no course will ever follow the scenario exactly; indeed, it is probably a sign of teacher inflexibility if it does. But sketching out the scenario helps you to clarify your objectives, see relationships among course components, and, in general, think about aspects of the course that would not be considered in a routine list of objectives.

➡ *Teacher objectives.* Why should students be the only ones for whom objectives are written? Each teacher is a "behaver" in a classroom; we are acting and reacting, directing and responding as we attempt to teach. It seems appropriate, then, that we develop some objectives for our own teaching. These objectives may be as simple as a list of the ways you want to change your teaching: "This term I want to be less (or more) directive than I was last"; "I want to do more with creative drama in my science fiction class." Or you might keep a set of notes in a journal, sketching out your aims and making note of your progress. This kind of "objective writing" may seem a bit removed from the rigors of composing behavioral objectives, but we think it is vital for both teaching responsibly and growing as a teacher-person.

Telling Why You Want to Do It

A much neglected aspect of teaching is describing the *rationale* behind doing what we do. In fact, it seems to us that much of the discussion of objectives has been misdirected; our concern should be less with specific goals than with explaining specifically *why* goals, methods, and techniques are appropriate in the schools. This factor has been overlooked in the accountability movement as well. In their zeal for getting teachers to write "satisfactory" objectives, accounters have too often failed to make certain that individual objectives are consistent and noncontradictory. Thus, in many programs you will see objectives that ignore research findings or have no obvious connection with English: "The student will demonstrate knowledge of nouns as a way of improving writing skill." "The child will demonstrate the ability to discriminate red from green as a reading readiness test." Does "knowledge of nouns" improve writing? (Research findings certainly give minimal support to that idea.) Is there any reason to believe color discrimination carries over to reading? (Differentiating red and green is an ability unrelated to reading.)

In short, a teacher can prepare elaborate lists of goals, all neatly phrased in behavioral (or other) language, yet still produce an ineffectual, inconsistent program. Most of the lists of objectives we have studied are, in fact, hodgepodge collections of statements generated "by committee."

A statement of rationale, like a list of objectives, can take many forms. It may be an informal "credo" or "manifesto": "This I believe about the teaching of English. . . ." It might be a statement of principles about language acquisition. It can be an informal or formal discussion or response to literature or the teaching of reading. Whatever its form, the rationale should answer the following questions for the reader:

Are the objectives consistent with one another? Do your goals reflect a coherent philosophy of teaching? Do they jibe with one another?

Are the goals consistent with a supportable philosophy of teaching English? Though the profession obviously doesn't know all there is to know about teaching English, teaching goals should at least be consistent with current thinking. For instance, including a unit on sentence diagramming on the grounds that it makes better writers is not supportable on philosophical grounds and is not reinforced by research.

Do these goals meet the real needs of students? Many courses are developed on the basis of what someone *thinks* kids need or *hopes* kids need. To include Shakespeare in a curriculum on the grounds that "Young people need it and won't get it after school" is a dubious proposition. In short, some discussion of *why* your goals are appropriate for your students is an important aspect of an accountability program.

We feel that statements of rationale will frequently ease the way for administrative acceptance (and public acceptance) of teacher objectives. If you simply list objectives for your Supernatural Literature course without a rationale, you still leave yourself open to the (very good) question, "Why should kids be reading this kind of stuff in school?" There are (very good) answers to that question, and teachers need to state them in support of their instructional goals.

Telling Whether or Not You've Done It

Assessment is perhaps the most difficult part of a good accountability program, involving a great deal of planning and imagination. In some respects it's not surprising that people have turned so readily to standardized testing as a measure; it's a lot easier than developing individual assessment devices for individual students and situations. Yet even here the English teaching profession has made rather considerable strides in the past decade and a half. Where fifteen years ago multiple choice, short-answer, quotation identification, and essay tests were about the only assessment instruments developed by teachers, we have a variety of ways in which to assess kids' (and our own) successes and failures in achieving stated objectives. Chapter 5, "Alphabet Soup," explores many means of evaluation. Here are a few more:

➡ *Logging.* One of the simplest solutions to the assessment problem is better record keeping. Instead of simply jotting down letters and numbers in a grade book, keep a *log* of student accomplishments, an annotated list of *what* students have done and *when* they did it. This record can be as detailed as your time and energy permit, and much of the actual work of logging can be done by students. Simply ask them to note, on a daily or weekly basis, what they have been doing in your course. When parents or principal ask about what's been going on in your class, show them the logbooks.

Several variations on the logging idea include:

➡ *Teacher and student commentary.* Have the students keep their log on the left side of the page, and you write your commentary and response on the right. This provides a running conversation with the student and allows you to offer feedback on a regular basis.

➡ *Portfolio.* Along with the log, keep documentary evidence: the papers and projects students create. Nothing "proves" that you've accomplished your aims more satisfactorily than showing a concrete product.

➡ *Mapping.* In Rita Hansen's *Writing Bug* (an activity kit published by Random House in 1972), classroom materials are described on a large poster or "map" that shows all the possible activities. Prepare a similar map for your class, showing the options available and leaving room for students to insert their names when a project has been completed. In addition to providing a manageable record of your whole class, this approach also helps kids see the organization and structure of your goals.

➡ *Intellectual history.* From time to time, ask students to describe what is happening in their minds as a result of the course. What ideas are they concerned with? How has their reading affected their thinking? What progress do they seem to be making in their writing? If "intellectual history" sounds too stuffy, just have the kids write you a letter telling where they have been in your course.

In an article titled "Testing Without Tears," (*The English Journal* 74 [March 1975]), Roberta Riles and Eugene Schaffer describe a number of alternatives to conventional testing including:

➡ *Discussion.* Small-group analysis of what is happening and what has been learned in a class.

➡ *Role playing.* A way of demonstrating mastery of a subject or understanding of a piece of literature.

➡ *Student observers.* With training, students can become skilled process observers, sharing assessments with each other.

➡ *Feedback forms.* Of all sorts: simple questionnaires that allow students to evaluate an activity and their performance on it.

➡ *Debates.* Through debating, students clearly demonstrate whether or not they have mastered your objectives.

➡ *Simulations.* To participate successfully in a simulation, one has to have mastered skills. Thus, a simulation of a daily newspaper allows students to show some of their writing skills; in a mock trial, students reveal their depth of understanding of characters in a novel.

Two forms of large-scale or mass testing deserve mention:

➡ *Criterion-referenced testing.* This is a term out of standardized testing. Increasingly, testmakers are focusing attention not on normative tests (where kids are compared to national norms) but on tests that simply measure whether or not the student can do something. You can adapt the idea for your own classroom by setting up a series of tasks that when done "correctly," according to criteria you and/or the students set up, demonstrate mastery of the subject. In simplest form, a criterion-referenced test might involve writing a business letter to demonstrate proper use of letter form. Your criterion is standard letter form; the student who does the task correctly passes. In more complex areas, a criterion-referenced test might involve demonstrating skill at responding to literature by sharing a response to a poem in a small group or showing organizational ability by creating an essay whose main purpose can be "discovered" by a reader. Once again, the emphasis is on doing, on showing skills in action.

► *Standardized tests.* Despite their frequent misuse, standardized tests *do* have a role in an assessment/accountability program. Before using them, however, you probably need to "educate" people—students, parents, other teachers—in their proper interpretation. For instance, it is widely believed that the decline in SAT verbal scores represents an absolute decline in literacy; English teachers need to note that, in fact, the decline took place in a set of verbal aptitude test scores that are at best only a marginal measure of literacy. Similarly, the public seems to demand that *everybody* score above national norms on standardized tests; we need to point out that, by the nature of the tests, 50 percent of the test takers will score below the norm.

Further, standardized tests have to be selected with great care, taking into consideration such questions as:

■ Is this test revealing information that will be useful to us in assessing our program? (If not, why use it?)

■ Is the test valid and reliable? Does it measure what it says it will measure? (Recall, for example, that almost no standardized tests of writing ability actually require students to write. Can a short-answer test be a valid measure of writing ability?)

■ Can we inform the public of the test results without having people misread the results?

Accountability, we think, need not be feared by English teachers. It is possible to develop a system of objectives, supported by a rationale and assessed through imaginative means, that allows us to be accountable to the public that pays our salaries, yet continue to teach in productive ways. We think, further, that a well-developed program will help you teach better, not worse, by helping you focus your beliefs and goals precisely.

At the same time, English teachers need to be skeptical of the accountability systems being introduced into the schools from outside, particularly those that do not allow teachers to participate in the development of the program in significant ways. The accounters, too, must be held accountable.

SUMMARY AND TROUBLESHOOTING

Dear Abby Fidditch

IN these "Summary and Troubleshooting" sections of *The English Teacher's Handbook,* we will attempt to recap the main ideas of each section and, more important, discuss some of the problems that may emerge when you move from the printed pages of this book to your own classroom.

In this section on curriculum and course planning, however, we'll let an old friend do the talking for us:

Abby Fidditch is an unwillingly unemployed former English teacher who lost her job when the voters in her district defeated their twenty-second straight school bond issue. The school board, in response, fired all teachers with less than forty-three years experience. Abby has taught in one-room schoolhouses and giant urban high schools; she has taught Shakespeare and Vonnegut, old grammar and new grammar, smart kids and not-so-smart ones, children who wanted to be there and those who didn't. Many of her former colleagues write to her for advice. We hope you'll find these letters and her replies helpful in your own teaching.

Dear Abby Fidditch:

What do you do to relieve pressures and tensions within a department to make it a more productive unit? If it's not jealousy, it's apathy. I'd like to get the department jazzed up and active on curriculum change, but my attempts have all been frustrated. I am . .

A Dangling Modifier

Dear D. M.:

Don't put yourself down. See your task as that of making a "unified paragraph." Despite their weariness and their jealousy, most of your colleagues are deeply committed to teaching well. What's needed is often just a matter of allowing people to channel their energies successfully.

Try these:

To set an example, be the first on your corridor to start dittoing off successful teaching ideas to give away. Don't worry if people steal ideas. Show that sharing can be productive.

Have a department meeting on neutral ground, preferably a tavern.

Unify the department by starting a public relations program, informing parents of your program. In talking to others, you'll begin talking to each other.

Respect other teachers' methods and ideas. Too often, I think, we are unfairly critical of people who teach differently than we do. For example, though I'm no advocate of forcing kids to do the term paper, I have seen teachers who do it, and do it well. I respect that.

If all else fails, look for kindred spirits, the people who *do* want to change and experiment. Look for ways of working closely with them through team teaching or experimental course work, or even just planning to lunch together.

Though the unified department is a positive goal, in some schools you may just have to dangle.

Abby

Dear Pedagogical Poetaster:

How do you handle the matter of externally imposed objectives? While it's all well and good to talk about teacher autonomy and meeting student's needs, both my state department of education and my school district have developed long and detailed lists of minimum skills that students must master. There's talk now of new eighth-grade and twelfth-grade exit exams which kids must pass to graduate. I think the skills lists are pretty inadequate, but I want my kids to be able to pass.

Subjected and Objecting

Dear S.O.:

You seem to me to hit the nail on the head when you say, "The skills lists are pretty inadequate." In fact, most of the lists I've seen deal only with surface trappings of English, not the substance of composing and reading. If you limit your teaching to those lists, you will be limiting the literacy of your kids. Most skills-writing groups admit that, by the way, and claim that their minimum list is just a "starting point" for teachers. Take that as your cue and try some of the following:

Concentrate your objectives writing on the matters other-than-basic. That is, since the imposed list is inadequate, develop your own goals that move well beyond it.

Don't let the skills list restrict the dimensions of your teaching. Keep the state or districtwide objectives in perspective. When I was teaching in California, where much of this mess seemed to originate, I simply reserved teaching the mandated objectives until close to test-taking time. While some people object to that as "teaching for the test," it seems to me to make a great deal more sense than letting a test dominate your instruction.

Integrate the required list with your own objectives. The fact is, you teach basic skills by the hundreds every day you enter the classroom. In the course of an ordinary composition or reading assignment, you probably cover dozens of skills on the mandated list. Develop the habit of noticing how your own teaching covers the minimums. Then jot down a few records to show how you've done the work.

Nobody wants to hold children back, and it <u>is</u> important that you satisfy the external demands that are placed on your students (and thus on you). The important thing is that you not let the demands themselves hold you and your students back from achieving all that you can.

Abby

Dear Superteach,

I teach in a school where the curriculum is largely predetermined. We have a fairly detailed curriculum guide and the three years of English are divided into three year-long courses: Introduction to Communications, American Literature, and British and World Literature. I find this framework very limiting, and I don't want to wind up teaching just communications, basic skills, or a chronology of literature. What can I do?

Guided by the Curriculum

Dear Curriculum Guide,

No matter how detailed the curriculum, you are still the teacher. I think the idea of teaching by units offers you a way out of your dilemma. Unless your curriculum guide (or department chair or principal) says you must teach literature chronologically, approach it from a thematic point of view. One set of textbooks, for example, divides American literature into themes like "Who We Are," "Where We Live," and "What We Believe," which allows the teacher to function with literature through ideas, rather than literature as mere history. Similarly, a course like Communications can be split up into numerous interesting units and packages. While I like the freedom elective curricula give you to plan new courses, most of the advantages of elective courses can be incorporated into a traditional framework. In addition, with your year-long courses, you have a great advantage over many folks teaching electives who find that nine- or eighteen-week courses are too short for them to get to know their students.

Abby

Dear Ailment Alleviator:

I keep up to date and try a lot of the "new" ideas. Some of them work pretty well, but at other times they're a dud. For example, I have a required American Literature class that I am trying to run as an open program. Everybody is on contracts, with periodic progress reports required. I have whole-class, small-group, and individualized reading programs. I'm not teaching Moby Dick. I let them respond to literature in a varity of ways. I'm doing all the "right" things.

And nobody's doing anything. The kids are, for the most part, faking the contracts or going through them with painful slowness. About all they want to know is, "Will we be graded on this?"

I am . . .

A Naive and Ambitious Teacher

Dear Teach (after all, we're all naive and ambitious):

I'm not going to try to propose exact solutions for your dilemma, because outsiders' solutions have a way of not working any better than what's already happening.

But I can strongly emphathize with your problem: I have had a number of classes like this. Once a group of kids responded so lethargically to my open techniques that I wanted to sell them as a matched set of pet rocks.

Analyzing my own failures I've reached four conclusions about why the "right things" don't always work:

1. Kids have been trained to work under pressure, under fear of grades, in a lock-step fashion.

2. Given number 1, "openness" is perceived by the students as either "disorganized" teaching or an invitation to do "nuthin'."

3. Reading and literary study have often been painful experiences for students. Why should they read, even in "free" settings?

4. English is an obligatory subject, and "required" courses tend to be disliked.

Elective English provides a partial solution to number 4, and I'd suggest that you talk to your colleagues about replacing the required American Lit. course with some sort of elective program, even if only a choice of different kinds of Am. Lit. If you can't do that, continuing to individualize would seem to be the only alternative.

For number 1, reverse training, or unconditioning, is needed. I'd start to work on a sequence beginning with where the students are (locked into a grade/pressure system) to where I would like them to be (self-motivating, independent learners) and literally teach them how to get from here to there. For an excellent description of helping students learn to make decisions, see Eve Moore's article "How to, Not What: A Course in Choosing," in the November 1975 issue of The English Journal.

For number 2, I think you (and your students) may have to adjust your ideas about "structure." "Freedom" isn't freedom if it simply leads to inactivity (or to chaos). I believe that in thinking of "openness" we also have to be concerned with control. Sometimes one has to impose certain structures (later to be removed) just to get things rolling. Contracts may be too unstructured for these kids at this time, in which case you have to return to more formal assignments. Once the kids are doing things, you can begin teaching them how to work without so many formal constraints.

Number 3 may be the heart of it. If kids don't see the value in books and reading, they won't read. With a group like this, I'd simply concentrate on getting the literature to them any way I could: reading aloud, playing recordings, showing films, etc. Instead of worrying too much about whether or not they are actually reading, give them literature on a silver platter, the best literary experience you can. It may be the only one they ever get.

Abby

Dear Teacher Advocate:

A while back I read Herbert Kohl's 36 Children and noted with interest (and sadness) his comment that at the end of the year, he wondered if he had done his children a disservice by teaching in unusual, if humane ways. What would happen to them next year when placed in ordinary classes? I worry about the same thing in my school. If I teach writing rather than grammar and emphasize responding to literature rather than routine comprehension drills, what will happen to my kids when they hit their next English class? Half as important, what will happen to me when next year's teachers learn that my kids don't know some of these "basics"?

Thinking of Tomorrow

Dear Thinking Teacher:

Your worry is a fair one, and one that a number of teachers share. To be reassuring, though, let me note that kids have a remarkable capacity for forgetting that which is useless, uninteresting, and unhelpful. The chances are when your kids hit next years' class they will be at no real disadvantage, since nobody will recall the drill material from the year before, and – muttering in disgust – the teacher will start all over from the beginning: "Class, the 'noun' is a name . . . " Further, children are remarkably skilled at adapting to differing teaching styles; you needn't worry that if you give them freedom this year they will be damaged or incapable of functioning in a more disciplined setting next. They'll adapt easily. Most important: I suggest you concentrate on making this year's English class a memorable one, and by that I simply mean focusing your energies on giving your students access to the best and most interesting books you can come up with and engaging them in the most positive sets of writing/speaking assignments they've ever experienced. That kind of class, like Kohl's classroom, is the one students will remember and profit from long after they have reentered "the system."

Abby

Dear Literary Junkie:

I got into it at Parents Night. I tried to explain my program, which involves lots of free reading and free writing and thematic units and all that. The only thing I got was objections. "Well, that sort of thing is well and good, but . . ." At the end of the night, I felt totally defeated, yet I'd tried my best to describe what I know is a good program. How do I cope?

PTO'd

Dear KO'd:

I think you have to play a bit of a rhetorical game with parents nowadays. Unfortunately, if you simply tell the parents what you think is right, they'll attack. "Humanistic" education isn't very popular, even when well justified. It sounds as if the parents were playing what Eric Berne calls the "Yes, but" game, where, no matter what you suggest they say: "Yes, but . . ."

One way out of the game is to transfer the responsibilities for answers to the person doing the objecting. Instead of letting them shoot down your ideas, ask them what they propose or suggest. Now this too has dangers, because all that many parents "want" is grammar. If you just say, "What shall I teach?" they'll say, "Basics."

But suppose you approach it this way: Tell parents, honestly, that you want to help their children get ready for college, for life, to master the basics. But express your concern, too, that you don't know exactly what they, the parents, want from it all. What do they expect? How can you help them achieve their goals. At that point, the burden shifts to them, and the "Yes, but" game ends.

Abby

Dear Lively Adverb,

What's your advice on the matter of college preparation? Our state university is complaining bitterly that entering freshmen can't read and write, and it is vigorously blamming the schools. We want to do a good job of preparing kids, but each college has its own book lists, its own style of Freshman English, even its own acceptable form of the term paper. What should we do?

College Bummed

Dear C.B.,

College preparation and school-college articulation are problems that go back as long as the history of the secondary schools themselves, and the colleges have never been particularly satisfied. Part of the problem and many of the solutions rest with the colleges themselves, for there is no way in the world any high-school English faculty can prepare young people fully to face the rigors of college life. I wish the colleges would stop spending so much energy on blaming and concentrate more on aiding students once they arrive on campus.

Still, what can you do as your share? I suggest that the best preparation for college is providing the richest set of language arts experiences you can. Instead of focusing exclusively on essay writing or term paper writing, invite your students to explore their experiences in many different modes of writing (including, but not limited to, the essay and term paper). Similarly, instead of designing your literature curriculum around a selection of books that "might" be useful to the students later on in college, teach a variety of books, including some classic literature. In the end, a fully literate student will win out over one who has spent all his or her high-school days concentrating on a narrow range of college-related tasks.

I'd also recommend that you hold an articulation meeting with representatives of a local college. Tell them of your concern and ask them to tell you about what it's like at their school. Warning: Don't ask them, "What shall we teach?" What you teach is your decision. Ask them to tell you what their institution is like, not to tell you what's right or wrong about yours. Further, you can also ask a very important question on behalf of your students: What can the college or university offer them? Quiz the college folks about their program. Is it broad or narrow? Does it offer individual choice? Is counselling adequate? Who teaches the undergraduate and introductory course – full professors or teaching assistants? If you are to send your students off to that school, you want to find out. Articulation, in other words, must go two ways. By seizing the initiative and inviting the college reps to meet with you, you can probably control the direction.

Abby

Dear Behavioral Modifier:

Why is it that nobody has much to say about the most pressing of teaching problems: discipline. You can't teach creatively until you have enough discipline to keep the class under control. So what about it? What about troublemakers, rowdies,, disruptors, malcontents, and all those types we real-world teachers face day after day after day?

Just Plain Tired

Dear JP:

Let me tell you what I learned indirectly from a methods class at Grimm University: The rules people give you about discipline almost invariably do not apply to real young people. You can't generalize about how to handle a class. "Don't smile for the first six weeks," they told me in college. I smiled by accident and found a class of kids smiling back. "Start tough and then let up," somebody advised. I started tough and when I tried to let up, the students were so afraid, they wouldn't talk. There are guidelines and limits, of course, but I've found that I can only deal with discipline problems one at a time, trying to be fair on one hand and true to my own values on the other.

A final observation: It seems to me that the "self-fulfilling prophesy" is especially true in the case of discipline. Kids behave the way the teachers expect them to. If teachers think they have "bad" and "troublemaking" students, sure enough, they <u>do</u>. Similarly, the teachers who take a positive view of young people and their energies seem to have fewer problems with behavior.

Abby

PART TWO

Ideas for Teaching English

SECTION A

Literature and Reading

INTRODUCTION

The majority of English teachers entered the profession because of a love of literature. Although teachers acknowledge the importance of writing and language studies in educating young people, our first delight comes in sharing books and ideas. Literature enculturates and enriches; it provides valid and useful leisure activity; it presents a storehouse of human values that must not be lost to future generations. Even though school boards and parents have not placed literary study high on their lists of priorities, English teachers have successfully and rightly preserved the importance of books and reading in their classes.

But like most subject areas of teaching, literature has grown more complex in recent years. The schools are no longer content to offer a watered-down version of college survey courses to students, and in the 1960s and 1970s the traditional chronological British and American Literature courses were augmented by courses that explore the dimensions of literature from many points of view. In addition, the past two decades have seen increasing interest in the problems of *reading* that associate themselves with literary study, for it's clear that young people cannot discuss issues, topics, or even plot until they have successfully made contact with the text, managing the vocabulary and ideas.

Unfortunately, in many schools (and in professional organizations as well) this has led to a division of interests: a split between teachers of English (meaning "literature") and reading (meaning "skills"). In the reading class or lab, kids often use worktexts and machines to master isolated skills about the process of reading, and when they read, it tends to be nonfiction: informational materials, the school prose of textbooks, or "basic" materials like application forms and assembly instructions. In literature class they read "important" books, hash over ideas, and write an occasional paper on symbolism or some other esoteric literary topic. Literature, in such circumstances, is seen as isolated and elitist, something only the better pupils can pursue with any degree of success. Most important—and disastrously—literature is perceived as something otherworldly, having little to do with "real life."

Fortunately, contemporary research into both reading and literature points to a resolution of the dichotomy, and we find it interesting that research is focusing on a single common element in reading, literature, *and* criticism: the *reader.*

For instance, the work of Kenneth and Yetta Goodman at the University of Arizona and that of Frank Smith at the Ontario Institute for Studies in Education suggests that in teaching reading we have placed entirely too much stress on "getting" meaning from a page and too little on seeing what skills the student brings to the page to make sense of it. In literature, Louise Rosenblatt and Alan Purves have written about the response-centered approach, which grants that the reader's reaction to a work of literature is as important as what the artist intended (or didn't intend). Finally, so-called subjective critics of literature—David Bleich and Norman Holland, for example—have shown that literary criticism is a subjective art, not an exact science, and that recognizing the subjectivity of criticism can still allow one to treat literature systematically and in scholarly ways.*

These concurrences help to cut through a number of traditional problems and issues that surrounded the teaching of reading and literature. Are we teachers of literature or skills? Are we teachers of great literature or can students read popular forms as well? Do we teach classics or contemporary literature? What are the differences between literature and nonliterature? Such questions now collapse, for we are teachers of literature *and* reading *and* the skills of literature *and* (so-called) nonliterature. We teach popular forms *and* classic works, for our concern is not so much the material being consumed as the functions print serves in the lives of the consumers: our students, the readers.

Our program is integrated around four central aims for literature and reading:

1. Get them reading. Nothing happens in either reading or literature classes until students make contact with print. We suggest making English classes places where students constantly encounter print (and "read" nonprint media), where they engage with and react to books. The English classroom must be awash in the materials of literacy.

2. Treat reading and literary study as meaning-making activities. When a

* See Appendix G for full references for the authors alluded to in this paragraph.

student meets a black-and-white printed page, something new is created, a set of meanings based on what the author said, meshed with the understanding and experiences and responses of the student. We need to concentrate instruction on helping students to explore their reactions intelligently and articulate them successfully for themselves and for other people.

3. *Let evaluation and criticism grow naturally from a person's responses to reading and literature.* To focus on the reaction of a reader or to say that critical response is subjective is not to ignore all standards or to say that any old response, no matter how sloppy or far out, is acceptable. Subjective criticism simply notes that great works become great because of the quality of response they consistently elicit in readers. Shakespeare is great not because of some inherent magic of his "black-and-white" words on the page, but because when we see his plays (or read them) we are moved—deeply and inexorably. Depending on how we are moved and on the author's success at moving us, we evaluate and critique literary works.

4. *Help students recognize that reading and literature are good for something: living.* Too often literature and reading programs wind up operating in a vacuum. Students read to learn to read better; they read literature only to learn to evaluate literature more successfully. Though we assuredly want to create good readers and good evaluators of reading, we must not lose sight of the fact that we read to accomplish things: to gain information, to clear out our brains, to find solutions to problems, to purge ourselves of emotions, to share great ideas, and so on. Literature and reading programs cannot afford to be otherworldly, and a good program will go to great lengths to put reading into the context of the real world, helping students see how the medium of print affects their lives and allows them to exert a measure of control over their lives.

Above all, *literature is dramatic.* We do not particularly fear that literature and print are dying forms. The booming paperback bookstores, the wealth of print available today, and the enduring interest of people of all ages in a rich variety of literary forms, all testify that books are dramatic, exciting, powerful stuff. A good reading and literature program will thus draw on the natural drama of literature, taking it out of the classroom and making it a part of the lives of young people.

CHAPTER 8

The First R

"My students can't read!" continues to be a major complaint from junior-high, senior-high, and even college teachers all over the country. In response, a multitude of books and programs has been written and packaged with the promise to eliminate reading problems—usually by "remediating" students whose skill development has been neglected in their earlier schooling. Unfortunately, prepackaged programs are often bought by schools for use by teachers who have had little training in the area of reading and who must, therefore, use the reading materials "by rote," or as an act of faith. Though considerable research about reading has been done by linguists and psychologists, research findings have not found their way into teacher-education programs or the prepackaged programs, with the result that reading programs, though well intentioned, often don't work in the schools.

In the past, most programs have been based on the assumption that reading is simply a process of decoding print into oral language. The result has been either to emphasize the relationship between letters (graphemes) and the sounds associated with those letters (phonemes)—the "phonics approach"—or to stress the sight recognition of the whole words—the "look-say" method. Both phonics and look-say approaches assume that if students can sound out or pronounce a word, they know what that word is and therefore understand what they are reading. In short, a good reader is one who perfectly reproduces what is on the page in oral reading. The emphasis on perfect reproduction has produced two kinds of readers: the *strugglers* and the *perfectionists.* The strugglers are those who have not mastered the rules of oral reading and thrash about trying to pronounce the words placed before them on the page. The perfectionists are performers; they've mastered word-recognition skills and can produce flawless oral reproductions, but when asked to explain what they have read, their comprehension may be quite low. Usually, the strugglers end up in a remedial program, where they may or may not learn to read, and the perfectionists are allowed to continue in regular classwork, where a teacher may or may not recognize that despite their fluency, they can't read very well.

Reading is getting meaning from the printed page; it is not a perfect oral reproduction from printed symbols. How does one get meaning from print? First of all, psycholinguists suggest we should see reading as an active, rather than a passive, process. Readers bring a whole language system to the reading situation. They have control over the grammar and syntax of their language; they have a host of meanings and experiences in their heads. All of these are brought to reading and play a role in the meaning readers create. Students' reading is an interaction between their own language and experience and the language and experience of the writer.

Reading is not a mechanical process, but a thinking process. Kenneth Goodman calls reading "a psycholinguistic guessing game" in which readers use all of their language systems (graphophonic, syntactic, semantic) at different times to make meaning from print. As people read, they predict what will come next (on the basis of what they already know from what they have read—or on the basis of knowledge that they bring to the reading—or on the basis of the structure of the sentence), and their predictions are either verified or denied by their reading. Readers make "mistakes" for different reasons when they are reading. They may be producing an "incorrect" response based on their experience or own language background, rather than failing to decode correctly. Often students' "errors" show that they are "translating" into their own language and experience, revealing their strengths as meaning makers.

Reading programs, however, generally fail to recognize the role experience plays, and the child with a reading problem is put in a program that ignores meaning and breaks language down into small parts that are word-centered or even sound-centered. Such students are thus limited severely in the kind of language they are "allowed" to deal with. In many cases, the materials they are allowed to read are limited and tightly controlled. Thus, while "good" students have "proven themselves" and are allowed to do free reading in areas that they enjoy, poor readers have not yet earned that right and so must continue to work with subskills and bits and pieces of language and teacher-selected materials until they have mastered "reading." Only *then* will they be allowed to enjoy reading.

Little wonder, then, that poor readers don't learn to read in the packaged programs. These kids don't like to read in the first place. Giving them exercises, drill, and selected readings merely reinforces their hatred of reading as dull, difficult, and totally unrelated to their lives.

Further, the bits and pieces approach contradicts the very purpose of reading. Reading is a communication process; people read to gain information, experience, ideas. When that element is removed from the activity, all reason for reading is gone.

Finally, a good reason for avoiding the bits-and-pieces approach is that it uses short selections that do not allow students to use their own language and experience in building meaning. Short paragraphs do not provide students with enough language to gain meaning. Students should be given readings that are long enough for building meaning as they read; longer readings give a context for predicting what will come next and gradually build understanding.

Current research in psycholinguistics offers an alternative to the bits-and-pieces approach for teachers who want to help students learn to read.

- Give students freedom to choose what they want to read. If what they are reading interests them, if it is about things they know something about, if it is related to their purposes for reading, then they are much more likely to gain meaning from their reading and thus build confidence in their ability to read.
- Allow students to stop reading something they are not enjoying. No single book is sacred or irreplaceable. Reading should be an enjoyable and rewarding experience for everyone, but especially for the student with reading problems. It will cease to be that (or never be that) if students are forced to read things they hate.
- Emphasize reading as communication rather than as a series of subskills. This means using whole language (stories, plays, articles) not fragments (letters, isolated words, phrases, or exercise paragraphs).
- Encourage students to become active thinkers, predictors, and evaluators in the reading process. Encourage them to speculate and anticipate on the basis of what they know about the subject.

Who Is the Nonreader?

The problem of the "nonreader" has been greatly exaggerated. Certainly, some students fail to read the assigned work, and others struggle through the assigned work but seem unable to understand what they've read. But many problems have more to do with the demands of the situation (tests, drill, and teacher probes) and the materials (textbooks and assigned literature) than with the students' abilities and skills. It is more accurate to say that nonreaders *don't* read or *won't* read rather than *can't* read. Again and again we have observed so-called nonreaders who, when given material appropriate to their needs and interests in a nonthreatening situation, are successful in making meaning from what they read.

Students who don't read exhibit some common characteristics:

■ Nonreaders lack confidence in their ability to make sense of what they read.

■ Nonreaders are afraid of making mistakes.

■ Nonreaders often overrely on graphophonic relationships and do not rely strongly enough on their own experience and their knowledge about what their world is like and how language works. For example, in an effort to be true to the graphophonic relationships, students will often produce a nonword or a sentence that doesn't make sense to them.

■ Nonreaders hate to read.

Solutions for aiding students who don't/won't read are quite different from those for students who can't read. Rather than sending students back through a series of exercises on phonics, word attack, syllabication, and vocabulary (which most of them have done for five to ten years), complete and engaging reading experiences are called for. Some solutions for the nonreader:

➡ *Individualize reading assignments.* It is pointless to put a student through a series of reading experiences that he hasn't the confidence to tackle. Such assignments insure failure. With the help of the librarian and surveys of the student's interests and previous reading experiences, locate materials appropriate for that particular student. (See chapter 9, "Reading Resources.") (Be wary of the student's grade-level reading scores and of readability formulas for assessing the difficulty of texts. They are often misleading in predicting a student's ability to handle reading materials. A student who is allowed to read what he cares about will read material that his test scores and a readability formula say he can't read.)

➡ Break down some of the old reading rules that have made students feel stupid, restricted, or trapped.

➡ Encourage students to guess words that they don't know and then move on. The meaning will probably become clear through the context.

➡ Encourage students to skip parts of a book that are too difficult or are not yielding interesting or useful information. They can come back to them later if they feel a need to fill in their understanding.

➡ Encourage students to put down a book that they are not enjoying or that seems too hard for them and to seek another book more appropriate for them. Explain, however, that the first part is always the hardest. Even proficient readers experience some confusion and discomfort at the beginning of a new book or story until they're familiar with the author's intent, style, characters, situation, etc.

➡ Encourage students to glance back to pick up what they've missed or to skim ahead to prepare for what's coming. Both help to build a fuller context through which students can create meaning.

➡ Provide context for readers who lack confidence and reading experience. The more insecure a reader is, the more "extra" information he or she will need in order to tackle and understand the material.

Other needs which you can provide include:

➡ *Tapes.* Several publishing companies have put out easy reading materials accompanied by audio-tapes so that nonreaders can read and hear the materials at the same time. You can save money and improve the quality of the literature by making your own tapes. Select a variety—in subject matter, style, genre—of short materials, practice reading them with expression, tape them, and catalog them for easy student access. Novels may be taped, but they are, of course, more time consuming to produce. Students can be enlisted, too. As a project possibility, have students prepare and tape dramatic readings of favorite stories, plays, and poems to be added to the tape library.

➡ *Films and records.* Allow students to listen to recorded and filmed versions of a literary work before they read it themselves. Some versions may be identical to the printed work and some may be adaptations. In either case, students will gain information that will help them make connections with what they know and what's on the page when they read. Moreover, films can be great motivators for reading. Note the jump in sales of books after the filmed version has appeared on television or in the theaters.

➡ *Prereading discussions.* Talking about the book or story before the students begin to read helps create a context into which they can fit what they encounter in print. You may wish to talk about the characters, describing which are major and which are minor, what they look like, something about their personality traits. Or you may wish to say something about the historical or social milieu of the work's setting and situation, describing events that took place during the same time, the important concerns of the era, the social conventions of the people. Or you may wish to say something about the language or style of the book, what you yourself find interesting or difficult about reading the book, perhaps pointing out some specific words that are important but that might give students difficulty.

There is some danger in prereading discussions. It is important to affect students' judgments, responses, or evaluations of the work as little as possible. When students encounter a work, it should be through their own values and sensitivities. There must be a balance, then, between helping create a context that will help students read without undue struggle and frustration and allowing students to discover on their own what's important to attend to in their reading. The teacher has to find such a balance independently and rediscover it with each book and student.

► *Picture books.* Many beautiful and informative picture books, fiction and nonfiction, are available for both young and adult readers. These books support and confirm what the reader sees in print. Make picture books available. Students need not read them or be accountable for them, but may use them for making their own connections between pictures and print.

► *Magazines, newspapers, and comic books.* Again, these materials provide lots of context clues with pictures, print size, subheadings, illustrations, and diagrams. Teachers who have allowed students to browse and read freely in popular, nonacademic materials have been pleased with their students' growing interest and time spent in reading. (Test scores and readability formulas become unimportant when students actually begin to read. After all, the goal is to get kids reading. As a friend of ours says, "I never heard of a kid who reads who can't read.")

The next section on language experience describes ways in which a student's reading may be strengthened by making connections between oral language, writing, and reading.

Practical Approaches to Teaching Reading: Language Experience

The language experience approach to the teaching of reading has been used more extensively on the elementary-school level than on the secondary level, but many activities in language experience are appropriate and helpful at all levels. In its simplest form, this approach consists of students sharing experiences through telling stories which are transcribed by a teacher or aide, and then using these student-written materials as part of the reading material in the class.

This technique has several advantages:

- Students who are intimidated by print and do not feel confident about handling printed matter are helped to see print as a written form of oral language.
- Written language is seen in the context of the total language experience; the same emphasis is given to speaking and writing as is given to reading.
- The subject matter of the reading is appropriate because it grows out of

the students' own experiences and hence is on their developmental level and often contains shared or common experiences.

■ The problem of controlling reading level through vocabulary is neatly eliminated, for the students' own vocabulary becomes the source of reading instruction.

STUDENT DICTATING TO TEACHER OR AIDE

Use class time when students are involved in group or individual projects to have students who are having trouble reading dictate stories to the teacher. Frequently, students who have trouble reading also have trouble writing; the same kids, however, have information, ideas, and imaginations as active as the very verbal students in the class. It is often surprising to discover the complexity and sophistication of style and vocabulary students have when released from the pressures and tensions of writing something down. In addition, because the story and the language are theirs, they are able to read the story back and build confidence in their ability to deal with print. Having the story published or posted helps students to see their writing as communication and of interest to others. Of course, the number of students involved in dictating will be small, and the teacher can use times when the class is involved in individualized projects or reading to take dictation. In addition, many teachers have found aides enthusiastic and helpful in using language experience with their students. (See chapter 4, "Outsiders In.")

Students may also be willing to dictate to other students. This may present difficulty if students feel that they are being forced to demonstrate inadequacy to a peer. If this is the case, the teacher can design activities that are oral, but that may be transcribed later for all the class to read. Students might interview one another on tape, and the tapes later be transcribed for a class booklet or publication. Or students might produce a radio program on tape to be transcribed for reading by the entire class.

Students who have trouble reading might also be engaged as tutors for younger students. Usually they have the confidence to deal with elementary-level reading and writing and can build experience in dealing with print in this situation. They may read simple stories to kindergartners or primary-age children; they may tell stories to younger children; or they may take dictation from younger children. The work already done in this area shows tutoring by older children to be a very positive experience for younger children; older children may advance by as much as two years in their language development.

COLLABORATIVE WRITING

Many kinds of collaborative writing projects have kids producing language that then becomes part of the class reading matter.

Divide the class into groups of three or four. Make sure that the groups are well balanced, with each having students who have confidence in their reading/writing ability and with no more than one "nonreader" in a group. In a common meeting, generate a list of possibilities for a story to be written by the whole class. After the class members have decided what they'd like to write about, let each group work on a section of the story. Allow enough time for groups to work so that there can be some discussion of the various ways to handle the story. It also helps both concentration and keeping each section of the story a mystery if the groups working on the story can work apart in a conference room or a library.

In an alternative version, a group begins a story and does as much of it as it can in the time the teacher has allotted. The story is then passed on to group two, which reads what group one has written and adds the second section, and so on. The only group that knows the whole story, then, is the final group. When the entire story has been finished, it can be read to the class and then printed so that each student can have a copy. Either way, you may want to have a handmade copy printed, illustrated, and bound to keep in your classroom. Teachers who have used the collaborative story-making project have been pleased and surprised with how prolific their students can be and with how complex and imaginative the stories are.

In a variation on the creation of the whole story, have groups of students write endings for a "professional story" that is read to them in class. There are several advantages to this: it is less time consuming than the creation of a whole story; it asks students to do in more detail what you want them to do in all their reading (that is, to predict and anticipate what will come next on the basis of what they already know); and it lessens the impression that print is "sacred" and encourages them to manipulate and interact with printed literature. The endings are read aloud or copied for the entire class. Students can then talk about why they ended the story as they did and compare the endings. The teacher may want to read the "professional" ending and compare that to the students' versions. This can also be done as a whole-class project, with students discussing the story and coming to a consensus on an ending. In a solo variation, students who have trouble reading and writing can be given the opportunity to tape-record their ending or dictate it to the teacher or another student.

Students also like to create concrete poetry, where the poem takes the shape of an object that is central to the poem, be it ice cream cone or statue or cat. Two practical small-group poetry-writing activities are *found poetry* and the *cinquain.*

Found poetry consists of writing from newspapers and magazines broken into lines to create a "poem." Students enjoy taking ads, articles, editorials, reviews and finding sections that can be broken down to look and sound like poetry.

The cinquain is a five-line poem that follows a formula. The first line consists of one word that names the topic; the second contains two words that define or describe the topic; the third has three words that express action related to the topic; the fourth consists of four words that express the poet's attitude toward the topic; the fifth is a one-word synonym for the topic. Of course, any of these can be done as individual projects with nonreaders dictating their poetry.

Reading with a Purpose

Packaged reading programs often lack purpose or direction for students. To "remediate" the programs (not the kids), design projects where reading takes on purpose, allowing students to read for information or personal interest.

Have a treasure hunt. Let one group of students go on the search. The larger the area in which the hunt can take place, the better. If your students can roam the school or community, so much the better; if not, the classroom will do. Create lists of objects for students to find, or write clues for them to follow in order to locate "the treasure" (comic books, teen magazines, poems, postcards).

Get a blueprint of the school or a map of your town. Have students trace the route they take to get from one part of the school to another, from school to home, or from one part of the town to another. Let the students write directions for getting from one place to another, and (if possible) have others follow the directions. Or let students make a map of their community or neighborhood marking hangouts they use. Have them write a "Hangout Guide" to be used by other students.

Have students create things, following directions. Bookstores abound with hobby and craft books. Collect some for your reading class and let students read on how to make: hammocks, puppets, candles, quilts, beanbag chairs and toys, looms, baskets, and flutes.

➤ Let students write a "How To" book in which they write about some of their own skills, from skateboarding to the breeding of tropical fish. Following the language experience approach, writing a "How To" book draws on familiar language and experience and encourages children to read their own writing.

➤ Have hobby fair days. Let students bring in their hobbies and display and teach what they do to the rest of the class. Have them prepare a booklet that can be dittoed for the rest of the class and allow time for students who wish to do some work with the hobby.

Reading in the Content Areas

The concept of reading in every classroom is one that English teachers should support and encourage among their colleagues in other subject areas. The organization of information disciplines other than English—science, math, social studies, the arts—may require reading strategies that the subject-area teacher is best equipped to teach. At the same time, however, the English teacher can provide valuable support in a variety of ways:

➤ Sponsor interdepartmental meetings to talk about reading, language, and learning. Share observations about the kinds of problems students have with reading in various subject areas and brainstorm for solutions in classroom reading materials or teaching methods. Unlike most content-area teachers, English teachers have usually received some training in reading. Share your knowledge of the reading process and of the relationship between reading and other language activities.

➤ Offer your help and expertise in book selection for the content areas. Suggest alternatives and supplements to the traditional single text, which is often a dull and lifeless tome not appropriate for the diversity of students within a classroom. Inexpensive supplementary materials for a variety of subjects can be found in popular magazines on history, sociology, science, psychology, music, drama, dance, painting, government, current events, law, politics, and religion.

➤ Broaden the kinds of materials you use in your own classroom. For free reading and within thematic units, offer nonfiction reading as well as literary selections. Many excellent trade books are available for adolescents on everything from black holes to King Tut, from puppetry to pet care, from ballet to vegetarian cooking. Reading a wide variety of materials for different purposes strengthens students' reading flexibility, as well as supplementing reading they may be doing in other classes.

➡ Cooperate with a teacher in a different subject area in teaching an interdisciplinary unit. Some administrative arrangements may need to be made so that you are teaching the same students at two different hours during the day or, if room permits, so that you can combine two different classes: English and history, English and art, English and foreign language, English and biology, English and civics. Work together in planning materials and activities that integrate the two subject areas.

➡ If it's administratively difficult or impossible to share an entire group of students in an interdisciplinary course, try some partial sharing. Find out what the civics, history, or art teachers are doing and coordinate efforts. Allow students to do joint projects, to read literature related to a specific historical period, to read about a particular artistic technique or an important artist, and to read a translation of a foreign work in its entirety. Such efforts need not be one-way. Request that teachers in other subject areas support your efforts from time to time, too.

Classroom Environment and Materials

It is important that the students who have trouble reading not be punished and penalized for their problems. Teachers should make every effort to integrate nonreaders into their classes by using a variety of methods, approaches, and reading materials.

We mentioned that many teachers have had great success with the use of comics, magazines, and newspapers, which are particularly helpful for nonreaders. Catalogues and large illustrated books are also available on a variety of subjects. If the class is working on a particular subject or unit, the teacher can find diverse materials that relate to that subject so that nonreaders can have a means into the subject and can make a contribution through the work that they are able to do. It isn't necessary to isolate and separate kids with varying verbal abilities. Create a classroom reading center as a place for students to go (figure 1).

FIGURE 1 A CLASSROOM READING CENTER

We have emphasized writing in describing ways in which teachers can help their students learn to read. In doing a good deal of writing, students will also be doing a considerable amount of reading—of their own and their classmates' work—and it will be reading that grows out of their own interests, experiences, and language. Developing the relationship between reading, writing, and speaking is helpful for those students who are verbally fluent and for those who struggle with language. If all language activities in the classroom were directed toward that end, we'd have a lot fewer "nonreaders."

CHAPTER 9

Reading Resources

One of the most important aspects of involving students in reading and responding to literature is having a rich learning environment that makes all kinds of reading matter available. We suggest a wide range of magazines, newspapers, books, and other materials for the reading program. As budgets get tighter, however, one may question where this "stuff" will come from. Some ideas on stocking and arranging the reading area:

- Rummage sales, garage sales, and auctions are good sources for teachers to pick up cheap used paperbacks, old magazines and comics, and other unique and interesting reading materials.
- Explore the idea of getting last month's unsold magazines from your local bookstore.
- County, state, and federal government offices have free pamphlets and booklets available on everything from nutrition to child abuse to scenic areas.
- Enlist students and parents in the effort to build the literature program and to increase the availability of reading materials. Parents are often willing to contribute old paperbacks, as well as magazines and newspapers, to the school reading room. We have read of a school system that uses parent-sponsored newspaper drives to raise cash for books. What other sources of community fund raising might you tap?
- When making decisions about the departmental budget, explore the idea of spending money on books that are bought in single copies or sets of ten, rather than whole-class collections.
- Make sets of titles available in a centralized location for teachers to use for thematic units. Rotate sets of seventy-five or one hundred titles from class to class.

➡ Very often reading centers are used only for students who have "reading deficiencies." Consider converting the reading center into an area that makes materials available to all students, as well as being a place where it is comfortable to read. See if students can be given a free hand in decorating the reading room or lounge in ways they find attractive and appealing.

➡ Get the poetry club or junior class or literary magazine staff to set up a paperback bookstore in the school. Most people who try this are astonished by the number of books kids will buy.

➡ Try to get funds alloted to furnish the library or the reading center with comfortable furniture, rugs, pillows. Have a decorating party for the reading lounge in which students and teachers make curtains, wall hangings, and large pillows.

➡ Make recorded literature readily available. AV catalogues list thousands of tapes and recordings of literature. Why not let kids experience literature through listening rather than reading (or through both, simultaneously)?

➡ Make tape players available so that students can listen to music while they read. Or get a record player for your room. Let the kids who want to read and listen to music do that; let the kids who want quiet go to the reading room or the library.

Library Resources*

A few years ago a "Peanuts" cartoon showed Charlie Brown carrying an enormous load of books. The caption read, "I always check out books during National Library Week. It makes the librarian feel needed." While those who work closely with librarians have some idea of the number of ways that libraries and librarians can be helpful to us, communication between teachers and librarians is not always everything that it could be.

Serving Youth, a recent book for high-school librarians by Lillian Shapiro (Bowker, 1975), includes some lists of what teachers think librarians *should* do and what teachers think librarians *do.* (Corresponding lists for librarians' perceptions and expectations of teachers are also included.) Here are a few listings from "What Teachers Think Librarians *Do*":

* Material for this section was drafted by Maggie Parish, the University of North Carolina at Wilmington, to whom we extend our thanks.

Stamp out cards.
Type cards and do other clerical jobs.
File things.
Guard the library's holdings.
Purchase materials for the library according to some secret formula bringing about a balanced collection that contains nothing the teacher wants.
Worry about overdue books.

Good rapport between teachers and librarians has too seldom been a reality, yet there are not only a number of ways in which they can help each other, there is also a great deal of information which each profession tends to accumulate that the other profession could find valuable. By working together, librarians and teachers can do their jobs more effectively. By talking together, each group can learn from the other about resources thus far unsuspected.

PUBLIC LIBRARIES

What can librarians do for you? What can you do that will make it possible for librarians to help you better?

There is an entire network of librarians beyond your school who can be of help to you. Precisely how that network is arranged, and what it has to offer you, will vary a great deal from community to community and from state to state. Public libraries almost always have a children's literature specialist and quite often have a young-adult's books expert as well. A large system will have a special young-adults' consultant for the whole system (city, county, or region). The services these people may provide include:

➤ *Bibliographies.* A free, easy way to keep up with books to recommend to your students. (You can ask your librarian to prepare a bibliography on a particular topic.)

➤ *Book talks.* Some libraries encourage their children's and young-adults' librarians to visit schools and give book talks and/or describe library services. (You can ask for a book talk geared to a particular topic that your class is studying.)

➤ *Field trips to the library.* Do this with the objective of either gaining an overview for you and your students of library resources and services, or also to investigate what is available in the library that would be of help to your students in particular areas that they are studying.

Deposits of books. Through your local, county, or state library, books are sometimes available for your classroom use. In one state, for example, a number of books on a topic can be borrowed by a teacher from the state library, with the school librarian handling the transaction.

What any public library will offer borrowers in general, and young adults in particular, varies widely from community to community, depending on citizen support for the library. Some public libraries loan toys. Some loan garden tools. Many loan records or tapes. A growing number loan framed prints or even original paintings or lithographs.

Many libraries plan special programs around young adults, and young-adults' librarians would be delighted to hear suggestions for programs. A 1973 *Idea Source Book for Young Adult Programs,* published by Boston Public Library, lists ideas for programs on such topics as "Ecology," "Body and Soul," "Women in American Society," "Cars and Driving," and "Original Writing and Music." Some public libraries have done innovative architectural planning for their users, so that materials and reading areas are more convenient and more inviting. The old gray public library—the one we remember from our childhood—often ain't what it used to be. The student-centered classroom and the people-centered library have both been growing at the same time, but libraries, like banks, can sometimes present an awesome facade, even to teachers. Find out what your public library can do for you and your students. Let your librarian know what you and your students need.

Students can discover and tell each other what the public library has to offer, too. Instead of the usual introduction to the card catalogue and the Dewey Decimal System, send students to look for material on the subjects they are most interested in—to find out about all the places and all the forms this information might be in. Or send students to browse, to explore, just to see what they stumble upon that looks interesting. People use paperback bookstores for browsing a great deal, while libraries, with comfortable chairs and librarians eager to circulate the books that their borrowers want to read, are too often thought of as "no nonsense" places. Perhaps they should be called "Book Parks"; then people would think of them as places to play as well as places to work.

SCHOOL LIBRARIES

You and your school librarian are the experts on what your school library (or media center) can do for you. Again, services and facilities will vary enormously (just as budgets do). But many resources will be used inappropriately or not used at all if you do not take responsibility for outlining your options and expressing your opinions.

There is, of course, some overlap in the services that school and public libraries offer, but there are also resources unique to each. It is quite possible that your school librarian will be more closely acquainted with nonprint materials, an area that has grown enormously in recent years:

➡ A school librarian or media specialist in a generously supported library or media center, for example, might develop a bibliography for your classroom use, including films, slides, kits, games, programmed instruction, television broadcasts, paintings, and human resources.

➡ Some media centers will cooperate with teachers in producing materials for classroom use.

➡ The school library or media center should never be overlooked as a potential learning environment in its own right, as well as a support system for classroom learning. Send your students there for help with project work.

Many librarians and educators believe that the best way to help young people become better readers is to let them read, and that the best way to insure that this happens is to make available books that are of special interest to them, and to give them time and space to read in:

➡ Having books all over the classroom (paperbacks, a deposit from your school or public library, books brought in by students, books begged, borrowed, or even purchased at book sales) is one possibility.

➡ Providing a chance for students to go to the library to browse, to read about whatever they *want* to read, is another. (Some good writing can come out of reading centered around students' own interests.)

There is also the question: "What can you do to help your school librarian help you better?" Since you are colleagues and partners in the same school, there are a great many ways for cooperation.

➡ Most librarians appreciate advanced word about an upcoming assignment that will bring many students asking for similar materials. The librarian can then make such materials readily available, obtain additional materials from other sources if they are needed, or advise you on additional resources. If learning is individualized and different students pursue different areas of interest, this is not as likely to be a problem, but even small groups working together on a theme or project might easily need to go beyond the library's resources; advanced warning makes it possible for the librarian to plan appropriate strategies and to offer alternatives.

➡ Librarians welcome suggestions for additions to the collection or for weeding. They will be pleased to be invited into your classroom as resource people, and doubly pleased if you make use of the media center yourself, for your own recreational reading and professional growth.

One important area where teachers and librarians must work together is that of censorship. Both groups recognize the danger of the increasing amount of "book burning" that has occurred in the last few years. Further, both groups are wary that tighter copyright laws might make it difficult to provide learners with cheap and readily accessible reproductions of materials. The areas of common cause for librarians and teachers are great; they have a much greater chance of gaining their chosen objectives if they pursue them together.

Multiethnic and Minority Literature

We'll close this chapter with what has been a special problem: including more ethnic and minority literature in the English curriculum. Courses centered on ethnic literature have too often come as the result of political pressure, and the response of educators in this country, English educators included, has often been practical rather than human or artistic; that is, it has been with some reluctance and only under pressure that schools have instituted courses in black, Chicano, native American, and Asian-American literature, as well as courses that focus on white ethnic literature and literature by and about women.

In addition, multiethnic literature courses have often been developed solely for the particular minorities who attend the school. For example, in the Southwest we find courses for Chicano and native American students. In large urban areas, black literature has become a popular course. But we haven't seen much black literature being integrated into the courses, or into the curriculum, of rural schools, or much Indian literature being taught in the urban East. Moreover, the courses exist almost exclusively as elective *options,* which may "satisfy" the minority groups who are involved in consciousness raising about their own roots and who want to read literature that reflects their own experience. But that experience with ethnic literature is not emphasized for the nonethnic student.

Certainly, teachers' impulses haven't been negative. They have begun to acknowledge more fully the importance of having students read literature that enhances self-image, that develops a sense of pride in the cultural heritage, and that demonstrates clearly the contribution of a group to American culture. But we have not gone far enough. Minority literature is too often peripheral, an extra, an option to what some see as the real or mainstream literature; it is separate but not equal. Ethnic literature should not exist just as an extra for those who are interested in it or who "need" it. We think the literature of different cultural groups in this country has the potential for enriching the curriculum immeasurably and deserves to be included across the English curriculum in all manner of courses.

We see three major reasons for integrating multiethnic and minority literature into the English curriculum:

First, it's *good* literature, easily measuring up to the artistic standards teachers want to apply in their classrooms. Whether we are talking of neglected literature by and about blacks, women, Chicanos, or Ukrainians, the literature has a richness and diversity of genres, styles, and creative uses of language.

Second, and more important, multicultural literature enriches experience. Students encounter values, life-styles, and conflicts that present new ways of viewing the world, new perceptual modes, and new perspectives on problems that people must solve or learn to live with. At the same time, students experience the universality of certain experiences. Recognizing how people share many common experiences—identity crises, falling in love, family conflicts, growing old and dying—is an immensely satisfying and humanizing experience.

Finally, teachers need to work toward an integration of multiethnic and minority literature for political reasons. Earlier, we used the word *political* in a somewhat pejorative way, but there is a sense in which it becomes a positive and useful term. We are a nation of diverse and interesting people. But the old melting pot metaphor has been replaced by a more realistic and exciting proposal: that we recognize and celebrate our diversity and richness of experience. As people find out about one another and learn to value differences, they will no longer fear and distrust one another. The understanding that replaces fear and distrust will make us infinitely stronger, both as a nation and as individuals.

Multiethnic literature can be integrated in many kinds of English classes: courses on genres, surveys in American literature, as well as courses in science fiction, the West, folk literature, and naturalism. In addition, minority literature works well in broad thematic courses and units, such as "Growing Up in America," "The Family," "Identity," "Conflict," and "The Generation Gap."

While the use of minority literature throughout the English curriculum is an important goal, it also seems appropriate from time to time to offer units and courses that acknowledge more directly the various experiences of ethnic groups in this country. Such units might be entitled "From the Old World to the New," "Into the Mainstream," "The Struggle for Equality," and "Racial and Ethnic Relations."

In choosing books for the literature curriculum, keep in mind some of the following questions:

1. Have I included literature that challenges my students' values as well as literature that reinforces them?
2. Have I made available literature that represents the ethnic backgrounds of the students in my class?
3. Have I included literature that shows peoples and life-styles new for my students?
4. Have I been attentive to the images of male and female presented in the literature I have chosen?
5. Have I been careful to balance stereotypical views of people, values, and life-styles with more precise, detailed, and authentic views?
6. Have I chosen literature that emphasizes similarities and universals as well as differences and unique qualities?
7. Have I focused on the work's literary merits as well as its social and political merits?
8. Have I been sensitive to stereotypes that might be damaging or hurtful to students who are in the minority in the class or school (be they Anglo, black, Oriental, male, or female)?
9. Have I provided a richness of alternatives so that students may have choices in their reading?
10. Have I provided opportunities for discussing images of people, their values, and their life-styles as they are presented in literature?

Book and Media Selection Sources

As we've suggested, books themselves are in plentiful supply, even in underbudgeted schools and departments. Often the question is not so much "Where do I find materials?" as "How do I know which materials to select?" Of course, the librarian can be of extraordinary help here, but there are some other book selection sources you probably should know about.

Whenever we're planning a new course or unit, one of the first places we head is the local paperback store to check on resources. In addition to offering a full line of paperback titles, the stores usually carry a number of magazines related to the topic, as well as a few hardbound books and reference tools. In an hour or two of browsing, you can frequently come up with a lengthy list.

And in using the bookstore as a resource, you have the advantage of knowing that all the materials are available locally.

➡ Elementary and junior-high teachers have a distinct advantage in having available a classic reference book, *Children and Books* by May Hill Arbuthnot (Scott, Foresman, 1972). Often revised, this is a treasure trove of information about children's books—their nature, their history—and includes extensive annotated booklists and bibliographies. Unfortunately, nothing quite like it exists for secondary teachers.

➡ Two excellent booklists published by the National Council of Teachers of English do offer help to the secondary teacher. *Your Reading,* (1976) junior high, and *Books for You* (1977), senior high, present extensive lists of books, subdivided into interest categories and annotated. These books are the work of committees, so they draw on the collective wisdom of librarians and teachers all over the country, and they have been through many editions, so the current list of titles has been "field tested."

➡ *The English Journal* offers numerous book-and-media selection reviews. Columns appearing regularly include "Books for Young Adults," "Pick of the Paperbacks," "Multi-Media," and "The Short Film." *The English Journal* also reviews literature texts on a regular basis and each January publishes a resource directory that includes annotations of new text, trade, and paperback offerings. Finally, once each year the *Journal* publishes *"More* Sources of Free and Inexpensive Materials," an extended list of low-cost teaching materials.

➡ Special-interest groups and organizations offer bibliographies. For example, the Children's Book Council regularly puts out bibliographies of notable children's books in the fields of science and social studies. The NAACP has booklists (and so, for that matter, does the John Birch Society). Keep an eye out for *usable* bibliographies of these kinds.

➡ Finally, NCTE publishes an extremely useful "bibliography of bibliographies," *Book and Non-Book Media* (1972) by Flossie L. Perkins, a well-researched guide to resources in many areas related to the teaching of English.

CHAPTER 10

Reading and Responding

IN her classic text *Literature as Exploration,* first written in 1938 and reissued by Noble and Noble in 1967, Louise Rosenblatt spoke of reading as "a performing art," with the performance coming, not from the literary artist, but the *reader,* who learns to "perform" upon a text, creating an interpretation for himself or herself. Thirty years later, a study group at the Dartmouth Seminar on the Teaching of English advocated a similar approach when it spoke of "response to literature," stressing that *how* a reader reacts to or engages with a text is at least as important as *what* the author "intended." As we have suggested, a response-centered approach is by no means inconsistent with evaluating literature (chapter 11, "What to Say about a Good [or Bad] Book") or with introducing students to "great" literature (chapter 12, "Teaching the Classics"). Nevertheless, it seems clear to us that at least throughout the secondary years, literature study should center on the reader and his or her response rather than examination of texts themselves.

Underpinning this belief are four basic assumptions about the relationship between literature and the reader:

1. Experience with literature is personal. A student's reaction to a literary work is based on a complex mix of past experiences. How the student responds to a play or poem or story depends, to a great extent, on who he is, where he has been, what he has read. If teachers want students to be moved by literature and be responsive to it, then they must help young people find literature appropriate to their emotional development, their age, their interests, their needs, and their reading levels.

2. Engagement with literature is a natural process. Teachers don't have to trick kids into reacting to good books; nor do they need to provide much background to spark the process. The experience with literature (as with most life experiences) doesn't begin with abstractions; it begins with absorption and involvement. Forcing young readers to abstract, generalize, and analyze an experience that is quite close to them or that they haven't had the time to digest frequently alienates and frustrates them. There is ample time in school for analysis of literature; but "exposing" kids to "literary discussions," especially in early stages, can be deadly when it detracts from literature as experience and emphasizes literature as object.

3. We read different kinds of materials for different purposes. People read to be well-informed citizens and consumers; they read out of curiosity and a desire to know about things unknown; they read to enter into new worlds and life-styles; and they read to feel deeply and to identify with others. Recognizing this, teachers should allow for and encourage students to read all kinds of materials, not just fiction and poetry. We believe the English class should be flooded with reading materials, including material of a distinctly "nonliterary" type. We'd like to see a classroom stocked with hometown newspapers and large city newspapers (the *New York Times* and the *Wilsonville Gazette,* for example); magazines on news, sports, fashion, crafts, hobbies, and skills (like auto mechanics); "how to" books on carpentry, macramé, exercise and diets, transcendental meditation, preparation of natural foods; informative paperbacks on weather, astronomy, home repair, mountain climbing, bicycle touring; large attractive books on artists, scenic trips, ballet in America, history of Navajo art; books on child care, a short history of the world, theories on the evolution of man; books identifying rocks, plants, cloud formations, and health problems; and catalogues, comic books, joke books; and pamphlets on government jobs, stocks and bonds, interest rates.

4. Students' reactions to what they read are based on both their purposes for reading and on the nature of their involvement with it. Sometimes the basics of the plot may be what excites a student. A story may be mildly interesting to one student but deeply moving to another. Teachers need to provide a variety of ways for students to respond to what they have read.

In *Response to Literature* (NCTE, 1968), D. W. Harding described three kinds of contact that a literature program must have to be successful: the individual reader with individual book; small group experiences with literature; and shared common experiences. We'll look at these in reverse order.

Shared Experiences

Having a group experience with literature allows for a wide range of response from people whose values and opinions are very different from one another, and exchanges among people with different interpretations of a common experience help all grow in self-awareness.

Sharing responses to a literary work gives students new insights into that work and into their own values and experiences. In addition, the common literary experience in the class can be a useful starting point from which to individualize. From that point, the teacher may provide various options in reading and writing that are stimulated by a whole-class activity.

Some alternative approaches to the shared class reading:

- Use short readings (a poem, one-act play, short story) that can be read and responded to in one class period. (This is an especially good way to kick off a thematic unit.)
- Use creative film shorts and feature-length films related to issues and topics of interest to the class as a whole; then follow them with selected short works.
- Assign TV shows related to issues and topics of interest to the class as a whole; then follow them with selected short works.
- Encourage students to bring in what they are reading and to share and discuss it with the entire class.
- Invite students to exchange (either orally or in some published form—ditto, mimeograph) things they have written with the class as a whole. After all, there is no reason why kids' writing shouldn't be treated as literature too.
- Encourage small groups to give presentations or dramatizations of literature as a starting point for the class discussion.
- Bring in records of plays, poems, stories, radio broadcasts, rock operas.
- Share things you are reading that you think the class might enjoy, including not only literary works, but newspaper items, movie reviews, magazine articles, etc. Encourage your students to do the same.
- Over a period of some time (a week or two) read a short novel to your students.
- Use bulletin boards and walls to put up poems, articles, student writing, and excerpts from plays and novels, as well as pictures and posters. Have students contribute literature they want to post.

Small Groups

The small-group experience is in many ways the most satisfying and productive way of handling longer works and long-range projects. As in the large group, students are able to share impressions and discuss diverse reactions and interpretations. At the same time, through the small group students have more choice of literature (with the teacher providing options), and they can work with material that represents various levels of difficulty and presents many different topics, life-styles, and experiences. In addition, students are better able to work at their own pace in their reading, writing, and projects.

➤ Within a large thematic unit, allow groups of students to choose from a broad range of fiction and nonfiction works; for instance, a unit on identity can include such diverse works as *The Outsiders; I Never Promised You a Rose Garden; One Fat Summer; Jane Eyre; The Invisible Man; Down These Mean Streets; Hamlet;* and *Tunes From a Small Harmonica.*

➤ Have a group of students become experts on a poet. Interestingly enough, biographical backgrounds seem to become relevant with this approach; small groups will study backgrounds that fail to interest the class as a whole.

➤ Let students explore a topic of concern ("Death," "Conflict," "The American Dream"), drawing on fiction and nonfiction, plays and poems, and media.

➤ Provide a list of interrelated short stories, poems, or plays for small groups to choose and read from according to their interests (sports, fantasy or science fiction, detective or mystery stories).

➤ Have students make a collection of their favorite writings or excerpts of writings on a theme for the rest of the class.

➤ Assume the students either have read or are about to read *The Lord of the Flies;* split them into small groups and pose certain problems for the groups to solve; then have each of the small groups report back to the whole class, using their reports to stimulate large-groups discussion. For example, one group might be given the task of creating a new society in which violence and force were nonexistent; another group might be faced with the problem of the novel (you have just been marooned on a desert island that has vegetable and animal life and fresh water; what are the first five or ten things that you must do to insure your survival?)

Individual Reading

There are too few opportunities in school for students to make entirely free choices about what they want to read. Teachers often talk about the importance of reading for one's own purposes, but rarely is the student allowed or encouraged to do so. Individualized reading is more than students isolating themselves with a book.

➤ Allow a week for students to read silently in class, or at the library or in the reading room. Set aside a conversation corner where kids who want to talk about their books can get together. Alternatively, set aside one day a week for, say, a few weeks (or even an entire term) when students read, in class, a book of their own choosing. Only ground rule: The reading should not be reading required of them in your or someone else's class.

➤ Hold a book seller's day. Divide the class into three groups and let each third, in turn, "sell" its books in book fair fashion. Encourage students to provide visual aids to accompany their "pitch": posters, book jackets, magazine spreads.

➤ Sponsor small-group book conferences. Have students get into twos or threes and tell each other about the book they have read most recently.

➤ Have individual conferences with students about the books they have been reading. Chat informally with individual students about their books. Don't worry about whether or not you've read the book; ask questions that follow the students' interests, rather than questions designed to make sure they have read the book or gotten all the "important" facts or information from it.

➤ Let individual students or small groups of students take turns setting up bookcases with materials on a particular topic displayed in a prominent place in the school building.

➤ Have students choose their favorite books to be put in a book cart that can be wheeled from classroom to classroom as recommended books for individualized reading.

A good English class will include a combination of these kinds of reading experiences. It will provide large-group sharing experiences that include diverse responses to a single work, small-group experiences that allow individuals with common interests and tastes to relate to one another about a literary experience, and completely individualized experiences that allow students to have complete freedom in the choice of reading they want to do.

Alternative Modes of Response

Many teachers who try the response-centered approach quickly run out of ideas. A large range of options and avenues of response must be available so that student work doesn't become stagnant and formulaic. Options for response must allow for different kinds of students and many types of reading materials. The suggestions below can't be imposed on a class as a whole, nor are they appropriate for all literary works. The teachers' knowledge of their students and the things they are reading will help determine how they use these suggestions.

TALK AND DRAMA

Much of the talk that goes on in response to literature will be informal and natural. Encourage students to:

- Talk informally about the characters they liked and the characters they can't stand, the scenes that made them cry and the scenes that were exciting.
- Have an informal talk with the teacher about an aspect of the book they are interested in.
- Tell the whole class about books they are particularly enthusiastic about, highlighting key scenes or describing major characters.
- Do improvisations of key scenes from the book they read, either for the whole class or just within their group.
- In a small group, take the various roles of the major (or some minor) characters from a novel, play, or story and allow other members of the group to interview them about: why they did what they did; whether they would do things differently if they had to do them over; what they think of various contemporary issues; what they most value in the world; and so on.
- Improvise and extend scenes not fully developed or scenes indirectly described in the work.
- Do a reader's-theater production of a work, preparing and reading key scenes to the class.
- Script a scene from a story, novel, or poem and lead the class in a production of the script.
- Videotape dramatizations of short stories, poems, scenes from novels and plays, newspaper articles, etc.

WRITING ACTIVITIES

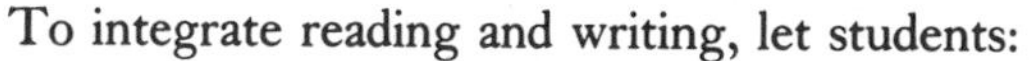

To integrate reading and writing, let students:

- Rewrite the ending of a story or novel, making it end in the way they wanted.
- Write a sequel to a story, novel, or play, describing the characters or actions that took place after the literary piece ended.
- Write an exchange of letters between characters from different books, plays, or poems.
- Write a newspaper account of a major event from the literary work they are reading.
- Write a poem based on the mood, images, or feelings aroused by the story; pretend they are one of the characters in the story and write a poem based on that character's sense of his experience.
- Write a story based on a play, using their sense of the play to fill in the physical description of people and places left undeveloped in dramatic form.
- Describe how they would film a scene from a novel, play, story, or poem; they might include camera angles, character movement, lighting, costumes, scenery, etc.

NONVERBAL ACTIVITIES

Students need not always respond to literature in words. Have your kids:

- Make a film based on a poem or story, trying to be more concerned with capturing the mood and the emotion than with reenacting the work.
- Make a poster or visual representation of a literary work, trying to remain true to the primary emotional and intellectual qualities of the work.
- Make a slide-tape show based on a literary work, using pictures and music appropriate to the mood, theme, and ideas of the story.
- Make book jackets, magazine spreads, or advertising posters that would attract the attention of a book buyer.
- Make a model of the location in which a story or poem takes place.
- Design and build a small-scale set for a play.
- Illustrate a poem or short story.

CHAPTER 11

What to Say about a Good (or Bad) Book

Learning the difference between a good book and bad is easy for many students: their teachers tell them. And if the teachers are "good" ones, they explain *why* a particular literary work is "good" or "bad." Teachers can make such judgments confidently, because they have a great deal of support for their evaluations: the word of their college professors and the scores of critical articles they read while fulfilling the requirements of an English major.

All of us, of course, want our students to appreciate good literature. Somewhere along the way we found pleasure in reading literature and satisfaction in understanding how it works, what makes it affect us. Understandably, we want to share this experience with our students. We notice how rhythm and sound patterns in a particular poem create certain moods and emotional responses, and we want our students to notice that too. We recognize how an author creates sympathy for a basically hateful character, and we want to explain to our students why their responses to that character might be mixed. We recognize how certain plot structures with their reversals, twists, or complexities create expectations in us and manipulate our response, and we want to show our students how clever and artful the writer was. Our impulses for "dissecting" literature, then, are often well meaning, and some of our students respond positively. More often, however, the teacher's analysis of literature ends up alienating students, reinforcing their belief that literature is boring and incomprehensible, and that they can't possibly appreciate it because they didn't see all that "stuff" that the teacher found. And if that's what appreciating literature means, who needs it?

The desire to have students love literature need not conflict with attempts to help them develop an aesthetic appreciation of it. We believe, in fact, that aesthetic awareness and the ability to evaluate a literary work follow naturally from engagement with literature. Even very young readers evaluate what they read.

They show preference for certain kinds of plots and characters; they respond to rhythm and sound by repeating and even memorizing pleasing sections of books; they ask questions about characters' motivations and make observations about their morality ("That wasn't very nice of him"); they laugh when they think something is funny, get angry at injustice, and sad when they see pain or suffering; and when they think something is "dumb" (if they're in a safe environment), they'll say so. When a child is questioned about his or her responses, the answer is seldom "I don't know," but an attempt to explain *why*. This, of course, is the birth of the evaluative process and the heart of all aesthetic awareness from childhood on: the ability to understand, both through looking inward at ourselves and outward at the text, why we respond as we do. The teacher can nurture the growth of this process, but the teacher's aesthetic judgments cannot be a replacement for the child's own.

How can the teacher nurture the growth of artistic awareness? Much of what we do grows out of our attitude. We think the following are important to keep in mind:

1. Both students and teachers have "taste," but their tastes are often different. Not only do teachers' tastes differ from students', but students vary in their tastes as do teachers; that's why some postbachelor students specialize in Victorian literature, some in Romantic; some in American, some in Comparative; some in poetry, some in fiction. Recognizing that there are differences in taste means taking a less dogmatic stand on what is "good" and what is "bad" literature.

2. Taste changes as people change. This is true for both young people and adults. As we have different experiences, our preferences change. As we learn more about ourselves and the world, we understand and appreciate more. And certain kinds of "real-life" experiences affect the kinds of "vicarious experiences" we seek. If students are allowed to follow their preferences, they will continue to do so as they mature.

3. Teachers who want their students to grow need to accept their students' tastes. Often it seems to teachers that what students appreciate is stereotypic and even simplistic. It's important to recognize, however, that students in secondary school are in a stage of development in which they are establishing their identity, breaking away from authoritarian ties, and trying to develop their relationships with the world out there. They are looking for answers. They are using literature for their own ends, and to undercut that is to underrate the importance of literature as experience.

4. Growth in aesthetic awareness comes as the result of consciously considering our tastes and preferences and reactions to literature. When a piece of literature delights, persuades, angers, or depresses us, we want to know why. We become curious about the inner workings of something when it seems powerful and important, and we look for answers about its power both within the literature and within ourselves. Of course, not all literature evokes that response in us or our students. Sometimes the literature is not sufficiently moving, either happily or sadly. And sometimes a piece of literature is too moving. When deeply affected by an experience, the last thing we want to do is sit down and analyze why we are crying or feeling joy; that comes later.

Recognizing the range of responses students may have to the literature they read, then, the teacher has to be very sensitive about when to ask questions and when to keep quiet. It is pointless to have students analyze and describe the affects of Tennyson's *Maud* if they hated or didn't understand the poem. It's even less valuable to spend time explaining literary techniques, no matter how masterful, to kids who didn't read or enjoy the poem. No matter how beautifully complex the character in Jane Austen's *Emma,* if students think she is boring, the teacher will make little progress in helping students appreciate Emma or any other character by telling kids—and then testing them—about how interesting she is.

If, on the other hand, a kid comes in having read Lipsyte's *One Fat Summer* and seems excited about the book and is chatting about incidents he or she recalls, the teacher has something to work with. Most likely, with many of the novels or stories or plays students read, the subject will be character or plot. Did you think that was going to happen? Why were you surprised? Did you feel sorry for Bobby? No? Angry? Why? You didn't like Pete either? Who was your favorite character? Why?

Poetry, too, evokes response from students when not out of their conceptual or emotional reach. Students reading Stafford's "Fifteen," for example, are led to consider what it's like to be too young, what it's like to have a fantasy almost fulfilled, that motorcycles can be poetic subjects, and how the language of poetry can capture much in little space. How did the poet do that? And topics need not be timely to be accessible to kids; loneliness, love, and death capture their thoughts and feelings. Poetry and its inner workings become important, not when students can define metaphor, symbols, onomatopoeia, cacophony, and iambic pentameter, but when they can feel the effects of those techniques and respond to them—whether they can label them or not.

What to say about a good book or bad, then, is not exclusively the teacher's responsibility. What to say about a good or bad book evolves, emerges, changes, and grows, as do students of literature and life.

Whole-Class Activities

It is valuable from time to time to have the whole class discuss an issue or respond to a piece of literature. Students bring a diversity of experience, insights, values, passions, and prejudices to your classroom. Discussing their very divergent responses to a literary work does several things.

First, because students bring unique experience to their reading of literature, the range of responses and feelings about what they have read enriches the literary work. Some student responses are a direct result of something that has happened to them. A student may have a strong visual or emotional response to Stafford's "Travelling Through the Dark," for example, if, like the poet, he has seen a dead deer along the side of the road or been in an accident involving an animal. Students who have experienced death, divorce, or illness are likely to have strong opinions, positive or negative, about a character in a similar situation. Of course, students need not have had direct experience with an event or place or person to care about what happens in literature. Their thoughts, daydreams, and fantasies, as well as those of parents and friends as they have grown, affect their response to literature. All of these are brought to bear when a whole class discusses their responses to a literary work, and the poem or story or play takes on new depths and levels of meaning as they discuss how and why they interpreted the language and events of the piece.

Second, discussing divergent responses mitigates the effect of "too personal" responses. Because of important personal experiences or prejudices, students sometimes will have a very strong reaction to a character or event, often opposite or at least very different from the responses of classmates. Discussing the source of those feelings both with reference to what happens in the book and what has happened in the student's past gives young people insight into themselves and into the workings of literature. Students offering divergent interpretations should not be interrogated or forced to show cause ("find it in the book"), but should have the opportunity to compare responses with other students whose interpretations differ. In such discussions, students move naturally from text to experience and back again.

Finally, class discussions spark enthusiasm and stimulate thinking. "I never thought about it that way," a student will say on hearing a new interpretation. And sometimes stories or poems that seemed silly or complicated are opened up for students by hearing their classmates talk.

The following activities are useful in involving the whole class in response to literature:

For whole-class discussions, short literary works—short stories, poems, one-act plays—are preferable. Then you don't have to worry about sustained interest over a long period of time or about the varying reading rates. Give students half the class period to read the piece, or read it aloud, and discuss the piece immediately while thoughts and feelings are still fresh and active.

Consider using recorded literature or films, too. Though it is better for students to have the text in front of them so that they can refer back to it when they need to, it is also useful to have them talk about what they remember. Replay the film or record after they have a chance to discuss it, and let them compare their initial response.

Read a novel aloud over a period of a few weeks. The popularity of "The Radio Reader" shows that we never outgrow the pleasure of hearing literature. Though many kinds of books will work, for a heterogeneous class a high adventure or suspense story will probably hold the audience best. Discuss what's happening after each reading, looking at how characters are changing and why, how certain scenes or places affect the mood of the book, how events advance the plot. Also have students conjecture and anticipate what will happen next, how conflicts will be resolved, how characters will end up. Discuss how and why students' versions differ.

Ask open-ended questions. It is often best to begin with questions on a literal level: What happened? Who were the most important characters? What was their problem? How did that happen? How did they solve it? Then move into questions of preference and interpretation: Who was your favorite character? Why? Did you agree with the way that character handled the situation? How would you have handled it differently? Have you ever been in a situation like that? What happened? Did you expect things to turn out as they did in the story? If you had written the story, how would you have ended it?

Follow student leads. Of course, students will determine the direction of much of the discussion, particularly if they have a strong response to the piece. "I hated Andy's father" or "I thought it was really dumb when Margaret told her teacher what happened" are the kind of remarks that can kick off a discussion that allows students to explore the text and their own experiences in detail. The teacher's role is to make certain that students are accounting for their responses and to help them articulate their thoughts and encourage them to refer to passages from their reading. It is also important that students who have particularly strong feelings not dominate the discussion, but that all students be given the opportunity to talk.

Avoid the impulse to force systematic discussion. Occasionally, discussions of literature seem to go off on tangents or seem to be chaotic, with students talking randomly about personal experiences or jumping around in their discussions of the literary work. Though it's possible to go too far afield, much of this talk is productive and necessary. Understanding of a literary work is not automatic and systematic, and flailing around with one's thoughts orally is a means by which people come to insights and formulate their thoughts. In addition, avoid the impulse to come to closure on every discussion. It is not necessary to explore every aspect of the literature and reach agreement on what the author intended to communicate, whether a character's motivations are pure or not, or whether the events were plausible. In fact, coming to closure usually involves denying the validity of divergent responses and reducing the complexity of the work.

Avoid teaching literary terminology a priori. One of the most unproductive ways of teaching literature has been the breaking down of literature into techniques or aspects, so that students talk about *plot, theme, character, narration, irony, symbol, setting, imagery, dialogue, metaphor, rhythm* as separate entities. The anthology that uses literary works as illustrations of techniques is a sad testament to what the teaching and learning of literature has become. In discussing a literary piece, technique is important only insofar as it creates a response in us. Rather than introducing the fact that there are various types of narratives—first-person, limited omniscience (and Wayne Booth has shown just how complex narrations can be)—allow students to consider narration when it's an issue that affects their thinking. In drama, students will obviously learn a great deal about dialogue and the use of language and dialects to reveal character. The teacher does not have to introduce formal definitions for students to raise questions about character, theme, or form. Similarly, defining metaphor and symbol before approaching poetry can sometimes interfere with understanding of poetry rather than promoting it. Students are often too concerned with finding language that fits the definition rather than understanding the poem. Again, considerations of technique will arise naturally as a student consciously considers his or her response. But it's most important to remember that poetry is so much more than the most careful explication of technique can ever discover.

Considerations of how the poet expresses emotion through punctuation and capitalization, how authors develop character through dialogue, and how they manipulate response through narrative voice are questions that arise when students grapple with meaning. Literary terminology may become important as a student struggles to express an insight; before that, it is at best meaningless and at worst a stumbling block.

Encourage comparisons of literary works. First, have students compare the quality of the books, stories, and poems they are reading. Ask them which piece they liked better and why. The discussion can go in any number of directions: the characters were more realistic; it was easier to visualize the setting—you felt like you were really there; it had a happier ending; it was easier to understand; there weren't so many hard words; it was shorter; it wasn't so serious; there were funny parts in it; the poet seemed to care more about the animals and nature. After students have described *why* they thought one piece was better than another, again, they can discuss why. What in them and in the literature affected their evaluation?

Also, have students compare how different genres or media affect an author's message and your response to it. How are the experiences of lost love, skateboarding, marine life, a view of the mountains, conflicts between parents and children, death, and sexual fantasies handled differently in poems, plays, stories, novels, essays, and films?

Refer to works that students have previously read and ask them to compare their reactions. Or while reading a novel that centers on death, bring in a few poems and take a day or two to discuss the poetic handling of a theme. Or bring in a pop-psych book on the subject for comparison.

Another possibility is to have students compare the book, film, or TV series handling of the same story. How do the constraints and techniques of the medium change the story? Comparative studies provide students with a variety of perspectives on ideas as well as sensitizing them to the effects of form on message.

Chat about what you're presently reading. Don't just talk about the heavy stuff, but let them know about a *Time* article you read that you thought was interesting, some modern poetry that you tried to plow through and ended up hating (and never finishing), a mystery novel that you couldn't put down, and a book review that made you want to read the book. Let students do the same. Take time at the beginning or end of each class period to talk informally about any sort of interesting printed matter; such chats are probably more effective than the formal book report.

Small-Group Activities

Small-group work is perhaps the ideal way to handle literature in the classroom, because it allows students to have a choice in the literature that they read, but still gives them other people with whom to share their reactions. Through large-group discussions, students will learn ways of talking about literature which they can carry over into the small group.

➡ Have the group set up a revolving leadership. Responsibilities of the group leaders may vary. They may be responsible for writing up a list of questions that the work provoked or evoked in them; they may kick off the discussion by describing a reaction they had to the work; they may find related writings they might want to bring in to provide a different perspective on the theme; they may want to do a dramatic reading of a section or scene from the work. Group leaders may also have the responsibility of meeting with the teacher or writing progress reports to keep the teacher informed about what's happening in the group.

➡ Group members may prepare weekly, or even short daily, writings to bring to the discussion. (See chapter 10, "Reading and Responding.") Discussion may focus on response papers as well as the literature.

➡ Begin a small-group "Review Board" or "Literature Newsletter." The small groups prepare reviews of the book they are reading to share with the rest of the class via the bulletin board or a weekly, biweekly, or monthly dittoed handout. Students in the small group may write collaborative reviews of the books they are reading, or if opinions differ, they may write competing reviews. Let students use their small-group discussions to discuss, write, and edit the reviews they will publish.

➡ Establish periodic class sessions for "Book Talk." Have group members prepare an informal presentation of their book to acquaint other class members with it. Even better, ask the school librarian or the public librarian to allow your kids to do "Book Talk" for a wider audience.

➡ By writing, students who are reading books on their own and don't have a group to bounce ideas around with can objectify, extend, or play with their thoughts. Students may become a part of the novel by writing as a character or the novelist might. (See chapter 10, "Reading and Responding.") Or they might take the position of critic or editor, describing what the author does successfully and unsuccessfully, what might have been changed, improved, or left out of the novel. Allowing students to participate freely in criticizing literature not only helps them develop their critical awareness; it also makes literature seem less intimidating and less sacred. When students feel free to express their preferences and tastes (rather than saying what the teacher wants to hear about this "good" book), it becomes easier for them to *like* a book rather than defensively hating everything they're supposed to like.

➡ For some students working alone, the interim between initial response and describing that initial response is difficult. To help students come to grips with their response, Alan Purves assigns a poem that students have not seen before and asks them not to look at that poem until they have a block of time—say, an hour. The students read the poem, writing down initial responses, associations, and thoughts elicited by the poem. Because they have alloted sufficient time, they are able to go back to particular words and phrases and trace their meaning both for themselves and in light of other parts of the poem. Students may do this with literature other than poetry, tracing their response to a character by reading various scenes and writing—essentially, freewriting—about their response. The teacher, during a free-reading period may set aside time for students to write as well as read. Such writing allows the student, in effect, to have a dialogue with himself or herself.

Conferences with students also provide a means for students to talk about literature. The teacher need not have read the students' books in order to ask intelligent questions and help the students clarify their thoughts and ideas. Again, your questions will be open-ended, allowing the students to express what *they* see as significant and following up on those areas.

Finally, one should never underestimate the power of a good book, poem, story, or play. In our experience with individualized reading programs, we have found that certain books spread like wildfire. Not only are kids telling you about the book informally and in individual conferences, but you also overhear them describing key scenes or reading "good" parts to one another.

It is important to remember in all this discussion of critiquing, evaluating, objectifying, and analyzing that many times the most appropriate response to literature might be laughing, crying, swearing, or dancing. As an English teacher, make room for those too.

CHAPTER 12

Teaching the Classics

IN recent years, teachers have turned more and more to adolescent fiction as the basis of their reading program, because they have recognized the importance of students' reading literature that is appropriate to their intellectual and emotional development, literature that is accessible in language and meaning, literature that "speaks to them." For most young people, understanding and appreciation of classic (noncontemporary literature dubbed by college English curricula as worthy of survival) comes relatively late because of its sophistication in language structure and concepts and because of its distance from the experiences and life-styles of the twentieth century. Though both teachers and parents want their children to be exposed to the best our culture and language have to offer, early pressure to read books that are too difficult often destroys students' interest in reading and the possibility that they will *ever* read the classics.

Teachers have been well advised, then, to diminish their dependence on the classics as the center of the curriculum. However, such books still have an important place; in fact, certain classics, well taught, are among the favorite reading experiences of many students.

When teaching the classics, it is important for teachers to recognize the kinds of difficulties students may encounter in reading. Because English teachers have had several years of college training in reading literature and studying historical backgrounds, they have become accustomed to what in student's eyes may seem odd or strange when first reading novels and poems of other times. The language, the values, the morals and manners of characters in such works as *Hamlet, Gulliver's Travels,* and *Great Expectations* are often confusing and inexplicable to a sixteen-year-old who lives in Fredonia, New York, or Athens, Georgia, who plays on the football team or leads the cheers, and who works at McDonald's for spending money. Perhaps the enduring themes of literature justify teaching the works, but we will have to do more than just say that to interest adolescent readers who live in a society as busy, as complex, as materialistic, and as media-oriented as ours. Moreover, to help students understand what they read, it is necessary for teachers to create contexts and build connections and relationships. As we have said elsewhere, understanding of reading grows out of what we bring to the work; meanings grow from what we already know and understand.

What then can the teacher in the English classroom do to create contexts and build connections for students reading "the classics"? We discuss three units in which classical literature can be taught: thematic units; interdisciplinary period studies; and great people studies. Within each, we offer sample readings, prereading, postreading, and class activities.

Thematic Units

A thematic unit is one of the best ways of organizing a reading/writing sequence, because it allows teachers to keep the class together, providing opportunities for students to talk together and work together, while at the same time allowing the teacher to individualize. Students may come together to share short pieces—poems and stories—as well as films, records, and speakers, but may also go off to read longer works of their own choosing.

Though certain classical works may be beyond the development of some students, many classics are accessible to youngsters. For example, *The Arbuthnot Anthology of Children's Literature* (Scott, Foresman, 1972), organized thematically, contains literature by the "greats" alongside the "lesser knowns." Short works by Blake, Browning, Keats, Yeats, Shakespeare, Whitman, Dickinson, Wordsworth, Longfellow, Kipling, and Stevenson are included in such units as "All Sorts of People," "Traveling We Go," "Magic and Make Believe," "Wind and Water," and "Wisdom and Beauty."

A bibliography for older readers, NCTE's *Books for You* (1976), organizes and annotates literature appropriate for adolescents in grades 9–12—fiction and nonfiction, poetry and drama—by theme and genre, and includes both "junior" and classical works. The section on "Love and Romance" includes, for example, such classic novels as Charlotte Brontë's *Jane Eyre,* Emily Brontë's *Wuthering Heights,* Thomas Hardy's *The Return of the Native,* and Leo Tolstoy's *Anna Karenina.* Classic plays include William Shakespeare's *Romeo and Juliet* and Edmond Rostand's *Cyrano de Bergerac.* Sir Walter Scott's long poetic legend

The Lady of the Lake is also on the list. Greek and Roman love stories also seem appropriate for a theme on love and romance, as do some biblical stories, stories from *The Canterbury Tales,* and other novels: Thomas Hardy's *Tess of the D'Urbervilles,* Gustave Flaubert's *Madame Bovary,* and Edith Wharton's *Ethan Frome.* A great deal of poetry is available, including Shakespeare's sonnets.

In a section entitled "What is Important?" is a variety of books that focus on characters exploring the meaning of their lives, their relationships to nature, their relationships to society, and the impact of their actions. Included are John Bunyan's *Pilgrim's Progress,* Joseph Conrad's *Lord Jim,* Fyodor Dostoevsky's *Crime and Punishment,* William Dean Howells's *The Rise of Silas Lapham,* Victor Hugo's *Les Misérables,* Plato's *Republic,* Jonathan Swift's *Gulliver's Travels,* William Thackeray's *Vanity Fair,* Henry David Thoreau's *Walden,* Anthony Trollope's *Barchester Towers,* Mark Twain's *The Adventures of Huckleberry Finn,* and Walt Whitman's *Leaves of Grass.* Twentieth-century classics include: Albert Camus' *The Plague,* Willa Cather's *Death Comes for the Archbishop,* Theodore Dreiser's *An American Tragedy,* F. Scott Fitzgerald's *The Great Gatsby,* William Golding's *The Lord of the Flies,* Ernest Hemingway's *The Old Man and the Sea,* Sinclair Lewis's *Babbitt,* Boris Pasternak's *Doctor Zhivago,* J. D. Salinger's *The Catcher in the Rye,* and Thornton Wilder's *The Bridge of San Luis Rey.*

Many excellent collections of poetry are available for individual students to use or from which poems may be taken for whole-class readings. Some that include a wide range of selections are Joseph Auslander and Frank Hills's *The Winged Horse Anthology* (Doubleday, 1949); Richard F. Niebling's *A Journey of Poems* (Dell, 1964); Milton Crane's *50 Great Poets* (Bantam, 1961); Paul Engle and Joseph Langland's *Poet's Choice* (Dial, 1962); Robert Penn Warren and Albert Erskine's *Six Centuries of Great Poetry* (Dell, 1955); Donald Hall's *A Poetry Sampler* (Watts, 1962); and William Stafford's *Traveling Through the Dark* (Harper, 1962).

The list of works for "What Is Important?" suggests many subcategories or more limited topics for young readers: "Heroes and Heroines," "Getting Ahead," "Man and Society," and "Man and Nature." Consider the following classics that might be given as choices for students in a theme on heroes:

Chaucer, *The Canterbury Tales*
Homer, *Iliad* and *Odyssey*
Joseph Conrad, *Lord Jim* and *The Secret Sharer*
Daniel Defoe, *Robinson Crusoe*
Sir Thomas Malory, *Le Morte d'Arthur*
Sir Walter Scott, *Ivanhoe*

Shakespeare's *Hamlet, Othello, Romeo and Juliet*
Cervantes, *Don Quixote*
Alexandre Dumas, *The Count of Monte Cristo* and *The Three Musketeers*
James Fenimore Cooper, *The Last of the Mohicans*
Stephen Crane, *The Red Badge of Courage*
Herman Melville, *Billy Budd*
Mark Twain, *The Adventures of Huckleberry Finn* and *The Adventures of Tom Sawyer*

PREREADING ACTIVITIES

In a thematic unit, students should, of course, be given the opportunity to select from a variety of reading materials. Since students will be reading novels, stories, and plays of varying levels of difficulty and focusing on somewhat different issues and ideas, it is important to make prereading activities help students think in advance about ideas and issues they will be encountering. At the same time, activities must be broad enough to encompass a variety of approaches to the same theme.

It is also important to help students think about the background that they already have, but it is equally important not to discuss too much, to create activities or discussions in which students come to closure too soon, to "preteach" what the work will develop in its own terms. Discussion should be open-ended. Consider the following ideas developed for the theme of "Heroes":

- Engage students in a discussion of the themes and ideas raised in literature they will be reading.

- Talk with them about their ideas, theories, and beliefs about heroes (and heroines): What qualities do you consider necessary for someone to have to be heroic? Are those qualities different for men than for women? In what ways? What heroes and heroines have you had in the past? Where did they come from? (Literature, TV, comics, movies?) Why did you admire them? Are there any public figures you consider heroic? Who? Why? What are the qualities of mass-media heroes and heroines? Who are mass-media heroes and heroines? Can a person kill another person and still be a hero? Can a hero lie or cheat or steal? Are heroes courageous? Can heroes and heroines be timid? Do heroes and heroines have to be physically attractive?

In discussions preceding the reading of literature, let students range widely in their comments. Encourage them to uncover the resources from past experiences, reading, and the media. Help them discover what they think and believe and why. Such discussions of belief, philosophy, and value may be helpful preceding readings and units on a variety of topics: "Love" (romantic, altruistic, humanitarian, platonic); "Morality" (personal, interpersonal, governmental, institutional); "Nature" (man's place in it, what's going to happen to it, what has happened to it, what "controls" it); "Violence" (who *is* violent, who's responsible, when is it approved).

Additional prereading ideas:

➤ Consider using filmed or recorded literature to kick off a unit. Recorded versions of *The Last of the Mohicans, The Red Badge of Courage,* Shakespeare's plays, *The Canterbury Tales,* and many other classics are available. Films are also available, though they are more expensive. It is important when using films and records that you have the opportunity to preview them. Nothing is worse for killing interest than a grainy B-grade film or a record in which the King's English sounds like Anglo-Saxon.

➤ Use the media as a point of reference for having students talk about their own ideas. A good movie can be used as the basis of comparison as students do their individual readings as well. When they come together as a large group, they can compare the heroisms of the characters in what they are reading with the character that they met on film.

➤ Use the public library and the school library to discover records, tapes, and movies. The libraries in medium-sized cities are expanding their resources and often have large collections of media resources.

➤ Finally, in preparation for a unit, read aloud short works of poetry or excerpts from novels (or, if time permits, the whole novel over a couple of weeks), as the basis for beginning to think about and discuss themes. Often students will want to read aloud, but don't put anyone on the spot. Or selected students who enjoy drama might be allowed time in advance of beginning a unit to prepare a dramatization for the whole class. It is interesting to note that after a novel-made-into-film has been shown on television, the sales of that novel leap.

➤ Involve students in improvisational drama and role playing in which they take the part of people whose experiences are unlike their own. For a theme on heroes, dramatic situations may include:

- characters involved in a controversy about whether or not to fix a ball game or a track meet
- characters involved in a cheating incident in school
- characters involved in a love triangle.

ACTIVITIES DURING READING

As students are reading novels and plays they should have the opportunity to discuss their ideas and to deal with matters that are confusing to them. Have students engage in . . .

➡ *Large-group sharing.* Let students share their books with the rest of the class as they are reading, talking about ideas and feelings toward characters, and notions of heroism.

➡ *Small-group discussions.* Students can work through unfamiliar situations and share reactions to the events of the novel. Articulating these ideas increases understanding.

➡ *Discussions with the teacher.* The teacher can act as a resource person for students as they encounter new words and ideas. Though the teacher may not know all the answers, he or she can use free-reading time to look up and provide resource material for students who have questions.

➡ *Writing.* Though writing is often thought of as a way of putting things together *after* reading, writing can provide an excellent way for students to gain control of ideas *as* they read and to log their reactions.

Writing is particularly helpful when a student is reading a longer work. For example, try these "in-progress" forms:

➡ *A reading log.* The student keeps a journal of reactions, projections, imaginings, and reflections as he or she reads.

➡ *Rewrites and additions.* Students can write the final chapter of the book *before* they read it; or they can rewrite sections that they would like to see changed; or they can add chapters or sections.

➡ *Diaries and letters.* Students may choose a character that they would like to be as they read and write that person's running account, through a diary or letters to a friend, of what is happening to them as the story progresses.

ACTIVITIES AFTER READING

As students read their individual books and complete their reading, encourage them to discuss additional themes, ideas, characters, and situations that had an impact on them. In addition, of course, you will want to bring the whole class back together to discuss how individual readings' explored the central theme.

➡ As a whole class, then, discuss how the novel shaped the students' thinking and affected their ideas: What characters and situations had the most impact and why? How have students' definitions and feelings grown and changed as a result of reading the novel?

➡ Dramatizations and composition are appropriate follow-ups, with students doing, say, a readers' theater production of key parts of the novel, rewriting and scripting parts of the novel into a play or acting out plays, possibly even with costumes and sets.

➡ Compositions may be evaluations of our responses to the work. Classic works set in other times and places allow the students to write about their own life-style, values, and assumptions. In more formal papers, they may wish to compare the values of their own time to those of another period. In imaginative papers, they may do comparisons by bringing together characters from different periods in an imaginative situation and write about the interaction, or they can, "Rip Van Winkle style," place a character from sixteenth-century England or nineteenth-century Russia into twentieth-century America.

Interdisciplinary Period Studies

While thematic units focus on helping students make connections and build contexts between their own experiences and those of another time, interdisciplinary period studies immerse students in a particular culture to examine connections among the arts, music, science, people, places, and events. Though the units may sound like college period courses—The Renaissance, The Age of Reason, Realism and Naturalism, The Romantic Age, The Victorian Age, The Puritans—the intent is to develop a much fuller and richer understanding of an age.

The reading in an interdisciplinary unit will be centered, then, not just on fiction, poetry, and drama. Biography, autobiography, children's literature, and nonfiction works on music, dance, art, architecture, popular culture, morals and manners, science, history, politics, philosophy, and religion will also be a part of the course. A course in the Victorian Age might contain, then, such diverse literature as:

Charles Dickens, *A Tale of Two Cities, Bleak House, Great Expectations, Oliver Twist*
Robert Browning, *Colombe's Birthday*
Elizabeth Barrett Browning, *Aurora Leigh*
John Ruskin, *Notes on the Royal Academy*

Charles Darwin, *Origin of the Species*
Alfred Lord Tennyson, *Maud, Idylls of the King,* or *In Memoriam*
Oscar Wilde, *The Importance of Being Earnest*
Emily Brontë, *Wuthering Heights*
Charlotte Brontë, *Jane Eyre*
George Eliot, *Adam Bede*
John Stuart Mill, *On Liberty*
Robert Louis Stevenson, *The Strange Case of Dr. Jekyll and Mr. Hyde*
Anthony Trollope, *Barchester Towers*
Dr. William Acton, *The Functions and Disorders of the Reproductive Organs in Youth, in Adult Age, and in Advanced Life*
A. C. Benson and Viscount Esher (eds.), *The Letters of Queen Victoria, 1837–61, 1907–08*
Frances Isabella Duberly, *Journal Kept During the Russian War*
L. Huxley (ed.), *Elizabeth Barrett Browning: Letters to Her Sister, 1846–59*
R. Ironside and J. Gere, *Pre-Raphaelite Painters*
S. E. Ayling, *Nineteenth Century Gallery: Portraits of Power and Rebellion*
F. D. Klingender, *Art and the Industrial Revolution*
J. Maas, *Victorian Painters*
L. T. C. Rolt, *Victorian Engineering*
Lytton Strachey, *Eminent Victorians*
C. Woodham Smith, *Florence Nightingale*
Brigadier P. Young and Lt. Col. J. P. Lawford (eds.), *History of the British Army*

PREREADING ACTIVITIES

Because reading choices will be so diverse—and perhaps foreign to students who have been locked in to a rigid departmental discipline approach—students will probably need direction and an overview before they make their choices and begin reading. Consider some of the following:

Bring in a time line of major events of the era that you are focusing on, both within the country under consideration and in other countries during the same time. (Students often know more about the history of America than other countries; include major events that were happening in this country during the period you're studying.) Several interesting books can provide you with the information you need to create the time line, and in fact, some kids might enjoy browsing through the books and creating time lines focusing on certain subjects (science, art, medicine) in more detail. Stanford M. Mirkin's *What Happened When* (Ives Washburn, Inc., 1966) is a human-interest reference book that arranges historical events by each day of the year, with years listed under the day. Students are always eager to see what happened on their birthdays. *Historical Tables 58 B.C.—A.D. 1965* by S. H. Steinberg (Macmillan and St. Martin's Press, 1967) contains a chronological listing of the history of tribes and geographical eras, ecclesiastical life, cultural life, and political life. By far the most comprehensive book of this sort is Bernard Green's *The Timetables of History* (Simon and Schuster, 1975), which contains important historical events in history and politics, literature and the theater, religion and philosophy, the visual arts, music, science and technology, and daily life. These reference books, or ones like them, are available in the library and are an invaluable resource to teachers as well as students to get a sense of the relationships among important historical events.

Invite speakers. Librarians, history buffs, art historians, philosophers, musicians, theologians, and genealogists and museum curators have knowledge and information that they are often willing to share through school speaking engagements. Check with local colleges and universities, museums, libraries, and historical societies for the availability of speakers. Be sure to give speakers guidance so that they discuss ideas appropriate to what students already know and what they are interested in knowing. Perhaps students can develop a list of questions they would like to have answered to help the speaker to prepare his or her presentation.

Slide shows and films are available that characterize a particular age. Again, be sure to preview. It is also important that students be reminded that these present a general characterization of a period. Ask them to check the view given in the film or slides against what they read. What inconsistencies or contradictions or exceptions to the rules do they find in their reading?

Bring in picture books and art books that characterize the period or aspects of the period and let kids browse through them. Discuss possible topics they may wish to explore further that appear in these books. For the Victorian Age, for example, a variety of books give inviting overviews of the period that would stimulate further exploration: Gillian Avery's *Victorian People: In Life and in Literature* contains black-and-white illustrations, etchings and engravings, and paintings from the period and describes the lives of the aristocracy, the middle class, the poor, and the criminal. Hilary and Mary Evans' *The Victorians at Home and at Work* is even more heavily illustrated with art from the period and contains additional information about such areas as education, recreation, health and sickness, and invention and exploration. Another coffee-table book, Robert Hart's *English Life in the Nineteenth Century,* contains large color reproductions of the age as well as descriptions of the life-styles. J. B. Priestley's *Victoria's Heyday,* a social history of 1850–1860, contains a year-by-year description of the decade accompanied by vivid art reproductions as well as black-and-white illustrations. This list suggests the kinds of library resources that are available to the general reader and provide much more interesting sources of information than textbooks in bringing an age to life.

In place of an introductory lecture, consider preparing a "collage" of literary works. What did various Victorians—Brontë, Dickens, the Brownings, Tennyson, George Eliot, Thackeray—have to say about death, romantic love, morals and manners, women, war? Consider using music and art reproductions to accompany your dramatization.

Circulate or post several art reproductions from the period you are studying. Have students describe the paintings and what they think the paintings are "about," what they say about the person who painted them, and the life and experience of the artist.

Take students on a field trip to an art museum or historical museum to look at the art and artifacts of a period. To help them focus their attention, give them some indication of what they will see. In addition, you might assign students a painting, art object, or artifact to describe or write about when they return.

ACTIVITIES DURING READING

Encourage students to keep a list of questions they have while they are reading. Set aside time every now and then for students to share questions and information. Students reading a novel may have a question about the incidence of a certain illness or the hullaballoo about an invention. Students reading nonfiction books on medicine or science may be able to answer those questions. (Keep resource books around for kids to answer their own questions, too.)

Again, let kids keep a reading journal to record things they want to remember and talk about later, or to enter into the book by participating with diary writing from a character's or person's point of view, or by rewriting the story.

➡ Let students draw or paint memorable scenes as they are reading. At the end of their reading, they can present their illustrations to the class along with readings from selected parts of the books.

➡ Break up reading time for periodic sharing of reading. Information from other sources will help students build the context to make their reading more meaningful and richer. Caution students against setting up one-to-one relationships between what they know about real life and what is happening in their novel or poetry. This might be a good time to talk about how authors use reality as raw material but feel free to deviate from it as it suits their artistic purposes. Paintings and sculptures will also aid in this discussion.

ACTIVITIES AFTER READING

Prepare a period fair: a Victorian Age Fair, a Romantic Period Fair, a Renaissance Fair, a Fair of the Westward Movement, a Fair of the Pilgrims, a Nineteenth-Century American Fair. Include the following in a display:

➡ A facsimile newspaper from the period (perhaps from a particularly memorable day), which includes articles, editorials, cartoons, drawings, advertisements, and features that would have appeared during the period.

➡ A display of art reproductions from the period, accompanied by short biographies of the artists. Student imitations of the art of the period may also be included in the display.

➡ A tape of music written during the period (biographies of the composers may be posted). Student reaction papers and mood pieces may also be a part of the display.

➡ A display of illustrations of inventions from the period with descriptions of what the inventions did and what became of them. Some enterprising students may wish to construct models of inventions (and give you the opportunity to include shop teachers in the fair).

➡ A book of biographies of famous people. Colorful and influential politicians, scientists, theologians, philosophers, musicians, and painters, as well as writers might be included in such a book. If possible, make copies available for visitors who wish to purchase them.

➡ A dramatization of a play from the period or an adaptation of a novel or a poem. Let students and their parents and volunteers make costumes, props, and scenery for the play. Or if your museum connections have grown, borrow from the curator.

Food. Let students who have researched home life prepare recipes that can also be copied and distributed or sold. (Consider putting poems or short quotes on the recipe sheets.) Prepare some of the simpler foods in class or encourage students to make food as homework. Or do an entire meal from the period for members of the class only.

Original writings: book reviews; poem reviews; imitations of authors; character diaries; reaction papers; original poems suggested by the science, art, or music of the period; essays analyzing and describing the period or some aspect of the period. Copy and distribute in book form or distribute as broadsides or pamphlets. (Include people in the school graphics and art department.)

A reader's theater production, perhaps similar to the teacher's introduction to the unit, but with student-selected literature forming the "collage."

Original musical compositions performed by students. (Enlist the music teacher for help in preparation.)

If you find it impossible to do an elaborate period fair, let your students pick and choose from the list of projects (with others you and they add) for their final projects in the unit.

Great People Studies

Great People Studies give students an opportunity to look at famous people from various angles: their life-styles and values, their work and their culture. Give students the option of reading about a wide variety of important people: artists, musicians, dancers, authors, philosophers, warriors, religious leaders, economists. To limit the unit, you may wish to have students explore only literary people. Or you may wish them to explore famous people who lived in a particular era. Present them with many ways of learning about the person: biographies, autobiographies, their writings, their writings about their work, their treatises, articles from magazines and newspapers, historical novels.

The unit may be taught so that everyone is exploring the same person, but of course, the person should be significant and important enough to have the interest of all the students and enough material available so that everyone can find something they want to read.

PREREADING ACTIVITIES

➡ Begin by having students identify people who interest them or pique their curiosity. Have them write a list of questions they would like to have answered about the person. (Note: If your library is a small one, or if it's difficult to get materials from the public library, you might like to begin with a list that you draw up from the card catalogue or that the librarian might have available of people about whom there is ample information. Sometimes students may have to be guided away from a topic because they won't be able to find enough on it.)

➡ For students who do not have anyone in mind, provide a list of topics or an interest inventory. With the librarian, develop a list of famous people for kids who are interested in such topics as science fiction, parachute jumping, skiing, baseball, Egypt, journalism, religions, women's studies, swimming, airplanes, child care, earthquakes, dancing, kings and queens, the trombone/violin/piano, the law, medicine and health, etc.

➡ Have students brainstorm for a list of ways they may find out about the person they are interested in: biographies, autobiographies, historical novels, historical societies, commemorative institutions, etc.

➡ Have students brainstorm for questions they may want answered about a great person. What has this person contributed to his or her field of interest? What is this person like in private life? How did these people go about making their contribution? How did they feel about their work? How was their work received? How did they grow or change as their careers progressed?

➡ Have students locate resources for reading about their person. If they need to write away for printed information or they wish to write to an expert in the field, help them get started immediately.

ACTIVITIES DURING READING

➡ Though students may be working individually much of the time, some of them may have common interests or be studying the same person; let those students work together from time to time, sharing information sources and describing what their sense of the entire field is—the baseball world, nineteenth-century British science, nineteenth-century American religion—and their great person's contribution to it.

➡ Have students keep logs and diaries.

➡ Begin a class correspondence, with students becoming their great person and writing letters to other great persons in the class.

ACTIVITIES AFTER READING

➡ Have students write a biography of their famous person, emphasizing the most important contributions.

➡ Have students make a scrapbook of their famous person, perhaps creating facsimile reproductions of mementoes the person might have kept as he or she was growing up, becoming successful, famous, or infamous.

➡ Spend a class period having students play the role of their characters. Establish a situation for them to act out their roles: a press conference, a fete put on by the president, the historical society, or the JayCees.

➡ Let students work out improvisations in small groups. For example, what would Abraham Lincoln, William Shakespeare, and Amelia Earhart talk about? Or Walt Whitman, Napoleon Bonaparte, and Emily Brontë? Or Queen Elizabeth, Charles Dickens, and Richard Nixon?

➡ Have students visit classes of younger children as their person. Let the student give a speech or presentation and/or answer questions that children might have about their character's life and times.

➡ Have students choose a current issue that their famous person might be interested in, and let them write a position paper on the topic from that person's point of view.

➡ If their famous person wrote, let them try writing something in that person's style.

➡ Have them imagine their person's spirit watching over the world. What would that person think of modern life?

➡ Have the students prepare a multimedia presentation characterizing the life and work of their person.

The classics can be taught successfully if students have the opportunity to make their own choices in what they read, have an environment and teaching that helps build context for understanding, and have ample opportunities for creative talk, writing, and drama.

CHAPTER 13

Teaching Popular Literature

Thank you *George* for . .
Soupy Sales and Bloomingdale's
James Moody and Howdy Doody
Frank Buck and Donald Duck
Edith Head and Grateful Dead
Elsie Borden and Flash Gordon
Margaret Mead and Allen Freed
Billy Budd and Elmer Fudd
Double Decker and Chubby Checker
Bar Bells and Orson Wells
Mason Jars and Hershey Bars
R. H. Macy and Dick Tracy
Jane Fonda and Satchidandanda
Gandy Goose and Lenny Bruce
Magic Marker and Charlie Parker
Benjamin Spock and Monte Rock
Betty Boop and Hula Hoop
King Kong and Ping Pong
Pinky Lee and Sandra Dee
Peter Max and Cracker Jacks
Babe Ruth and Spooky Tooth
Lady Day and Sugar Ray
Herbie Mann and Charlie Chan
Frankie Lyman and Neil Simon
Huckleberry Finn and Rin Tin Tin
Henry Miller and Phyllis Diller

Sarah Bernhardt and Werner Erhard
Stanley Kubrick and Dave Brubeck
Larry Parks and Groucho Marx
Jungle Jim and Tiny Tim
Satchel Paige and John Cage
Buddy Holly and Toonerville Trolley
Buckley's Nazz and Satchmo's Jazz
Gil Hodges and Buck Rogers
Easy Rider and Duke Snider
Fatty Arbuckle and Artie Garfunkel
Liz Taylor and Popeye the Sailor
Willy Mays and Gabby Hayes
Paul Bunyan and Damon Runyon
Submariner and Ike and Tina
William Boyd and Pink Floyd
Lauren Hutton and Willie Sutton
Carmen Miranda and Andy the Panda
Helen Reddy and Ferlinghetti
Admiral Byrd and Mortimer Snerd
Mack Sennet and Tony Bennet
Lucille Ball and Huntz Hall
Bill Haley and Barnum and Bailey
Clarence Darrow and Mia Farrow
Joe Papp and Al Capp
Red Grange and Dr. Strange
Freedom Train and Frieda Payne
Claude Rains and Lionel Trains
Johnny Carson and Greer Garson
James Dean and Mr. Clean
Don Knotts and Alan Watts
Count Basie and Edgar Cayce
George Meany and Harry Houdini
William Cody and Truman Capote
Amos N' Andy n' W. C. Handy
Fred Astaire and Buddy Baer
Pearl Buck and Daisy Duck
John Lindsay and Alfred Kinsey
James Cagney and Jerome Ragney

Al Capone and Vic Damone
Johnny Cash and Ogden Nash
The Human Torch and Larry Storch
Ticker Tape and Moby Grape

—from an advertising circular by
Acropolis Books, Ltd.

The above "thank you" list begins to express the variety and richness of the American experience, not only as seen in the great historical events or the great art produced in the United States, but as reflected in its popular arts: the entertainments, diversions, and aesthetic experiences of the masses. Though the popular arts, by definition, appeal to a large number of people, they are not necessarily inferior or mediocre in quality. We think that the study of the popular arts, both those of today and those of previous periods in American history, can be not only an enjoyable but also a rewarding experience in the English classroom for several reasons:

The study of popular culture enriches students' understanding of America and Americans. The fiction and poetry, magazines and newspapers, radio and television programs, movies and plays that Americans like provide insight into their tastes, values, and beliefs. Through a study of popular culture, students can begin to answer the questions: What is peculiar or unique about Americans? How have Americans changed and developed throughout their history? What traits and beliefs have endured? How have we come to be what we are today? What traditions seem strongest in America? How do I reflect those traditions? In what ways am I different?

The study of popular culture helps students understand their own tastes and values better. Students can examine their own interests and compare them with the interests of their peers, their parents, and people in other times. The study of popular culture also gives students an opportunity to examine some of the sociological, economic, and commercial roots of their own and others' tastes.

Popular culture is diverse and rich. Students of varying interests and abilities will be able to find something that they are interested in and that they would like to explore in more depth. In addition, popular culture resources are at our fingertips: paperback books, magazines, newspapers, television, radio, and movies are a part of everyone's daily lives; all can be used in developing students' awareness of their culture and their own values and preferences.

To show the potential of these materials, we will review three approaches to popular culture in the classroom: the historical, the literary, and the genre.

The Historical Approach to Popular Culture

Use interest in history as the jumping-off point for a study of American arts. Consider some of the following possibilities:

► Choose an important historical period. Break the class into small groups to explore the popular culture of the period. What were the American fads and fancies, for example, during; the Revolution? the Civil War? Prohibition? World War II? the Kennedy presidency?

Have students go to primary sources as often as possible: magazines, newspapers, novels, stories, poems, dramas of the period. (For some of the earlier periods, the original works will no longer be extant, and students will have to rely on secondary information and collections of artifacts.)

After students have reached their areas, have them prepare original materials representing the popular art of the time. They can create magazines, newspapers, stories, poems, and plays, and even electronic displays. Students might want to include fashion, games, and fads of the time as well as popular writing.

► Choose a single, important day in the history of the U.S.—the deaths of Jefferson and Adams (on America's fiftieth birthday in 1826); The assassination of Lincoln; the hanging of John Brown; the landing of Lindberg; the bombing of Pearl Harbor; the assassination of Kennedy—and have students discover as much as possible about that day. Choosing later events provides students with the opportunity of using primary resources. If your library doesn't have the appropriate back issues of magazines and newspapers, take a trip to the local paper, the city library, or a local college or university library. Have students ask: What other important events occurred on that day? What was being advertised in entertainment? In fashions? What sorts of fiction and poetry were appearing in the periodicals that month? What were the best-sellers? The most popular songs? Who were the heroes, stars, and idols? What names appeared frequently? Who were they and why were they important? Have students write their own magazine or newspaper which reflects the events and circumstances of the time. Or have them present improvisations or scripted dramas of the events of the day they are researching, reflecting both the mood preceding and following the significant event.

► Have students who have studied a particular era produce a popular art form of their era: a Horatio Alger short novel; Civil War ballads; sentimental and didactic verse and fiction; minstrel shows; vaudeville; dime novels, cartoons, and comics. Have students collaborate on projects, producing the art, staging, music, as well as the writing.

➡ As a part of the study of a particular period, have students create or re-create a play, a minstrel show, or a tent show representative of the period.

➡ Involve the class in writing and producing a television series based on a historical period. The series could be a serious one or a situation comedy. Most students are familiar with the situation comedy depicting the fifties, "Happy Days," which could serve as a model for their own. Fads, pastimes, music, heroes and heroines, fashions, and social and political values might be represented on the show.

➡ Students might enjoy discovering the history of popular culture through their own families, houses, and neighborhoods.

➡ Have students interview parents and grandparents about the things they did when they were young. What books did they read? What did they listen to on the radio? What movies did they see? What were their favorite TV shows? Who were their heroes and heroines? What comics did they read? What games did they play? Have students develop a chronology of popular culture on the basis of the answers they get from their families. Then they may enjoy doing some research to see how their parents and grandparents memories compare with what they can find about the period.

➡ Have a treasure hunt in which students search attics, basements, and bookshelves in their houses for books, magazines, and newspapers saved by their families over the years. What has survived? Are there common books that seem to endure? Classify the books according to years and try to discover common elements in reading material.

➡ Visit garage sales and rummage sales to pick up old books and magazines. Start a class library of "the survivors."

➡ Have students bring in parents' and grandparents' school yearbooks and picture albums. What can they discover about the values, interests, and fads of the times through looking at these? Verify or extend their view of the period by reading the best sellers of those years, or reading magazines and newspapers from that period, or researching the Academy Award winners over those years.

A Literary Approach to Popular Culture

The study of popular literature complements and augments students' sense of the literary past.

➡ Some of the American fiction that has survived and become classic was also popular in its own time among a large audience. Have students read literature popular in its own time which is considered highly today. Ask them to account for its popularity in its own time. Why was it widely read? Why has it continued to be important? What qualities appeal to readers today?

➡ Provide students with both popular and elitist poems from a particular period. Have them compare and contrast the poems read by a large audience with the poems read by only a few. Ask students which poems they prefer and why.

➡ Encourage students to read magazine fiction spanning a period of years. Ask them how the fiction changes. What is the difference between fiction popular in the twenties and fiction popular in the thirties or forties? Let students try writing fiction appropriate to different time periods.

➡ Teach a best-seller unit. Allow students to read books from the best-seller list for designated years. Have them characterize the literary interests reflected by the books on the best-seller list. Then have them compare the books on the best-seller list with publishers' figures of numbers of books sold. Are the best-sellers the most popular books? What discrepancies do they find?

➡ Have students read novels that have been made into movies. Ask them to consider why the novels were chosen to be made into films. Discover which were the most successful among large audiences. Try to account for the popularity of the movie. Whenever possible, choose films that will be shown on television, at movie theaters, or that you might be able to rent.

➡ Sponsor a literature revival for which students choose popular fiction and poetry from a period to repopularize. Let them do advertisements, posters, and book reviews touting their literature.

➡ Explore popular children's literature. After students have read popular magazines and books for children, let them write children's stories for children of other times. How do those stories compare with interests of children today?

➡ Divide the class by decades or historical or literary periods. Have each group research the most popular plays during their period. Let them choose one play from their period to present to the rest of the class.

A Genre Approach to Popular Culture

A genre approach to the teaching of popular culture allows students to choose an area of popular culture or popular art that they are interested in and to pursue it in depth. Consider some of the following possibilities when teaching units or courses in humanities, popular culture, American literature, or American history.

FICTION

The Western

Read all the novels by a popular writer of westerns, such as James Fenimore Cooper, Zane Grey, Henry Wilson Allen, Jack Schaefer, A. B. Guthrie, or Ernest Haycox. Describe the heroes of the novels. How is the West depicted? Do some research on the West. How does the real West compare with your novelist's depiction?

Choose one of the real-life heroes of the old West, such as Buffalo Bill, Kit Carson, or Daniel Boone. In what ways are these heroes depicted in fiction? Trace their influence on the heroes of the western novel. Use one of these heroes as the basis for your own work for western fiction.

How are women or minorities—Indians, Orientals, and blacks—depicted in western fiction? Write a minority-viewpoint critique of a popular western.

Compare the western tradition in fiction with the western tradition in movies and television. Choose a particular hero of the West and compare his depiction in fiction with his image on TV, radio, or movies.

Read a series of short stories by various western writers. What are the common elements? How are they different? Write your own western short story using the elements common to the popular western.

Detective and Spy Fiction

Read a series of detective or mystery novels by the same writer, such as Arthur Conan Doyle, Mary Roberts Rinehart, Willard Huntington Wright, Frederick Dannay and Manfred Lee, Agatha Christie, Erle Stanley Gardner, or Mickey Spillane. Characterize the type of mystery that your writer creates. What are the qualities of the main character? Of the villain? How does the writer create suspense? How does the writer provide clues? Read novels by more than one author and compare the heroes, crimes, and solutions.

Choose one of the major heroes in detective fiction—Charlie Chan, Ellery Queen, Perry Mason, Sam Spade—and trace his career both in fiction and in the electronic media. Does the hero change over the years? In what ways? How do the kinds of crimes he likes to solve and his mode of solving them change? Create your own episode using your favorite hero.

➡ Read a series of short stories from mystery periodicals. Try to categorize the various types of detective fiction and heroes. Look, too, at the other aspects of the detective/mystery periodical. What do the articles and advertisements say about the kind of reader who reads this magazine?

➡ Compare the detective/police stories on television with the detective stories of your favorite novelist. Do the same with movie mysteries.

Science Fiction

➡ Read a series of science fiction stories from different periods (by such writers as Hugo Sernback, H. G. Wells, John W. Campbell, G. Stanley Weingaum, Philip Wylie, Jules Verne, Isaac Asimov, and Ray Bradbury) and discover how science fiction changes over the years. What are the major themes of science fiction stories? What values and beliefs about existence are offered? How does advancing technology affect the science fiction story?

➡ Compare the science fiction of television and movies with the science fiction you read. What do they have in common? What's different?

TELEVISION

Soap Operas

➡ Watch several soap operas for a week. What seem to be the main problems that characters in soap operas encounter? Describe the status and professions of characters in the programs. What variety do you see in life-style and status in soap operas? Try to account for the kinds of characters, life-styles, and problems presented on soap operas. What do you conclude about the type of audience that watches these shows?

➡ Write and present an episode for a soap opera that solves a problem in a way you would like to see it solved. Or resolve all the problems occurring on a particular soap opera in a single episode.

➡ Write a soap opera for children or for teenage boys or for native Americans or blacks. How would the problems and issues and life-styles be different for these different audiences?

➡ Compare the issues and problems presented in soap operas with the issues and problems presented in nighttime television.

➡ Do a study of the history of the soap opera, including the radio soap opera. How has it changed over the years?

Situation Comedies

What's funny about situation comedies? What kinds of characters, experiences, and life-styles are represented in situation comedies? To what types of audiences do they appeal?

Do a historical study of types of situation comedies, such as domestic comedy, military comedy, minority comedy, etc. How have situation comedies developed over the past twenty-five years?

Design and present one episode of a series for television creating your own cast of characters and your own unique situations.

Drama

Do a historical study of TV drama. How have the types of programs changed over the years? What sorts of heroes or heroines have remained? What new types of characters appear on television that weren't around in the fifties?

Describe the image of minorities as seen on TV. How are minorities depicted on situation comedies? On dramas? Which shows have minority characters as central figures? How are their values and life-styles represented?

Describe the American woman as represented by television. Look at soap operas, advertisements, situation comedies, and dramas. How has the image of the woman changed in the past five years? In the past ten?

Characterize the TV hero. What does he value? What does he want from life? How does he go about pursuing his wants? Are there various kinds of heroes on television? Categorize TV heroes.

FILMS

Which movies in the past ten years have had the greatest success at the box office? What types of movies seem to be most popular? Why? What does this say about the American tastes and values?

See as many movies starring the same character (James Bond, Dirty Harry, or Inspector Clousseau) as you can. What accounts for the continued success of these characters? Write a scenario for a movie starring your favorite movie hero.

See as many movies as you can in the same genre—Walt Disney movies, Clint Eastwood movies, nostalgia movies, rock and roll films. Describe what audiences you think these movies appeal to and what their appeal seems to be.

➡ Do a study of Academy Award winning movies, actors, and actresses. What common characteristics do you see in award winners? How are they different? What relationship do you see between the movies that were well received and the historical period or events occurring at the same time? What characteristics do you see in award-winning actors and actresses? How has the notion of "the star" changed over the years?

➡ Do a historical study of a particular type of film: the romance, science fiction, westerns, mysteries, history-biography. Describe how the genre changed and developed.

➡ Choose an actor or actress that you like and research his or her career.

MUSIC

➡ Do a study of the history of rock and roll, jazz, or the blues. How has the music changed over the years?

➡ Choose a musician who has influenced popular music. Research that person's career and do a recording collage of the performer's music.

➡ Do a musical collage of the best-selling rock-and-roll singles in the past several years. Describe the recurring themes in hits over the years.

➡ Study a classical musician to determine whether he was "popular" during his own time. Describe how he became popular.

➡ Do some research on song writing. Where do writers get their ideas for words and music? Which usually comes first? How do they combine the two?

➡ Do a study of record production. By what process do the sounds that go into a tape become the sounds that come out on a tape?

SUMMARY AND TROUBLESHOOTING

Education's Wax Museum

For this section, we want to draw on an essay that appeared in *The English Journal* a little while back. It explores the problems associated with a "response centered" literature curriculum in detail and does it imaginatively. Come with us, then, as Margaret Verble, a member of the Department of Curriculum and Instruction, the University of Kentucky, takes us on a tour.*

Tour guide: If you will just step this way ladies and gentlemen, we will continue our tour through Education's Wax Museum. This next exhibit is entitled, "The English Teacher and the Poet, a Preview of Purgatory." If you will just step a little closer, you will be able to see the fine detail of the figures. Notice the curl of the Poet's lip. He almost looks mad. Note too, if you will, the realistic coloring of the figures; our artist was able to achieve that haggard look on the teacher's face primarily through the use of shading. You should be able to see the blue tones under her eyes and in the hollows of her cheeks. These figures are so realistically done that if you stand here long enough they almost come alive. The books and furnishings, of course, are real.

Poet: I've told you time and time again, they can't see us as we really are. They've been through your educational system; all their imagination has been blunted. The only time you have to worry is when there are children in the group. (*Orating*) "What a distressing contrast there is between the radiant intelligence of the child, and the feeble mentality of the average adult." Freud said that, if you want to write it down.

*Margaret Verble, "Education's Wax Museum . . . Only a Step Away," *The English Journal* 65 (May 1976): 28–33. Copyright © 1976 by the National Council of Teachers of English. Reprinted and excerpted by permission of the publisher and the author.

Teacher: I'm sick of you quoting to me as though I were some kind of idiot. I'm a perfectly well-educated, rational adult. Just because I won't teach your poetry and the contemporary poetry of your friends you act as though I'm a mental incompetent. I'm not, you know. I'm at least as well educated as you are, and a lot saner.

Poet: Exactly my point, dear lady. You are, granted, most sane and educated. That's precisely what's wrong. Your rational education makes me want to bounce around the room on my ear. Why can't ——

Teacher: (*Interrupting*) That's a good example of what I'm talking about. My rational education makes you want to bounce around the room on your ear. That sounds just like something you'd say in a poem. How can I explain that to my students? It doesn't make sense.

Poet: It makes perfect sense to me. What you mean is that it doesn't make sense logically and analytically. There are other ways of making sense. Now, admit it. In saying that, I communicated to you. You understood it immediately. Didn't you?

Teacher: Well, yes, I suppose I did, but I can't explain it.

Poet: (*Banging hand on table and rising*) Well, for god's sake, teacher. You don't have to explain it. It makes sense intuitively. You can't explain it analytically. Even if you could, it isn't necessary. There's more than one way of knowing. (*Orating*) There's the knowing of the turtle and the knowing of the kangaroo.

Teacher: That confirms it. You're nuts. I don't know why I'm talking to you. Except, of course, because we're locked in.

Poet: You're locked in.

Teacher: And you're not, I suppose?

Poet: No. I'm not a turtle. I'm a kangaroo, lady. "Stone walls do not a prison make." That's Lovelace. You're locked in your own rational mind. I, on the other hand, am free to jump about. (*He jumps on table.*)

Teacher: Completely gone.

Poet: Perhaps. Perhaps. But it's a problem for you, not me. What are you going to do with us "nuts," teach? What, by the way, have you done with our fathers, Blake and Yeats?

Teacher: I don't teach much Blake and Yeats. They're too hard for the kids to understand.

Poet: (*Deflated*) Geeez.

Teacher: Look. Try, I mean really try, to understand. I have to teach my students how to think. To think—analytically—to problem-solve. That's what it's all about. I admit that every time I tackle a poem like it were an algebraic formula I die a little somewhere inside. But that's how I was taught to do it in college, and I don't know what else to do.

Poet: Ah! College. That's the problem. It's those damn formalist critics and their True Believers. They think poems are frogs to be dissected and pulled apart. They pull out a line, hold it up to the light and say, "Now what we have here is a paradox. Notice how the paradox is connected to the theme by the vehicle of the concrete image. All of this is part of the metaphoric system." The metaphoric system is, of course, the circulatory system of poetry. Actually, you could probably study the circulatory system of a frog and find out as much about poetry as they do by approaching poems that way.

Teacher: There you go again. That's not fair. Not fair at all. We owe a great debt to the New Critics. They taught us to pay attention to the text of the poem again and to read without judging a poem's worth by some outside criterion, like our favorite moral system.

Poet: (*Thoughtful*) Hum. You're right. I apologize to the Vanderbilt crew. But my point is that the principles and tenets of the New Criticism have become rigidified into another "outside criterion." And on top of that, they simply won't work—particularly with more recent American poetry. Nor will they work with Spanish poetry and French poetry.

Teacher: I know that. Probably better than you do. Why do you think I have these circles under my eyes? I want my students to read poems that are contemporary and relevant to their lives. But who can make sense out of what you are writing today? (*She picks up a book.*) Just listen to this. This is from your friend, David Ignatow:

The Life Dance

I see bubbling out of the ground
water, fresh, a pure smell. My mind
too begins to spring. I take
small hops. I enjoy myself
partly because I have the nerve.
Is anybody watching?
I care and don't care,
as I hop, and soon
because nobody is looking I'm leaping
and twisting into awkward shapes,

letting my hands make signs
of a meaning I do not understand.
I am absorbed in getting at what
til now
I had not been aware of.
There is a feeling in the world
I sometimes think I'm grasping.
I find myself holding a hand or
as I take a deep breath
I think it is there*

Poet: That's nice. I like that. (*She looks quizzical.*) Don't you understand?

Teacher: I understand there's something there, something I can't get to even if I explicate it. But no, I don't understand what, and neither does the speaker.

Poet: But it's there, isn't it? You know it's there, intuitively, just as the speaker does.

Teacher: But what does it mean?

Poet: Ach! You know a poem doesn't mean, it simply is! Or shall I give you that quote?

Teacher: Spare me, please. What I meant to say is, how can I lead my students to analyze that poem so that they will grasp its significance?

Poet: That's just the point. You can't. At least not in the way you've been talking about. After living with that poem for a long time there are some things that can be said about it that are akin to analysis, but you're not ready for that yet because the first step is missing. There has to be an intuitive understanding of the poem first.

Teacher: Intuitive. Intuitive. That's what you always say. But what does that mean?

Poet: It doesn't mean, it is. I am. I don't mean. It is, like a kangaroo is.

Teacher: Come on now. Get serious. I've been reading up on intuition since being trapped in here with you. Even the people who talk the most about it don't know anything about it. Take, for instance, Carl Jung. He thinks intuition is just as important as thinking and feeling and sensation as a way of knowing, but

*David Ignatow, *Poems 1934–1969* (Middletown, Conn.: Wesleyan University Press, 1970), p. 247.

when put on the spot about how it works, do you know what he said? He said, "I don't know how it works." Take Jerome Bruner. He came out of the Woods Hole Conference proclaiming the necessity of fostering intuitive thinking in students. Yet he admits he doesn't know what it is, either. He says it's even hard to identify when it's taking place. And then to make things even more difficult, contemporary poets write poems that aren't logically associative. Ignatow's poem is the mildest of examples. I could have taken Mark Strand, Gary Snyder or Robert Bly. Bly even calls his poetry "leaping poetry," and says, "The real joy of poetry is to experience this leaping inside a poem."

Poet: Look who's quoting now.

Teacher: Quoting is the only way to cope with your arrogance. And don't dodge the question. What is intuition?

Poet: (*Quietly*) I don't know. There is a mystery in the middle, like the mystery in the middle of a poem. I can't define it. But I can say things about it. When I write, I write through an intuitive process. My poems come to me. The Muse used to get credit for it, but since the discovery of the unconscious, we poets usually say that our associations and images come to us out of the depths of our unconscious minds. You see, it's as if the mind jumps back and forth constantly from the conscious to the unconscious. Bly's right. It's a leaping process. You start grounded in your conscious mind—jump—and land grounded in your unconscious. We give you that ground in the images of our poems, but we can't give you the air to leap into. Only you can jump that barrier between your conscious and your unconscious. That's why intuitive thinking is more important in reading contemporary poetry than is analytical thinking. The turtle can't get over the wall—or out of his own shell.

Teacher: Hum. Jung talks about the role of the unconscious in the intuitive process, too. He says intuition is sort of perception that goes by the unconscious, rather than by the senses.

Poet: I expect he's right.

Teacher: (*Rises and walks in thought*) You know, I was reading Darwin's autobiography the other day ——

Poet: (*Interrupting*) Geeez, lady, you read a lot.

Teacher: There's a lot I want to know.

Poet: And books are the only way?

Teacher: I know your point before you make it. There are other ways of knowing. That's possible. I'm beginning to see that, but you act as though rationality is the enemy. Why can't analysis and intuition be supportive of each other? (*Smiling*) My intuition is that they aren't antithetical. (*He starts to interrupt.*)

Wait. You haven't heard me out about Darwin. Darwin brooded over his biological data for years before he saw the pattern it fit into. Then, one day during a carriage ride, his theory came to him in a flash. He grasped the structure of it in that instance, and then spent years more fitting individual pieces of evidence together to build that structure analytically. In Darwin's case, that intuitive leap came in a moment of exhaustion after years of frustrated analysis. Then that intuition guided the rest of his analysis. Do you see what I'm saying? Intuition and analysis are not mortal enemies—they can support one another.

Poet: I see what you mean. It's like working a jigsaw puzzle without looking at the picture on the box. You look at all those little separate pieces long enough and you start to get an idea of the pattern and that idea of the pattern helps you fit the pieces together. Then, the more pieces you fit together, the better idea you get of the pattern.

Teacher: Right. That overall pattern, picture, or structure is what intuition gives us. You know, Bruner talks about intuition having to do with grasping the structure of a situation without resorting to analytical tools, and Jung, too, talks about the intuitive attitude as the one that takes in the whole of a situation through unconscious processes. Do you think that's true?

Poet: Probably. I know from my own experience that when I read somebody else's poem I know immediately if that poem fits together as a whole. But the thing that has always impressed me is the immediacy of that intuitive perception. There's nothing interposed between the poem and me. When you analyze a poem you have to interpose some logical apparatus between yourself and the poem. In contemporary poetry that's one of the things that keeps the associations from hopping around the way they should. It stills the frog, so to speak.

Teacher: I thought you were the one who's against poems as frogs.

Poet: Not alive leaping, hopping frogs. Only dead, cut-up frogs.

Teacher: Then, to follow our logic through (you can squirm at that word if you like, as long as you realize that's just as narrow minded as me protesting against intuition), to follow our logic through, I can find out a lot about a frog by dissecting him—by analyzing him—but I can also find out a lot about him by letting him live and watching him hop around. If I only saw dead, dissected frogs and never saw a live frog jumping through the air, then I wouldn't know much about frogs. There would be something—what should I call it—a *frogness,* that I would be missing.

Poet: That's it, Teach. It takes awhile with you, but you eventually plod on through.

Teacher: Thanks. It takes awhile with you too, but you eventually can be led to make sense. But I still have a problem.

Poet: What's that?

Teacher: How do I keep the frog alive in the classroom?

Poet: (*Irritated*) There you go again, lady. And just when I thought you understood. You keep the frog alive just like you keep anything alive. You don't kill it. You let it live.

Teacher: I'm going to ignore that outburst because I've discovered that with a little prodding you really can be rather helpful.

Poet: Geeez. Look who's being arrogant now.

Teacher: It's the only way to live with your ego. Exactly what does "let it live" mean?

Poet: Just that. Let it live. Don't analyze it to death. Don't bring outside criteria to bear upon it. Don't enclose it and yourself in a shell. Let the reader and the poem be . . . together.

Teacher: What does that mean? No, don't tell me. It doesn't mean, it is. Can't you see, that doesn't do me any good. I've got thirty students an hour. I can't throw a poem in the room with them and tell them to watch it. How does all this translate into my classroom? How can I bring a poem, or for that matter, any piece of literature, together with my students' intuitions?

Poet: Well, the first thing you have to do is to break their shells. By the time they get to you they're used to thinking analytically. You've got to get them out of their turtle minds and into their kangaroo minds.

Teacher: Easier said, than done. I don't know how to do it.

Poet: Well, you have to start with yourself. Do you trust me?

Teacher: Do I trust you? What is this, "Fiddler on the Roof"?

Poet: Look who's being cute now. Do you trust me?

Teacher: I . . . Well . . . I . . . well. What is it you want me to do?

Poet: Never mind, you don't trust me. (*He turns away.*)

Teacher: (*Feeling rather silly*) Okay. I trust you. (*He turns back around.*) Well, sort of. I mean. Yes. Yes. I do. I trust you.

Poet: Sure? You'll have to take a risk.

Teacher: I'm willing.

Poet: Okay. Read the poem slowly. Out loud.

Teacher:

The Life Dance

I see bubbling out of the ground
water, fresh, a pure smell. My mind
too begins to spring, I take

small hops. I enjoy myself
partly because I have the nerve.
Is anybody watching?
I care and don't care,
as I hop, and soon
because nobody is looking I'm leaping
and twisting into awkward shapes,
letting my hands make signs
of a meaning I do not understand.
I am absorbed in getting at what
til now
I had not been aware of.
There is a feeling in the world
I sometimes think I'm grasping.
I find myself holding a hand or
as I take a deep breath
I think it is there.*

Poet: Look at the crack in the floor. Relax. Think of nothing but the crack. It's a crack in the ground. . . . The ground is so dry that it has cracked open. . . . your mouth is as dry as that crack. . . . Every part of you is dry and shrivelled. . . . There is very little air. . . . Deep down under the ground you can hear a sound. . . . It's a long way off and getting closer. . . . It's water and it's coming up. . . . You can feel it in your mouth. Water is bubbling up out of the crack in the ground. . . . Notice how it makes you feel. . . . Now hold your hands in front of your face. . . . The lines in your palms are like the crack in the ground. . . . Close your eyes and move your hands like the water that comes out of the ground. . . . Now move your arms. . . . Now, your whole body. (*She rises, but in doing so opens her eyes and sees him watching her. She stops, embarrassed.*)

Teacher: Oh!

Poet: Tell me about the poem.

Teacher: It's about joy. About rising up. I felt as if I were coming up out of myself. Like everything that is me was getting wider and moving out into the world. Like almost.

*David Ignatow, *Poems 1934–1969* (Middletown, Conn.: Wesleyan University Press, 1970), p. 247.

Poet: Almost?

Teacher: Just, almost.

Poet: You feel "almost"? (*She nods*) My dear lady, that makes no sense at all.

Teacher: But. . . . (*They laugh*) That's what it's about. That's right isn't it?

Poet: I don't know. There is no right or wrong; rather there is the opening of possibilities at which to guess. I think you have guessed at a large possibility.

Teacher: I see. Guessing. That's important. That's what we do when we use our intuitions. We have hunches, we guess, we leap out a little into time. And with guessing, there is always the possibility that our guesses won't get us very far. Wow. That opens up vistas I hadn't thought about.

Poet: You just jumped ahead of me.

Teacher: I'm talking about intuition as a mode of knowing that requires the courage to guess. If I want to foster intuitive knowing in my classroom, I not only have to bracket out a priori answers to questions, I also have to allow my students the freedom to guess. And that means I have to throw out the whole system of rewarding the right answer and not rewarding the wrong. That system inhibits intuitive thinking.

Poet: I imagine there's a lot more than that that inhibits intuitive thinking in the high school classroom. You've got to be pretty secure to step away from the comfortable certainty of analysis. Secure not only in yourself, but secure in your surroundings, also.

Teacher: I was getting to that. Even I stopped when I saw you watching me. My students, hedged in by peer group pressures on one hand and by the personal uncertainty of adolescence on the other, are much less likely than I to exchange the safety of their turtle shells for the risks of intuition. I need to start them off with little hops before I ask them to broad jump. Hum?

Poet: Why don't you start with metaphors? Ask them what things are like. Common, every day things—like the principal, for example. As them what kind of animal the principal reminds them of. They'll say, "He's like a walrus," or "He's a bear."

Teacher: Actually, he's more like a penguin than anything else. They even call him that. But I can hardly ask them about the principal.

Poet: Ah, but you see my point. They use the metaphoric mode intuitively all the time and never think about it. The principal is a penguin. You can build on that every day intuitive use of the language. And after playing with metaphors they use all the time, unconsciously, you can lead them into wider and more sophisticated metaphors. For instance, if I were a chair, what kind of a chair would I be?

Teacher: If you were a chair, what kind of chair would you be?

Poet: Yeah. What kind of a chair would I be? Describe me.

Teacher: Well, let's see. You'd be a large chair. One of those chairs that insinuates itself into a room and refuses to be ignored. You'd probably be rather gaudy, and a little ragged. And, asymmetrical, too. I don't think I'd be comfortable sitting on you. (*They laugh*) What kind of chair am I?

Poet: That's easy. You're a solid chair. A little plain, perhaps, but very solid and sturdy . . . and, oh, yes, rather comfortable after you're broken in. One certainly couldn't lounge all over you, but you'd sure be nice and warm to settle down into.

Teacher: (*Flushing*) You've just hopped over into an entirely different metaphor.

Poet: So I did. Forgive me. But that's how language is, you know; it sometimes betrays us by saying more than we want known—or even know ourselves.

Teacher: I know. Sometimes it seems to move all on its own, like your frog. I guess that's what metaphors are all about—movement. The word, itself, even means "to move beyond."

Poet: To jump. To leap. Intuitively, not logically, from Teacher, to chair, to the sexual.

Teacher: So that's why you told me to start with metaphors. Metaphors and intuition work in the same way—by leaps and bounds.

Poet: That's it, although I didn't consciously realize the connection when I said it. I think we've just explicated my intuition. (*Pause*) Uh, Oh. Here they come again. I can hear the pitter-patter of little feet. Children, this time. (*The Poet and the Teacher quickly resume their initial position.*)

Tour guide: Come around here and you can see better. This one is called "The Teacher and the Poet." Come a little closer and you can see how real the figures look. Notice the curl on the Poet's lip. He looks quite mad. Notice too, the realistic coloring of the figures; our artist was able to achieve that haggard look on the Teacher's face primarily through the use of shading. Notice the blue tone under her eyes and in the hollows of her cheeks. They look so life-like that if you stand here long enough they almost seem like real people. Are there any questions?

Child: The Poet doesn't look mad to me. And the Teacher is smiling and happy, not tired.

Tour guide: No, no. Step a little closer and you can see better.

2nd child: Hey, mister, are they suppose to move? The Teacher winked at me.

Tour guide: No, son, they don't move. Your eyes are playing tricks on you.

2nd child: But I saw her.

Tour guide: You can't always trust what your eyes see. You gotta think about things and use your brain. These figures can't move because they're made out of hard wax. They're rigid and inflexible.

1st child: Look, the Poet's laughing. They're alive! (*The children hop up and down, excited. The Tour Guide smiles condescendingly, and wisely shakes his head.*)

SECTION B

Teaching Composition

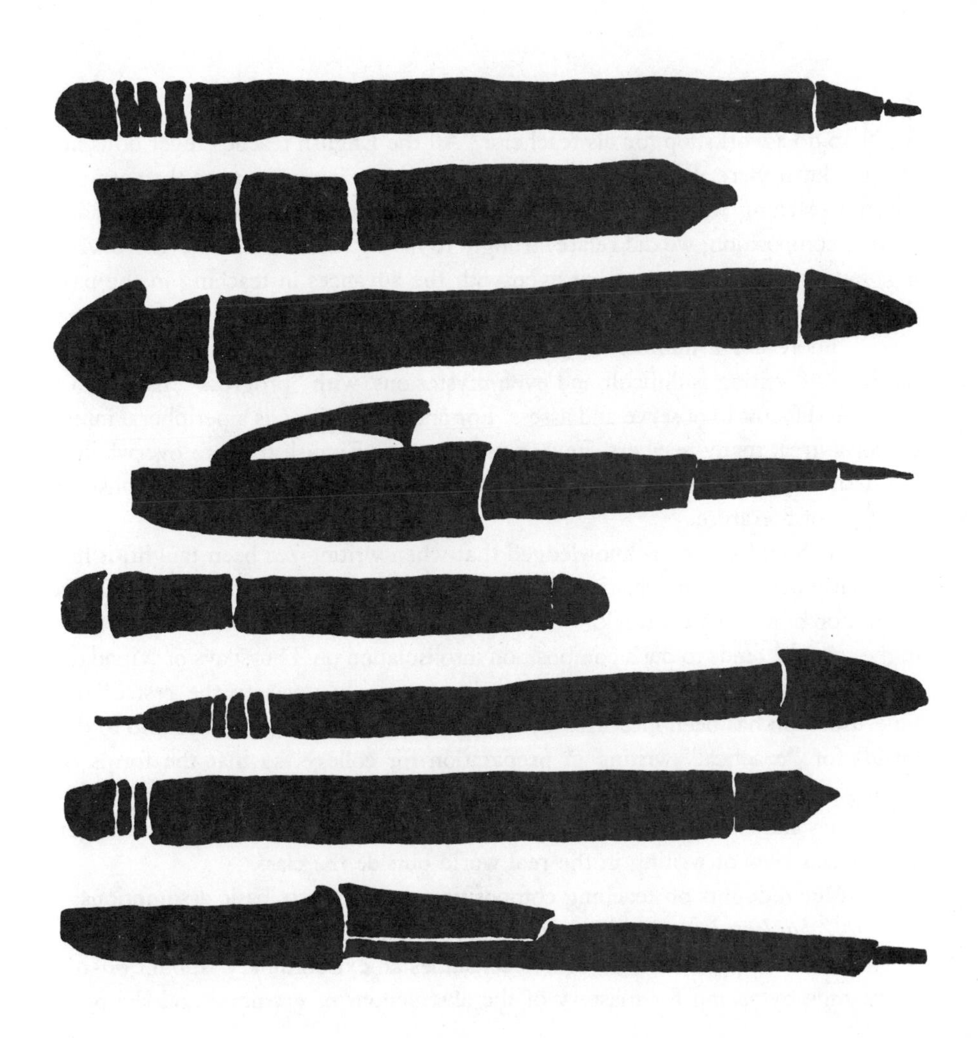

INTRODUCTION

Not too long ago we heard from a superintendent of schools who wanted us to do a workshop for his teachers: "All the English teachers ever do is literature down there. What I want is a good workshop in grammar so they can get back to teaching writing!" While we're hardly sympathetic to the "grammar" path to composition, we did relate strongly to his expressed desire for more writing, for it seems fair to say that even with the advances in teaching in the past decade or so, writing is still a neglected area in English classes.

There are a number of good reasons for this, of course. For one, the teaching of writing is difficult and even mysterious, with "progress" that is both slow and difficult to observe and assess. For another, writing is a peripheral interest for a great many teachers. Few of us came into English from an overwhelming desire to teach basic skills. Most of us came to English teaching because of our love of literature.

It should also be acknowledged that when writing *has* been taught, it has frequently been done in relative isolation from the rest of the curriculum. Thus the notion of a "theme a week," itself designed to increase the amount of writing in the schools, tends to push composition into isolation on Thursdays or Mondays or Fridays, while other things—mostly literary study—occupy the rest of the time. Isolation has been increased by the tendency of teachers to succumb to demands for "practical" writing in preparation for college, so that the forms of writing practiced by students with any degree of regularity turn out to be expository essays and examination English. Little wonder, then, that many students get a jaundiced view of writing in the real world outside the class.

Our thoughts on teaching composition center on six basic assumptions:

1. Students learn best by doing, not by examining principles. The structured or "handbook" approach to discourse consumes an extraordinary amount of students' time by asking for mastery of the abstractions of grammar and rhetoric, abstractions that may or may not apply to real writing situations. The best way to solve a writing problem or assignment is *to do it,* not study *about* it. To teach Johnny and Jane to write, then, we need to offer them a rich variety of involving, engaging writing experiences.

2. *Students need help with actual writing forms, not textbook fabrications.* The formal, structured, academic paper that most of us were taught (and probably have taught) is largely a myth. Seldom are students asked to write the "outlinable," neatly paragraphed essay with topic and clincher sentences. Each writing project, each writing audience, creates different demands for content and form. Instead of telling students that a single, mythical form will do for all situations, we should teach students to assess the demands of content and form for a variety of writing tasks.

3. *"Practical" writing programs must extend beyond the immediate demands of test-taking and paper-writing situations.* One unfortunate side effect of the back-to-basics movement is that it is cutting into the breadth of the writing program. A course that never extends beyond the formal essay—important though that may be for some tasks—will be narrow and, we think, unsuccessful.

4. *Students need to develop an awareness of and sensitivity to the linguistic milieu in which they live.* Few adults are sensitive to the nature of "the word," how it shapes and is shaped by experience. Thus, to borrow from the general semanticists, they become "word bound." A writing program, then, needs to be concerned with more than paper production. It ought to help students develop a feel for the context in which papers are produced and read.

5. *Students need to develop a consciousness of their own writing habits and the techniques and strategies that help them find success.* Each of us writes in individual and idiosyncratic ways, and each of us takes different routes to success in communication. If we help students recognize their own patterns, we provide them with much more help than knowledge of form.

6. *Students can learn to serve as their own editors.* The traditional writing program relies heavily on the teacher as theme grader and theme corrector. The result, ironically, is to make students dependent on outside appraisal of their writing, appraisal that is frequently unavailable outside of the safety of the school classroom.

Throughout this section, we will stress a single point that draws together our premises: For students to write well, they must see that composition is a regular, natural, pleasurable part of the English class, not just an add-on. Thus, even in literature classes, students should write regularly and with real purposes in mind.

CHAPTER 14

Teaching the Basics

The revival of interest in the so-called basic skills of English must be of deep concern to all of us. Increasingly, teachers find themselves confronted by alarmed school administrators and parents and college instructors who claim that English classes have neglected fundamentals, that today's young people are poorly prepared because of a failure of English teachers to concentrate on basics. "Stop emphasizing 'frills,' " is the cry. "Why, in my day we diagrammed sentences and knew the difference between a noun and a verb." Because English teachers have too frequently been the self-appointed guardians of standard English, we now find our competence seriously questioned: "English is a required subject for ten or twelve school years. Is it too much to ask teachers to produce kids who can write a 'decent' paragraph or spell common words or speak 'good English'?"

In one school after another, teachers find themselves being pushed toward the development of courses or units in basics which stress such matters as the distinction between *lay* and *lie,* how to spell *recommend,* and the art of filling out a job application (even though the local factory may have laid off half its work force because of economic conditions).

We do not want to see young people excluded from jobs because they can't write applications; nor do we want to see them denied access to "the good life" because they have not mastered the conventions of standard English. Nevertheless, we feel that the push for basic skills instruction is misguided for two fundamental reasons:

First, the frontal attack on basics through grammar drill, workbook exercises, remedial reading activities, communication skills classes, spelling lessons, or the red penciling of themes has clearly *never* been successful in changing the language behavior of young people. English teachers *haven't* ignored basic skills;

historically, they have taught very little else, *and it manifestly hasn't worked.* Whether they have taught functional grammar, structural grammar, transformational grammar, contemporary usage, or bidialectism, the direct method of teaching basics has not produced the desired results.* Given the fact that direct instruction hasn't worked, the outcry appears to be little more than a misplaced nostalgia for teaching methods that never worked in the first place.

A second, much more important concern is that the entire basic skills issue has been rather badly muddled because of some fundamental misconceptions about the nature of basics held by a great many parents, some administrators, and far too many teachers. What is a "basic skill" anyway? We argue that the real basics of literacy are *not* conventions of spelling and mechanics and usage (important though they may be in some social situations); the true fundamentals are a complex mix of cognitive, psycholinguistic, and social processes that are demonstrated whenever one human being communicates with another.

A person who has truly mastered the basics of English is one who can converse and write successfully for his or her own purposes. Thus, a child of six who engages in conversation with another six-year-old (or a twelve-year-old or an adult) successfully has mastered basics even though he or she doesn't necessarily speak with the sophistication of the twelve-year-old or an adult. The fully literate person is one who is comfortable in a wide range of speaking and writing situations, not just a master of correct grammar.

Further, it seems clear in the light of recent research that the true fundamentals of literacy are learned *naturally* and *intuitively* to a great degree. For example, we now know that by the time they are five or six, children have mastered an astonishing range of linguistic transformations that allow them to generate new, original English sentences at will. All this is done, without the benefit of workbook or drill or instruction in basics, through a learning process that involves everything from gurgling and babbling to interaction with parents and peers. Recent research in psycholinguistics indicates that even reading may be self-taught to a greater extent than we had imagined. For instance, it is commonly observed that students make fewer reading errors toward the end of a

* For a more detailed discussion of the fruitless attempts to make people talk and write better through basic skills instruction, see Stephen Sherwin, *Four Problems in Teaching English: A Critique of Research* (National Council of Teachers of English, 1969); Richard Braddock, Richard Lloyd-Jones, and Lowell Schoer, *Research in Written Composition* (NCTE, 1963); and Elizabeth Haynes, "Teaching Grammar: A Review of Research" (*The English Journal* 67 [January 1978]). We also recommend that you collect "gleanings" from these books to show parents and administrators concerned about the learning of "basics."

story than at the beginning, demonstrating in simple fashion that *people learn to read by reading.*

The skills "crisis" has also been complicated by a sort of negative-think that tends to ignore the enormous skill mastery demonstrated by virtually every student in the schools. The very worst speller in a typical secondary school class can probably write several thousand words unerringly. The students whose vocabulary is said to be "deficient" know ten to fifteen thousand words at sight. Even the least fluent writer in the class can turn out oral discourse at the rate of 150 words per minute. While such students may not operate at a level of literacy that is entirely satisfactory to parents or administrators or teachers, it points out the absurdity of saying that kids "can't spell," "don't know" vocabulary, or "can't" create ideas in language. Most teaching begins with students whose skill acquisition is vastly greater than teachers have been willing to acknowledge.

By comparison, the so-called basics—matters of correctness—are relatively few in number. Most handbooks list something like sixty or seventy usage items—most of the *lay-lie, sit-set, who-whom* variety—which separate the speaker of standard English from the speaker of nonstandard. Spelling "demons" are fewer in number than the words most fourth-graders know "by heart." Black English and standard English differ by only a couple of dozen phonological and syntactic features. When teachers concentrate instruction entirely on the surface niceties of literacy—usage, spelling, mechanics—they neglect the true fundamentals of speaking, writing, reading, and listening effectively. This, in turn, helps explain why years of teaching phonics, spelling, vocabulary, grammar, usage—well-intentioned though it may have been—has never worked particularly well.

The most satisfactory program of teaching the skills of literacy is, we think, one that engages young people in the fullest and richest possible array of language activities, creating new and interesting opportunities for them to talk and read and write and listen; for the more students "language," the more fundamental literacy they will acquire. Such a program is based on two premises about the relationship between literacy and surface correctness:

1. The fundamentals of literacy are mastered only in an environment that invites skill development rather than penalizing it. Too often schoolrooms inhibit the development of literacy by punishing kids for skill deficiencies rather than concentrating positively on extending the range of skills students have already mastered.

2. Matters of surface correctness can be learned if placed in context of a literacy program that values articulateness first and places correctness in perspective.

In this chapter we sketch out a two-step approach to teaching the basic skills of writing: *first,* engaging students in the writing process in an environment that encourages and supports the development of literacy; *second,* approaching surface correctness through editing and response.

Engagement: Teaching Skills "In Process"

Traditionally, composition programs have offered skill instruction at two points: before the fact of composition (through lessons in grammar, rhetoric, style, etc.) and after the fact (through evaluation and error correction). Thus, students have been given instruction in paragraphing and paragraph forms; the organization of narrative, expository, and argumentative prose; outlining form; research techniques; and the like. Following a writing assignment, errors or problems in executing these forms are discussed and skill deficiencies corrected. We are convinced, however, that the most important part of the skill-acquisition process comes during composing, while the writer is struggling with ideas and words and a conception of what he or she wants to say, developing skills through the actual production of a composition.

Prewriting Ideas

It is a cliché—but an important one—that "students must write about things they know." Less easy is locating substantive topics that interest kids but which rise above the level of "My Summer Vacation" or "How to Raise Hamsters" (though in some circumstances both of those topics will lead to involved writing). We've had good experience locating writing activities through some of the following techniques:

- *Interest inventories.* Use questionnnaires to ask students about interests and concerns, likes and dislikes, loves, hates, fears, worries, hopes, ambitions. Guarantee confidentiality (just as you would with a journal-writing assignment), but use this information to locate ideas about common personal concerns.
- *Values clarification.* The techniques of value clarification popularized by Raths, Harmin, and Simon (*Values in Teaching,* Charles Merrill, 1966) provide practical ways of eliciting expressions of genuine interest from a class.

Activity cards. A number of commercial programs—among them the *Interaction* series (Houghton Mifflin), *The Writing Bug* (Random House), and *Write Away!* (McDougall-Littell)—have shown how individualized assignment cards can engage students in a wide range of motivated activities in a manageable way. (See chapter 3, "Beachcombing.")

Offer writing options. Almost any writing topic, from a description of a personal experience to a report of "research," can be developed in many different forms and styles for many different audiences. As you increase the number of options available, students are more likely to find a form with which they feel comfortable. Further, you can encourage students to develop their own writing topics in addition to yours. After listing six topics on the board, ask the kids to list six more. Or allow the students to depart from your assigned topics in new directions. (See chapter 15, "Extending the Dimensions of Composition.")

The Writing Process

Develop strategies to break down the common writing period. Although there are times when students will need to write on a single topic within a specified time limit (mainly in examinations), most writers need a degree of freedom to compose, and that includes time. We suggest:

Establish a "works in progress" file. Students can keep one or several papers in a file for future revision. We've found that letting papers "cool" in the file for a bit allows the student to approach his or her work with fresh insights and helps develop critical awareness. Some teachers who have tried this system report that a bit of external pressure is sometimes necessary to move papers from the "in progress" file to completion, though our experience indicates that if the satisfactions of publication are offered, students will often finish up works on their own.

Use the "contract method." This allows one to individualize writing assignments while maintaining structure in the class. With contracts, students prepare a series of writing projects which they want to undertake. The contract between student and teacher helps to insure "progress" while allowing students freedom to proceed at their own pace.

Create writing "sequences." Frequently students like to exhaust a writing idea or genre through a series of related pieces. Allow your playwrights or short-story writers or essayists to take off on writing "jags." Or encourage a student to build one piece of writing on another: if a student does an interesting poem, help him or her to see ways the same issue, topic, or theme might be explored in other genres.

➡ *Establish "experimentation" days.* These are relatively unstructured sessions where students are encouraged to explore new avenues in writing.

Additional ideas for engaging students in their writing:

➡ Discuss the realities, unrealities, and difficulties of writing with your students. Help them understand the kinds of expectations audiences have for writing, as well as some of the difficulties involved in putting together a well-written paper. An especially useful technique is to share your own pains over the writing process with a class, helping them see there is no magic or simple route to "good" writing.

➡ Allow time for free talk during the writing process. Instead of having students work away in silence, encourage them to seek help from each other and from you as they think through, organize, write, and revise. While some teachers fear plagiarism in this sort of environment, the fact is that if writing assignments are truly individualized, the danger of copying is slight. (If, on the other hand, a teacher has every kid in a class of thirty analyzing the metaphors in "Stopping by Woods on a Snowy Evening," plagiarism seems inevitable.)

➡ Whenever possible, guarantee from the start that papers will be read by more people than the teacher. All kinds of audiences are available in your school and community: your class, other classes, the school as a whole, the neighborhood, the city. If students know that their writing is intended to be *read,* the writing process takes on reality. Furthermore, when they know that their writing will appear in print—be it on classroom ditto or in the school magazine—their concern for surface correctness increases as well.

➡ Set up a writing center with a good supply of paper, writing tools, and reference books (figure 1).

The Follow-Up: Revising, Editing, Correcting

Engaging students in the writing process goes a long way toward solving traditional concerns about skill instruction, for if students are truly involved, they simply write better than they do when the writing process is an exercise in grammar or rhetoric. But there still remains the question of what to do with the writ-

FIGURE 1 A WRITING CORNER

ing students produce. If red penciling doesn't work, what *does* the teacher do? What can young people learn about writing by analyzing their own successes and failures? We find that, ironically, few kids need to be told about the "importance" of correct spelling or "standard" usage; if anything, they have heard so much about "good English" that it frequently inhibits their writing. The key to after-the-fact analysis, we think, is to keep matters of correctness in proper perspective, providing help and assistance when needed by writers, but keeping surface correctness second in importance to the broad fundamentals of literacy. Here are some techniques and strategies that seem helpful to students. (See also chapter 19, "The Red Pencil Blues.")

Take the mystery out of matters of correctness. Many young people have problems with standard English only because instruction has been a confusing mixture of grammar study, workbook drill, and discussion of elaborate rules that supposedly help a person speak or talk "right." Encourage kids to ask questions about spelling or usage or punctuation; then answer their questions as directly—and helpfully—as possible. Don't use students' inquiries as an opportunity to slip in some "instruction."

Make information about correctness readily available. Establish a writing center where students can get help in proofreading. Such a center can include:

- posters or fliers with hints on how to proof a paper;
- a cassette library, with students and/or teachers talking about how they write and revise;
- many samples of student writing; and
- neatly indexed information about matters of correctness. Handbooks are last resort; few people want to take time to look things up in the midst of composing. Pull the basic information out of the handbooks and put it in file folders, labeled with questions students might ask: "How do you spell it?" "What do you do with commas?"

Let students edit each others' work. If writing assignments are individualized and the kids engaged in the writing process, the writing produced is interesting, and the students in the class can function successfully as each others' editors. However, this process has to be approached cautiously; one cannot simply throw kids together in small groups and expect miracles. We have found it useful to introduce groups to the editing process by setting down initial guidelines for discussing writing:

For the writer. Talk to the people in your group about the "pleasures and pains" of your writing. What do you find most satisfying about this piece?

What gave you trouble? What audience were you trying to reach? Do you think you reached it successfully? What help can the group give you in refining your paper?

For the readers/editors. Don't attack the person whose writing you are examining. It's easy to find mistakes in *anybody's* writing; it is much more difficult to provide another person with help. How can you help the person with his or her writing? What are the most exciting parts of the paper you are reading? Tell the person about them. Can you guess which parts of the paper pleased the writer most? Why? Have you ever written a paper like this? What, from your experience, would help the writer with the problems he or she has described?

Things to avoid. Comments that try to make the writer "a better person" by changing his or her writing . . . worrying about spelling and punctuation . . . comments that don't directly help the writer . . . comments that sound as if a "teacher" uttered them.

Here are other techniques for encouraging students to think critically, yet responsively and humanely, to each others' work:

- Hold a writing fair where students display their writing portfolios for informal discussion in a relaxed atmosphere.
- Submit writing to national contests. Not just the best writing, but *any* writing that *sincerely* moves an audience.
- Let students collect and bind their writing into a book or anthology; then have them write a preface or introduction.
- Publish, publish, publish. Duplicate single pages and booklets by ditto, mimeograph, or offset. Display writing on chalkboards, bulletin boards, fliers, and posters. Publish monographs, leaflets, greeting cards, broadsheets, newspapers, and magazines.
- Provide students with realistic information about dialects and about language in society. Don't tell kids that standard English will get them a good job or bring health and wealth. Do help them understand what standard is and why it is important to some people. Conduct a unit—"Standard English: Myths and Realities"—where students explore dialects.
- Badger the administration to establish a "HELP!" center staffed by older students, community members, and, if available, college tutors—a place where any student in the school can go to get concrete, specific help with reading and writing assignments.

CHAPTER 15

Extending the Dimensions of Composition

IT has always seemed to us unfortunate that the range of school composition is quite limited when compared to the universe of discourse available outside the school. Young people and adults find themselves confronted daily by a dizzying array of language forms: radio broadcasts, commercials, plays and dramas, signs and placards, musical lyrics, essays, articles, poems, books, captions, soap operas, news stories, letters. In school, however, we tend to focus on a single form of composition—exposition—usually in the hopes of getting students ready for the imagined rigors of college or "real-world" situations.

The function of the written word in society is changing and has changed dramatically in this electronic century. We don't rely on print the way we used to, but at the same time, print is anything but dead, and language use—composing—is expanding its dimensions just as rapidly as the electronic media find new horizons to explore. (As we drafted this statement, for example, the radio was broadcasting a report on a two-way cable television system, which would allow people to talk back directly to their television sets via a computerized hook-up. Imagine the delightful possibilities this offers the teacher of composition!)

While we cannot possibly teach every student every discourse form likely to be encountered in the remaining sixty (or will it be two hundred) years of his or her life, we *can* prepare students for this expanding world of discourse (and for the realities of college and business and industry) if, instead of restricting instruction in literacy, we see that our aim as composition teachers is to do everything we can to offer diverse composing experiences. A good comp program, we think, will set as its goal allowing students to compose in as many forms as possible, in imaginative forms as well as expository, public forms as well as private, informative writing as well as writing for entertainment, speech and drama as well as writing, and popular and media forms as well as traditional literary genres. A list of just a few of the possibilities is provided in figure 1.

PERSONAL WRITING
Journals
Diaries
Sensory writing
Writer's notebook
Feelings
Sketches
Observations
Reminiscences
Autobiography
Monologue
Free response
Calendars

IMAGINATIVE WRITING
Fiction
Fantasy
Adventure
Science Fiction
Riddles
Jokes
Poetry
Collaborative novel
Stories
Dialogues
Epitaphs
Songs

INFORMATIVE/PERSUASIVE WRITING
Essays
Editorials
Reports
Letters
Telegrams
Bulletin boards
Labels and captions
Reviews
Newspaper articles
Magazine essays
Booklets
Directions

POPULAR FORMS
Ads
Commercials
Propaganda
Posters
Flyers
Popular journalism
Satire
Imitations
Song lyrics
Concert reviews

DRAMA/ORAL ENGLISH
Mime
Charades
Improvisation
Creative drama
Writer's showcase
Debate
Discussion
Show and Tell
Interviews
Puppetry
Game shows
Choral reading
Reader's theatre
Conversations

MEDIA COMPOSITION
TV scripts
Radio programs
Slide-tape
Soundtape
Montage
Collage
Animated film
Commercials
Videotape
Bulletin boards
Magazine layout
Storyboard

FIGURE 1 EXTENDING THE RANGE OF COMPOSITION

To develop a rich variety of composition assignments, simply pick a topic or idea—politics, love, the family—and "noodle," glancing at the list of forms in figure 15–1, and seeing how your topic could lead to an interesting composition in that genre. A sample form for developing your own topics form is provided in figure 2.

But extending the dimensions of the composition program involves more than simply creating long lists of topics. You also need to find diverse situations and settings to make writing assignments, to engage students in the composing process, to provide audiences for student writing, and for offering response and feedback. In the remainder of the chapter we will present a potpourri of composition ideas in many forms and media, collected over the years from teachers who have shared our interest in extending the dimensions of composition.*

➡ The TV networks make much commotion over their new fall program offerings. Have your class organize to review the new shows. Especially interesting is to assign teams to each of the three major networks to produce a set of comparative reviews.

➡ The *paired biography* works well as an activity for early in the year. Have students pair off, interview, and write each others' stories. This is a particularly good way to get kids started responding to their own writing, since in this case, both interviewer and interviewee have a stake in the final product.

➡ Writing warm-ups:

1. If you could have your name and a slogan printed on a lapel button, what would it say?

2. You have just been told you can fly anywhere in the world for supper. Where to? Why?

3. Yesterday's newspaper headline was about *you*. What did it say?

➡ An alternative to "My Summer Vacation": "What I *Didn't* Do Last Summer." Or in the spring, "What I *Won't* Do On My Vacation." Or "What I Wish I Had Done."

➡ Let students choose *pen names* for their writing early in the year. On those occasions when writing is personal or private, the students can cover themselves under the pen name. This is also a useful way to help students learn to critique each other's writing. In most cases, by the end of the year or term, most students will be quite willing to expose their secret identities.

➡ Label a box "Let's Talk About . . ." and let students drop in dis-

* We wish to thank teachers at the Gull Lake English Festival, sponsored by Michigan State University and the Michigan Council of Teachers of English; the Michigan Council of Teachers of English Writing Conference, Kalamazoo, Michigan; and the Michigan State University Summer Workshops for the genesis of many of these ideas.

List Composition Topics for: Exploring "Our Town"

PERSONAL WRITING

Visit your old elementary school and write about your memories.

Write about some of your favorite "haunts."

Tell about what makes your neighborhood unique.

IMAGINATIVE WRITING

Write a poem about your street.

Imagine Our Town in 2001. What will it be like?

Write an imaginary story about a crime or mystery set in Our Town.

INFORMATIVE/PERSUASIVE WRITING

Write a letter to the editor of the paper about a change that is needed.

Describe the resources of Our Town to a person who has just moved here.

Investigate the entertainment sources available in Our Town to a person your age.

POPULAR WRITING

Write an ad or commercial for Our Town.

Interview a public official about his or her role in Our Town.

Debate a needed improvement in Our Town.

DRAMA/ORAL ENGLISH

Dramatize the founding of the city in 18--.

Prepare a reader's-theater reading of writing about Our Town.

Bring in historical artifacts from the "early days" and discuss.

MEDIA COMPOSITION

Borrow the videotape unit to prepare a short program about the community.

Prepare a feature story - with photographs - of the downtown area.

Create a slide-tape introducing a stranger to Our Town.

FIGURE 2 DEVELOPING COMPOSITION TOPICS

cussion suggestions. Some kids, of course, may suggest ideas that are not entirely suitable for school talk, but the teachers we know who have tried the idea found that some interesting and profitable discussion and study topics emerged.

Early in the year, establish one bulletin board as the *student writing board* reserved exclusively for young people's writing. Invite the students to post anything they write to create a constantly changing display.

A good icebreaker role play begins with one person pantomiming an action (changing a tire, making pizza, sewing something); as students in the class catch on to what's happening, they join in.

Start an *open-ended story* as a team project. Someone in the class leads off with two or three minutes of narrative. On succeeding days (or even weeks or months), students can, during free times, go to the tape recorder, listen to the most recent installment, and improvise further adventures and misadventures. For time to time play back the most recent chapters for the whole class.

As part of a unit on *values* or as a get-acquainted activity have students bring in an object that represents them, something very special or important to them. They can either talk or write about why it represents them.

Writing or improvising a modern, satirical version of a fairy tale is a good warm-up activity for writing or drama.

Try a *nonverbal communication hour* in your class in which students communicate only through gestures, pantomime, charade. Students enjoy this because of its novelty, but the session will also bring about a useful discussion of the nature of language.

Let students make a "TV show" or "movie" of a story using shelf paper attached to a cardboard box to create a "screen."

End an advertising unit by having students sell an *egg*. Each student creates an ad campaign to sell his or her egg. Students from other classes come in with enough "money" to buy five or so eggs—the eggs of the most persuasive salespeople.

Students love to do *interviews.* Make up a series of topics of current concern and have the students conduct sidewalk (or school corridor) interviews.

This is your life. Kids are often astonished to learn that their parents actually have a *past.* Set your students to the task of preparing a "This is Your Life" script for one or both of their parents or of an older acquaintance or relative.

Have your students *research your town*—buildings, events, people. In many communities, local arts committees have a bit of cash to support such work. Your students might be able to get money for photographing, xeroxing, even printing an historical collection. (See figure 2 for more ideas.)

➡ Borrow a set of art slides from the art department and let students put together a slide-tape with well-known paintings and their favorite poems.

➡ A *story-starter* box includes a set of story openers typed on index cards. Create your own story starters or borrow opening lines from the stories in your favorite anthology.

➡ For a quick and easy classroom magazine, simply supply colored ditto masters (they come in red, green, blue, black, and, of course, schoolroom purple). Have each student select his or her best writing in recent weeks and hand copy it on the ditto. Kids can pass around unused scraps of the ditto backing sheet so that each can create a multicolor print of the writing. Ditto them off, collate, staple.

➡ Borrow from the world of Dr. Seuss and have students write about *imaginary animals* (have your class artist illustrate the project) or have younger students create a *new zoo*. Or take off from *If I Ran the Circus* and have students write *If I Ran the School.*

➡ Checkbook characterizations offer a good starting point for writing. Create a fictional checkbook register showing dates, amounts, and places where spent. Students create a character sketch of *the mystery spender.* Slip in a copy of your own check register if you dare.

➡ *Superheroes* are a natural for motivating writing and initiating a flow in kids who are reluctant to write. Have students create a superhero and a corresponding series of adventures or misadventures.

➡ *Bag skits* work well with junior-high young people. Bring in paper bags containing junk: egg cartons, squirt gun, banjo string, buttons, baby rattle. Each small group picks a bag and creates an improvisation using the contents as the props for the scene.

➡ Explore the idea of *stereotypes* by having students write the most clichéd, stereotyped short stories or plays they can think of. As an alternative, dig out scripts from early stage melodramas (a number of good anthologies exist) and have the students read or act them.

➡ A practical approach to the *class newspaper* is to place a limit of one two-sided sheet each week. How much can editorial groups get onto two sides of an 8½ × 11 or 8½ × 14 page using either ditto or mimeograph? (Limiting to one page also saves you the problem of collating and stapling numbers of sheets together.)

➡ Stimulate creative writing by playing *sound-effects* records or *mood music.* Bring in photographs or paintings or films and ask students to write about what they see, imagine, feel. Play records of old radio serials; then let students write contemporary versions. Give students a minimystery or adventure setting and let them write conclusions.

➡ A seventh-grade teacher introduces a *body language* unit by having students watch a TV show with the sound turned off. Based on what they see in gestures, facial expressions, and the like, the students try to reconstruct the plot. Soap operas and shows *low* in action work best, since overt action (a sock in the jaw, for instance) conveys too many clues. If possible have your school's AV person tape the show, with the sound, for purposes of discussion later.

➡ For a *creative writing stimulus* a teacher in high school simply has two hundred or so *magazine pictures* laminated by the school's graphics department. The pictures can be used for descriptive writing, as essay starters, even as a source of "settings" and "plots" for improvisations.

➡ Use the *photographic essay* as a composition project. The students choose a topic or theme, take their cameras, and create a series of illustrative photographs. These can be mounted, with or without captions, to create a display. A surprising amount of verbal composing takes place in the process of completing this nonverbal project.

➡ A cut-and-paste activity: Clip *cartoons* from the daily paper, blank out the words in the balloons, and let kids write in their own dialogue. This works especially well with the "soap opera" cartoon strips like "Rex Morgan, M.D." or "The Heart of Juliet Jones."

➡ An old but effective idea is having students describe a simple activity so that another person can execute the task. Try telling about tying a shoe, for example. A variation, just as old and just as effective, involves describing a common appliance or gadget—eggbeater, bicycle, typewriter—so that another person would recognize it.

➡ Little-used writing forms to explore: children's storybooks, satire magazines, sports stories, craft articles, community newsletters, ghost story anthologies, one-act plays, travel folders, menus, auto repair manuals.

➡ Send students to the microfilm collection of newspapers to write a summary of the world and local news on the day they were born.

➡ Send students to a shopping mall for a period of observation, followed by writing.

➡ *Correspondence as a composition course:* Consider developing an entire composition course around the *letter*. Give students a list of possible correspondents ranging from personal and known audiences to impersonal and more abstract audiences to imaginative and created audiences. Rather than having students write a theme a week, have them write a bundle of letters, running the gamut in writer roles and voices. In order to avoid the "dummy run," you might want to require that *half* the letters to be sent to the addressee. (Even with the foibles of the postal system, the price of a stamp to reach a *real* audience is about the cheapest, most effective form of communication around.) Part of the course might be devoted to designing personalized stationery that presents the image the student wants to project of him or herself. Instruction in proper letter format can be accomplished with a couple of dittoed handouts showing alternative forms. Consider the following range of audiences for a letter-writing course:

- yourself
- someone very close to you
- an archrival or enemy
- your mother or father
- your brother or sister
- a grandparent or aunt or uncle
- someone you haven't seen for awhile
- an adult you admire
- a teacher
- your boss
- a minister or social leader
- a political figure
- a scientist or inventor
- a hero or heroine
- a movie or TV star
- a rock star
- an imaginary person or animal
- the child you may have someday
- a person who lived in the past.

Students may benefit from a list of topics which also suggest a range from the concrete and personal to the abstract and impersonal:

- an important childhood memory
- a problem you're having
- something you are angry about
- something that scares you or is worrying you
- an important event that happened to you recently
- someone who is important to you
- something that you've been thinking about lately
- something you've always wanted to do
- what you want out of life
- your home or school or community

- a book you've read or a TV show or movie you've seen
- a play, a sporting event, or a concert you've attended
- something you'd like to see changed
- a new product or invention
- a crazy idea you have
- an important social or political problem you're concerned about
- what you will be like in 2001
- an ideal world
- an imaginary world.

➡ We have developed an integrated writing program based exclusively on *script writing.* As we observed, in preparing a script, students use a rich variety of writing forms and styles, from the exposition required for plot backgrounds, to detailed descriptions of stage sets, to conversation. With its emphasis on dialogue, script writing is an especially comfortable mode of discourse for young people; they can write as they speak, and in the process their fluency increases. Begin the course or unit by having students write thirty-second playlets, an idea taken from *Writing Incredibly Short Poems, Plays, Stories* by Norton and Greton (New York: Harcourt, Brace Jovanovich, 1972); then move on to short one-acts, group serials and melodramas, radio plays, finally to full-length scripts that can often be presented in full-dress, or, at the very least, performed by a reader's theater group.

➡ Peter Elbow has based an entire college course on sending essays to concerned people, then inviting those people to talk to the class about their reactions. This might work well with secondary schools as well. See "A Method for Teaching Writing," *College English* 30 (November 1968).

➡ Have your students make a *class anthology* of writings they do during the year. Blank bound books of various sizes can be purchased at school supply stores and give the anthology a "real book" look. Pages at the beginning and end of the book can be left blank for a table of contents and index at the end of the year when the book is completed. All students can contribute, with some doing illustrations, lettering, and printing in addition to writing. The completed book can become a part of the teacher's class library or, preferably, the school library, where it can be circulated to all students.

➡ Allow students to do some *public writing.* Tack up a large piece of butcher paper (graffiti-style) and let kids spend a week or so writing a collaborative story.

➡ Encourage nonwriters or students for whom writing is particularly painful to *record stories on cassettes.* Their writing may be transcribed and published in written form and/or you can make it a part of a cassette library.

CHAPTER 16

Composing through Drama

Creative drama can help students become more imaginative, extend their perceptions and awareness of what is around them, make them more conscious of themselves and how they relate to the world, help them become more flexible and self-confident, and help them clarify their feelings and ideas. Above all, creative drama is an act of composing that strengthens all language arts skills. Teachers can make the English classroom a place in which the development of the whole person is important, in which language development is tied to social and emotional development, in which thinking, feeling, perceiving, and conceptualizing are part of an integrated process of growth. In addition, drama in the English classroom supports and reinforces the natural desire of students to relate to one another.

Our belief in a more extensive use and integration of creative dramatics into the classroom has as its basis three premises about the nature of the dramatic experience:

1. Creative dramatics emphasizes process rather than product or performance. In creative dramatics, the role of the student is that of participant rather than performer, and the dramatic experiences provided are extensions of dramatic and social relationships and expressions of individual feelings and thoughts. Although it is acceptable to use audiences and share dramatizations, the emphasis is on individual exploration and expression (either alone or in a group experience) rather than on a polished presentation for the entertainment of others.

2. Creative dramatics involves the development of the whole person. Practices in creative dramatics encourage students to become more aware of the physical surroundings and environment with activities that help kids draw on sensory experiences—what they see, hear, smell, taste, feel. In addition, creative drama can be used to help students explore and experiment with nonverbal expression. Drama exercises encourage students to become more aware of their bodies, of how they can use their bodies to express themselves, and of the ways people use space as a part of the communication process.

3. Creative dramatics encourages new and vital uses of language. The mode of drama—dialogue—again emphasizes the importance of process, of being and becoming. Role playing and improvisation, central activities in creative dramatics, place the student in the role of participant; he must be involved in exchanges and situations that cause him to qualify what he is saying, to support, extend, develop his ideas, draw on feelings, and develop fresh ways of using his language to express and project the role he is playing.

Carefully chosen dramatic situations allow young people to gain emotional release through becoming totally involved in the ideas they are expressing in a relatively safe way. They don't have to reveal personal difficulties or conflicts directly, but they may take on a personality or character that is feeling those conflicts and act out their feelings through that character. Or students may take on roles or characters very unlike themselves and try to project themselves into values and life experiences foreign to them. Such experiences can make kids more tolerant and sensitive to people unlike them.

Creative dramatics can also help the literary experience become more personal, immediate, active. Sensory and movement exercises, role playing, and improvisation can all bring kids to new insights, to a new sense of what is going on in a poem, play, short story, or novel. It can help them visualize the action or scenery of a literary piece; it can provide them with ways of identifying with characters and experiences unfamiliar to them; it can provide them ways in which they can imaginatively project themselves into new situations; it can help them feel and experience directly rather than merely intellectualizing about what is happening to characters. In short, the dramatic experience, used in conjunction with literature, is *participatory.* Such experiences with literature can provide students with a *Gestalt*—an integration of action, movement, feeling, ideas—that can make literature a more personal and intense experience.

As a personal exploration and heightening of awareness, creative drama has obvious advantages in helping students toward more vital uses of language and can have direct effects on students' writing. Both writing and drama emphasize the use of concrete, sensory detail and encourage students to draw on their own experiences. Exploration of environment, of the senses, of movement and space, and of the body, and role playing that emphasizes values, conflict, and interaction feed directly into writing. Students can write about their own personal lives and about broader issues in vivid and concrete ways based on thoughts and feelings they have experienced—dramatically.

Getting Started with Creative Drama

It's easy to be intimidated by the use of dramatics in the classroom. For one thing, the traditional role of the student in the classroom is fairly passive. The teacher gives the assignments and does most of the talking, and what goes on in the classroom is predictable. In using creative dramatics, however, the teacher may be opening a Pandora's box. The desks and chairs are pushed out of the way; the students are out of the seats and encouraged to move around and make noise—and sometimes they make lots of it. The teacher can begin to feel that the classroom is out of control.

In addition, because teachers have often had little experience with dramatics themselves, they feel unprepared and unqualified to introduce dramatics to their students. Teachers may feel shy about taking on dramatic roles or doing movement exercises or sensory activities, and feel hesitant about asking their students to try them. And there's always the student who, in the middle of an introduction to a new activity, will pipe up, "This is ***dumb!***"

For these reasons, teachers should begin with activities with which they feel comfortable and confident. Gradually, as teachers and students feel safe working together, there will be greater willingness to try new things. In the beginning, teachers will want to provide activities and exercises that give students some measure of anonymity and don't make them look foolish in front of other students. Performance situations are best avoided, especially at first. The teacher should be patient and supportive in helping students relax. But by continuing to use dramatic activities as a regular part of the classroom routine, both teacher and student can gain the self-confidence and assurance to move into new kinds of experiences. Creative dramatics should be fun as well as useful.

Because teachers and groups of students differ, the teacher may want to pick and choose from the following lists of suggested activities. Although they are often presented in a sequence in creative dramatics classes, they don't have to be done in any particular sequence in the English class. The activities are merely suggestions that are meant to give the teacher starting points that should be adapted according to the needs of the classroom situation and the students. The imaginative teacher will learn to develop activities appropriate to his or her own teaching style, the content and materials of the subject, and the interests of the students.

Activities for Sensory Awareness/Imagination

The following activities invite the student to explore the world through use of his or her senses. Students begin by exploring actual, physical objects and then move to activities in which they imagine themselves handling and using objects from the physical world. These activities often provide a good prelude to writing activities in that they encourage awareness of concrete detail. They are also good warm-ups for mime and improvisation.

- Students lie on the floor and as the teacher names parts of the body, students are asked to become aware of that part of the body, investigating how it moves, what they can do with it (moving from toes, ankles, feet, legs, hands, neck, head, eyes, etc.).
- Students lie or sit on the floor, close their eyes, and listen to all the sounds they can hear, first inside the room, then outside the room; they try to identify the sound and then try to invent *new* possibilities for what they could be; they then try to create a scene or situation around the sounds they hear.
- Students get in pairs or small groups; one person makes a sound (rubs hands together, scrapes wall, taps pencil) while the others try to identify the noise with their eyes closed; students can then relate the sound to an incident or create a story around the sound.
- The teacher brings in a bag of objects (hairbrush, sponge, spatula, toothpick); one student identifies the object by feel and describes it; others try to guess what the object is.
- Students close their eyes and find designated places in the room (the door, the window, the blackboard); then everyone finds one person and without talking and using only touch tries to get acquainted with that person.
- Students lie on the floor and pretend they're on the beach. Using side coaching (talking from the sidelines), the teacher talks students through a series of experiences: Students are asked to imagine the warmth of the sun, the feel of the sand beneath them. The teacher gives the students time to imaginatively project themselves into the situation. Students are then to imagine that they have a beach ball, which they get a "feel" for and then toss and catch: Teacher repeats the instructions with a tennis ball and a medicine ball.
- Students pair off and take turns doing mirror images of one another, imitating gesture, movement, and facial expression.

Activities in Movement and Mime

Movement activities provide a bridge between developing sensory awareness and using mime. When doing movement activities, the student has to use sensory data and information to create an imagined physical setting or object. Becoming aware of the body and how it moves helps a student develop concentration and control that are useful in mime and improvisation. Movement activities are usually specific and imitative, with the emphasis on the action rather than on emotion.

Mime emphasizes the development from movement as controlled action and imitation to movement with expression of emotion or personality. For some students, movement is more comfortable than mime, because they are reticent about expressing feelings, even through actions. In giving instructions to students involved in movement and mime activities, the teacher should be clear in explaining the activity and at the same time encourage free response and individual interpretation.

In *Creative Dramatics and English Teaching* (NCTE, 1974, p. 131), Charles Duke suggests simple movements for students to try as warm-up activities. Have students demonstrate how they would do the following: eat an ice cream cone, cotton candy, a hot toasted marshmallow, a boiling-hot ear of corn; walk through deep snow, through fallen leaves, through a driving rainstorm, across a plowed field, in a windstorm, up and down sand dunes, across pebbles in bare feet, in high heels, in sandals, in army boots, in slippers, with a cast on one foot or leg; touch a hot radiator; handle a handful of dirt; pick up a heavy suitcase.

Movement and mime activities can be done as brief, controlled activities in which the student does things alone, or they can be done as longer sequences. Some examples of longer sequences:

- Teacher has students imagine they are blocks of ice; the air gradually gets warmer and warmer and the ice begins to melt. It continues to get warmer and the ice becomes water and then begins to evaporate; now the water is vapor and forms a cloud; finally the vapor of the cloud becomes rain.
- In an activity combining sound and movement, the teacher establishes a drumbeat and the students pretend they are soldiers. The teacher tells the students: "March to the beat; a loud beat signals that you should change directions; when the drumbeat changes to a faster cadence, pretend you are trying to escape to the rhythm of the drumbeat. Now become a soldier trying to get through a sandstorm; now pretend your leg is wounded as you are trying to make a shelter so that you can sleep; you go to sleep; when you wake up, you are able

to escape (by whatever means you wish—by becoming a bird, insect, airplane; discovering a jeep; seeing a town nearby)."

➡ Teacher instructs students: "Pretend you are swimming under water; enjoy investigating and seeing all kinds of unusual things under water (animals or fish, sunken vessels, a treasure, pieces of coral, rocks, shells). Find something you want to take to the top; try to swim up with it." Try making, building, or repairing something under water.

Some movement and mime activities combine both individual and small group efforts.

➡ Every student in the class becomes a spaceman or a spacewoman. The teacher then directs the students: "Become aware of the spacesuit's bulkiness and of the difference in the atmosphere; pretend you are in your spaceship; eat and drink from the plastic containers and tubes used in space travel. Now pretend you have landed on a planet or on the moon. Prepare your gear to go out and investigate the planet. Examine the rocks, plants; climb boulders and small hills; investigate craters and caves." The students now get in small groups of four, and two students become spacemen and two become creatures from the planet. Creatures and spacemen discover one another, react to each other, and try to communicate (without using words).

➡ *Movement to music.* Students begin my moving freely to the music; then, in small groups or in a large group, they take turns leading the rest of the group in movements to the music. In small groups, students create a story around the music, beginning by plotting the changes in mood and rhythm in the music and devising actions appropriate to the changes.

The following are activities for small and large groups in movement and mime:

➡ Small groups of students (six to eight) line up one behind the other; the teacher establishes a rhythm, and the person in the front of the line establishes a movement to the rhythm which the rest of the group imitates. The teacher signals a change in leader with a loud drumbeat, and the person in front goes to the end of the line and a new leader begins a new movement.

➡ Students divide into small groups. Half the group works together to create a rhythm, and the other half works together to create a series of movements to the rhythm. Then the two groups reverse.

➡ The class creates a machine with one or two students establishing and repeating an action; one by one, students become parts of the machine by adding actions and movements to the ones already in motion.

For pantomime in small groups, have students:

➡ Stage a bank robbery. Students can be bank tellers, robbers, customers, policemen. Do the same scene as a comedy.

➡ Put up a prefab building. Have them do it as a comic scene and as a serious scene.

➡ Perform a rescue operation. Two students are on a cliff above; a third student is caught on the ledge below and is afraid to move.

➡ Act out a restaurant or banquet scene. Some students are waiters, serving drinks and various courses of a meal; others are being waited on.

➡ Become fishermen. One is catching all the fish and others are catching nothing; or people are fishing from a boat in which one person is patient and the other impatient and can't sit still.

➡ Act out parts of salespeople, selling shoes, furs, jewelry, etc. Customers are trying on all kinds of merchandise while the salesperson is convincing the customer to buy.

➡ Become patients in the waiting room of a doctor's or dentist's office. Some patients are nervous; some are sick; some are impatient.

➡ Act out the scene of an automobile accident or bicycle collision.

➡ Without using words act out a play, poem, or scene from a story they have read.

Involve students in a whole-class activity in which everyone is doing different kinds of things. Examples: an amusement park, a county fair, a parade. As a whole group, the class establishes the things that they might find there, and then the class breaks into small groups to become various parts of the scene. For example, in an amusement park scene, the students could use rides, games, traveling musicians, clowns, food vendors, and customers. Students communicate their aspect of the fair or park without using words.

Role Playing and Improvisation

Role playing and improvisation combine gesture and movement with language. Improvisation can be used in conjunction with many different kinds of classroom activities and units. Students can explore their own values and feelings in a "Who Am I?" or a values-clarification unit; students may gain insights about an issue or topic by setting up improvisational situations in which various aspects of the issue are represented by various roles or characters; students can become personally and concretely involved with the characters, predicaments, and issues of a literary piece by role playing the characters and acting out some of the situations in literature. In addition, writing ideas may grow out of dramatic situations in which a student participates: dramatizations of parent-child conflicts, television stereotypes, or occupational situations may provide new perspectives for students to explore in writing.

For some students, no matter how supportive the environment and the teacher, the role-playing situation in which he must express himself physically and orally is intimidating. Even if the improvisation is not going to be "performed," some students are shy and feel inadequate in having to take on a persona in front of even a small group of peers. Those students should be allowed to participate in some other ways of role playing.

Some possibilities:

- *Tape recording.* Often students who are self-conscious about doing dramatic activities can enjoy the privacy of tape recording. It's helpful for the student to be able to take the tape recorder to another room to tape a radio discussion or a radio play in which he takes on a new role or a new character.
- *Puppetry.* Using puppets also gives students some anonymity. They can be invisible to the audience and often find this liberating for expressing the ideas and feelings of a character. In addition, students often enjoy creating their own puppets and can express the nature and personality of a character through their creation of a puppet.
- *Shadow screen.* Some improvisations can be behind a shadow screen. A sheet (or large lightweight paper) is stretched between two poles and the performers stand or sit behind the sheet. A light behind the players casts their shadow on the screen, and the gestures of the characters can be seen without the players having to appear directly before an audience.
- *Panels.* Some improvisations work very well as round-table discussions with people taking on different characters and discussing issues and ideas talk-show style. Not having to move and gesture is a comfortable introduction into improvisation for some students.
- *Simulations.* Some simulation games are very helpful to the shy student because they often involve simultaneous actions in which everyone is involved. In that way, students may choose how they will interact and how involved they want to become.

The following is a list of suggestions for improvisational situations. Although the suggestions are divided into groups or general categories, the situations overlap in some cases.

PERSONAL EXPERIENCES/VALUES

➡ A younger brother has been begging to drive his older brother's new car; the older brother finally gave in, and the younger one has just wrecked the car and has to break the news.

➡ The boss is reprimanding the wrong employee on a shoddy repair job on a TV; the person really responsible enters the scene.

➡ The doctor is telling a nervous, fearful patient that he or she must have surgery.

➡ A teacher and principal have called in a student to talk about a paper that is just like one the teacher got the previous year.

➡ A salesperson has given an ill-tempered customer the wrong change during a rush period; other customers are waiting.

➡ A teenage girl has been invited to a party in a nearby college town; her parents don't want her to go.

➡ Two students are confronting a teacher over what they think is a badly taught course.

➡ A distraught single woman is discussing the bad repair job done on her car with a patronizing service manager.

➡ A father is telling his family that he has been fired from his job.

ISSUE-ORIENTED IMPROVISATIONS

➡ Student council officers are having a meeting with school administrators about establishing an open-campus policy.

➡ A politician has been invited by local concerned citizens to explain his stand on abortion.

➡ An ex-military man is having a discussion with a pacifist about why the draft should be reinstated.

➡ A policeman is talking with some law students about why he resents having to read arrested people their rights.

Local and school newspapers, as well as national magazines, can provide sources for improvisations based on current issues.

IMAGINARY SITUATIONS

➡ Create an improvisation in which the situation, scene, and characters are suggested by a piece of music.

➡ Create an improvisation in which opposites are personified (love and hate, war and peace, poverty and wealth, meekness and strength, pride and humility) and argue for their power, goodness, usefulness.

➡ Create an improvisation in which a line from a poem, play, story, article or an adage are used as the beginning or ending line of the scene.

➡ Create an improvisation in which two or more animals (lion, giraffe, cat, dog, pig, sheep, turtle) argue about who is most powerful, most beautiful, most intelligent.

LITERARY IMPROVISATIONS

➡ Dramatize a poem, song, story, or scene from a novel.

➡ Interview various characters from a story, poem, play, or novel about their interests, experiences, and/or why they act or believe as they do.

➡ Take the parts of various poets who have written on the same theme and let members of the class ask questions about their interests, experiences, and/or why they act or believe as they do.

➡ Take the parts of various poets who have written on the same theme and let members of the class ask questions about their different approaches to the same theme; or let the poets discuss their different approaches among themselves.

➡ Create an improvisation in which the unhappy characters from a novel or story confront their author about the way he made them.

➡ Place characters from an older novel into a situation in a modern novel; or vice versa.

CHAPTER 17

Brass-Tacks Writing

Brass-tacks writing? What's that? We debated the phrase at some length before selecting it as a title for this chapter. We were searching for a word to describe a particular kind of writing that has never had a suitable label.

Some call it "practical discourse," the writing of business, academia, and society-at-large, but such a title has the unfortunate implication that writing like poetry, fiction, and drama is somehow "impractical" or useless.

Some simply call it "exposition" or "expoz," but that implies a sternness and formality that is not characteristic of much good twentieth-century prose.

We thought about calling it "serious writing" and rejected that because much successful practical discourse is light and playful.

So we settled, with reservations, on "brass-tacks writing" (you can call it "nuts-and-bolts prose" if you wish), to suggest that we're talking about what the public generally regards as "basic" writing, the kind that will help kids succeed in the verbal situations of school and society, the stuff that Johnny and Jane allegedly can't produce.

But we want to note that there has been an unfortunate division between brass-tacks writing and the other kinds—personal writing and so-called creative writing—and this is reflected in much of the teaching methodology we have observed. When teachers are seeking personal and creative writing from their classes, they often draw on a pedagogy that sees ideas and content as more basic than form, that places self-expression at the center of the writing process. When they turn to brass-tacks writing, however, the pedagogy shifts. Suddenly, the outline, the topic sentence, and the structured paragraph take priority. The structure approach is the sort demonstrated by conventional grammar and rhetoric handbooks, which have been enjoying their best sales in years as a result of the back-to-basics revival.

We feel that this division is unfortunate and unnecessary, that nuts-and-bolts writing can be taught in creative ways. We feel that creativity is not synonymous with chaos, that discipline can come from within the self as well as from the laws of grammar or rhetoric, that correctness is not inconsistent with expressiveness. Our central premise in teaching *all* kinds of writing is that personal experience—whether it be the experience of a chemistry lab or of a love affair—is the stuff out of which both content and form grow, in essay or exam, in poem or story, in letter or memo. Further, the need to communicate with an audience—lab instructor or lover—creates the need for form and structure in writing.

We think, then, that writing programs can meet the demands of back to basics in new and intriguing ways. If we use a consistent, sound pedagogy for teaching writing—poem *or* essay, nonfiction *or* fiction—we can help students prepare to meet a wide range of writing tasks, "serious" ones, "practical" ones, "nuts-and-bolts," whatever their opposites and contraries may be.

The Word in Society

"Print is dead," cried the prophet from north of the border. "Then teach media," responded the pedagogues. Of course, media study is an important part of an English program, and a later section of this book explores "Multimedia English." But print is hardly dead in the world. While inflation has driven up the cost of just about everything, including paperbacks and newspapers, print is cheap and, thanks to contemporary technology, getting relatively cheaper. Perhaps kids watch TV in the evenings instead of settling by the fire to read a novel (did they ever really do that?), but they are saturated with print words in their daily lives. To help students understand the role of print in their lives, try some of the following:

➤ *Collect words for a day.* Have students keep an informal log of their encounters with language, from the label on the toothpaste tube, to the writing on the dashboard of the car, to the dozens of signs on every block in the downtown area, to newspapers and magazines. Have them compute a rough estimate of the total number of words that pass by their eyes each day.

➤ *Examine word sources.* Follow up the previous activity by asking students to prepare projects or displays indicating the sources of the words with which they make contact. How important is, say, *packaging* in bombarding them with words? What role do *newspapers* play, even if not read front page to back page?

➤ *Explore the role of the printed word on television.* Advertisers have long known that purely pictorial ads are not as effective as those that include print. Ask your students to figure out the pattern of print use in commercials.

➤ *Conduct a unit on the contemporary magazine.* Study the writing in *Ms., Psychology Today, Sports Illustrated.* How often does a piece of exposition actually begin with a stretch of narrative writing? What techniques of creative writing are found in brass-tacks writing? You may be surprised yourself to discover the extent to which the distinctions between the formal essay and fiction have been blurred—to good advantage—by contemporary magazines.

➤ *Study the new journalism with the same idea in mind.* How do writers such as Tom Wolfe rework language and what are they trying to accomplish?

➤ *Discuss the language of advertising.* In making claims for products, advertisers must, by law, not falsify or misrepresent their products. This, in turn, leads to very clever linguistic manipulation. For instance, an ad claims, "If it's not finger lickin' good, it can't be Kentucky Fried Chicken." Now, on first reading, that phrase might seem to mean that no fried chicken, even your mom's, can be finger lickin' good (if that's a virtue in the first place). But in fact, the "finger lickin' " phrase is a trademark of the Kentucky Fried Chicken franchise and thus can be used *only* by them in advertising to describe their product. Their claim, then, means about as much as: "If it's not a Chevrolet, it can't be a Chevy."

But, you may note, rightfully, that those are reading and language activities, not writing. We submit, however, that while examining language in this way, students are becoming more sensitive to the realities of how language operates in society. This, in turn, helps them use language more successfully.

Producing Persuasive Language

One of the myths perpetuated by the grammar and rhetoric handbooks is that we are all perfectly rational and logical in our thinking, and that when making decisions, we carefully inspect assertions (topic sentences) and analyze the reasons for or against them (supporting evidence) and come to agree with the writer (clincher sentence). While that form is occasionally appropriate, politicians and advertisers have long known—and exploited—the fact that decisions are not made in totally rational ways.

There are ethical, unethical, and shady ways of persuading people; there are rational appeals and those that center on emotional and intuitive responses.

While we're not advocating the teaching of unethical and irrational means of persuasion, we think it important that students become acquainted with the brass tacks of contemporary appeals.

One technique for developing this awareness that we have used successfully with students, grades 7 through 12, is called "The Campaign." It is described in detail in Stephen Judy's *Explorations in the Teaching of Secondary English* (Harper & Row, 1974). The unit can last a day or a week, or can even constitute the work of an entire term. The procedure is direct and simple:

Working in groups or teams, students select an idea or issue or concept that they want to promote. Students we have worked with have selected such diverse issues as promoting bikeways, abolishing required courses, abolishing grades, and encouraging the use of nonsexist language.

Next, they produce and coordinate a campaign to push the idea, using as many different forms and media as possible. They may choose to make bumper stickers and buttons, banners and placards, write speeches, conduct television interviews, hold debates, launch letter-writing campaigns, develop laws and legislation, and so on.

Frequently, participants in the project start off with campaign items that are gimmicky and simple (buttons and placards), but most groups come to realize that the expository word is an important part of any campaign. While people are vulnerable to the short and snappy, they also seek ideas and information, and few campaigns can succeed on emotional appeals alone. Thus, students come to see the role of the word in persuasion.

The final step is presentation of the campaign materials. This can be done with a class or across several classes, with students serving as evaluators of the probable success of each campaign.

Even more effective, we think, is to make the campaign a *real* one from the start, with students actually presenting their materials. Often local agencies or organizations will offer campaign topics. The Red Cross wants to advertise a blood drive, or a conservation group wants to alert public attention to the potential destruction of a nature area. Such groups will welcome help and sometimes even provide supporting funds. (Working within a budget also heightens the reality of the project.)

Variations on the campaign activity include: school elections; promoting school activities and programs (concerts, car washes, PTO nights); developing ad campaigns for local businesses; and persuading the school administration and teachers to make alterations in the structure or program of the school.

Writing to Somebody with a Face

It seems to us that writing is most motivated (and the need for surface correctness most evident) when students are writing for real audiences, whether large or small, close or distant. Working on this premise, some graduate students at the University of British Columbia in Vancouver developed a plan for a course called "Writing to Somebody with a Face," aimed at having *all* writing read by somebody else (generally, someone other than the teacher). Their course involved students in writing all manner of letters, memos, notes, and essays. It was relatively easy to create a list of audiences for student writing. The course was augmented with parallel literature, from epistolary novels to the Earthworm Tractor Company correspondence of Alexander Botts, an old *Saturday Evening Post* short-story hero.

Some people and places to write:

➤ Other students, of all sizes, ages, and geographical locations. Set up a letter exchange within the class or between classes or between schools. The idea of pen pals is old hat, yet productive; you can get names for as little as fifty cents apiece through pen pal associations.

➤ Political figures. Guaranteed to bring a response, even if only a form letter. Let students write congressmen and representatives, aldermen and mayors.

➤ Business leaders. Ask community members to tell students about the writing demands of their chosen profession.

➤ Television executives (to critique programming).

➤ Celebrities and movie stars (though don't expect much of a response).

➤ Newspaper editors.

➤ Members of the school board (but for heaven's sake, make certain there aren't any typographical errors).

One way to launch a "Writing to Somebody with a Face" program is to supply the class with attractive stationery (ask a local store to help you out) or to get blank paper in many colors and let students design their own rubber-stamp or wood-block monographs. One teacher we know buys up quantities of old postcards at garage sales and makes them available to students.

Set a basic objective: "In this course, you'll write ——— letters, ——— each week." Then brainstorm for audiences for letters. Costs need not be prohibitive; many letters will be hand delivered within the school or community, and even a first-class stamp can be purchased by most students once or twice a week.

Even if you don't choose to make the writing in your program exclusively to somebody with a face, this kind of interchange adds enormously to a course and the teaching of brass-tacks writing, as well as providing solid evidence to administrators that you are concerned with the teaching of basics.

Exploring Issues and Problems

"The Campaign," described above, centers on persuasive discourse, on convincing another person of the rightness of an idea or the importance of taking action. Yet, in the wake of the activist sixties, many young people and a lot of strife-weary adults are more interested in exploring and solving problems close to home than shaking the universe. The focus is on information, frequently of a personal sort, rather than public persuasion.

What about . . . careers? Marriage and family? Women's rights? Getting into college? Getting a job after college? Living with somebody? Abortion? Relating to people? And there are a host of practical concerns. How do you change the oil in your car? What do you feed a turtle? How do you sew a blind French seam? How do you make yourself up to appear sixty on stage? Where do babies come from? The medium of explorations of these, and a thousand other topics, is *the word*—printed, spoken, written.

Somewhat akin to a course in "Writing to Somebody with a Face," consider a course or unit investigating "Issues and Problems 'With a Face,' " real issues and problems generated by students:

■ Prime the pump by suggesting the kinds of topics listed above. (Hint: Scan the subject index of the card catalog to get as broad a list as possible.)

■ Then ask the students to suggest questions and problems in a public brain-storming session or, if preferred, by submitting topics on index cards.

■ Group students by common interests.

■ Let the groups seek answers to their questions, exploring as many different information sources as possible, looking to community members, social agencies, experts around the school, libraries and media sources.

■ Finally, have students present their answers, as imaginatively as possible, to the assembled class, in panel or position paper, media show, or dittoed magazine.

Is this a writing project? Perhaps not in the strictest sense; but it is clearly a *language* project, having students draw on the word both as information source and as a mode of presentation.

In a variation, have your students create a *Question-Asker's Yellow Pages.* Every community and/or county in the country has a wealth of resources for finding out about things. If you want to learn how to tie flies or footnote a research paper or adjust a lawn mower or understand yourself or your body, there are people and organizations or agencies that provide answers. As a project, let your students discover what your community has to offer; then prepare a book showing people where to go to seek answers to their questions. This project, in addition to teaching students a great deal about the word and about information sources, is also a valuable community project, and your *Yellow Pages* can frequently be distributed in quantity to an audience—with a face.

The Academic Writing Scene

Thus far we have concentrated our discussion on brass-tacks writing in society, certainly an important concern, for all our students will, at thousands of times in their lives, be required to use language successfully in practical situations. At the same time, there is the academic scene, a rather different, sometimes abstruse language milieu. The writing that students do in school frequently has little to do with the practical demands of their lives. Ken Macrorie once remarked that all academic writing, from kindergarten on up, seems geared toward the writing of Ph.D. dissertations, which nobody reads. When young people spell badly or punctuate abominably, it is frequently in school or college where this "execrable" writing is observed.

Teachers need to be concerned with the academic writing scene for several reasons, then: first, and most important, because they want to help kids succeed, in school (and elsewhere); second, because the profession is under fire from teachers of other subjects, from administrators, from parents; third, because some, but by no means all, students will face the academic writing scene in colleges or postsecondary schools.

At the same time, we feel strongly that much *mis*direction in the teaching of writing has taken place because the concerns of academic writing have long dominated secondary-school teaching. Without losing sight of the earlier discussion, then, we want to suggest the following strategies for preparing students to deal with academic writing in school or college:

1. Survey the kinds of writing demands placed on students. This is a study, like the study of the word in society, that students can conduct. Ask your students to keep a detailed log of the writing required of them in other courses. Just how often *do* they write in history . . . in science . . . in health and safety ed.? What papers/exams/reports/worksheets are required? Does *anyone* (other than the English teacher) require secondary-school students to write the formal, documented term paper? Pool the results from one or several classes and discuss with your students to help them understand exactly what they are facing.

Note: This survey will also provide you valuable information for the next faculty meeting, when someone complains about the quality of student writing. As a review of the National Assessment of Student Writing observed, if students are not required to write in other courses, it is not likely that they will be impressed with the importance of "good writing" in English.

2. *Prepare a writer's gallery of college writing.* Ask your former students to contribute their freshman papers to a "museum" you prepare. Such a collection will help students see the range, the consistency, the diversity of college assignments and to see what they're up against.

3. *Teach students to use a good short handbook of usage, spelling, and writing form—from business letter to research paper.* Such books exist in paperback, freed from the grammar/rhetoric discussions of school texts. They provide advice on getting papers into publishable, correct form, and they use a minimum of terminology.

4. *Teach students to analyze the stated and unstated requirements in assignments.* The teacher says, "Analyze the poem any way you wish, but use supporting evidence." What does that really mean? What will happen to the student who presents an offbeat analysis rather than the one discussed in last Tuesday's lecture? Like TV commercials and political pledges, assignments often say a great deal more (or less) than the surface structure implies.

5. *Help students evolve an inventory of strategies for success.* Students learn (but are not often conscious of) the techniques and strategies that they and other students use to get good grades in academic writing situations. Ask students to save their A (and D) papers for a postmortem. What went right (or wrong)? What can one learn from the comments on the paper?

Further, students can assess their own writing and study habits. Cramming is not something sinful; for many people cramming is the only way to remember huge quantities of information. Other people can study on a regular basis and do well. Some people can outline a term paper the day it is assigned; others will pound out a first, final draft hours before it is due. Writing and study habits differ, and each person needs to discover what will work for him or her.

6. *Encourage students to think about the audience for academic writing.* The

teacher is not the usual audience; he or she is reading with a narrowed purpose: to discover if the writer "knows the stuff." That's not like the audience for a novel or essay or editorial. Sometimes the "audience" is a graduate assistant who is simply looking for key points, the items stressed in recent lectures. Such audiences are reading for a different purpose, and students need to know it. (See next item.)

7. *Teach formula writing.* We argued earlier that the structured, topic-sentence essay is largely a myth. Yet there are advantages to knowing how to do a formula piece, an essay designed not for publication, but for grading, be it exam or term assignment. Ideas for formula writing include:

■ *The Dale Carnegie Approach.* In paragraph one, you "tell 'em what you're gonna tell 'em" (explicitly stake out your central thesis). Then you "tell 'em" (block out your points with evidence). Finally, you "tell 'em what you've told 'em" (summarize). This formula works, because the teacher or prof or assistant can quickly determine whether or not the student knows "the material." (If students don't know the stuff, suggest that they eschew clear writing.)

■ *Transitions.* Teach a number of "finger-pointing" transitions: "in the second place," "thus," "on the other hand," "nevertheless," "however," "therefore." (Eschew "In conclusion. . . .") Suggest that writers plug in an appropriate transition at the beginning of each paragraph; it helps theme graders find their way.

■ *Language.* Avoid informality (but don't teach pomposity). Academics see red over informal language. Students are generally well advised to avoid contractions, colloquialisms, informal expressions.

8. *Delay teaching formula writing as long as possible.* The formulae can be taught quickly and easily to young people who have had broad experiences composing. Teaching the formula too soon simply leads to gobbledygook.

Finally, it is crucial to remember that the mastery of academic writing skills is not an end in itself. Too many units on the term paper go awry because the focus becomes mastery of research strategies and footnote form. As you teach academic writing, then, try to integrate the formal instruction into the truly basic processes of exploring, researching, probing, helping students come to know something of interest that can be shared with another person. If students write to *know* they will also write to *share,* and the conventions of the research process will be mastered while students learn and share. Try some of the following alternatives to the traditional term paper unit:

Science writing. Collection a dozen or two science books for young adults on popular topics (space exploration, animal life, computer technology, air and water pollution) and have the students brainstorm for additional problems or topics. Students may then work individually or in pairs exploring and researching the subject. Instead of having them write a formal science paper or report, have them cast their material into the form of a magazine (but following accepted conventions for documentation, formal writing, etc.).

➡ *History writing.* Elicit interest in historical periods by bringing in collections of historical novels clustered about a particular era or series of eras. After students enjoy reading one or several novels, encourage them to move in the direction of historical *non*fiction and finally toward the preparation of monographs or reports, or possibly even composing a historical novelette or short story themselves.

➡ *Cultural history.* The enormous popularity of the *Foxfire* books in this country is a testament to the interest both adults and young people have in cultural history. For *Foxfire,* Eliot Wigginton, a Georgia English teacher, simply had his students research skills, arts, and crafts from the mountain tradition by interviewing their elders. The resulting materials found their way into a student-produced series of magazines that incidentally demonstrate extraordinary mastery of "research skills."

➡ *Literary research.* In *Transitions: A Literary Casebook* (Random House, 1974), Richard Peck took a common literary theme, "Coming of Age," and collected a number of short stories, poems, and essays on the topic. After students explored the issue itself, Peck presented a series of writing topics exploring aspects of the theme and introduced, in an incidental manner, both literary terminology (theme, genre, etc.) and the characteristics of good academic writing about literature. Since the theme was itself of great interest to adolescents, their response to literature drew them quite naturally into more formal discussions (research) about it.

➡ *Community Problems.* Peck has also prepared a parallel research casebook called *Urban Studies* (Random House, 1974). Following the same pattern, he introduced students to the topic by offering a collection of articles on the urban problems of contemporary society, then moved them into more formal reading and research writing on topics identified by the students themselves.

CHAPTER 18

Writer and Audience

English teachers are more concerned than ever with helping young people learn to meet future demands and expectations—the next grade, the social studies teacher, college professors, potential employers—yet we still want students to see writing as an important, creative activity in their lives. Though it's impossible to predict *all* the demands students are likely to confront in their writing career, it is possible to help students expand their literacy, to become more flexible and confident in dealing with a wide variety of writing tasks. In recent years, teachers have begun to broaden writing in the English class beyond the theme-a-week and/or book-report format to a wide variety of discourse forms. Another means of developing students' literacy is to expand the audiences, both in number and kind, for which students write.

Writing, like reading, is an interaction between *writer, subject,* and *reader.* The writer presents information, ideas, or experiences in such a way that the reader will understand them, respond to them, benefit from them. When students write for the teacher alone, the interaction between reader and writer will remain constant, perhaps even stagnant. Changing the audience, however, creates new ways of conceiving the subject. On the basis of the type of audience for which they are writing, students have to make decisions about the kinds of information they must include or exclude, depending on what the audience knows or needs to know about the subject. For example, in writing about "What I Like (Or Don't Like) about Wappawanna High School," students will provide very different information for a teacher than they will for their parents or for the local elementary or junior-high kids. Because the audiences have different experiences and different perspectives, the point of view and the selection of information the student makes will differ from audience to audience.

Audiences affect the voice the students use and the styles of writing they employ. When writing to or for friends, voice and style are likely to reflect oral language use—chatty, casual, informal. In writing for the teacher, the language is likely to be in a somewhat more formal register, reflecting the language and more structured relationships of school. Students will naturally adjust their style to their reader; helping students become aware of their range of voices will help them refine that range and make the choices consciously.

Providing students with audiences for their writing helps them develop a notion of appropriateness of various forms and usages of language in different contexts. The importance of eliminating sentence fragments, capitalizing proper nouns, and getting subjects and verbs to agree is not always apparent to students; students (and people in general) often communicate precisely what they want without following the formal conventions of language. Full sentences are not necessary for providing answers to a short-answer quiz, for proving to the teacher that you read your assignment, for writing a lab report in biology, for writing a letter to a friend, or for filling out a job application. Conventions of form *are* important, however, when writing a letter to a politician about a problem in your community; when writing a textbook or storybook for third-graders; when writing an invitation to a community leader to visit your school; when writing an article for publication in the class or school magazine; when writing a letter of application, complaint, or praise that you want the recipient to take seriously.

Most important, expanding audiences for writers gives students a genuine reason to write; writing assignments are less likely to be contrivances or gimmicks and more likely to be motivated and involved *communication.* Adolescents have many ideas, experiences, and feelings that they are willing to share. But they don't want to write to a vacuum, and they don't want to communicate with people to whom they have nothing to say.

The audience, in short, is perhaps as important as the topic.

Some Audiences for Student Writers

PEERS

Using students in the classroom as the readership has become increasingly popular. Too often, however, the main function of that audience has been to edit or proofread or correct the work of their peers. Though this is one important function of student readers and student respondents, it should not be the sole function. Students should also share writing with each other purely for the pleasure and enjoyment of it. Adolescents have many experiences and feelings that they want to discuss with one another. They enjoy dramatizing what happened after school yesterday, and what Mr. So and So said to the school goof-off after sixth hour, and what awful thing happened at Greg's party Friday night. And they are willing to share these things in writing, if they don't have to worry about being judged and criticized for their behavior or the way they expressed themselves.

The importance of this type of expression—sharing experiences with peers in an informal situation—should not be underestimated by the teacher who wants students to write better. Learning how to express their thoughts, relate their experiences, and interpret their feelings is an important part in the process of establishing identity as a writer and developing voice in writing.

KNOWN ADULTS

Teachers and parents are important in young people's development, and known audiences—adults who are familiar to the student—can act as a sounding board for students as they are developing ideas and interpreting experiences. The relationship with known adults is sufficiently informal for the student to feel secure about using that (adult) audience to try out opinions and theories. At the same time, communicating with a known adult, particularly in a school setting, requires a greater degree of formality than communication with peers.

UNKNOWN ADULTS

More opportunities should be provided for students to direct their writing to people outside the range of their immediate personal experience. Often teachers try to have students project a general audience as the audience for their writing. A more helpful approach is for students to specify an audience or for teachers to suggest a variety of audiences for the student. Audiences can include:

local politicians
national politicians
inventors
industrial leaders
movie and television stars

scientists
rock musicians
classical musicians
dancers
artists
directors
magazine and newspaper editors
ecologists
athletes
authors
journalists
businessmen
lawyers
doctors.

Students may write to these people to complain, to express opinions, to seek advice, to ask for changes, to express appreciation, to suggest solutions, to share experiences, to obtain information.

IMAGINARY CHARACTERS

Students may direct their writing to characters or people they create or to imaginary figures from literature, movies, television, or comic books. The variety of characters in media and literature allows for many different voices and approaches. Letters students write to adolescent TV characters will probably be very different in topic, style, and tone from what they might write to a super hero or a tough detective. Creating imaginary characters even allows students to project an audience that meets the needs of an idea or concept; thus, the creation of a mad scientist as audience allows students to develop an imaginative idea or even to take on the voice of the mad scientist themselves.

YOUNGER STUDENTS

Teachers have had a good deal of success having junior-high and high-school students write books for elementary-school children. A younger, less experienced audience allows students to write as experts, to take on the voice of authority. Such writing requires students to develop their ideas more fully than they might in writing to a peer. Whether they are describing an experience or situation at school or a concept or theory they have learned, older students writing for younger ones will need to develop their writing in terms of a less experienced reader.

SPECIALIZED AUDIENCES

Much of the writing traditionally done in English classes has been on literary or research topics, with the teacher as sole audience. We think, however, that expanded audiences are appropriate even for this more academic prose. Thus, students who enjoy reading and writing about literature can write for each other as a specialized audience; students who have a research interest in chemistry or biology or history can write and review each other's work. But specialized audiences need not be limited to academic writing; in any class you can find writers and readers on a host of special interest topics: sports, science, jewelry, banjos, jai alai, mushrooms, partridge hunting. . . .

Providing Audiences: Practical Suggestions

LETTERS

A form implied by the expanding of audiences for student writers is *the letter.* There are many possibilities for using correspondence as a part of your writing program. (See also chapter 17, "Brass-Tacks Writing.")

➡ *Letters as response to literature.* Have students express their ideas and feelings about a piece of literature by writing a letter to a character in a novel, play, story, or poem. Or have them write a series of letters to different characters. Students can tell the characters what they thought of their actions, what they would have done in the same situation, what solutions or advice would be helpful to the character. Another possibility: Have students take on the role of the character and write from the character's point of view, developing his or her response and using his or her voice.

➡ *Letters as a research tool.* Too often research projects are a dull collection of second-hand information that students gather from limited sources without much thought about the research, the project, or the sources. But research can be a vital and interesting way to learn. Let students decide what they want to know about well in advance of any due date for finished papers, provide them with sources for gathering information, and start them writing letters. Some letters may merely be "To Whom It May Concern," asking for pamphlets, booklets, and free materials. But *people* are the most exciting source of information: their ideas, their opinions, their facts, and their theories. For example, juvenile delinquency can be an interesting topic, with letters written to social workers, lawyers, judges, psychologists, and staff members of detention homes. Students interested in child abuse can correspond with doctors, lawyers, and legislators about the seriousness of the problem and what's being done about it. Students can begin their search for authorities on social, medical, political, and ecological problems through many federal, state, and private organizations. Correspondence with authorities provides students with a real and vital way of gathering and evaluating data, and it also provides them with a new communication process.

Correspondence as a journal. Though the journal is a good place for students to experiment with their writing and to keep track of their ideas and experiences, it is limited by the use of the self-as-audience. Certainly, writing as a means of personal reflection is extremely important. It might be interesting and helpful for students, however, to experiment with trying out different voices and approaches for different audiences in their journal. A list of audiences and topics like the ones above also make good experimental writing suggestions for the journal.

Letter exchanges. These may be set up among students in the same school and different classes, among students whose schools are across town from one another, among students who live in different states or different parts of the country, and among students who live in different countries. An in-school exchange may be between "mystery correspondents." Set up a letter exchange between your students and the students of another teacher in your building. Tell the students to give information about themselves, but not to tell who they are. Allow students to continue correspondence until they have been able to figure out who their mystery correspondent is or until they give up. Have a common class meeting or a party for mystery correspondents to meet. This is especially good in a big school, where students might not know one another.*

* Thanks to Betsy Kaufman, Queens College, who piloted this idea in a summer writing workshop.

PERFORMANCES

Another way to provide student writers with audiences is through the use of public performance of students' work. Performance may be as simple as having students volunteer to read their writing from time to time to the whole class; it can be as complex as a program in which students' writings are integrated into musical/drama/media programs done for the community. Consider the following possibilities:

Class readings. Set aside one day every week or two in which students do free writing; then ask volunteers to read their writing to the rest of the class. Such spontaneous situations encourage students to relax about sharing writing (particularly since they can't expect a "perfect" piece in just a single class period). After students have begun to enjoy sharing their writings and are comfortable with one another, establish a more normal way of sharing writing. Set aside a period every few weeks in which students make a dramatic presentation of their writings, using a reader's-theater format. Eventually, try a more elaborate program with the use of costumes and media effects (slides, music, tape recordings of sound effects, etc.). Student performance days can be developed around themes or serve as the culminating activity for a unit.

School performances. Drama, music, art, and athletics give students an opportunity to show their talents and abilities to their peers and adults in the community, and young people derive a great deal of satisfaction and feeling of self-worth through their accomplishments. They are also willing to devote a great deal of time and energy to perfecting their skills in those areas. Their work in writing can provide the same sort of satisfaction if they are given opportunities to share what they have done. Consider ways in which student work in writing can be opened up to the whole school. Perhaps student-written plays can be performed by the drama club in an afternoon meeting. Many schools have lunch-hour movies; use one day a week for students to present their stories, plays, and poems during the lunch-hour break. Perhaps various departments can encourage students to participate with music, drama, and readings. Use school assemblies for students to present their work and to recognize achievement in writing as well as music, forensics, and athletics.

Parent-teacher meetings. Often parent-teacher meetings involve sharing what students are doing in school. Again, emphasizing the importance of student writing and sharing student writing with parents will lend encouragement and motivation for writing and develop students' sense that they are writing for *someone,* not just writing to develop a skill or to eliminate a problem.

➡ *All-kids' TV show.* Programs for the community can include student writings. A program of drama, composition, music, and media by student creators and performers is also a good candidate for public access television. Call or write the local cable TV people to find out the requirements and uses of public access television, and help your students develop a program using their own writing.

PUBLICATIONS

Publications provide a variety of ways that students' writing can be shared with a variety of audiences.

➡ Mimeograph books for special occasions: for the class Thanksgiving book, end-of-term book, winter book, Valentine's love-stories book.

➡ Use prebound blank books that the class can spend the term filling with their best writings and illustrations.

➡ *Class magazine or newspaper.* Have students publish magazines or newspapers once a marking period or semester. Rival groups within the class can compete for readers.

➡ *Individual books.* Have students collect a portfolio of their best writing. Bind the book and share it with other students in a writing fair. Students can write prefaces for their own books for each other. Books can be reviewed for the class magazine.

➡ *Class books.* Have the class as a whole publish a book. Set up different committees within the class: typing, proofreading, illustration, editorial, cover, and dittoing. (You can usually get by with one or two reams of paper if dittos are run back to back.)

➡ *Class reading assignment.* Have students put a writing of their choice in a pile. Each student responds to a classmate's paper with a collage, free writing, poem, or drawing.

➡ Use class bulletin boards and school bulletin boards to display student writing that has been edited, proofread, and illustrated. Make the most of interesting graphics and art to "show off the writing."

➡ Add student books to your class library or to the school library (to be checked out like other library books). Make use of students' expertise by setting up days in which students who are experts may share their knowledge. Some kids may be expert cooks; some may know about trail bikes and snowmobiles; some may know about rocks and shells; some are experts on bugs or plants or birds; some know about hunting and fishing in all their subtleties. Allow students to prepare a presentation in which they share with the entire class (or more). Along with their demonstration and presentation, have them write and illustrate a booklet providing the information to the novice. Such communication involves the writer in making conscious and explicit what he knows for someone who does not share his expertise.

Get money from the arts council in your area to do more elaborate books of student writing, using offset printing to reproduce colorful booklets to be distributed throughout the school and community at a minimal price.

Use already existing publications. As a possible course requirement, have students submit writing to two of the following groups: school paper, school yearbook, school literary magazine, newspapers, magazines, and contests.

Create new publications. Develop your own magazines, newspapers, or writing contests. This is a good way to get students talking about criteria for good writing.

Swap writing between classes. Exchange class magazines, newspapers, broadsheets, and direction-giving papers (how to make peanut-butter sandwiches or how to tie a shoe) with other classes. Sponsor a "Penny a Poem" fair and invite other classes to buy poetry.

Swap writing between schools. Have students write children's books and read them to preschoolers or elementary students. Have students send their writing to junior-high students. Exchange writings between your class and a class of college students preparing to be teachers.

Have students write "texts" in history, botany, zoology, general science, geography, art, music for students. Provide writers with the teacher's objectives and with the text that the students use. Have them develop more detailed (and more interesting) booklets that give an in-depth or specialized look at one of the areas of study of their particular audience.

CHAPTER 19

The Red Pencil Blues

"Wad-ja-get on your Hamlet paper, Susan?"

"I don't know—probably failed. I can never figure out what he likes. I thought my last paper on Lear was good and I got a D. The paper I thought was rotten, he liked."

This conversation, between a yearbook editor and her friend, is reminiscent of many conversations among students when they get back their papers: The talk generally centers on the grade, not the content; on the teacher's "wants" rather than on the intellectual growth of the writer himself or herself. Yet the same two students, overheard in a Journalism class, engage in a much different kind of discussion about writing: "Read this story, Susan. I'm happy with the beginning, but I'm not sure about the rest. Do you think this point is clear, or does it need to be explained more? Should I talk to Mrs. ——— about it?"

Why is it that we don't seem able to get our students to talk about the effectiveness of their writing? It seems that whether we use comments, conferences, proofreading symbols, green ink rather than red, or profuse praise instead of criticism, students focus primarily on the grade and only secondarily on the comments. How many long evenings and warm sunny Sunday afternoons have teachers spent commenting on and correcting student papers that will be pitched in the trash or filed into a notebook unread after the grade has been noted?

One clue, we think, is to note the difference between writing in English and writing in a Journalism or Yearbook class, where the aims of writing apparently differ.

Much of the material for this chapter was prepared by our colleague, friend, and former student Pamela Waterbury.

1. The writing for the yearbook or school paper is vital and real to the students—it is alive. It is done with the purpose of communicating to an audience what the students considered important. Writing done in classrooms is often dead writing, a mechanical exercise performed to satisfy requirements or to get a grade, not to communicate.

2. In the yearbook or journalism setting, the incentive for improving or working on writing comes from the students' desire to reach their audience. They want to make *this* particular piece of writing successful with their fellow students, their parents, and their teachers. In the classroom, on the other hand, students are told to work on their writing so they can get a better grade on papers in college or write well enough to obtain a job. Instead of writing for success today, they are writing for success in the faraway future.

Convinced that students can be encouraged to discuss writing, and not just grades, we have experimented with other approaches to student writing. Our goal has been to recreate the yearbook-writing setting in the classroom. We want our students to write with the purpose of communicating their ideas and observations for an audience. One of us has described this as "writing for the here and now" (Stephen Judy, *Explorations in the Teaching of Secondary English* [Harper & Row, 1974]). Approaching writing in the here and now means that instead of viewing writing merely as themes to be corrected and graded, we see it as wanting to be read, responded to, and shared with a larger audience.

Our reasons for approaching writing in this way center on the following premises:

1. Students should learn to write in order to better explore themselves, others, and their world and to communicate their observations to others.

2. Writing, like other skills, is learned by doing and then learning from the results of the doing. In writing, this means you discover what effect your words have on others; if your words don't work, you try again.

3. The issues of writing—content, form, and "basics"—become a natural concern for students as they prepare their writing for publication. It becomes important to organize your thoughts, spell words correctly, and use standard punctuation to ensure your paper will be read easily and achieve success with classmates.

Experimenting with a here and now response to writing won't always produce ideal results. In fact, the unexpected is bound to happen. Most of the unexpected will be valuable; it will show that writing is more than stringing together words. But sometimes writing is painful for the audience and the writer. You can expect some nightmarish experiences when students write about real and delicate subjects and you haven't the faintest idea of how to respond, but their writings will be vibrant with real concerns and issues. Johnny may hurt Susan's feelings by telling her, "This is boring," but Susan will learn about the effect of her writing on an audience, and you'll be there to direct the criticism in a more helpful way. Johnny will get negative responses from his audience, but he'll also receive an abundance of positive comments that will tell him other students understood and enjoyed his writing. And sometimes students will never go beyond talking about the content of the paper to discussions of its form and mechanics. But they will be talking about their writing and the issues of writing and not "Wad-ja-get?"

Once you've decided to experiment with a here and now approach to writing, where and how do you begin? The most helpful way we've found to start is by following stages in processing manuscripts suggested in *Explorations in the Teaching of Secondary English.* The teacher roles in this process revolve around the teacher as *personal responder, manuscript manager, technical advisor,* and *stage director* or *manager.*

The Teacher as Responder

Step 1: Decide If the Writing Is "Honest."

Usually you can tell how sincere (or "honest") the writing is by deciding how involved, interested, or excited the student was in the writing. When the student is communicating a message that is real, his or her voice or personality comes through the writing. (Sometimes it is hard to find the message amidst all the layers of static, but as a skilled reader, you should search and dig out the meaning with its metaphors and symbols.) Questions we've found helpful in determining the sincerity of the writing are: Is it interesting for me to read? Can I picture the student saying this? Is it fresh and lively? Did I get involved in the paper as I read? Can I picture the student involved in it?

Step 2: What Do You Do If the Paper Didn't Work?

Realizing that most people (including students) do not like to waste time purposely writing insincere papers, we've found responding honestly yet gently is most effective. Let the student see the paper didn't work, not that he failed. React positively to those parts you find valuable and show the student places where you have difficulty responding. Usually if you give your honest reaction to it without attacking the student ("It seemed as though you weren't involved in this," or "Did you have trouble getting interested in this paper?"), the student answers honestly and you can go on to try another assignment or approach. (See the later section on "Praise and Criticism.")

Step 3: Respond Honestly to the Paper.

Begin by listening to what the writer has said and let him know that you have heard; that means responding as a human being rather than a teacher-evaluator. Your reaction might take one of the following forms:

- *Reflection.* Reflecting means to retell the message in your own words, letting the writer know that you understand his or her message. This technique is especially useful when responding to very personal papers.
- *Give impressions.* Tell the student your impressions (not evaluation) of the writing. What is the main idea or shape of the paper? What intent does the paper seem to have? In general, give specific feedback: "This dialogue makes me see this character as a braggart rather than a confident person."
- *Give reactions.* Tell your personal reactions. This can take the form of a stream-of-consciousness or a running dialogue with the paper. What do you feel or think as you read the paper? Let the student know what ideas you find convincing and unconvincing, and why. Tell your own ideas.
- *Identify interesting and confusing sections.* Let the student know what parts most interest you. Be specific by pointing out lines, phrases, or images you find effective. At the same time, let him or her see what doesn't work for you. Show the specific places you find confusing as a reader, not as an evaluator.

Step 4: Decide If the Paper Should Be Published.

Most often this means deciding if the paper is public or private writing. Is it something the student would feel comfortable sharing with others? If you have doubts, discuss it with the student. If you think the student would have a positive experience publishing his paper, then encourage him or her to do so.

Step 5: What Should You Do If the Writing Is Not for Publication?

Return it to the student with your honest reactions and responses. Since this writing most often will be private and personal, it will call for the teacher responding in the role of trusted adult and/or interested advisor. This does not suggest that teachers should act as counsellors, but it does mean they must respond as caring and concerned human beings to calls of help from students. Another role the teacher fulfills in this situation is that of resource person. The teacher can suggest other readings on the same theme (poems, short stories, essays, or novels about loneliness, for example); or indicate other ways of approaching the topic; or have the student read papers by other students on the same theme. This allows students to realize that they are not alone in their feelings, and at the same time, it expands their thinking.

The Teacher as Manuscript Manager

Step 6: Decide What Form of Publication Is Best

In deciding this question you will want to consider the students' skills and the nature of their papers. The following questions will help decide which medium would work best: What form would be best for the particular student considering his or her skills? Does the paper need reading aloud (dialogue, skits, plays, some poems, speeches)? Or does it need quiet reading to be understood (character sketch, short story, essay, some poems)?

The Teacher as Technical Advisor

Step 7: What Technical Advice Can You Give the Student for His or Her Paper?

The teacher now functions as editor by helping the students prepare their papers for publication. They must be made aware of the strengths and weaknesses in the paper that will affect its success. Here you must consider the audience and the form of publication, as well as the student. If Johnny has difficulty forming sentences, then probably you would urge him to do an oral reading of his paper and help only with the most basic problems; whereas, if Susan is a skilled writer, you would urge her to use dittos and work with her on more technical problems.

Step 8: How Can You Best Offer Information as a Copy Reader?

When giving information about polishing grammar, punctuation, and wording, the teacher should again keep in mind the student, form of publication, and audience. If the audience extends beyond the class, then more rigorous proofreading standards will be applied than if the student is reading the paper aloud. Whenever possible, encourage students to help each other with proofreading. At first students will be reluctant, but as they achieve success with their papers, they will be comfortable using each other as proofreaders.

The Teacher as Stage Director or Manager

Most students don't automatically begin to share their writing. It's up to you to set the machinery in motion and help them discover ways of giving meaningful responses to papers (something other than misspelled words).

Step 9: Create the Atmosphere

Let the students know at the beginning that they will share papers. Explain why you think it's important. Once they've begun doing it, they'll see why. Help students trust each other and you by using getting-acquainted activities. We've found the following activities help students talk and share with each other:

- *Interview sheets.* Have students interview five students they do not know. The interview sheets can be partially made up beforehand by you. Including funny questions helps remove the strain and threat from the interview.
- *Profiles.* Have students pair up doing profiles of someone they don't know well. Then have the student interview the person and include the information around the profile.
- *Object day or uniqueness day.* Have students bring in an object that shows something they enjoy doing or are good at doing. This is a great way for them to realize the skills they already possess.

Step 10: Develop a Format for Talking about Writing

Discuss how sensitive people are about their writing and the need for sensitive praise and criticism. Sometimes setting a ground rule that there can be no criticism during the first three or four sessions relieves tensions and fears. Effective questions for getting students to discuss writing are: What did you like? What did you identify with? How did you feel as you read it?

Step 11: Set the Process in Motion

Begin by having everyone (including the teacher) share something so that the sharing of writing becomes an accepted and desired part of the class. Sometimes it's helpful to have the first paper remain anonymous (although the writer usually reveals himself). Begin with a short writing that most students find easy and enjoyable. Examples of writings that have worked are: free associations, free writings to pictures of music, short dialogues, brief descriptions of places and people, and concrete sentences.

Step 12: Publish and Share

Student papers can be shared as part of an in-process editing step or as a final product. The in-process sharing involves students helping each other prepare their work for publishing (usually this takes place in the form of small groups or individuals helping each other), while the sharing of writing as a final product means the student has completed his revisions and is ready to share the results.

Suggestions for Those Unresolved Issues

ISSUE 1: PRAISE AND CRITICISM

For most writers, especially beginners, papers are intimately linked to identity: "Criticize my paper, you criticize me." The following suggestions are "gleanings" from Haim Ginott's *Between Parent and Teenager* (Avon, 1971):

Praise: Dos and Don'ts
DON'T . . .
Evaluate: "You are the best writer in the class."
Glorify: "You are such a good poet. I always enjoy your poems."
DO . . .
Describe: "Your description of walking on cinders was vivid; I could feel them cutting into my feet."
Deal with specifics: "I like the line 'kite wonderful and flower luscious days.' It reminded me of how I felt last Monday."

Criticism: Dos and Don'ts
DON'T . . .
Attack the person: "You are a bad speller."

Attack personality traits: "You don't spend enough time on your work. When you go to college, you can't be this lazy."

Evaluate: "This is bad writing. Your reasoning is ridiculous."

DO . . .

Describe what you see: "This paper seems less developed than other writing you've done. Did you enjoy doing it?"

Describe what you feel: "I had trouble responding to the end of the paper. I had expected more and felt let down when it ended so quickly."

Suggest approaches: "This character doesn't seem developed enough in this section. Maybe you could think about how a younger brother would react in the same situation."

ISSUE 2: TECHNICAL ADVICE

Many of the ideas for giving technical advice we've discovered from helpful responses people have given our own writing; some we've gathered from information our students have given us on what they have found most helpful; and others, we've learned from Peter Elbow's chapter "The Teacherless Writing Class" in *Writing Without Teachers* (Oxford University Press, 1974).

➡ *Summarizing or describing comments.* Tell what went on in the paper—describe the writing. For example, give your impressions of the character described; or explain your impression of the main idea or theme in the paper.

➡ *Telling.* Show the writer your response as you read the paper. What things do you think or feel? What experiences of your own come to mind? What ideas does the paper give you?

➡ *Pointing.* Point out specific lines, ideas, or words that you find successful. (They strike you as being powerful or effective.) Try to let the writer know why: "This line reminds me of what mud feels like when it oozes between my toes." "This dialogue helps me see how selfish John is." "This point convinces me of your argument."

➡ *Unanswered questions.* Raise questions that weren't answered. For example: "I would like to picture this more fully. What did it look like? How did he respond in this situation?"

➡ *Possibilities.* Give comments that show the student possibilities in his paper. "This is an appropriate metaphor; can it be developed even more?" "I like the religious symbolism; can it be used throughout the paper?" "This might be an interesting place to begin the story; it's where I first became involved."

➡ *Weaknesses.* What aspects of the paper are unclear or confusing?

➡ *Showing.* Elbow proposes that a reader respond to writing by using a stream of metaphors; for example, the reader describes the writing in terms of weather (foggy, clear, sunny, crisp) or in terms of voices (dull, loud, gentle). Other metaphors he suggests are: locomotion, clothing, terrain, color, shape, and animals.

ISSUE 3: PROVIDING SKILL INFORMATION

➡ *Find out the questions students have.* Try using a survey to find out what problems students have as they rewrite and polish their papers. Some of the revising problems my students identify are: developing ideas, making dialogue realistic, and finding ways to show rather than tell. Questions they ask when polishing their papers concern: using quotations, using commas, and creating paragraphs.

➡ *Use students as teachers.* Identify experts in the class to help with specific problems: poetry expert, paragraphing expert, and spelling expert.

➡ *Develop a buddy system.* Encourage students to help each other by setting up a partner system or have them set one up. Before a paper can go to press, it must be proofread and countersigned by the buddy or several buddies. Eventually students will work together automatically on editing and proofreading problems.

➡ *Provide resource material.* Develop a fund of operational advice that describes ways of writing essays, short stories, poems, and plays in terms the students can understand. Have a fund of professional writing and student writing available for students to explore when they encounter problems. Develop Unipacs that deal with grammar and punctuation problems. Have different grammar books available for students.

ISSUE 4: GETTING STUDENTS TALKING ABOUT WRITING

To help students develop techniques for responding to writing, we find it helpful to first talk about papers in a large group. Sometimes we use examples of student papers from previous years to introduce assignments, and then we approach the examples in the way we want students to approach their own writing. Once you've established a basic approach for discussing writing, you can break into smaller groups using guided discussion sheets. The following questions can be used: What was the main point of the paper? Summarize the paper. What parts of the paper did you especially like? What parts of the paper were vivid or detailed? What mood or feelings did you get as you read the paper? Were there sections you found confusing?

➡ Help students recognize that different writings have different purposes, and encourage them to respond appropriately to those purposes. The paper itself or the writer may provide clues about the paper's intent. A student writing about a terrible fight with a parent or best friend is probably not interested in stylistic advice; and a spontaneous collection of images of autumn is probably not in need of mechanical markings.

➡ When a student has indicated that he would like group input or advice on a project, a good place to start is with the group's immediate emotional or intellectual response: "This paper made me sad"; "I had an experience like this, but I didn't respond the way this writer did"; "I really hated the main character in this story"; "I got confused about what was happening in the middle of the poem." From there, the readers may move back to the original paper or further into their own experience to explain more about what made them respond as they did. Responses and interpretations will differ, and the conflicts among readers will help the writer to know the effect his writing had on others and to evaluate what he might have left out or added for a different effect. In addition, the writer may wish to clarify his purposes and aims and get help from others on what he might do to better communicate the experience or idea. Most important, the interplay between reader, text, and writer involves the participants in exploring experience and heightens awareness of the effect that the telling has on the experience.

➡ Discussions of style and structure should—and will—come up naturally when students are discussing each other's papers. When considering how a paper affects them, students often come to see how a particular image, the organization (repetitions, flashbacks), the use of details, or certain sentence structures work effectively in papers. For example, a discovery that students often make when learning to discuss papers is how sentence length affects rhythm and movement. Often this kind of recognition leads to an enjoyable playing with language and style in their own writing. Enriching and expanding use of language enriches and expands experience.

➡ A word on the value of tangents: Occasionally teachers are discouraged by student discussions of writing which seem to take off on unrelated tangents. A teacher leading or overhearing such a discussion should be very cautious about interfering and getting the discussion "back on the track." For students to relate their own experiences because their response was triggered by reading someone else's paper is a healthy and positive sign. First, the reader has been affected by someone else's writing; the writer is able to see how what he has done has been interpreted by someone else and how it squares with someone else's experiences. Second, students' imaginations are stimulated, and related assignments and spin-offs occur to them.

In helping students learn to talk about each other's papers, clarify the difference between responding to content and copyreading the paper. Unfortunately, for many students, matters of superficial correctness have taken precedence over ideas and feelings they have expressed. Students should be helped to see that correction of mechanical and usage problems has a place when the end of the writing process is some sort of publication.

SUMMARY AND TROUBLESHOOTING

Meditations on an Empty Briefcase: Excerpts from the Journal of a Composition Teacher

AUGUST

Each January first, like most folks, I sit down and write a list of New Year's resolutions. Though I've never had much luck at keeping them (especially quitting smoking), the idea of starting the year with a fresh slate has a lot of appeal for me. It occurs to me, too, that summer is like New Year's for teachers. As I sit here in my study my briefcase is empty, my body is relaxed, and I can give some thought to my teaching for the coming year.

I resolve to be a better composition teacher next year. I have to face it; I've always been more interested in literature than writing, and I've neglected the written word. But everybody's concerned about "Why Johnny Can't Write," and I ought to be doing my share. I've thumbed through my old journals and reached the conclusion that what I ought to be doing, first and foremost, is getting the kids writing more. So my objective for the year will be for each student in my classes to write twice each week: once in an informal setting, a kind of rough draft or journal-style entry; once as a paper that will be revised, properly spelled and punctuated, and neatly copied. It will be as close as I can get to the old idea of "a theme a week."

SEPTEMBER

My god, but their writing is awful. During the first two weeks of school I collected two writing samples (on popular topics like TV shows, not "My Summer Vacation"). I'm really appalled. It's true, the kids can't write. They can't spell; they can't organize; they can't write complete sentences. It is as if they've never been asked to write before. I think I'm going to ask them to write about writing—what they have done, how they feel about writing, what they think their strengths and weaknesses are.

OCTOBER

Well, with my kids, writing seems to be the least popular indoor sport. They hate it with a passion. Furthermore, they haven't done very much of it. While I don't want to snoop on my colleagues, it's clear from the kids' papers that very little composition is done any place in this school. I suspect that some of the badness of the writing results, then, not from stupidity or inarticulateness, but from inexperience and lack of confidence. To remedy that I'm already going to change my agenda, cutting down on the formal papers and just having the kids write and write and write on a range of personal topics.

NOVEMBER
I'm beginning to see some growth, but damn, it's slow! I've been trying to concentrate my comments on the positive that I find in the kids' work, and there are some genuinely bright spots—good metaphors, moments of truth, and so on. But I've also hit a snag: I don't know how to put grades on the papers. For instance, yesterday one "nonwriter" turned in a paper that, for the first time, revealed something of him as a writer and human being. Yet the paper was poorly punctuated and spelled. I certainly didn't want to give it a C, for that would discourage the student; but it wasn't an A paper either. And I can't stand the idea of double grades: one for content and one for mechanics. I think I'm going to try a system that I read about someplace where papers are either graded A (for accepted by the teacher) or ? (If there is some doubt about how hard the student worked). While I can see some flaws, maybe this system will give me the freedom to think writing rather than grades.

DECEMBER
I've got the end-of-term blues, I think. My A/? system worked well on individual papers, but in the end, the grading system got me: I couldn't give kids all As so I wound up having to punish some kids for being nonwriters in the first place. The teacher in the next room tried some sort of contract system and I believe I'll try that next term. That is, if I even continue the program next term. I'm really weary of carrying home a briefcase full of student writing night after night.

JANUARY
Trouble! I got called down to the office today to talk with the principal. He was waving a page of kid writing around in front of me and talking about morality and public opinion. It seems he got his hands on one of my kid's informal writings from earlier in the term, a piece that used a couple of four-letter words and openly discussed the fears of an unwanted teenage pregnancy. I had written back empathizing with the writers' feelings, trying to show understanding, but not judging or offering advice. The boss says that I should have condemned both the language and the very thought of teenage "fornication." I am, he says, "condoning immorality" by not censoring the kids' thoughts and their behavior. I guess for my own protection I'll have to caution the kids about their writing topics.

More trouble from on high. The statewide assessment scores come back last week, and our school ranked among the lower percentiles in the district. Nobody seems to acknowledge that we're competing with some high-power suburban schools, where all the kids come from academic or professional homes in which literacy is prized. Somehow, we're supposed to make our kids perform just like those from Plasticville. The principal says he wants more basics: more spelling, more grammar, more vocabulary, and we are to document the regularity with which we teach this stuff. Of course, I teach all of these every day when I am having my students write, but that's not what The Man wants. How can I teach writing if I have to spend all my time on drill?

FEBRUARY
I set up something I call Correctness Corner (one of my kids wanted to call it Korrecknus Kawner) in my room, stocked with all the handbooks, plus some proofreading posters. The kids are to go there whenever they are polishing a paper for reading by an audience. The principal saw it, and although he frowned at my jazzy posters, he thought the whole idea was just fine. The kids don't mind it, and it has gotten me back in the good graces of the administration.

MARCH
There's just no other conclusion possible. I've got to empty out my briefcase. I can't keep bringing home 150 essays a week. I'm bitchy around home, and I'm spending all my time as a theme grader. I'm depressed about my teaching, even though the kids' writing is getting demonstrably better. This isn't a matter of good or bad teaching; it's a matter of survival.

I heard about "teacherless teaching" at a conference today, and it may be my salvation. The speaker argued that we must help students learn to edit their own writing rather than always doing it for them. She puts the kids into small groups and has them react to their writing. She also does a lot of publishing of kids' writing, which provides an outlet and makes writing seem real. I think I'll give it a whirl.

APRIL
We saw the first robin of spring today, and one of the kids said, "Don't look at that bird, 'cuz in here you'll just have to write a poem about it!" Everybody laughed. Me too. The kids still grumble about having to write so much, but they're getting better at it, and I think they are finding it genuinely satisfying, at least much of the time. The small editorial groups have made the point to the kids that they have to take responsibility for their own work, and it allows me to make my criticism and commentary oral, in class, rather than on the papers, ex post facto. Of course, I'm still reading everything the kids write, but when I don't have to put detailed comments on each and every paper, the burden is tolerable.

MAY
We published our first classroom magazine today, and the kids (and I) were really excited. It was no masterpiece as far as magazine design is concerned: just mimeographed pages with a linoleum-block cover done in art class, but everybody is happy about it. I'm certain my kids never believed they would see themselves in print, the

school literary magazine being out of bounds for all but advanced placement kids. Each student got two copies and almost everybody wanted more. We may have to print a second edition. Most impressive to me was that somehow – by hook or crook – the kids got their writing into creditable shape: The book is "properly" spelled and punctuated and so on. Only one blight on the day: I showed the book to the principal, whose only comment was that the poems must have been plagiarized, since average students aren't supposed to be capable of writing that well.

JUNE

Last day of classes. It has been a pretty good year, and the kids and I knew it. This week I asked them to select their best piece of writing for the year and to recopy it into a blank bound book that I circulated. Told them I wanted to keep some of their writing as a souvenir. The kids also added some autographs, yearbook-style, that were fun. All in all, the classes seemed like an episode of "Welcome Back, Kotter," rather than the real-world place where I've met those 150 kids the past 180 days.

I'd like to be able to claim smashing success in making the kids writers, but I can't. Out in the "real world" many of my students won't write any better than they did last September. But on the other hand, many of them will, and I'm pleased to claim some of the credit for that. I can also say with certainty that every kid who walked in the door last September has had at least one, and in most cases several, smashing successes with writing.

If I had to pick an average specimen from my souvenir book, I suppose it would be this piece by Bill Willis, a kid who came to me as a nonwriter – hostile, in fact – and who will never do much writing beyond high school.

> This is the last week of school. In another week I'll be getting a job. Then I will be able to buy a bike.
>
> Not a Japanese bike. Not an English bike. But an all-American machine, a Harley-Davidson; the biggest, the heaviest, and the classiest hunk of iron ever built.
>
> Not a store-bought bike, but something that you build and know inside out. Something that you make with your own hands, and your own imagination, after you sweat and swear and make sacrifices for.
>
> You take a big, bulky old hog, and make a lean, lithe, athletic, bone-jarring machine, a chopper.
>
> You love it because it is part of you. Part of your mind and part of your body. It becomes your best friend. It may seem funny that you could love a hunk of metal, but I know I will. You can't feel that way with store-bought bikes.*

*Thanks to Rita Hansen, the Chicago Public Schools, who shared this writing with us.

Deathless prose, it isn't. But it is powerful and vigorous, and above all it is literate. I enjoy its natural rhythm and imagery. Bill can now use English with confidence.

All in all, I'd have to rate my August Resolution Project as a modest success. I haven't succeeded all the way down the line, but the satisfactions were enough that I plan to be a writing teacher again next year as I start out with an empty briefcase.

Besides, I'm still smoking about a pack a day. I wish I could be half as successful at kicking that habit.

SECTION C

Language Study

word ;(and) ing?...

INTRODUCTION

Notes on a Language Activities Curriculum

We've been on a "back-to-basics" kick, right?

Right!

And that means back to *grammar,* right?

Wrong!

Or at least, let's hope it's wrong. There's no hard evidence to suggest that formal, traditional grammar, taught for so many years, made students better users of language in speaking or in writing. Indeed, one can even argue that the repetitive, year-after-year study of the same approach to language may actually have been harmful because it kept students from other classroom language experiences. Yet we've seen evidence that a number of different secondary-school grammar texts popular a decade or two ago are threatening to regain that popularity *now.*

And we fear their return, less because of the approach to language they fostered—though their attention to "correctness" is, we think, terribly misguided—but more because the series texts seemed so identical from volume to volume, from year to year. The grammar approach begins each year working from small particles (parts of speech) to "wholes" (whole sentences, whole paragraphs) with a repetitiveness that is bound to destroy an interest in language in even the most able student.

What is needed in language study is great flexibility, freedom for teachers and students to pursue all kinds of classroom language experiences, among which one—but only one—is grammar. In a time of great national attention to the ways in which our students use (more often, say critics, *misuse*) language, we must phil-

Portions of this section and chapter 20, "Language Fun and Games," were drafted by Professor Ted Hipple, the University of Florida.

osophically and practically commit ourselves to classroom language study. Quite properly, the days when we turned to language only as a break from literature are gone forever.

At the same time, however, we have to remember that teaching is time bound. We must order our priorities at least partly along temporal lines: class periods spent in teaching A cannot be used to teach B. A valuable period spent in teaching, say, grammar, cannot be recalled for a lesson on dialects. And there's the rub. There's a lot to do in the study of language, much more for us to teach and our students to learn than there are days available for that teaching and learning. There's fascinating information about dialects we want our students to have, not the least of which is the liberating knowledge that the dialect people use is but a poor guide to their characters. There's the study of semantics and of doublespeak, of usage, of language history, of vocabulary, of the language of literature. And we haven't even mentioned writing.

The bottom line is a profound question: From the plethora of riches, what language do we choose to teach to assure that our students become better users of language? The plural "explorations" suggests that no one exploration, no one field of study, no matter how thoroughly taught and learned, will adequately answer the bottom-line questions. Instead, there are to be *many* explorations, chosen according to some guidelines we feel comfortable about using. Time must be one of the guidelines. Do we have time for this study? But other guidelines are important, too. We'd like to suggest these six:

1. What we choose to teach must be learnable by our students. Some concepts in language study are rather sophisticated: the writing of thesis sentences, for example, or the language of subtle persuasion. If our students can't handle them, teaching these concepts should be delayed. Astonishing amounts of time in language-study classes have been wasted trying to teach difficult abstractions about language to young people who, quite simply, weren't ready.

2. What we choose to teach is not necessarily incorrectly chosen if it happens to be fun for us and for our students. Fun in school doesn't need to be a Friday afternoon commodity "when all the serious work is completed." It can and should be a part of the total plan. As we'll argue in the next chapter, "fun" is an intrinsic, not frivolous, part of language exploration.

3. What we choose to teach should be directed at least as much toward increasing student comfort with language as toward achieving surface correctness. Too many teachers today, in seeking the latter, lessen the former. Students become almost tongue-tied in their fears of misusing a pronoun or saying "lie" instead of "lay." When comfort is our goal, correctness will follow naturally.

4. What we choose to teach must be based on our understanding of how the language works. For generations teachers have presented half-truths to their students about the nature of "good" English and "correct" speech. With the number of good language and linguistic books and courses around, there's no excuse for a teacher not giving students accurate information about language.

5. What we choose to teach must permit evaluations that focus on the positive, on what students can do, and not exclusively, or even mainly, on what they cannot do.

6. What we choose to teach must be centered on student's actual use of language. This is a language *activities* program, by which we mean that we believe students come to know and use language more successfully not by studying it or doing exercises about it, but by using it and coming to understand how their language use succeeds and fails, how it naturally employs a wide range of interesting language principles.

All of these guidelines may be subsumed under one goal: No matter what our area of language study, *we want our students to feel better about themselves as users of language as a result of that study.* Students who believe that they can use language effectively are right more often than not. They *can* use language effectively. Perhaps not always *correctly* from a purist's point of view. There may be an occasional fragment, a run-on sentence, or some unconventional spelling, but a continual focus on language explorations that meet these six guidelines will go a long way toward removing or lessening the incidence of these kinds of errors.

Our language is one in which the teacher has a large and ever-growing collection of language activities that meet all or most of the guidelines we've suggested. In this curriculum, some activities may take several days or even longer, others only a few minutes. Some activities the teacher plans carefully in advance of the class period; others come to mind and are used spontaneously.

It would be impossible to provide more than a few activities, but in the next four chapters we present some we've had success with, and possibly they'll be equally successful for you. At the very least, they'll provide you starting points for your own repertory.

CHAPTER 20

Language Fun and Games

Mrs. Jaypher

A poem to be read 'sententiously and with grave importance':

Mrs. Jaypher found a wafer
Which she stuck upon a note;
This she took and gave the cook.
Then she went and bought a boat
Which she paddled down the stream
Shouting: "Ice produces cream,
Beer when churned produces butter!
Henceforth all the words I utter
Distant ages thus shall note. . . ."
—Edward Lear (1812–1888)

To Make an Amblongus Pie

Take 4 pounds (say 4½ pounds) of fresh Amblongusses, and put them in a small pipkin.

Cover them with water and boil them for 8 hours incessantly, after which add 2 pints of new milk, and proceed to boil for 4 hours more.

When you have ascertained that the Amblongusses are quite soft, take them out and place them in a wide pan, taking care to shake them well previously.

Grate some nutmeg over the surface, and cover them

carefully with powdered gingerbread, curry-powder, and a
sufficient quantity of Cayenne pepper.

Remove the pan into the next room, and place it on
the floor. Bring it back again, and let it simmer for
three-quarters of an hour. Shake the pan violently till
all the Amblongusses have become of a pale purple colour.

Then, having prepared the paste, insert the whole
carefully, adding at the same time a small pigeon, 2
slices of beef, 4 cauliflowers, and any number of oysters.

Watch patiently till the crust begins to rise, and
add a pinch of salt from time to time.

Serve up in a clean dish, and throw the whole out of
the window as fast as possible.

—Edward Lear

Edward Lear knew just about as well as anybody that language use is fun and games, and in this era of "back to basics," it is important for teachers not to forget the very important role that language *play* has in our mastery of English. Both adults and children enjoy the humorous use of language—puns, riddles, jokes, rhymes, puzzles, and satire. Children naturally create humor through language, and they respond to it with ease, without the intervention of teachers or instructors.

Language play, of course, goes well beyond humor, for most good speakers and writers have a sense of "the play of language," that is, a feeling for words and language which allows them to explore and exploit the richness of English to make their meaning clear. Secondary students, we think, also need to gain this sense of the play of language. We propose, then, that a regular feature of the English class be the use of language and word-play games. While the resources are too numerous for us to list, the following sampler of games will give you an indication of the possibilities:

Word Games

Many newspapers carry the anagrammatic JUMBLE each day. Not only can you direct students to these, but you can urge that they create their own. Similarly, the *word-seek* or *find-a-word* puzzles in the papers can be challenging for your students, both as exercises to complete and as games to create. Later, you can take the better jumbles or word-seek puzzles developed by your students and put them on dittos. Seeing their own creations in print, with their names attached, can go a long way towards developing pride, comfort, and skill in language.

So also will other games, like these:

Hink-pink. In Hink-Pink, students create a rhyming adjective-noun combination and provide its definition, with the other students and you trying to guess the rhyme. For example, the *chief of police* is the "top cop" (or, as some students say, the "big pig"). A *short poem:* a "terse verse." A Hinky-Pinky (the name of the game expands according to the number of syllables in the combination) for a *more stupid hitchhiker* is a "dumber thumber"; a *tax on pulchritude* is a "beauty duty." A Hinkety-Pinkety for a tree surgeon is an "organic mechanic." A Hinketetie-Pinketetie for a *middle European farmer* is a "Bavarian agrarian"; a *New Yorker's whiskey cabinet* is a "Knickerbocker liquor locker." Students can create their own hink-pinks and test their friends.

My gramma's game. My gramma likes apples, not oranges; books, not magazines; floors, not ceilings; pillows, not beds. Why these strange likes and dislikes? When the clues are written, it's not difficult to see that Gramma's preference is for things identified by words with double letters in them. Spoken words are another matter entirely and some of your students may need twenty or thirty clues. But then let them create their own "Gramma likes" lists. Gramma can prefer things named with words that begin with vowels, have three syllables, contain a silent letter, etc.

Odd man (person) out. Who doesn't belong in the following scheme: (1) J. Randolph Adams, (2) P. Nelson Kennedy, (3) C. Arnold Jackson, (4) D. Edward Blake, (5) L. Clark Grant. Did you choose number 4 because all the others had last names that were also the names of presidents? What about this one? (1) Grace H. Iverson, (2) Rachel S. Turner, (3) Diana A. Nelson, (4) Alice B. Croft, (5) Janice K. Long. Did you note the alphabetical order of all the initials except number 3's? Let your students write their own odd man out schemes and share them with their friends. (Caution: Sometimes more than one answer can be defended.)

Panagrams. A panagram is a sentence that contains every letter of the alphabet. When you change ribbons or clean the type, you probably have typed a panagram to test out the typewriter: "The quick brown fox jumped over the lazy dog." That panagram requires thirty-five characters to squeeze in all twenty-six letters of the alphabet, and language gamers have delighted in trying to write shorter ones, such as: "Pack my box with five dozen liquor jugs" (thirty-two letters). Some years ago, the *Saturday Review* conducted a contest with a case of soda crackers as first prize for the shortest panagram. (You might conduct a similar contest with a reward of a Burger King "Whopper" or a McDonald's "Big Mac.") The *SR* winner came in with this twenty-eight-letter gem: "Blowzy frights vex and jump quick." Unfortunately, its semantics—its very Englishness—is marginal. The following twenty-eight-letter panagram is more comprehensible, but it violates an unwritten rule of panagrams, that the use of proper names is not allowed: "Waltz, nymph, for quick jigs vex Bud."

➡ *Single-letter words.* Try this quiz with your students: What letter of the alphabet is . . . a bug? (B); a beverage? (T); a vegetable? (P); something to look with? (I); a cry of surprise? (O); to be in debt? (O); the person one speaks to? (U). Let your students make up more of these homonymic letter quizzes.

➡ *Teakettle.* Have your students develop lists of homonyms: marry/merry; sea/see; bark (dog's noise)/bark (tree cover); play (drama)/play (to entertain myself); ball (round object)/ball (fancy dance). Then have them make up sentences either orally or in writing, replacing the homonym with the word *teakettle* (the word can be changed to represent inflections):

"My mother is *teakettling* the dress I am going to wear to the party."

"*Teakettle* is a very import element in making steel."

Or, to make it easier (or harder) throw in a third homonym: "My dad prefers his nine *teakettle* when he's this close to the green." Answer: iron. Students playing make guesses and the one (won) with the right (write) answer presents the next pair (pear) of sentences.

➡ *Hominibles.* In *Word Play* (New York: Hawthorne Books, 1972), Joseph Shipley describes the game of "hominibles," which involves finding homonyms of words and phrases, then using synonyms of the sound-alike words to create puzzles and "chains" of language like:

Why is a sheet of paper like a lazy dog?

A *ruled sheet* is an *ink-lined plane.*

An *inclined plane* is a *slope up.*

A *slow pup* is a *lazy dog.*

➡ *Spelling and vocabulary games.* While the purpose of language games is expressly *not* to overwhelm students with instruction about language, we would be remiss if we did not point out that a great many language games also *teach.* Thus, "Scrabble," an enormously popular word game, reinforces vocabulary and spelling and pushes students into exploring new words. The old parlor game Ghost does the same orally. Participants sit in a circle and add letters onto a one-letter base. The person who cannot think of a letter to add that might lead to a word, or the person who adds a letter that actually makes a word, receives a letter from the word G-H-O-S-T. When a player has spelled GHOST, he or she must drop out of the game.

Crossword puzzles and word searches, both extraordinarily popular with students, also fit into this category of games that teach—through fun.

Punctuation games. Again with caution, we will mention that punctuation skills can also be taught and reinforced through games, though it would be a disaster if teachers attempted to convert language games into a "method" for teaching difficult or abstruse skills. In *Fun with Words* (Prentice-Hall, 1972), Maxwell Nurnberg poses some of these traditional puzzles which involve punctuation problems:

> . . . Punctuate the following, once as a request for information, once as an insult.
>
> What's the latest dope
>
> [Answers: What's the latest dope? (Inquiry)
> What's the latest, dope? (Insult)]
>
> . . . Punctuate the following so that instead of forbidding, it allows aquatic activity:

To invite swimming:

There are numerous other kinds of language games, some commercial, some made up. It's well worth noting how many of these meet all the guidelines for a language activities curriculum. That they both require and encourage some concentrated thinking is an added bonus.

Exploring the Alphabet

Writing in *The English Journal* (April 1977), Diana Mitchell described a junior-high project that involved both children's literature and language play. She brought in a number of alphabet books to her class and asked the students to analyze the patterns of presenting the alphabet to young children. Sometimes, for example, the writer will present one object for each letter (A is for Apple, B is for Ball). Another strategy is to combine a number of words beginning with the letter to create what's known as an *Alphabettor:* "Avery's animals attacked altogether, biting the bees, bears, and birds, caught and captured by Cooley's cautious company, . . ." The students then developed their own illustrated alphabet books with original rhymes, verses, and patterns of instruction.

We think this unit might also be a good unit in which to introduce an informal discussion of sound-alphabet relationships, helping to disabuse students of the idea that every letter represents a single sound, or that there is a necessary connection between alphabet symbols and the sounds they have have chosen to represent.

Kids might also enjoy exploring the evolution of the contemporary alphabet, seeing, for example, how the various letters have progressed from pictographic forms ages ago to their present shape and significance.

Language and Pictures

Many teachers have had their students write concrete poetry, a word-play variation in which students write the poem in a shape to represent the topic so that, say, a poem about a flower looks like a flower. For an excellent resource, see Milton Klonsky's *Speaking Pictures: A Gallery of Pictorial Poetry from the Sixteenth Century to the Present* (New York: Harmony Books, 1975). Lavonne Mueller, an English teacher in DeKalb, Illinois, took concrete poetry a step further and made it three-dimensional. She describes having her students create a "Word Museum" for the school library (*The English Journal* [May 1974]). The students studied early examples of visual language—pictographs, hieroglyphs, etc.—then created three-dimensional rendering of words. "*Wax*" was created of chunks of candle wax, then melted into a droopy sculpture where the medium was the message. One student carefully shaped dirt into letters and grew a rendering of "*grass.*" "*Boxed In*" came in the form of a series of Chinese boxes, and so on. Students created puzzles of cookies, embroidered words onto cloth, and sculpted words into clay. Fun and games? Yes. But Mueller also reports that in the process the students' understanding of the relationship between symbol and object—word and thing—grew enormously.

Graffiti Wall

Visit your local newspaper and ask for a newsprint end roll. This is the core of the huge rolls on which the newspaper is printed. When these get small, they are discarded, but typically enough paper is on them for you to put three-foot-wide strips on one or two walls of your classroom. (Shelf or wrapping paper will also do.) This becomes your graffiti wall, the wall on which your students can write or draw or paste anything—so long as it will not get you fired or in trouble. (The profanity or obscenity they can save for the rest room.) Also, they can't put anything on the wall that will embarrass another student. Things like "Call Sally for a hot time" are no-nos. But, otherwise, it's the students' wall. They can write slogans on it or verses of songs. They can draw on it, using crayon or paints. They can paste things on it, cartoons or pictures or newspaper items. Whatever they put on it, they'll be communicating. And that's the goal.

In a slightly more structured variation of the graffiti wall, Lavonne Mueller, whose interest in graphics and language was described in the previous section, covered the walls and even the *floor* of her creative writing class with butcher paper and brought in a variety of writing implements—pencils, pens, felt-tip markers, crayons, grease pencils, charcoals, and so on—to encourage students not only to experiment with writing but to gain a sense of how writing with different kinds of instruments affects how one composes—and even thinks and feels.

The Language of Advertising

As much as we lament the crude appeals of many advertisements on television and in the papers, advertising language is among the most innovative around. Ad people are constantly working to come up with new slogans, pitches, and jingles to attract us to their products. Studying ads is thus a good language activity. Such study has a real-world dimension. Ads do, after all, exist in the daily newspaper, on TV, and on billboards. Students are aware that they attend to and are influenced by advertising. Thus, your classroom focus on those advertising techniques frequently will strike responsive chords in your students, who see that they are persuaded by these very techniques.

Have your students create their own ads, a natural follow-up activity to a study of advertising methods. Their creations can cover the gamut of advertising, including fully developed and choreographed commercials that are captured for perpetuity (or at least until the end of the year) on the school's videotape machine. Simpler assignments, however, can do much the same job. Here are several activities:

The radio commercial. Ask students to use tape cassettes to record their carefully planned thirty-second or one-minute radio "message." What background music, if any, will they have? Will their talk be loud or soft? Fast or slow? To what age group will they pitch their commercial? To what socioeconomic level? To what educational level? What will they use as their attention-getting opener? Their closing pitch? Best question of all: What words will they use? Questions like these can provide the impetus for some good thinking and learning about language.

The billboard. Talk about billboards. What makes them eye-catching? The colors? The use of white space? Their placement? The product they are advertising? The language on the billboard? After such discussions your students may be primed to create their own billboards, either for existing products or for ones of their imagination. These can then be displayed for the rest of the class.

Classified ads. Let students write their own classified ads. Using newspaper models will provide them with an understanding of the need for precision, clarity, and economy in word choice. Their ads can be on any topic—help wanted, personal, whatever—but we've experienced the most success with the "for sale" type, which leads to an actual "classifieds" paper. If Tom has a basketball for sale, he writes an ad and turns it in. When enough such ads are available, put them on a ditto and give students a copy. A student who wants to buy a basketball then contacts Tom. For both seller and buyer this transaction illustrates a real purpose for language proficiency. (If you want, you can even charge students so much a word—say, a nickel, with a fifty-cent maximum—and use the money to buy paperbacks or posters for your classroom.)

Study the jingles of commercial ads. What does it mean to say "Winston tastes good like a cigarette should" or "Ford has a better idea"?

Examine double meaning and word play in ads.

"The quickest way to a man's heart is through his feet." (SLIPPERS)

"Decorate your family tree with Polaroid Colors." (FILM) (A picture of a family in a Christmas ad)

"Ever wonder what your panties say behind your back?" (PANTY HOSE)

"Who could make light of themselves better?" (LOW-TAR CIGARETTES)

"They begged for it, so we bagged it." (DOG FOOD)

Look for truth in advertising. Some secondary-school classes have investigated the claims made in advertisements. *Does* ZIP code make the mail move faster? *Does* Ford offer "a better idea"?

Examine "waffle" words in advertising. Many ads use words that seem to make a claim but do not. Thus, to say "No toothpaste gets teeth whiter than Bright-O" implies, but does not state, "Bright-O gets your teeth whiter than any other kind of toothpaste." Similarly, words like *new, bigger, improved, brighter, whiter,* and *tastes better* frequently leave out comparisons that would make realistic assessment possible. Better than what? Brighter than what? By collecting examples of waffle words, students can become more sensitive to the abuse of language, not only in advertising, but in other kinds of writing as well.

CHAPTER 21

A Curriculum for George (Orwell)

> Most people who bother with the matter at all would admit that the English language is in a bad way, but it is generally assumed that we cannot by conscious action do anything about it. Our civilization is decadent, and our language—so the argument runs—must inevitably share in the general collapse. It follows that any struggle against the abuse of language is sentimental archaism, like preferring candles to electric light or hansom cabs to aeroplanes. Underneath this lies the half-conscious belief that language is a natural growth and not an instrument which we shape for our own purposes. . . . [The English language] becomes ugly and inaccurate because our thoughts are foolish, but the slovenliness of our language makes it easier for us to have foolish thoughts. The point is, the process is reversible.*

More articulately than most writers, and certainly with more vigor than many linguists, George Orwell discussed the problems of the use and misuse of language. Unlike some contemporary writers who talk of language use with wailing and gnashing of teeth (see Edwin Newman's petulant discussions of language misuse or any of Jacques Barzun's tirades on contemporary English), Orwell recognized the complexity of the interrelationship between thinking and language and avoided the simplistic thinking that argues that if we "correct" people's use of English, we will somehow have solved the problem of language misuse.

Some would argue that not much has been done to reverse the process of

* From "Politics and the English Language" in *Shooting an Elephant and Other Essays* (1946) by George Orwell. Reprinted by permission of Harcourt Brace Jovanovich, Inc.

language "decline" during the thirty-odd years since Orwell wrote "Politics and the English Language." Whether or not there is "decline" in English is not an issue to be debated here. "The point is"—to borrow from Orwell—"the process is reversible." And given the current nationwide interest in honesty in public language, there may be no better time for English teachers to make a major contribution to language use by developing "A Curriculum for George."

Our "curriculum" is, in effect, a program to increase language consciousness. We think it important for young people to develop a fairly sophisticated understanding of the complexities of language and meaning making. The traditional language curriculum, with its emphasis on *naming* (parts of speech, types of sentences) and *fixed usage* has had the negative effect of diminishing people's awareness of the complexity of language. While there are hundreds of exciting activities that one can use in the English classroom (see the previous chapter), we will concentrate this chapter on two areas of language study that seem to us central to "A Curriculum for George": language and mind control, and the meaning of meaning.

Language and Mind Control

Orwell spoke extensively about language and mind control in *1984,* an excellent novel for study in secondary schools.

Doublespeak, his term for language that says one thing and deliberately means another, exists not only in the imaginary world of *1984,* but in contemporary real-world language. Each year the Committee on Public Doublespeak of the National Council of Teachers of English presents "awards" for gross misuse of English. One year, for example, the committee gave the Doublespeak award to a terrorist leader who said, "It is precisely because we have been advocating coexistence that we have shed so much blood."

Your students can quickly come up with doublespeak examples at least as dreadful, and collecting examples sharpens their sense of the pervasiveness of doublespeak and the ways in which it subtly works on people's minds. One of our favorites comes from an official of the College Entrance Examination Board attempting to mask CEEB's bafflement over the SAT decline by saying, "I cannot think of a single explanation that does not seem implausible, or at least, unlikely, given some of the data available."

Antidoublespeak activities for your classroom can include:

- Let kids write doublespeak, the most abominable, two-faced, misleading prose they can manage. This activity is *not* meant to justify the use of doublespeak, but to help students understand it through actual use. (A variation we've tried with success: Have Students write a Super-Patriotic All-American speech for a politician trying to woo the folks back home on the Fourth of July.)

► John H. Clarke had students prepare a media show, "One Minute of Hate," similar to the indoctrination sessions described in Orwell's *1984*. Another class watched the presentation, and calloused kids were astonished at the extent to which the program successfully aroused and manipulated their emotions. (See "One Minute of Hate: Multi-Media Misuse Pre-1984," *The English Journal* 63 [October 1974]).

► The morality of persuasion has been debated for thousands of years. Without attempting to force kids to reach "definitive" conclusions on age-old questions, invite students to consider problems like the following:

- Are politicians unethical when they use propaganda and advertising techniques to "sell" themselves?
- Is there any time when the use of doublespeak is justified?
- Is it legitimate for a public speaker to "bend" the truth or tell only half the truth in order to make a point?
- Is it right for an attorney to persuade a jury of the innocence of a person whom he or she knows to be guilty?

► Let students write two essays arguing the different sides of a hotly debatable issue. What do they feel happening to themselves when they argue the points they don't believe?

► Have students write two versions of a proposal—say, a request to the principal to subsidize a new publication or a student lounge—one done in very simple, plain language, the other done as eloquently and persuasively as possible. Is it possible to write a proposal in a "high" language without falling into the clutches of doublespeak? What techniques, ideas, and strategies do they discover in the process?

► Collect a batch of newspaper editorials or columns and ask students to analyze the use of emotional language, doubletalk, and overgeneralization. Students may enjoy rewriting biased editorials in "neutral" language.

The Meaning of Meaning

It is important to engage students in the analysis of language in daily use—collecting examples of doublespeak, assessing the media, analyzing ads, and so forth. But to place "A Curriculum for George" on a solid foundation, one needs to go further, helping students gain some understanding of the nature of language and how it shapes and is shaped by human thought. "The meaning of meaning" is the field of study of general semantics, best known in this country through the writing of S. I. Hayakawa, such as *Language in Thought and Action* (New York: Harcourt Brace Jovanovich, 1972). Among the skills with which the semanticists want to equip people are:

■ recognizing that words are symbols, not things in themselves;

■ knowing that words are abstractions, and that any abstraction is necessarily inaccurate to some degree;

■ seeing how the misuse of words can create misunderstandings among people;

■ recognizing the differences between connotative and denotative language;

■ seeing the importance of defining terms; and

■ moving away from "two-valued" judgments to perceive that things need not always be judged on a simplistic "good-bad" basis.

Some classroom activities:

➡ Let students play with the difficult task of defining *language.* What is language? Where does it come from? How does language mean? What does meaning mean? While engaging in this kind of discussion, students will sharpen their awareness of the nature of language and the role it plays in shaping and being shaped by thinking.

➡ A corollary activity is to ask the students to speculate about how life would change if language and communication were different than they are presently. What if we communicated solely by telegraph rather than words? Or used gestures exclusively? What if we communicated directly—mind to mind—without the use of language?

➡ An exciting language unit based on science fiction has been described by Beverly Friend in "Strange Bedfellows: Science Fiction, Linguistics, and Education" (*The English Journal* 62 [October 1973]). Friend explores ways in which language has been treated in science fiction, including languages of color, music, and computers. She also describes several science fiction works that discuss the use of language as a means of thought control.

➡ Assign your students the task of keeping a one-day or several-days log of their encounters with language. What language forms (speech, writing, media) do they encounter most frequently? What kinds of ideas and information enter through those various sources? Which means of "languaging" do they select most frequently for their own purposes?

➡ Pick a common household word—*television, dog, cat, mother, spoon*—and ask the students to list every possible association they have with the word. Compare lists to help show how a single common set of symbols—*d-o-g*—can create an incredible range of "meanings" for different individuals.

➡ Assign the students the task of expressing an opinion about which they feel very strongly *without using words.* They may use collage or montage, film, photo essay, slide tape, or sound tape. In what ways are the students' abilities to "say" things limited? In what ways, if any, does composing in a nonverbal medium *enhance* the ease with which they can communicate?

➡ Explain to the class how dictionary makers collect citations (examples of a word in daily use) as a way of creating definitions. Then assign the class a common word—*run, walk, sleep, car, ball*—and have them create a definition based solely on examples of use that they find in speech or print. How long does it take them to get enough citations to create a definition? (Hint: Choosing a word that functions as two parts of speech—e.g., *run*—nicely complicates the issue.) Use this activity to help students see the ways in which "meanings" come into existence.

➡ Have kids look for examples in speech or print of clashes or struggles created, in part, by misunderstandings about the use of words or terms.

➡ As part of a journal-writing assignment have students write an analysis of what they see as one of their own deep-seated biases or prejudices. Where in their past did this bias come from? What kinds of emotionally loaded words are associated with the prejudice? In what ways do students feel that this bias was "created by the misuse of language"?

➡ Have the students collect the words that are used to demean racial and ethnic minorities—*nigger, wop, spic, dago, kike*—and discuss how these words distort perceptions.

➡ Let students create nonsense languages like the one used in Lewis Carroll's "Jabberwocky." How do words in such languages come to take on "meaning"?

➡ As a class project, let the students create a new "mystery word," a new symbol for something common, say, calling a hamburger a *snurfburn.* How do other people react to the mystery word?

➡ Martin Luther King, Jr. once wrote: "A riot is the language of the unheard." Ask students to discuss the possible meanings of that statement; then engage them in conversation about the ways in which language and communication failures produce violence.

➡ A number of semanticists have argued that the *popular song* is a form of deceptive language, creating images of love and life that are simply not accurate. Have students analyze contemporary song lyrics with this in mind. Or let students study the images of love and life projected in songs of different eras. How has the vision of American love changed from "Toot-Toot-Tootsie, Goodbye," to "Havin' My Baby"?

➡ Have students eavesdrop on a conversation. How do ideas build upon one another in free-floating conversation? Who controls the direction of discussion? How does he or she use language to accomplish it?

➡ Edward Hall has written of the "silent languages" that affect our lives (*The Silent Language,* New York: Doubleday, 1959). He describes silent languages of *time* (we have set rules and expectations about punctuality) and *space* (we resent, for example, the intrusion of strangers in our turf). Get a copy of Hall's book; browse through it; then get students to discuss some of the other "silent languages" that surround them. For instance, there are languages, codes, and rituals that surround *dating,* and students can explore approved and disapproved messages that people send to each other. Professional sports also abound with silent languages. Your students can probably analyze in detail when it is appropriate for a defense cornerback to help the offensive tight end to his feet just seconds after having knocked him down.

CHAPTER 22

Teaching about Grammars

Grammar probably consumes more time and energy and generates more discussion, debates, and downright hostility than any other component of the English curriculum. We have teachers who say they are *for* grammar and those who are against. We have traditional grammarians, who argue for a return to basics; structuralists, who hold that the traditionalists are inept and inaccurate grammarians; and transformationalists, who claim that the structuralists are conceptually simplistic and linguistically unimaginative. Then there are the so-called eclectic grammarians, who neatly avoid taking a stand and say, "I'll teach whatever works. Have you any interesting handouts?"

The brouhaha over grammar has had a debilitating effect on the English profession. Instead of talking about how to get kids to read more, write more, think more, and speak more, we've spent entirely too much time debating whether or not students ought to be studying *transitive* and *intransitive verbs, subject-predicate agreement,* and *pronoun reference.* (Graffiti: Do English teachers lay or lie better?) Seldom have combatants in the Great Grammar Debate bothered to begin their discussion by following a simple ground rule from general semantics: *Define your terms.* As dictionary makers know, words used in diverse situations take on multiple meanings. What an angry parent means when he or she asks, "Why don't you teach my kid *grammar?*" is not what a teacher means when he or she says, "I do not wish to teach formal *grammar,*" which is not what a linguist means when he or she says, "My *grammar* is superior to their *grammar.*"

In case you've never looked it up, here's what *Webster's Collegiate Dictionary* says about *grammar.* First, the derivation:

> OF. *grammaire,* fr. L. *grammatica,* fr. Gr. *fr. Gr. grammatike,* fem of *grammatikos* skilled in grammar, fr. *gramma* letter, fr. the root of *graphein* to write.*

It is interesting for us to note the very close historical ties here among *grammar,* the written language, and skill in language use. As we will show, this three-pronged emphasis has presented a great many problems for teachers.

Now the definitions:

1. The science treating of the classes of words, their inflections, and their syntactical relations and functions. . . .
2. A treatise on grammar.
3. Manner of speaking or writing, with reference to grammatical rules.

The key distinction is between the first and third meanings. The first definition is essentially that of a linguist or an informed teacher: Grammar is a study of the system of English, how words and sentences fit together in our language. (From here on, we'll call that grammar[1].) Grammar[3] has to do with language in actual use in society. In the eye of the public, this grammar[3] is incredibly broad in scope, ranging from whether to say "may I" or "can I" (before grabbing seconds on the mashed potatoes) to good penmanship to writing an essay that somebody else can understand.

Grammar[2] is a textbook, technically a "treatise" on grammar, but as often as not, you'll find that a grammar book contains a wide range of information about the language. Some of the material in a typical grammar book will have to do with the way sentences are put together, but often grammars or handbooks contain matters that are quite nongrammatical in focus (for example, how to look up a book in the library).

It seems clear to us that for generations teachers have been presenting grammar[1] (the system of English) through grammar[2] (textbooks that purport to be grammatical treatises) in an attempt to get students to master grammar[3] (speaking and writing correctly with reference to grammatical rules). Has it worked? Generations of school children know intuitively that the answer is "No."

* "Translation": *Grammar* is derived from the Old French *grammaire;* from the Latin *grammatica;* from the Greek *grammatike,* the feminine of *grammatikos,* meaning skilled in grammar; from *gramma,* letter; from the root of *graphein,* to write. *Webster's New Collegiate Dictionary* (Springfield, Mass.: The G. C. Merriam Co., 1975).

Presenting textbook rules does not help people speak and write more correctly or more accurately. Further, as any conference-going or journal-reading teacher recognizes, research on the connection between grammar[1] and grammar[3] has proven generally fruitless. It seems worthwhile to quote from a recent exhaustive review of the literature compiled by Elizabeth Haynes of the University of South Carolina:

> One of the chief ways used by teachers to improve the writing of students has been the study of traditional grammar, with its rule memorization, drills, diagramming, and the learning of grammatical terminology. In 1935 the Curriculum Commission of the National Council of Teachers of English reported that scientific studies had not shown that the study of grammar was effective in eliminating writing errors. Strom in 1960 published a study of over fifty studies which deal with whether the formal study of traditional grammar improved written composition and other skills in English. Summarizing studies by Hoyt (1906), Rapeer (1913), Segal and Barr (1926), Catternwood (1932), Cutright (1934), Frogner (1939), and many others, Strom concluded that a knowledge of traditional grammar has had little effect on accurate expression in writing and speaking.

But what of the newer grammars[1]—structural and transformational? Do they make a difference in students' performance with grammar[3]? Haynes concluded her summary:

> . . . *While traditional grammar may be included in the curriculum as a humane and interesting discipline, or as a body of knowledge worthy of study, it should not be taught as an aid to writing.* Likewise, . . . while there may be legitimate reasons for the teaching of transformational or structural grammar, teachers should be very cautious about the incorporation of this subject matter into the curriculum on the grounds that it will improve writing.*

* Elizabeth F. Haynes, "Using Research in Preparing to Teach Writing," *The English Journal* 67 (January 1978), pp. 82 and 86–87.

The conclusion is, to our way of thinking, abundantly clear: The evidence simply does not justify teaching large amounts of grammar in an effort to make children write and speak better. Nor does the clamor of parents, administrators, and school leaders for more basics affect this research. What the public and outsiders have been demanding will not produce the results that they would like to achieve.

Does this mean that teachers should not teach grammar at all? Or that they should, with suicidal commitment to principle, tell administrators and the public that they are not planning to inculcate students into the good grammar of English?

Not at all. Each of the grammars, [1], [2], and [3], has a place in the school program. Teachers would be wrong (not to mention naive) to say that they don't care about correctness or that "grammar doesn't matter." The problem, it seems to us, is in blurring distinctions between grammars, in teaching grammar[1] (the system) thinking that it will change grammar[3] (language use), and in teaching grammar[2] (the textbook) as if it were a sole arbiter of grammars [1] and [3].

The first two grammars—the system and textbooks—will be the subject of the remainder of this chapter. Grammar[3] encompasses a wide range of issues and problems and will be examined in detail in chapter 23, "Dialects and Correctness."

Teaching Grammar[1]: The System of Language

A key point in Elizabeth Haynes's review is her note that grammar "may be included in the curriculum as a humane and interesting discipline, or as a body of knowledge worthy of study." By that, she simply means that studying how English is put together is, in its own right, something interesting for students. We've found in our own teaching that when grammar study is separated from an obsession with correctness, students find it intriguing. Try something of the following with your students:

Linguistic explorations. "Linguistics" is a word that intimidates a good many teachers or reminds them of "new grammar" courses where they found themselves studying abstruse analytic systems that seem to have little to do with the real world of teaching. Yet in its simplest form, linguistics simply means the study of language—examining the language as it really is—and when isolated from attempts to improve students' syntax, linguistic explorations can be a delightful, informative variation of word play.

For example, a great many teachers have used Lewis Carroll's "Jabberwocky" with its nonsense words to help students see intuitive linguistic principles at work in their own minds.

> 'Twas *brillig,* and the *slithy toves*
> Did *gyre* and *gimbal* in the *wabe.*
> All *mimsey* were the *borogroves*
> And the *mome wrath outgrabe.*

The italicized words themselves were coined by Carroll to create particular images, and the students enjoy talking about words like *slithy, toves,* and *brillig* to discuss where the words come from and why they carry meaning, even when they don't appear in the dictionary.

Further, in an elementary parts of speech lesson, the students can understand that *outgrabe* is some sort of action; *toves* are things; *slithy* is an attribute of a *tove.* If the words are nonsense, how is it that we *know* how they work in the sentence? In this way, the teachers show students how much they know about English and its sophisticated structure without having to know definitions of *noun, verb, adjective.*

Ruth Taylor, who teaches in the Birmingham, Alabama, Public Schools, has described "Linguistic Experiment in the English Class: Easy, Interesting Exercises to Do (*The English Journal* 65 [December 1976]: 45–51). Among the activities she suggests are:

Excluded combinations. Have students create a series of nonsense words, e.g., *wonkalooney, brigabobble, marmulate.* Then help them see that many possible letter combinations—*zl, cm, pd*—were not selected. Thus students can see that English words are formed according to a *system,* and not just a random collection of letters.

Pluralization. Let the students write plurals of nonsense words. (Taylor uses a list developed by psychologist Jean Berko with words like *glot, ost, wug,* but you could just as easily use your own nonsense words from the previous list.) Thus: "One *wonkaloony.* Two __________." How is it that students can automatically supply the "correct" word: *wonkaloonies?*

Changing parts of speech. Students can also intuitively change nonsense words into other parts of speech, creating an opportunity for discussion of the "rules" that English speakers have mastered. Thus: "If a person *marmu-*

lates, he or she is a __________." Taylor proposes a range of intriguing related activities: "What would you call a man whose job is to zib?" (We'd add: "What would you call a woman who had the same job?") In this activity it is probably not even necessary that students realize that they are altering "parts of speech." Just recognizing the rule-governed nature of language is enough.

➡ *Artificial languages.* Continuing in her discussion of linguistic experiment, Ruth Taylor proposed having students study artificial languages to understand the principles of language structure. In exploring these, students come to see some of the sophisticated ways in which the language systems are formed.

➡ *The QV language.* The syntax or grammar of this language is based on two rules:

Each "string" or sentence begins and ends with Q.
Each string alternates Q and V.

Thus QVQVQVQ is grammatical, while QVVQVQ or QVQV is not. The students, not knowing the rules, generate test strings until they have deduced the rules.

➡ *The KIPO language.* Given the following matrix, the students try to create a set of rules that explain all the "regularities," a set of rules that would allow another person to create grammatical strings:

L A N T O K I P O S E D
G O P L E K I P O R I T
Z U G M A K I P O F A K
H I R V A K I P O M U G

In addition to the obvious "K-I-P-O" in each string, the students can create grammar rules to describe length of sentences, relationships among vowels and consonants, and so on.

➡ *Kalaba-X.* This game involves a bit of grammatical terminology, but makes teaching the distinction between subject and predicate clear. Kalaba-X sentences are generated as follows:

Predicate *Object + Modifier* *Subject + Modifier*

In Kalaba-X "Mary had a little lamb" is translated as follows:

Owns lamb little, Mary
Loves lamb, Mary little
Loves Mary pretty, lamb
Owns lamb, Mary pretty

Students can have all kinds of fun translating everyday sentences into Kalaba-X: "Going class history person this."

Most readers, too, will recognize that Kalaba-X has some elements in common with Pig Latin. Students can produce samples of Pig Latin or other artificial language forms which they know, then deduce the grammatical rules.

Among other things, such studies will help students come to understand what grammar[1] is and how and why it is so completely different from grammar[3].

Foreign languages. Each language has its own way of signaling connections, from highly inflected Latin, where endings of words are crucial and word placement is flexible, to English, where word placement is more important than endings. Depending on your own foreign language training and the availability of experts to help, conduct an informal series of investigations of foreign languages, say French, Spanish, German, Italian, Chinese, Japanese, or Russian. How do the signal systems differ?

Structural grammar. Structural grammar, first popularized in the early 1950s as an alternative to Latinate traditional grammar, was attacked in some linguistic circles for its inadequacy in explaining the generation of original utterances in English. Nevertheless, in contrast to both traditional and transformational grammar, structural grammars are especially useful in classifying the forms of words and phrases. It seems to us that structural definitions of parts of speech are more accurate and comprehensive than the conventional—"a noun is the name of a person, place, or thing"—and are much more comprehensible to students.

This book is not the place for us to go into a detailed explanation of structural grammar and its applications in the classroom. Instead we will recommend and briefly review an excellent school text (a grammar[2]), *Words and Sentences* by Mark Lester (New York: Random House, 1973), which suggests possibilities for classroom exploration.

Lester begins by presenting "words describing words," a discussion of good and bad definitions that explores some of the basic elements of classification. This groundwork is used to engage students in inductive classification of words in English, words showing traits as:

ending in *thing*
following *a, an, that*
ending in *ly*

From such study, the students develop elementary word classes (the structural grammarian's alternative to parts of speech). Eventually, the classes of words are refined and sharpened, so that the students develop a rather full structural English grammar, including some basic sentence patterns.

By treating grammar[1] as a subject for scientific study rather than the mastery of rules and regulations, Lester has written a book that, to our mind, is inviting and engaging, and we know of a number of schools where the approach has been tried successfully. In the process, of course, the students learn a great deal about the nature of language, but they also pick up a surprising amount of terminology.

Transformational grammar. Again, this is not the place for us to produce a transformational grammar for schoolroom use. In contrast to structural grammar, transformational grammar is especially useful in helping students understand the complexity of English syntax, its "rule-governed creativity" (the ways in which our knowledge of grammar helps us create new sentences), and understanding how a human being comes to master his native grammar in the first place.

Once again, Mark Lester has written a good little book, *Constructing an English Grammar* (New York: Random House, 1973), which provides a pedagogical structure for teachers. He presents the students with *Tobor,* a computer (whose name is *Robot* spelled backward), and the students are challenged to teach the computer to generate English sentences. (The problem is, in a sense, similar to the students' decoding of the Q-V and KIPO languages mentioned earlier.) Lester carefully guides the students in the writing of more and more complex phrase structure rules, then shows them how individual phrases and sentences can be "transformed" through computer operations.

These past few pages have, in essence, been a sampler of the kinds of grammar^1 study in which students can engage. In the appendices to this book, we have listed a few of the many good texts helpful to the teacher. Finding interesting, linguistically sound materials for exploration is no problem.

Once again, however, it is important to stress (in the manner of the semanticists) that grammar^1 is not grammar^2 is not grammar^3. In particular, if you teach grammar^1—whether an abstract exploration like Kalaba-X or a grammar of English, such as structural or transformational—emphasis ought to be on helping students understand how their language works. Don't expect that they will write better or speak correct English. Don't expect that the usage errors will disappear from their papers.

You can expect, however, that your students will develop a better understanding of their language, the symbol system they use day by day, minute by minute in their lives, and such study can be enriching, enlightening, and thus, in the long run, quite practical.

Teaching Grammar[2]: Books about Language

Not too long ago, a major publisher reissued its basic high-school grammar book in the umpteenth edition with the advertising slogan: "It's passed the test of time with millions and millions of students." That's the kind of sentence we'd like to turn over to a group of high-school kids for linguistic analysis, for, like many advertising statements, it implies much and explains very little. By almost any measure, the conventional schoolroom grammars have flunked the test—you name the test—and the failures are documented by the research presented earlier in this chapter. Generations of students have plowed through the volumes of these series without learning how to use the language significantly better.

As we have argued, that is partly because grammar study does not and will not produce changes in language use. But part of the problem lies with the grammars[2], the books themselves. The typical school grammar is an odd mixture of description and prescription about language, a mismatch of instruction and drill, frequently presenting half-truths that describe English in the terms of Latin grammar and describe the writing process in mechanistic terms that make composition writing an assembly-line affair. Why these books, which really have not changed significantly in the past two centuries, continue to dominate in the schools is a puzzle to us, particularly in light of research.

Nevertheless, there are some good books about language around, books that can be genuinely helpful to students if we keep in mind *why* we are presenting the material and what we expect to accomplish. In the remainder of this chapter, then, we will describe some books that present an alternative to the traditional schoolroom grammar. Instead of spending (literally) tens of thousands of dollars buying (literally) tons of grammar books, suggest that your school district buy smaller numbers of some of the following:

Adult books. No, these are not X-rated. They are simply advanced books that help a teacher build the kind of linguistic background he or she needs to teach about language with intelligence. For example, Suzette Haden Elgin has written a short, accurate, informative pamphlet, *What Is Linguistics?* (Englewood Cliffs, N.J.: Prentice-Hall, 1973) that helps to clear up some basic confusion about this field. Her *Primer of Transformational Grammar for Rank Beginners* (Urbana, Ill.: NCTE, 1974) is also a useful introductory text. Jean Malmstrom's *Grammar Basics: A Reading/Writing Approach* (Rochelle Park, N.J.: Hayden Books, 1977) is a sound introduction to modern grammar that emphasizes, appropriately, that the real *basics* of English are reading and writing, not study of abstractions about language. If you feel a need to review traditional grammar, we recommend J. R. Bernard's *A Short Guide to Traditional Grammar* (Sydney University Press, 1975), a book that presents information quickly and concisely, without exercises or moral advice. Peter Farb's *Word Play: What Happens When People Talk* (New York: Bantam Books, 1973) deals with the social uses of language (not grammar) and helps to put the entire discussion of grammar in context. Finally, we think every teacher should have a look at either J. L. Dillard's *Black English* (New York: Random House, 1972) or Geneva Smitherman's *Talkin' and Testifyin'* (Boston: Houghton Mifflin, 1977), both describing the linguistic origins of black English in America.

Usage handbooks. Schoolbook grammars often fail because they lose focus on their stated target: helping students learn to speak and write correctly. They present complex information on nouns and verbs, predicate nominatives and intransitive verbs, which the student is somehow supposed to translate into action. But the "problem" with student writing is *usage,* not *syntax* (the social choices of words, not grammatical function). The kid, in short, says "ain't" when his hearers expect "am not." While the times at which teachers and others ask students to write and speak in standard will vary (chapter 23, "Dialects and Correctness"), a usage handbook is far more useful to most students than a grammar book.

Most usage handbooks are arranged alphabetically and present troublesome choices—*lay/lie, sit/set,* and so on. A good handbook describes contemporary use rather than trying to legislate good usage. Adult books by Bergen Evans, Eric Partridge, and Theodore Bernstein probably belong in every classroom, but several short usage handbooks for high-school students exist. (See, for example, Virginia McDavid's school edition of the *Random House English Handbook.*) We suggest, then, that you place a few usage handbooks on your class shelves and spend some time teaching students about their function and use.

It is important to emphasize that students do not need to know a lot about grammar to use a handbook successfully. While the handbooks refer from time to time to basic parts of speech, most of the explanations are presented in nongrammatical terms. Thus, in reviewing usage books we looked up our old nemesis, *effect/affect.* After a few grammatical distinctions, the author told us that *effect* means somewhat the same thing as *execute,* which also begins with an *e.* That mnemonic device stuck with us and has strongly affected our ability to use the two terms according to contemporary usage. The handbooks can effect changes in your teaching, too.

Dictionaries. Most teachers introduce students to the dictionary routinely, so we won't dwell on their use in much detail. We don't believe in penalizing students for their asking questions about words by saying, "Look it up! You know how to use the dictionary!" Nor do we have much faith in dictionary exercises to teach dictionary skills. We do think it is useful to show kids how dictionaries work and what's in them. (We also think it's OK for school dictionaries to contain, and for students to look up, the definitions of four-letter words.)

Spelling guides. The big trouble with dictionaries is that you have to know how to spell a word to be able to look it up. Yet writers most frequently use dictionaries for spelling, rather than to discover meaning. A useful alternative is a spelling guide such as *Webster's Instant Word Guide* (available at most bookstores), which simply lists the correct spelling of thousands of words. Spelling guides work because without the definitions to fill page after page, it is much easier for a student to find the word in question. Lists of commonly misspelled words are also helpful, though each of us has his or her own quixotic list of such words. However, the practice of giving spelling drill based on these lists of "demons" seems guaranteed to produce a confused and muddled group of students. Get several good spelling guides; teach the students how to use them; and display the books prominently in the classroom.

The thesaurus. The use of the thesaurus gets students entering essay contests and writing expository papers into a lot of trouble. The students have the general feeling that their writing isn't sufficiently sophisticated, so they try to gussy it up by introducing polysyllabic synonyms found in the thesaurus. What they do, of course, is pick words with the wrong connotations and wind up wrecking their essays. Occasionally the thesaurus is useful for finding just the right word or to locate a word that is just on the tip of your tongue (you look up its synonym). It can also help with spelling, for if you look up the synonym, you will probably also find the word itself spelled. Show students a thesaurus; explain how it works; caution against the misuse; and keep it on the reference shelf.

Secretary's manuals. These little volumes, available for under two dollars in paperback, are a gold mine of language information. A secretary's manual contains all of the advice of a schoolroom grammar, but places it in a less pedantic, more useful form. A typical secretary's manual contains spelling lists, some basic rules of usage, disputed usage items, letter form, information on the library and its use, and tips on manuscript preparation. Dollar for dollar, they are the most practical grammar[2] around.

Style and research manuals. For the older students and the college bound, a brief introduction to style and research manuals is probably helpful. Strunk and White's *The Elements of Style* (New York: Macmillan, 1973) remains a classic—and probably the most widely used—style book on the college level. It presents the basics of the plain style (good, solid, readable prose) as well as any book around. Kate Turabian's *Guide to the Writing of Term and Research Papers* (Chicago: Phoenix, 1974) is the classic in that genre. In presenting these texts it is important that the teacher not overstress their importance. Not every essay a student writes in college will be done in "the plain style," and few college undergraduates actually write an elaborate formal research paper with bibliography and footnotes.

We intend grammar^2 to include a lot more than syntax rule books. We're suggesting that the teacher seek out accurate informational books that will provide student writers and speakers the help they need when they need it. This kind of individualized approach will never fit into a research design, so we can't claim that a multitext approach will bring about a radical change in your students' test scores. We can predict with confidence, however, that you'll see results as students, one at a time, seek out the grammar^2 that will help them achieve success with their work in your classes and in other classes as well.

CHAPTER 23

Dialects and Correctness

People often confuse grammar[1] (description of the structure of the language) with grammar[3] (usage of the language) (see chapter 22, "Teaching about Grammars"). Students, uneducated people, or people who are not a part of a "status" group are often criticized because of their language, because, the attackers say, they don't speak "grammatically." Often critics refer to such "aberrations" as: "He don't know where to go" or "I be tired of goin' to school every day" or "What would youse like?" Such *faux pas,* however, are not a violation of grammar[1] but a variation in usage, one of the varieties of grammar[3].

The distinction is an important one: Grammar[1] consists of a multitude of "rules" that describe the structure of language. These rules are so numerous and complex and so much a part of us that we are not even able to say what they are, let alone memorize them and apply them to our speaking. We don't have to. The rules of grammar are what allow a baby at three years old—probably before—to know that "Ain't spinach going eat to I my" is not a sentence and "I ain't going to eat my spinach" is. The structure of grammar is constant and shared by all speakers.

English usage, on the other hand, is not constant. It varies from one part of the country to another. English usage in Tennessee is not like English usage in Maine is not like English usage in New York is not like English usage in Texas. English usage also varies according to ethnic origins, social levels, the amount of education a speaker has had, and with context and situation—with the relations among speaker, listener, and subject.

Moreover, the rules of usage change over time. Whereas the structure of grammar is relatively fixed, the conventions of usage change. When most of us were in school, for example, the use of "shall" as indication of future intention in first-person singular and plural was still on the books. So our texts taught us to say: "I shall study tonight; you will study tonight; he or she will study tonight; we shall study tonight, you will study tonight; they will study tonight." Rarely did we hear anyone—educated or uneducated—use that verb form. Indeed, rather than sounding correct, it would sound pretentious.

Like speakers of any era, we are presently seeing changes in what is considered proper usage. Consider the case of whom: How often do you hear someone say "To *whom* are you giving that present?" or "From *whom* did you get that letter?" or "To *whom* did you wish to speak?" More often you hear "*Who* are you giving that present to?" Similarly, most have been trained to use the objective pronoun following a predicate nominative: "It was *he* who brought the cookies." "It was *she* who danced in the ballet." "This is *he*" or "It is *I.*" Yet in actual speech situations, we usually use the objective case—"It was *him,*" "It's *me*"—or avoid using the pronoun in that situation and repeat the name of the person under discussion. Sometimes our training even causes us to overcorrect, and we are accustomed to hearing from college-educated acquaintances such utterances as "Now this is just between you and *I* . . ." or "My mom got that for my husband and *I* for our anniversary."

The point is that usage is determined not by hard-and-fast rules or a set of absolutes with which everyone agrees and to which everyone adheres. Usage differs from community to community, and proper usage grows out of what people within the community say or write. Usually, then, when one person criticizes the language of another, it is because the speaker uses language unlike the norm that the hearer is accustomed to, whether the hearer's language be Pennsylvania Dutch, Detroit Polish, New York Jewish, Chicago Black or White Appalachian.

For many years, far too many teachers have taught the status dialect—the dialect of the educated, upper-middle-class white—as if it were the only dialect. The problem with the emphasis on Standard Dialect (also known as Edited American English or Broadcast English) is that it ignores the complexity of language use and the language user. The very limited and limiting instruction students receive in standard grammatical structures (via the textbook grammar[2]) and spelling and vocabulary drills and exercises have little to do with helping students expand and explore the development of their language. Nor does the training have anything to do with the varieties of language situations and experiences that students are likely to encounter as they live out their lives.

Instruction in language usage, then, should not be a matter of training students to produce perfect English according to a mythical standard, but to help students become conscious of language use (their own and others') and the multiplicity of situations in which they will be called upon to use language in appropriate ways.

In *The Five Clocks* (New York: Harcourt, Brace and World, 1947), Martin Joos describes five styles of English usage ranging from informal to formal, with the emphasis on how language changes according to the relationship among speaker and listener and the situation in which they are involved. Most adult speakers, according to Joos, function in the middle level of the informality-formality scale, at the *consultative level.* Here the speaker provides background information that he thinks the listener will not have, and the listener participates continuously with verbal cues that allow the speaker to know whether or not he or she is being understood, what is approved by the listener, what needs further clarification, what is being questioned. The main focus of such interaction is an exchange of information in which both speaker and listener share in advancing the conversation.

At the *formal level,* the speaking/listening group is normally larger, six or more people, and the speaker is likely to be presenting information without continuous and direct feedback from the listeners. This affects the speech, for the speaker will have to know more precisely the direction this talk will take him or her, rather than using the cooperation of the listener as the means by which he determines what will come next. The entire structure of the presentation, including sentences, is likely to be more complete.

Frozen style is the most formal of language styles and appears in print. There is no opportunity for the receiver to participate; nor can the receiver rely on the intonation pattern of the speaker. Understanding will come from rereading rather than interaction.

Perhaps the style used most by adolescents is the *casual* style. While in the adult community language is used for the exchange of information in order to get jobs done and to keep the community running smoothly, young people use language to establish and maintain a comfortable and secure peer group or society. Casual style, characterized by ellipses and slang, treats the listener as an insider and therefore eliminates the need to provide background information or to rely on response: the speaker assumes the listener's interest and understanding, so he or she can leave out parts of sentences or parts of words: "Would you like to bring him with you?" becomes "Why doncha bring'm?"

While casual and consultative usually center around public information, with the most informal style, the *intimate,* there is no use of public information. Here two speakers share the code, and grammar is not necessary; meaning is extracted by the listener from context and intonation.

According to Joos the labeling of formal and frozen styles as "good English" or "exemplary English" or the *only* English students should learn ignores the realities of language usage of appropriate shifts in style of language according to situation. Each style offers the speaker/writer different possibilities:

> Good intimate style fuses two personalties. Good casual style integrates disparate personalities into a social group which is greater than the sum of its parts, for now the personalities complement each other instead of clashing. Good consultative style produces cooperation without the integration, profiting from the lack of it. Good formal style informs the individual separately, so that his future planning may be the more discriminate. Good frozen style, finally, lures him into educating himself, so that he may the more confidently act what role he chooses.*

Rather than teaching students "proper" English, then, English teachers should be developing opportunities for students to explore language use and practice in a broadening range of language along the formality/informality scale.

Activities for Teaching about Language Style

Have students analyze their own language. Use charts or notebooks for students to keep track of their language in various situations. How do they adjust grammatical structures for different audiences? When do they leave words out? When do they seem "wordiest"? Do they ever shift to "improper" usage for different audiences (double negatives, *ain't,* lack of subject-verb agreement)? What differences do they note in their phonological patterns? How does the sound change? Do they drop out letters and compact sentences (*gonna, gotta, wanna, dontcha, cm'on, gwan, comin', hopin', likta*)? Do their intonation patterns change? How does their vocabulary change? Are there levels of slang that change for different audiences? Have them list words that apply to only *one* audience. What about swear words? Have them examine how their language changes for:

* From *The Five Clocks* (1947, p. 40) by Martin Joos. Reprinted by permission of Harcourt Brace Jovanovich, Inc.

their parents; their parents' friends; their best friends; peers who are only casual acquaintances; teachers; the principal, coaches; service people in restaurants, stores, and gas stations.

► Create improvisational situations in which students become characters and act out situations unlike their own: a college professor talking with students describing what they don't like about his teaching style; a factory manager describing changes that need to be made in procedures to two workers; a college student trying to convince her parents to let her go to Europe; a cocktail party scene at the home of a General Motors executive; three ten-year-olds making up rules for a secret club; an airport information desk where a variety of people come to ask questions—a woman dressed in fur looking for the nearest bar, a couple in blue jeans with knapsacks as their only luggage, a janitor angry because he can't find the manager. Have students discuss the language of the various participants and the conclusions they drew about speakers on the basis of their language.

► Tape-record the improvisations and do a systematic study of the language students used to represent other characters. Discuss what we can learn about people through their language and how people can become stereotyped because of the way they express themselves.

► At different times let both boys and girls play the same role—a business executive, an angry parent, a person trying to get a job, a person trying to find directions in a strange town—and tape-record it. Have students look for differences in the language they use. How does a girl confront, persuade, question in ways that are different from males? Tape-record several experiments before beginning to analyze the results so that you don't bias or change how students perform in the role playing.

► Have students make slang dictionaries. Or have them make dictionaries of words that apply only to certain situations or are used in particular contexts. Have them create a book of slang that applies only to their group. Compare the slang books of kids from different groups: the band kids, the athletes, the intellectuals. The purpose here is not to draw lines, but to promote understanding across lines that already exist. (Note: The issue of censorship might arise here. Some kids' slang contains what might be considered obscene language. The idea *is* to discover the real language people use, but for your own protection you might have to limit reality.)

► Use literature as a means of discovering how authors use dialogue to reveal character and to reflect relationships and social contexts.

► Provide students with opportunities to adjust their language and adapt their style. Invite not just guest speakers to the class, but guest participants to share in whatever unit or theme the class is discussing. Provide situations where students and guest may interact: small-group discussions, question-and-answer sessions, group or individual interviews. Invite a variety of people representing various vocations and interests: parents, local politicians, local artists, poets, novelists, journalists, dancers, singers, editors, store managers, architects, stamp collectors, foreign-language speakers, bicycle racers, historians, photographers, restaurant owners. Students will not only hear a new vocabulary and gain interesting new information, but they will also be placed in a *consultative/formal* language situation in which the exchange of information requires a new verbal style.

Learn about areas in which your students have expertise and set up cooperative situations in which your students may visit the classrooms of elementary schools and junior-high schools to share their interest with younger children. Here they are placed in a *consultative/formal* language situation in which they have the responsibility for preparing and presenting information to strangers; at the same time, the strangers are young enough not to be threatening.

Allow students to take charge during parent visitation nights and open houses, acting as hosts and hostesses for a small audience of parents or talking individually with parents (not their own) about the activities of the class.

Age is another factor that affects usage. Have students explore the language development of young children, of small brothers and sisters. Have them examine the grammar, syntax (the regularizing of the *-ed* past tense ending around ages three to five—*goed, gived, runned,* for example), the developing vocabulary (the way in which small children, for example, will misuse a word in a variety of contexts trying to pick up clues from adults about its proper usage), and phonological development (Which sounds seem easiest? Which more difficult? Why is it that so many little tykes say *witto* for *little,* for example?).

Dialects

In the past, English teachers have been responsible for teaching the prestige dialect, the proper dialect, the dialect that will supposedly grant a speaker entry into social circles of consequence. Moreover, it was once thought by English teachers (as well as the man or woman on the street) that the inability to speak correct English—the language of the middle class and the grammar books—was indicative or a reflection of an inability to think clearly. Variations in language—in phonology, in lexicon, and in grammar and syntax—were thought to be at best peculiar, at worst, signs of stupidity or barbarianism.

Modern linguistic and psychological research has changed our attitudes about language. We now know that variations in language patterns grow out of a complex set of factors: geographic regions, social structure, and ethnic background, and that people learn from birth the variety of language that is spoken by their family and their cultural, geographic, and social group. What appears unsystematic and chaotic to a speaker unfamiliar with a dialect on analysis proves to be a systematic, regularized system which can be described and explained by linguists and other students of language.

No dialect seems to be the object of as much prejudice and suspicion in this country as black dialect, and "what to do about it" continues to be a controversy. Geneva Smitherman's *Talkin' and Testifyin': The Language of Black America* (Houghton Mifflin, 1977) provides a precise and thorough discussion of the history, development, and current notions of black English. It is her belief (shared by many social critics and historians) that language is used as a tool of oppression, as one of many barriers by the white middle class to keep blacks from entering the mainstream:

> The "national mania for correctness" is, after all, a useful tool. The speech of the blacks, the poor, and other powerless groups is used as a weapon to deny them access to full participation in the society. Teachers harp on the "bad" English of their students; potential employees are denied jobs because they don't talk "right"; future college graduates become force-outs because they write in "nonstandard" English. Yet what is "nonstandard" English is simply the language of "nonstandard" people.*

And, she goes on to say, language was learned from babyhood, was fixed by five or six, and is nearly impossible to change without giving up a large part of one's identity.

Much of Smitherman's book discusses the roots of black language and the closeness of language and identity. The language of black culture grows out of

* From *Talkin' and Testifyin'* (p. 199) by Geneva Smitherman; published by Houghton Mifflin Company. Copyright © 1977 by Geneva Smitherman. Reprinted by permission.

the complex interweavings of African language and the conditions of slave life and oppression in this country. Black dialect, like all dialects, is a way of thinking, a way of perceiving reality, a way of dealing with conditions of life, a way of surviving, a way of establishing and maintaining relationships. Smitherman concludes: "Thus to deny the legitimacy of Africanized English is to deny the legitimacy of Black culture and the Black experience" (p. 175).

The question of what to do about black dialect, then, is not a simple one. On the one hand, we hear that to be upwardly mobile, to enter the mainstream, one has to speak the language of the dominant group (even if racism is the basis of such a demand). "Be realistic; be practical; make this concession; play their game," the advice runs. On the other hand, we hear that to abandon or to adjust one's (perfectly legitimate) language is a violation and loss of one's identity.

The arguments extend from one extreme to the other, and all have implications for the teaching and learning of language. At one extreme is the eradicationist who believes that standard English correctness should be the goal of all language instruction, in which case the goals and values of society take precedence over the identity, goals, and values of the individual. The bidialectical advocates emphasize a "be practical" attitude: "It's true that all dialects are a legitimate form of English, but be realistic; the values of the society and the workings of the society demand a certain sort of behavior in order for the speaker to achieve success. Learn the dialect in order to achieve success." The hidden message, or course, is: "Your dialect is just as good as everybody else's—but not really. If it *really* were, you could use it!" At the other extreme are those who advocate that black language is a legitimate form of language that can and should be used by its speakers and that language instruction should concentrate on helping speakers become more articulate in their own dialect, rather than focusing on the learning of a new dialect.

Teachers of language who have dialect speakers in their classes, then, have important obligations. First, they must acquaint themselves with the dialects of the speakers in their classes. Second, in making decisions about how language instruction should proceed with a speaker of another dialect, they should carefully weigh the psychological, emotional, cultural, and practical aspects of that student's language development.

We cannot provide any simple solutions for what to do with dialect speakers in your classroom. We do, however, have two large, general solutions:

First, the goal of any language instruction should be to help students increase their confidence, flexibility, and articulateness in their own language, in the language with which they feel most comfortable. All students, no matter what their dialect or sophistication in language, should be involved in whole language activities—speaking, writing, reading—which require them to grapple with and create meanings, rather than in exercises and drill which limit students' actual use of language.

Second, all students, no matter what dialect they speak, should become increasingly conscious of language variety and language complexity. Students should be helped to recognize the cultural and psychological implications of language use and the styles of language used in various situations so they can make intelligent decisions about their own use of language.

Moreover, in a democratic society, it seems especially important that we break down the barriers of language prejudice, a prejudice, like most, which grows out of misconceptions, fears, and hostility, rather than out of a reasoned, intelligent, thorough exploration of language development and use. The language choices students make then become a matter of the relationships and roles they wish to take in society rather than a judgment on their worth as a human being.

Activities to Teach about Dialects

Two excellent books are available for helping both student and teacher explore the nature and varieties of American dialects. Roger W. Shuy's *Discovering American Dialects* (NCTE, 1967) is a casebook for explorations in the study of dialects which could probably best be used at the upper-senior-high level. Bill Reynolds' *Dialects in America* (Random House English Series, 1973) provides activities for younger students. The ideas in both books could be adapted for students throughout secondary school. The following list is suggestive of the many possible directions students can take in studying language usage.

Students can learn a great deal about regional dialects within one class. In order to discover the effects of geographical area on language, explain the three major dialects—Midland, Northern, and Southern—and have each student list the places in which they have lived and the length of time they lived there. In addition, have them provide the same information about their parents. Then give students opportunities to listen to one another talk (and read) in order to note the differences in one another's language in the three aspects of dialect.

Pronunciation. Both Reynolds and Shuy provide lists of words that speakers from different parts of the country pronounce differently. Some of those include: *part, ask, marry, merry, not, greasy, any, washed, sore, many, paw, out, door, water, tomato, roof, with, these, Miss, humor.* Though these words contain elements that are likely to be pronounced differently, students will hear differences in many other words. Have them write down words that they hear pronounced unlike the way they or others in the class pronounce them. (For sophisticated students, Shuy provides symbols for transcribing variation in sounds. Dictionaries also contain that information. For most students, sharing variations can be done orally.) Have students work in small groups to try to match phonological patterns with descriptions of regional origin.

Vocabulary. According to Shuy, vocabulary varies not only in accordance with geographical and cultural origins, but also with age, sex, education, and occupations. Have students listen to one another's variations in vocabulary for such words and expressions as: *cobweb, bucket, spigot, baby buggy, dad, my family, freeway, soda, string beans, blue jeans, bermudas, couch, purse, teeter-totter,* and *swimming trunks.* Again, have students listen for other differences in words that stand for the same concept or object. Have them work in small groups to try to determine geographical origins or differences that seem to be the result of sex or perhaps educational and occupational differences in their families.

Grammar. Though grammatical differences may not be as marked as differences in vocabulary and pronunciation, students will be able to note some. Have students note different uses of prepositions (it's *after/past* nine; sick *to/at* her stomach; we're waiting *for/on* her); plurals (five *foot/feet*); pronouns (it wasn't *he/him;* what would *youse/you* like? he did it *hisself/himself;* he gave it to Janet and *I/me*); and verbs (*dived/dove; rode/rid; spoiled/spoilt; lay/laid; ate/et/eat; saw/seen/seed/see*).

After students have had practice tuning their ears to the dialect differences, have them do a community-based project, taking perhaps a block or two in their own neighborhood to describe the dialects they find. By now, of course, students will have learned that some people may be sensitive to language variations and self-conscious about their own variety of speech. Students doing field-based studies should be sensitive to this possibility.

Use records, tapes, and taped television shows for students to listen to in their study of language varieties. In recent years, television has made available a wider number of language varieties, particularly in situation comedies. Have students compare varieties of language on TV shows. Use tapes of presidents or other political leaders to show variations in dialect among highly educated speakers. To check students' language prejudice progress, have them characterize speakers on the basis of their language only. Then reveal the person's identity.

➡ Have students examine literature to see the ways in which authors represent (or misrepresent) the language of characters from particular regions or from particular socioethnic backgrounds. Roger Shuy provides an excellent list of books that make use of dialects in some way:

■ *Norwegian/English:* John Van Druten's *I Remember Mama;* Ole Rölvaag's *Giants in the Earth* and *Peder Victorious;* Martha Ostenso's *The Mad Carews.*

■ *Nebraska:* Willa Cather's *O Pioneers!* and *My Ántonia.*

■ *Yiddish:* Arthur Kober's "That Man Is Here Again" and "Bella, Bella Kissed a Fella"; Leo Rosten's *The Education of Hyman Kaplan,* Bernard Malamud's *The Natural,* and Saul Bellow's *Herzog.*

■ *Chicago Irish:* Finley P. Dunne's *Mr. Dooley Says* and James T. Farrell's *Studs Lonigan.*

■ *Tennessee:* Mary Murfree's *In the Tennessee Mountains* and Mildred Haun's *That Hawk's Done Gone.*

■ *Quaker:* Jessamyn West's "The Battle of Finney's Ford" and Mable Hunt's "Little Girl with Seven Names."

The novels of Chester Himes, Richard Wright, and Ralph Ellison and the music and poetry of many many black artists provide many avenues for the exploration of black language to reveal character and views of reality.

➡ Have students explore their own language origins, their language roots. They might not be able to gather enough personal data to become very specific, but they can still explore the general history of their cultural-ethnic group in this country. Have them try to discover the following: What language or languages did your American ancestors speak? Where did they come from? What part of the country did they first settle in? Where did they go from there? What English words have come from the language of your ancestry? How did those words become a part of American English? How do these words differ from their original meanings? Have any grammatical or phonological patterns been assimilated by American English?

➡ Have students survey community attitudes toward language variations. Let them develop a list of variations in syntax, vocabulary, and pronunciation and ask people to describe their reactions to variations in English. Have students write up a summary of their findings.

➡ Much has been made about the employability of speakers of nonstandard dialects. Have students in your class survey employers in your community or write away to managers of large corporations to discover what expectations and demands employers have for workers in various jobs. Students might like to try different kinds of questioning to see what gets more helpful results—a series of open-ended questions or a carefully constructed language attitude survey.

➡ Have students begin a campaign to stop the discrimination against speakers of nonstandard English usage on the part of American institutions: the schools, businesses, the government.

The teacher of language is on the horns of a dilemma. On the one hand, we have solid linguistic research and a concern for our students' integrity which tells us to help them develop the language of their nurture; on the other, we have a competitive (albeit racist) society that demands that students and workers speak "standard" English and discriminates against those who don't. It's important to keep our wits (and ethics) about us. Helping students "get the sense right" should be our major goal. As the saying goes, "Richard Nixon had all his basic skills."

SUMMARY AND TROUBLESHOOTING

The Students' "Right" to Their Own Language—A Dialogue

The Scene

A convention hotel somewhere in America. The room is large, decorated in hotel rococo with plush, red carpeting—threadbare in spots—and wallpaper flocked with gold and red. A huge chandelier with plastic baubles casts a pale orange glow over the crowd of a hundred or so persons who have gathered to hear a panel discussion.

The Participants

A Moderator, a Linguist, a High School English Teacher, a Parent, and a Journalist.

The Topic

"Do Students Have a Right to Their Own Language?"

(*The Moderator, who has been fidgeting with a cigarette burn hole in the pea green tablecloth, pours water from a black plastic pitcher* (*embossed with the hotel logotype*) *into plastic tumblers* (*also embossed with the logo*), *which are passed along the row of panelists. The Moderator rises and speaks into the microphone, which immediately screams back a high-pitched note of feedback. After adusting the mike, the Moderator tries it again.*)

Moderator: Well, it looks as if it's time, so I guess we'll begin. Can you hear me out there? (*Affirmative nodding from the back row.*) Good. Well, you all know our panelists, so I won't waste any time with introductions. We're here today to discuss the students' right to their own language. Or more accurately, we're here to consider the implications of a statement by that title issued and approved as a policy statement of the Conference on College Composition and Communication. I'll read the statement:

> We affirm the students' right to their own patterns and varieties of language—the dialects of their nurture or whatever dialects in which they find their identity and style. Language scholars long ago denied that the myth of a standard American dialect has any validity. The claim that any one dialect is unacceptable amounts to an attempt of one social group to exert its dominance over another. Such a claim leads to false advice for speakers and writers, and immoral advice for humans. A nation proud of its diverse heritage and its cultural and racial variety will preserve its heritage of dialects. We affirm strongly that teachers must have the experiences and training that will enable them to respect diversity and uphold the right of students to their own language.*

That statement, as we all know, has aroused an extraordinary amount of controversy since it was issued. Our purpose is to explore its ramifications and to evaluate it. Would any of our panelists like to lead with a comment or a question?

Journalist: Yes, what does it mean? (*Laughter from the crowd.*)

Linguist: Let me take a crack at that. In simplest terms, "The Students' Right to Their Own Language" says that we need to recognize dialect diversity, that people of different national, ethnic, regional, and social origins speak differently. This statement acknowledges that there is no fixed, immutable standard English, but many different standards that are appropriate for different groups of people.

Teacher: Yes, and from the point of view of a teacher, it suggests that instead of trying to correct every "error" a student makes, I recognize and respect the dialect origins of what he or she is saying.

Parent: I was afraid of that. I am baffled by this statement. I went to public school for twelve—actually thirteen—years, and there was none of this kind of talk. There was right and wrong, and everybody learned it. I don't see why kids nowadays are any different.

Teacher: I can understand how you feel about that, because I went through the same kind of training myself. But as the Linguist can probably tell you better than I, research conducted in this country over the past fifty years has

* Adopted April 1976. Published in *College Composition and Communication,* Fall 1974.

suggested that for a vast majority of children, attempting to impose standard English simply hasn't worked.

Linguist: Actually, whether or not the instruction "worked" is beside the point. The message in this statement is that imposing dialects is not just a question of teaching, but of *morality*. Even if you were the most effective teacher in the world, it would be immoral to make every kid in a class speak alike. In the first place, linguistics confirms that English is flexible and changeable; there's no such thing as *a* standard English anyway. Second, and far more important, the language that we speak is very much bound up with our concept of what and who we are. To eradicate a person's dialect is to eradicate a part of that person's identity.

Journalist: All that sounds vaguely permissive to me. When I write a story for publication, my copy editor blue pencils the hell out of my stuff. He doesn't worry about my identity, and after twenty years in the trade, neither do I. Furthermore, I think my stories are better because somebody around the shop has standards and will exercise them.

Teacher: But you're blurring all kinds of important distinctions here. In the first place, you're an adult who's been practicing your trade for twenty years. In the second, you're talking about editing—probably for structure, content, and style—not standard English. You've probably been speaking standard English all your life.

Parent: There! The Linguist (*pointing down the table*) says there's no such thing as standard English. Now (*points at the Teacher*) you are saying that the Journalist has been speaking it all his life. You two (*points at the Linguist* and *the Teacher*) need to get your stories straight.

Linguist: All I said was that there is no *fixed* standard English. Actually, there are many standards with flexible characteristics. For example, there are dozens of standard kinds of black English, which vary from Detroit to Chicago to Mobile to Albuquerque. There's standard Southern English and standard New England Yankee, too.

Teacher: But I'd be more than willing to admit that there is also a kind of "standard standard." Some people call it broadcast or publications standard, because most newspapers and television news shows use it.

Journalist: Right, and *ain't* is a no-no at my paper, at any time and any place. So why should a student have a right to say "ain't"?

Moderator: We've got two issues cooking here. First, there's the question of standard English and what it is or isn't. Second is the question of the students' rights to using whatever language they want to.

Teacher: Good point. Let me address myself to the first. Yes, a broadcast standard exists, but it is not all that rigid. For example, although the schoolbooks say that intransitive verbs take nominative pronouns—"It is I," for example—*everybody* says, "It's me," and we all feel comfortable with it. This is because the idea of "standard" varies from one situation to another, and this is where the students' right comes in. Students learn the dialect "of their nurture" and that is a dialect with which they have come to feel comfortable. It is a standard, too, because everybody around the student speaks it! A kid who spoke Walter Cronkite-brand standard English back home in a neighborhood where black English is standard would be out of step.

Linguist: One of the things left out of the CCCC statement, it seems to me, is pointing this out. The authors of the statement were not forbidding the children to use *any* kind of standard. Rather, they seem to have intended to eliminate the common practice of imposing what amounts to white, middle-class English on all students regardless of their backgrounds. They object, quite rightly, to taking black kids or Mexican-American kids and trying to make them all speak uniform Anglo. Further, although the statement doesn't say so, it seems to me that the schools have been very guilty of discriminating against kids who *don't* speak Anglo. The statement calls for a reversal. It says we must "respect diversity and uphold the right" of students to speak a standard of their own choosing.

Parent: OK, I can see that. I can be a pluralist, too. I see why, for example, black people have been insisting on having their own literature included in the schools. Black pride and all that.

Journalist: Still, what are the schools for anyway? Isn't the purpose to *teach,* to present new information? How can the schools sit back and legitimize *doing nothing?* We have to face the fact that one reason a lot of inner-city students don't get jobs is because they don't speak and write good English. They can't fill out application blanks. The schools have to do something to help students change their socioeconomic status, and there can be no debate that standard English is a way out.

Linguist: I'm afraid that there is some debate on that. As the CCCC group documented in its report, standard English (or "broadcast English" as the Teacher calls it) isn't required as many places as some would like to believe. More important is the fact that giving minority speakers standard English is *not* in any way going to open new doors to them. It is racism and ethnicism in this country that prevents minorities from getting jobs. Nonstandard English is just an excuse.

Journalist: Even so, it would seem more useful for the students to speak standard than to go on speaking nonstandard. Why give an employer an excuse not to hire you?

Parent: And we parents have a right to expect that the schools prepare students to face real-world situations. Whether or not the schools believe in a student's right, the employers *don't.*

Teacher: That gets me back to a point I wanted to make earlier. It would be wrong to take this as a do-nothing statement. It talks about respecting and not interfering, but it doesn't say anything about what the schools should do in a positive vein.

Linguist: Yes, and in this sense, the statement is politically naive. As soon as it came out, journalists jumped all over it. The writers should have made some positive statements too.

Journalist: Well, let's hear them.

Parent: I'm all ears.

(*At this point, a side door swings open and two hotel employees barge into the room, speaking loudly in a minority dialect. When they realize they've gotten into the wrong place, they beat a quick retreat. All four panelists smile knowingly at one another, each assuming the episode has proven his or her point.*)

Teacher: First of all, I (and the CCCC statement writers) believe in helping students extend options. So that while I am convinced students have a right to their own language, I also feel they have a right to learn as much about language as possible.

Parent: What does that mean?

Teacher: It means, among other things, that instead of trying to impose standard English, I will spend a lot of time helping them come to understand how dialects work, where they come from, and what the social and economic implications of dialects are.

Journalist: In other words, instead of imposing a standard, you're going to frighten them into using it.

Teacher: (*Angrily*) I certainly hope not. All I want them to do is understand how language works, which is a lot more than most parents and journalists know! (*Points at them.*)

Moderator: Now . . . well . . . ah, the Linguist has something to say.

Linguist: From my point of view, if we spent one half the time teaching kids to understand how language works that we spend trying to impose a standard, everybody would be a lot better off.

Teacher: (*Still angry*) I'm not passive with my kids. I have them writing all the time, speaking all the time. They are constantly engaged in using language in new situations. We talk about job skills, too, and even look at application blanks to make certain they know how to fill one out properly. So I am extending options, all the time. I'm not imposing a standard. But I'm convinced that in the process, my students are going to learn the language they need to operate successfully in the world of jobs.

Parent: We keep talking minorities. Actually, my kids use pretty good English, because I've always insisted on it around home. But I want somebody to correct and grade their work so they'll get ready for college, not some namby-pamby who'll say, "That's lovely" to everything they write.

Moderator: Let me point out here that we're blurring that distinction between editing and standard English again.

Parent: So what! The point is that somebody's got to teach something.

Teacher: And I repeat, we are teaching something: options. I want for your kids the same thing I want for minority speakers; that is, I want them to be able to function effectively in a wide range of language situations. If your kids were in my class, I wouldn't red pencil their papers, but I would put them in discussion groups to talk about the effectiveness of their work. I'd want them to learn about dialects, too, to understand their own. I think you've acknowledged an important point when you've stated that they learned their English at home. That is the dialect of their nurture. Suppose that dialect were different from mine. Would you want me telling your kids that what they learned from their mom and dad was wrong—nonstandard, inadequate?

Parent: No, but I'd still want my kids to be able to function——

Teacher: Of course you would, and that's what a conscientious teacher is trying to give you. Again, by respecting students' language we're not advocating a do-nothing approach. As a matter of fact, it is much more difficult to teach understanding and options than it is to correct students' English.

Linguist: That's right. The CCCC statement really calls for much more intelligent, informed teaching than the old correctness approach.

Journalist: Maybe so, but that doesn't make good copy. It's test scores that my readers——

Teacher: If only you'd look——

Linguist: Perhaps if we had the research funds——

Parent: I have my doubts——

Moderator: This isn't a topic on which we are likely to reach closure, but our time is up. I think we have extended the discussion of students' rights to their own language quite a bit, but it is clear that this issue needs more and more and more examination. I'll recommend to the program chair that we continue with this session next year.

(The session ends, but the discussion continues as the audience files out into the hall. At the speaker's table the participants continue to talk with animation, and we can pick up bits of conversation: "You still can't persuade me . . ." "But don't you see that . . ." "Well, I appreciate that but . . ." "I'm glad we had the chance to. . . ." The hotel employees enter and begin rearranging the furniture for the next session, a panel discussion, "Has English Become an Electric Circus?")

SECTION D

Multimedia English

INTRODUCTION

About a decade ago, Professor Neil Postman angered and outraged a good many people when he published an essay called "The Politics of Reading." He proposed that the teaching of reading had, in effect, become a political act. Few students bother to read anymore, he claimed, and by clinging to the nineteenth-century medium of print, the schools were serving as a social sorting device, ensuring that the "haves" would continue to "get" while the "have-nots," by being classified as nonreaders, would be doomed to failure.

In the future, he argued, things would have to change, and he envisioned the classroom as "something like an electric circus." It would be

> arranged to accommodate television cameras and monitors, film projectors, computers, audio and video tape machines, and radio, photographic, and stereophonic equipment. As he is now provided with textbooks, each student would be provided with his own still-camera, 8 mm. camera, and tape cassette. The school library would contain books, of course, but at least as many films, records, video tapes, audio tapes, and computer programs. The major effort of the school would be to assist students in achieving what has been called "multimedia literacy."*

* From Neil Postman, "The Politics of Reading," *Harvard Educational Review* 40 (May 1970): 244–52. Copyright © 1970 by the President and Fellows of Harvard College; all rights reserved. This essay has been reprinted in *The Politics of Reading: Point-Counterpoint,* Rosemary Winkeljohann, editor (International Reading Association and ERIC Clearinghouse on Reading and Communication Skills, 1973).

Postman, who has a habit of being deliberately outrageous, was attacked both for his view of literacy as a upper-middle-class tool of oppression and his vision of the electric circus, which sounded to many like a betrayal of all standards. Nevertheless, beneath the overstatement lay a good deal of perceptive truth.

Teachers have a wealth of data and statistics about the number of hours young people spend watching TV, seeing movies, and listening to records. We have confusing and sometimes contradictory information about how all this time spent with the media affects the values, attitudes, and behavior of individuals. We are in conflict about possible detrimental influences on the reading ability of students and on their standards of taste and judgment. Yet the fact that media have enormous impact in undeniable.

Unfortunately, the complexity of media-related issues has led to a variety of practices in the English classroom. The attitude of many schools and teachers has been to ignore the media altogether, hoping to offer the "superior" values of traditional literature as an alternative to the "superficiality and insignificance" of the mass media. On the other hand, we have the media freaks. For them, media are "where it's at," and in their attempts to be relevant, some teachers have turned exclusively to film, TV, and rock music, to the detriment of print-related studies.

At times the media have been used in the classroom for their own sake; at times they have been used as a means of manipulating students into conventional studies. For instance, it has been common practice to use rock lyrics as a way of showing kids that they "really do like poetry" or to analyze rock as a conventional study of poetic devices. Such practices are a disservice both to the individual media—print and nonprint—and to the students' values and interests.

Given the concern of English teachers for the effective use of language, the English classroom is an ideal place for students to sort out and develop their experiences with the world of mass media. We think that four points about media should be emphasized and used as a basis for an integrated media-in-English program:

1. Media provide people with instantaneous, abundant information about the world in which they live. Whether they (or we) like it or not, young people receive information about all manner of products and services in the world of consumerism. They learn about pollution, politics, superstars, strife, violence, kidnappings, hijackings, social affairs, religious holidays, the weather, disasters, drugs, sports. All of this information carries an aura of truth, and the ubiquitous presence of the media causes young people to absorb it, often without choice or critical discrimination. Obviously, this information is an important source of vicarious experience (young people nowadays *do* know more about the world than previous generations). But media bombardment makes it crucial that kids learn to separate the truth from the lies, the important from the unimportant, the objective from the subjective, and the useful from the useless. Young people must learn to deal with that information in productive ways. Rather than being confused or misled, they need to be enlightened by it.

2. *Media provide people with a rich mosaic of experience.* The newspaper, the magazine, radio, film, and most notably television present reality in a kaleidoscope of facts, stories, opinions, advertisements, games, images, and propaganda. For most children and young adults the world is not one of sequentially related experiences but of seemingly unrelated experiences—juxtaposed or simultaneous. They watch television while they read the paper, engage in telephone or face-to-face conversations, play "Monopoly" or make love. They listen to the radio while they are talking, riding in a car, doing homework, and reading. Students are accustomed to a fast-paced world in which they tune in to whatever information or experience seems most valuable, interesting, pressing at the time.

3. *Mass media have effects on the values, attitudes, and behavior of people.* It is difficult to determine what role media have in the development of values and attitudes (and hence behavior) of their audiences—whether they shape, reinforce, or merely reflect values. The question is particularly important when dealing with young people in the process of developing values. Though we don't know for certain what specific effects are, it is axiomatic that young people need experiences that will allow them to reflect critically on the values being promoted (overtly and subtly).

4. *Media have an effect on the development of aesthetic standards and judgment of their audiences.* Through their contact with the media, the young learn to like certain kinds of music, stories, and even people. They respond emotionally and intellectually to the music they listen to, the TV shows they watch, the films they see. They learn to appreciate a variety of art forms and artistic experiences. At the same time, media inundation *can* have a numbing effect when used uncritically, unconsciously, and in too large doses. Young people need to become more conscious of what they like and why they like it.

When Postman spoke of a "circus" of electronic media in the classroom, many people picked up on the fun-and-games connotations—clowns and cotton candy—rather than a metaphoric possibility that a circus offers a person a variety of interesting choices at any given time. If one takes that second meaning, we're inclined to agree that English *should* be an electronic circus, offering many different media experiences. At the same time, we should hasten to add that as we have shown in previous sections of this book, English ought to be a reading, writing, and languaging circus as well. The media, we think, will never destroy literacy, and teachers need not create an adversary relationship between print and non-print forms. There is plenty of room for both in the three-ringed circus of English.

CHAPTER 24

Media in the Classroom

The media have so many applications in the English classroom that we'll simply begin this chapter with a potpourri, a listing of possibilities. The English teacher should create an environment that allows a student to work with, talk about, think over, and use media in new and creative ways, manipulating electronic (and print) media, creating new forms and expressions, examining the quality of media information and entertainment he or she is receiving. Obviously, interesting topics in mass media and popular culture are unlimited, and students should be encouraged to explore areas of interest. Some possibilities:

- Examine the role of sports in American life. Compare the way sports are presented through different media. What do various sports say about American values and interests?
- Examine popular religion in America. What kinds of perspectives are presented on the Sunday morning religious shows? To what kinds of audiences do they appeal?
- Do an in-depth study of a popular hero. Or compare various heroes, e.g., sports heroes, political heroes, comic-book heroes, TV heroes, heroes in history, heroes in best sellers. Do there seem to be common characteristics? Which do you find most appealing?
- Do a study of the occult as it appears in magazines, fiction, movies, and TV.
- Explore monsters. Do a historical or comparative study of Dracula, Frankenstein, the Hulk, King Kong—in novels, movies, comics, TV shows, etc.
- Analyze a popular rock group or a particular type of popular music.
- Write the history of the soap opera or of a particular soap opera.

➡ Examine the roles of females on soap operas, evening drama, game shows, and various types of commercials.

➡ Compare the Perry Mason of Gardner's novels with the Perry Masons on TV.

➡ Study Saturday morning cartoons and commercials and determine the kinds of appeals that are being made to kids. Look at the visual appeals made to kids as well as at the content.

➡ Compare the fiction found in school books with the fiction found in various popular magazines.

➡ Compare the editorial stance of *Newsweek, Nation,* and *U.S. News and World Report.*

➡ Compare ads in *Ms., True Romance, Woman's Day,* etc. What do the ads say about the audiences?

➡ Analyze the image of blacks (and other minorities) presented on TV, in movies, in magazines, in newspapers.

➡ Study the changes in the most popular types of shows over a ten-year period (western, detective, medical, minority, situation comedies, variety).

➡ Analyze the images of adolescents on television (or in movies, or in popular fiction).

➡ Compare TV news programs.

➡ Make a collection of articles and news stories on an event of local or national importance gathered from various sources.

➡ Describe American humor; look at television, comics, movies, joke books, etc.

➡ Examine popular psychology as represented in books, magazines, radio and TV shows.

➡ Examine advice columns in magazines and newspapers. What seem to be people's major concerns and problems?

➡ Explore public access television. Find out how "ordinary people" can use television.

➡ Look into organizations and groups of people who are trying to have some influence on programming in the media. Gather information about the progress and problems of public input into television and other media.

➡ Choose an area or issue of interest (pollution) and evaluate and describe how it is presented in various media.

The Media-Integrated Classroom

Although it is important and helpful to have students look directly and analytically at media, study in isolation is not enough. Rather than merely offering media courses separate from the rest of the students' experiences, it seems more productive and vital to discuss and consider media along with students' literary and personal experiences. The effective integrated classroom contains media equipment (videotape, slide and film projectors, record players, tape recorders), magazines, newspapers, comic books, as well as all manner of traditional and popular fiction, poetry, and drama. It allows students various ways of exploring experiences, ranging from analytical to expressive ways of ordering reality.

A Word of Caution

When opening up the classroom to various options in forms of response, you run the risk of allowing your classroom to become fragmented, with the student doing something just because it's there, rather than because a particular form is appropriate or worthwhile to his or her true response. The teacher will need to offer some guidance in helping students move from experience to experience and in helping them make best use of what's available to them.

Teachers should not avoid using media because they are not experts in the technology. It is necessary, of course, to know how to operate the machinery or to have someone available who can (your AV person can help). And it is helpful, too, to have experimented with media. Teachers, like students, learn best by doing, and to feel comfortable bringing media into the class, the teacher probably needs some firsthand experience. But little about the teacher's own learning need to be passed on to their students. After some basic pointers about how to make the equipment work, students should be able to do some experimentation and playing with the media to discover the effects they can achieve on their own.

FILMMAKING

Although filmmaking has become very popular as a separate course, it can be successfully integrated into traditional classes in literature and composition, as well as more broadly thematic or topical classes.

Because of the difficulty of coordinating sound track and picture, it is best for students to play films that have a musical or narrative sound track. Senior-high students seem to use film best as a visual image concentrating on mood or theme in general. Often this means a poem or a piece of music provides the basis for the creation of the visual image. For junior-high kids, this seems more difficult, and they do better at creating stories with film. Some ways of using film in the classroom:

- Capture the images of a poem; choose music appropriate to the poetry.
- Re-create the mood of a story, song, poem, drama.
- Use visual images to express an emotion, such as love, fear, anger, hatred.
- Explore the physical world with film, capturing subtleties, details; subjects might be cats, toes, old buildings, walks, fences.
- Explore an issue on film, such as conflict, pollution, conspicuous consumption.
- Retell a short story or fable on film.
- Create a sequel or parody of a film you've seen.

VIDEOTAPE

The advantages of videotape over film are that the tapes are reusable, so that after the initial investment, videotaping is inexpensive; mistakes can be corrected easily merely by rewinding and retaping; it has sound, so dramatizations, talk shows, and interviews can be done. Though the picture is not as clear and precise as with film, videotape can be used to capture or create interesting images. Students feel much freer to experiment and play around with videotape, and the results in the practice runs are often as enjoyable, creative, and exciting as the finished product. In addition, when given the chance to redo something, students may work and work polishing and manipulating an idea, often changing it in conception as well as quality.

Some suggestions for videotape:

- Create a TV series based on a novel or short story.
- Creat parodies or satires of fiction or TV shows.
- Make a TV movie based on real experiences that you have had or that you have read about in magazines or newspapers.
- Do a talk show in which you interview characters from literature about how they feel about their lives and times; or do a "Famous Authors" series in which various authors (from Shakespeare to Zindel) meet and talk about writing.

➡ Create advertisements to sell a movie, book, poem, or short story to the American public.

➡ Write, direct, and produce a play, and televise it; explore the possibility of doing it on public access television.

➡ Videotape a poetry reading or play production; explore the possibility of making the videotape available to other English classes.

➡ Research an issue; videotape a documentary that includes on-the-scene filming, interviews, and analysis.

➡ Videotape short improvisations and dramatizations based on novels, TV shows, short stories, poems, movies, songs.

SOUNDTAPE

Like videotape, soundtape can be used to produce both expository and artistic pieces. Its great advantage is that it is both inexpensive and easy to operate. In addition, students have an anonymity with soundtape that they don't have with videotape.

Some uses of soundtape:

➡ Produce radio plays, both student written and published drama; or re-create short stories and novels for radio.

➡ Do fictionalized interviews with characters and authors, either about their literary life or about their views of contemporary issues and concerns.

➡ Make a tape of songs or music appropriate to the thematic unit being studied (images of women, isolation, identity) or to a piece of literature being studied.

➡ Tape sound effects for a classroom play production.

➡ Interview friends, neighbors, family as part of your research on issue or topic of interest to you.

SLIDE-TAPE

The slide show has exciting potential both as an artistic medium and a medium of social-political commentary. Using photo slides and handmade slides, a student can gather images from his personal world and the larger world. Students can do an effective show with relatively few slides (40–50), or they can do an elaborate show using a couple of hundred slides, more than one screen, and a film shown simultaneously. The soundtrack can be made by taping television, radio, records, conversations, or readings of poetry, fiction, political speeches, letters, or magazine articles.

Some ideas for slide-tape:

➡ Illustrate a current issue with slides and sound tape using newspaper articles, editorials, TV newscasters' reports, and politicians' speeches.

➡ Explore various approaches and perspectives on a broad theme, such as *"Time," "Beauty," "Honor," "Death."* Use poets', philosophers', and historians' writings for your sound-tape.

➡ Illustrate a song, poem, or story with visual images.

➡ Choose a particular group in American society (women, blacks, farmers) and explore the images of that group projected by mass media.

➡ Use slides to create a personal narrative, an illustration of an experience or value that is important to you. The sound may be your own writing or writing that you think says something about you.

➡ Create an editorial with slides—on poverty, hunger, consumerism, nationalism.

WRITING

While students are exploring their world and experience through new media and new composing processes, writing continues to be a direct, accessible, and immediate means of creating and communicating. In the integrated classroom, students will continue to write, write, write:

➡ reviews of movies, TV shows, records, books, plays (not book-report style, but in the form of popular reviews).

➡ magazine articles, advertisements, short stories—for a particular magazine, or create your own.

➡ a poem in response to a movie, a TV show, or some music.

➡ a satire of a TV show or a movie.

➡ a letter to an editor or a guest editorial on a current issue.

➡ advertising copy to sell a movie, book, poem, short story.

➡ letters to superstars or politicians.

➡ scripts for TV shows, movies.

➡ papers, including narratives, dialogues, expositions, on themes and issues that draw on both popular and traditional art . . . on artists, violence, changing values, animals, dreams.

A Note on the Media and Aesthetics

Critics of the media, especially those in the arts and humanities, have a habit of dismissing the content of the media as aesthetically inferior. Critics praise television and films that present classic or established works but tend to discount those that appeal to mass audiences. The elitist often views the mass audience as a bunch of Charlie Tunas unable to distinguish "good taste" from what "tastes good." In the critic's eyes, the mass audience is only interested in what "tastes good." A major concern of the critic, then, becomes one of improving or raising tastes, of developing critical standards.

The fact is, however, that people have already developed their own critical standards. Whether the elitist likes it or not, people *choose* what television shows they want to watch, what records they want to hear and what movies they will cry over. They read the fiction that moves or interests them and buy the magazines and newspapers that tell them what they want to know about. By denying the validity of these experiences, the elitist cuts himself off from participating in a relationship that could lead to the mutual growth of individuals of differing tastes.

Young people, too, have aesthetic experiences with popular art, and they have standards that relate to those experiences. But they are not necessarily those of the elitist. The standards are based on the individual reader, hearer, viewer in a particular developmental stage, with a particular set of experiences, some particular needs, in a particular time and place. It is true that some people may live largely through fictional characters or prefer vicarious experiences that do not help them clarify reality and may actually distort it. Television or movies or fiction may become an escape from the real world. But television programs, movies, music, popular fiction all provide young people with important emotional, psychological, and artistic (patterns of feeling, knowing) experiences. They provide relationships and identification with characters; they become sources through which young people deal with and expand their fantasy worlds; they provide intellectual stimulation; they provide new ways of knowing. In short, much of the content of mass media from soap operas to evening dramas, from rock music to jazz, from *Willy Wonka* to *The Godfather,* provides experiences that remove young people from the realm of their own existence and help them view their own and others' experience in a new way.

One of the important roles of the English teacher and the English classroom is to help students become aware of those experiences that are productive and important (in their own terms) and that are not helpful or useful (again, in their terms). It is through accepting and valuing kids' experiences that the teacher can enter into such a shared exploration, an exploration that helps the student grow intellectually, psychologically, emotionally.

CHAPTER 25

TV and English

Thanks to television, the next generation will be born with four eyes and no tongue.

—Fred Allen

Although Fred Allen's prediction has not taken place (yet), what he says is metaphorically true. Our children spend countless hours watching television shows, and because viewing is a spectator, rather than a participatory activity, there is little time for any verbal interaction during prime time. Because there has been some massaging of eyes and ears as a result of television, the ancient arts of speaking and writing may have assumed a less important place in the lives of our children, and they may appear to have "no tongues."

If television forces children into passivity, and passivity is considered to be an unhealthy mode, why would we teach television in the classroom? Perhaps it is the duty of a good teacher to encourage students and their parents to limit the number of viewing hours or attempt to discourage the practice of viewing altogether. Realistically, neither one of these suggestions can be taken seriously. As the major form of American communication and entertainment, television can be held accountable for both good and evil; either way, it is as important a facet of our current culture as the automobile and the bathtub.

Whether we like it or not, commercial TV and educational TV do as much to educate or miseducate our children as any other institution in our society. That seems reason enough for language teachers, who are dedicated to the analysis, production, and criticism of language, its uses and effects, to focus some classroom attention on one of the greatest language-transmitting machines devel-

Much of the material for this chapter was drafted by Betsy B. Kaufman, director, the Academic Skills Center, Queens College, Flushing, New York.

oped by man. The English classroom is one place where students can explore the uses, functions, and product that comprise what we call TV.

In 1961, in a book titled *Television and the Teaching of English* (National Council of Teachers of English), Neil Postman said, "In any elementary or high school classroom in the United States, the teacher is probably the only member of the group who can recall vividly a time when life was lived without television." This statement is no longer necessarily true. There are more and more teachers who, like their students, were born since the advent of television. For them the word *channel* means something to switch, not something to swim or sail across. We should ask ourselves how that fact alone has changed what goes on in the classroom. Do teachers who grew up on Howdy Doody, Captain Kangaroo, and the Mickey Mouse Club regard school and the things supposed to happen there in a different way than those who grew up prior to 1947? What is the difference? Can those of us born in the twenties, thirties, and early forties understand what it means to a child to watch war in the living room?

As a major source of continuous communication through visual and auditory stimuli, TV is a part of the curriculum whether the teacher recognizes it or not. Because so much time in English is devoted to the study of other forms of communication—speech and print—it seems appropriate for the English teacher to assume responsibility for this form of communication too. In the past, many English teachers who devoted any time to the teaching of television, took the "if you can't beat 'em, join 'em" approach. The teacher assigns students to watch a Shakespearean production or an adaptation of a Galsworthy novel on television. This way the student can learn the content of the books without having to go through the painful process of reading them. There is nothing wrong with using TV for this purpose; in fact, it is a good place to begin discussion of what TV is and how it is used. But other ways to use the medium are equally effective, powerful, and worthy of study. Frequently overlooked by educators, these alternatives increase students' awareness of their own viewing habits and those of the people with whom they live. They get a sense of the role of TV in their lives and should begin to analyze its effect on them and on the environment in which they live.

Learning about how television affects our lives is probably the most important reason for studying it, but some English teachers still need to feel reassured by the knowledge that the traditional skills of the English class will not be ignored or go undeveloped. There may even be some students who ask, "If we study TV, when will we get the real English?" For the skeptics it is good to remember that students who write scripts and edit the works of their peers will learn reading, writing, and speaking through practical experience.

Three general categories may help in describing the alternative uses of TV in the classroom. These are effect, analysis, and production. They are interrelated and are divided here merely for the sake of discussion.

The Effect of Television on Human Beings

This area still remains virtually uncharted. Because so little is known about the effect of television, studying TV effects is both appealing to the adventuresome students as well as revealing for most students and teachers alike.

Some of the questions still unanswered are: How does TV change our lives? What do our lives change from? To what? To get at some answers to these and other broad questions about the effect of TV, students can engage in some fairly simple activities that help reveal what TV has done to the individual.

➡ Begin by asking students to do a survey of the programs that they watch and other programs viewed by other members of the family. Ask students to keep a careful record of who watches what, how often, etc. (Students can add to the questions in the survey, but for the first activity try to keep the survey fairly simple.)

➡ Have students compare the results of their surveys. Is there any favorite show for a certain age group? Sex? Ethnic group?

➡ Ask students to keep a TV log for a fixed period of time (two days or a week). Unlike the previous activity, when the purpose of the survey was to determine *what* shows were being watched, by *which* members of the family, this survey is meant to determine who does what while the set is on; who determines when the set will be on; and what will be viewed when it is on. Students should be asked:

1. Is there only one set in the household? Do people have to share the use of the television? Who decides what show will be watched? How are those decisions made? Is it always the same person who makes that decision? What happens when the set is on? Does everyone watch together? When do they watch alone?

2. Does anyone try to watch television and do some other activity at the same time? What other things do people try to do? Do women tend to try to do two activities, TV and something else, more frequently than men? Is this choice contingent upon the program being aired?

3. Who is the first person in the house to turn on the set in the day? What program is turned on? For what purpose?

4. In what room do you watch TV? Why? Is there another room you

think would be a better choice? Why? What would you do if there were no TV in your home?

5. What did your parents do before they had TV? What did your grandparents do before they had TV? Does your family discuss the TV programs that you watch? Do you discuss TV with your friends? Do people tend to talk or remain silent when the TV is turned on?

➡ Students can do a study on how television has changed our buying habits. What has happened to cigarette sales since cigarette companies are no longer permitted to advertise on television? Is there a vast difference between the effect of television commercials and the advertisement of other media? Have schools, or what is taught in them, changed as a result of television? How? How has our attitude about time been altered by watching the one-handed clock on the "Today" show?

➡ Students can engage in some primary research on the effect of television on human behavior. For instance, if a person does not watch TV at night for the period of a week, do his sleep habits change? Does he go to bed earlier or later? Does he sleep longer? Does he eat more before going to bed? Have students try this kind of experiment on a few willing subjects to see whether they can note any trends. The result can then be reported in the school newspaper or the local paper.

➡ Another piece of research that students might want to investigate is whether certain programs tend to induce insomnia in children. Are there certain nights of the week when large numbers of children in a particular locale have difficulty in going to sleep? Do they all watch TV? Have they all watched the same program?

Analysis of Television

The following suggestions are meant to encourage students to think in terms of what the program or programs we watch are about and how they project the ideas that are being put forth.

➡ Bring the school television set into the classroom. Choose a program for the class to watch and analyze together. Sometimes it is a good idea to pretape a program so that you know what to expect and are able to help students begin their analysis.

The following questions are intended to help begin the analysis with emphasis on the values and morals that seem to be inherent in the program:

Who are the characters? How many of them are men? How many are women? What are their ages? Do there seem to be more young people? How are the older people portrayed? How many children have lead parts? How are they characterized? How many characters are members of minority groups? What characteristics of speech do you associate with a given character? What values seem important to the characters on the program? How do you know? What morals are expressed?

After students have had the experience of doing at least one analysis in a group, they should try a show on their own. Then they are ready to do some longer projects.

► Ask students to watch a series for six weeks or a daily soap opera for two weeks. They may use the series of questions that they developed in the previous exercise and add questions to them that pertain to shows in a series, or they may wish to amend the questions. Some questions that students might ask about a series would include: Is there a formula for the show? In other words, can you see a pattern in show after show? This kind of examination can be done for almost any series, and it helps make students aware that either there are only a few patterns that writers choose from or that a particular show offers a variety of story lines. If this exercise hinders their own viewing, it may encourage students to create new patterns through scripts of their own.

► If students have established that different series have different patterns, then students may want to compare patterns. For instance, are the patterns for all situation comedies the same? Are all mysteries the same?

► Another, and probably the most ambitious project that we can suggest here, is to analyze or monitor the offerings network by network. Does CBS have a point of view that differs from that of NBC or ABC? What bias can be detected? How is it expressed? Are there certain subjects that seem to go unnoticed by some stations that are frequently discussed on other channels? How many hours of programming are devoted to political issues? How many to drama? How many to music? What kinds of programs does each network air?

► Have students study the format of new shows to see how networks express bias, even when they may not intend to do so. What news story comes first? Is the lead story on one channel the same as the lead story on another? What visuals are used with the story? What do the visuals underscore in the story? Can you think of other visuals that might have been used?

► Encourage students to analyze the biases of the noncommercial stations, such as PBS. What programs are aired on this station? Who makes decisions about programming? How does the station get funded?

► An important form of analysis for students, and one that they seem to enjoy doing, is the analysis of advertising. This can be done by watching television and discussing the commercials, or by obtaining the CLIO Award film for any given year and showing it in class. This 16 mm. film contains about fifty commercials, each of which won a prize for good advertising. When seen in a collection, the viewer becomes aware of the impact of advertising and the various approaches used to sell products on television.

➡ Have students develop their own category system in defining various advertising techniques. The old labels, "bandwagon," "glittering generalities," etc., may no longer be the most appropriate descriptions. Students may be interested in learning about these labels but should be encouraged to invent their own.

➡ Students should be helped to become more aware of the language of television. What words have been added to our language as a result of TV? This can be explored both from a technical and semantic view. For instance, words and expressions such as "tune out," "flip the switch," "boob tube," and "plug in" can be examined, and students can research when they first appeared and where they first appeared.

➡ Ask students to analyze the language of specific shows. What questions are asked on a talk show? Are the questions directed toward members of one sex different from the questions directed toward members of the other sex? Are the words used to introduce men different from the words used to introduce women? How can you describe or account for the difference? Do doctors on TV talk differently from policemen? Is the difference in pronunciation, vocabulary, or speech pattern, or a combination of many of these? Are there any noticeable differences in the way in which a TV teacher-actor speaks and the way a teacher on an educational TV program speaks? How do the actors on children's programming speak as compared to those actors on other educational shows? Do they use different vocabulary? Are there any words that are heard in normal conversation that are *never* heard on television? Does the vocabulary and use of the vernacular seem to change after 10:00 at night? If so, what do you think might account for this?

Television Production

An increasing number of schools own TV equipment. Most schools that have purchased equipment have bought portable units: video rovers or portapaks. This equipment is as easy to use as reel-to-reel tape recorders. Frequently the equipment is hidden away in the storeroom of a library or in the corner of one of the book rooms, so that it takes detective work by the teacher to find one. Once found, it is a joy to see students, some of whom have not been interested in any of the other work of the classroom, suddenly become engrossed in planning videotapes.

Before they begin to work with the camera and other equipment, students should be given time to learn how to use it. A few hours in a classroom is usually sufficient. Learning to thread the tape, holding the camera steady, and taking care not to drop equipment are all the mechanical instructions that most people need. However, students *do* need to plan programs in advance. Dialogue and camera shots are more effective if preplanned. Some rehearsal time is also a good idea, for in the beginning, students tend to forget that the microphone (often built into the camera) will pick up all sounds, planned dialogue and off-camera direction alike.

► A popular use of the portable camera is to do documentaries. Have students record events in the school or community. If there is a local theater group, ask the director or producer to allow your students to tape productions. The theater group may enjoy the publicity, and the show may be worth airing in the classroom later on.

► Have students ask the coach of the football team whether he would be willing for them to do a documentary on the team. This will require learning some interview techniques. Good questions are essential.

► Ask students to ask various teachers such as the drama teacher, the librarian, the music teacher, or the home economics teacher whether they can make a documentary about his or her course and the students in it.

► Have students go to the local paper and do a documentary on how the paper is published. What decisions are made about what is newsworthy and what is not? Have students check to see whether the local radio station is in any way connected to the newspaper. Does this constitute a monopoly on news reports? What effect does it have on what the public learns as news?

► If you live in a commuter area, have students go to the train and bus stations and ask commuters about the commuter service. Are these services as good as they could be? How can they be improved? Local politicians may not be too pleased with the answers, but this kind of program may serve a very useful service to the community.

► After studying about advertising, ask students to make up their own commercials for a new product or invent a new way of selling some already existing product.

➡ Have students identify a skill or concept that elementary or junior-high students have difficulty in learning. Ask the students to write, direct, and produce a tape designed to teach the skill or concept. They may want to use "The Electric Company," "Sesame Street," "Mr. Rogers," or some other educational programs as models. The tape might be tested on actual students in the elementary or junior-high classroom to see whether or not it is effective. If this works, students might produce a number of tapes for this purpose.

➡ Finally, students can write, direct, and produce their own original television plays.

In this chapter we have concentrated on offering some practical ideas for the use of TV in the English classroom. We have not begun to touch on the use of materials such as *TV Guide.* Nor have we discussed the place of TV criticism in the study to TV; that is a print-oriented exercise, and we think teachers have a good foundation in using that medium.

One idea that bothers us slightly about making suggestions on how to teach TV is that whenever someone creates a curriculum to teach something, the mere fact of writing lessons for the idea seems to institutionalize the process and eventually results in turning students away from the study. In fact, if we teach TV for a long enough period of time, someone will surely invent an objective test that will tell you what grade level a student has achieved in his viewing aptitude and ability. It is only a small step from there to courses in Remedial Viewing. Basic Skills Centers all over the country will be running courses in The Vocabulary of TV, Reading the TV Program Schedule, or How to Tell One Headache Remedy from Another. In other words, don't make the study of TV into a rigid discipline. TV is, and always has been, a leisure activity. Don't let us, or anyone else, become so analytical about it that we all lose the joy of watching.

CHAPTER 26

Dirt-Cheap Media

One of the most frequent complaints about the possibilities for media use in the classroom is expense: "It just takes too much expensive equipment and too much expensive material to run a media-centered classroom." There's no denying that media is somewhat more expensive than print. In fact, we're convinced that print literacy will survive because of its low cost. Nevertheless, teachers frequently overestimate the expenses of media use and underestimate the availability of low-cost or no-cost equipment.

Many media projects are surprisingly inexpensive if you know a few tricks of the trade. While it may cost a half million dollars to shoot a single episode of "The Bionic Woman," your kids can produce their own thriller on film for half a sawbuck, and can do it on video or audio tape for even less. Alert teachers will always be badgering the administration for an increased media budget. In the meantime, try dirt-cheap media projects.

Slides

There are several sources of slides that range from very inexpensive to fairly expensive.

- *Students' or teachers' own collections.* Color slides from vacations, scenic trips, and growing up can be used to illustrate a variety of themes and ideas in a slide show.
- *Purchased slides.* Vacation spots, museums, and art galleries are good sources for slides.
- *School or public libraries.* Some libraries have slide notebooks, collections of slides that can be borrowed.

➡ The best way to get just the right slide for your show is to make it yourself. Even if you have an inexpensive Instamatic, you can purchase film specifically for slides to photograph your own sights and scenes. A more expensive process, but one that increases your variety, is to photograph pictures from books and magazines. This process requires a 35 mm. camera. Your school or district AV person probably has the equipment and expertise to do this for you or show you how to do it yourself.

➡ The cheapest way to get slides (aside from bringing in your own) is to make them by hand, by using Contac paper and two-inch pictures from magazines or by drawing on clear plastic with magic markers. Again, see the AV person.

Films

➡ *Home movies.* Though home movies are often jiggly pictures of baby's first step or the bears at Yosemite, there may be students in the class whose families have other kinds of interests. In addition, for some purposes, bears or babies might work.

➡ *Colleges, universities, and the public library.* Libraries and colleges often have short films that can be checked out for several days. Check in your area to see if there are film libraries and look through catalogues to find films that seem to fit your themes and ideas. Often they are free; sometimes there is a minimal fee.

➡ Check your school or district AV department or media library to see what kinds of films are available. (Be on the lookout for films other than those designated as related to language arts.)

➡ *Television stations.* TV stations often have outdated commercials or public-service announcements on film that they throw away; sometimes they are willing to pass them on to schools. Students can come up with interesting juxtapositions with other materials, edit them to make their own films, or draw on "useless" ones to make handmade films

➡ *Handmade films.* Handmade films are most useful for expressing moods through colors, shapes, and symbols. Outdated film, exposed film, and leader can be used to bleach, dye, and perforate. See that omniscient AV person again.

Soundtapes

Students can record all manner of things with a simple cassette recorder:

- Interviews with friends, parents, teachers, strangers.
- Records of music, comedy albums, poets reading their own poems, dramatizations, sound effects, etc.
- Television programs, commercials, news announcements, and programs.
- Themselves reading poems, stories, plays, excerpts from novels, editorials, essays.
- Their own writings, or narrations to connect other recorded sources.
- Outside sounds: trains, cars, crowd sounds, birds, dogs barking.

Videotape

If you have the equipment, videotape is the cheapest visual medium to use, because the tapes can be used over and over, just as soundtapes. Videotape equipment can be hooked up to a television set, and you can record TV programs, commercials, news and sports shows; or you can videotape your own world, everything from interviews to dramatizations to documentary shows. (See chapter 25, "TV and English.")

Putting Together an Inexpensive Media Composition

Let students create their own world of all-at-onceness! The possible combinations and juxtapositions for a media project are endless. What you include depends on the purposes you or your students have in mind for the project, and how much time and money you have. You, as a teacher, may create a slide or media presentation to illustrate ideas, concepts, themes, or issues that you wish to introduce to your students. More valuable and productive use can be made of media by having students create their own media compositions:

- responses to literature
- development of themes and topics of interest to them

- illustration and presentation of research
- presentation of their writing
- illustration of literary works, eras, regions, themes.

A popular and simple use of the media show is to illustrate a poem or a song. In this case, the sound track becomes the basis of the show, and pictures are chosen to illustrate the images or ideas in the poem or song. In the simplest version, just the poem or song and the slides that illustrate it are used. A more elaborate version may include a poem, background music to accompany the poem, a large number of slides, and either a professional film (with the sound turned down) which illustrates the ideas, or a handmade film that reflects the mood of the poem.

A related media project involves using instrumental music in which the feeling or meaning grows, not from the words but from the music alone. In this case, students use prepared slides or create slides and film that reflect the feelings the music evokes in them.

After students have done a simple version of the media presentation, they may want to try something more elaborate and comprehensive. A thematic unit, a social issue, or a literary figure or period may provide the general topic for students to work on. If students have a broad topic, they can choose their own approach and their own focus on the theme. The following description of a media composition is illustrative of the process of creating a media project:

1. The first step in planning the presentation is for the students to decide the central feeling or idea they want to communicate. They might look through poetry or fiction anthologies that focus on the topic or theme they've chosen.

2. After they have done some reading, students will be able to decide the aspects of the subject they want to pursue. Perhaps they will want to create a project around poetry, around excerpts from novels, or around their own writings. Or perhaps they will want to do a combination, writing their own narration to connect and combine ideas.

3. While they are looking through print forms, they may also consider what role they want music to play in the production. Perhaps they would like to integrate songs relating to the thematic narration, or perhaps they would like to use music as a background to their words. They might want to use excerpts from several songs, or they might want to have one piece of music running throughout.

4. When they have found all the materials they want to include in their sound track, they begin to order and combine them in the way that best expresses their ideas on the subject, writing the narration they feel they need. At this point, they may find that there are things that they originally thought they could use

that they will want to discard; or they may feel the need to find additional materials to strengthen their focus and ideas. As they sharpen and clarify their thoughts, their original conceptions may change. When they have completed their narration, they record their sound track. They may record the music separately and mix the words and music, using a third tape recorder, or they may wish to do both simultaneously. (Often, doing both simultaneously involves turning the tape recorder off and on more often, which produces a click on the sound track, but that's a relatively minor problem.)

5. After the sound track is completed, the students begin looking for pictures that best express the images and ideas on their tape. The easiest way to do this is to have a typed version of the sound track, so that they can refer to the words on the script to decide what pictures best fit. The length of the sound track will determine how many slides are needed. To maintain interest, it is probably best to have slides on the screen for no longer than twenty seconds, and the time that the slides are on the screen should vary, perhaps with some on the screen for only a few seconds. A ten-minute slide show, then, would require thirty to fifty slides.

6. If the creation of the slides involves taking photographs and having them developed, students should allow enough time for processing the slides that didn't turn out right. When all the slides are completed, students put them in order for the slide show and number them. This makes it easier to place them in the projector (and simplifies matters should someone drop them all).

7. When the sound track and slides are completed, it is time to synchronize. There are two ways to do this: The first simply involves playing the sound track and running the slides, marking on the typed or written-out script where the slides should be changed. A second technique, automated, involves attaching the projector and tape recorder and using a synchronizer with which an electronic impulse is recorded on the tape. (Most media catalogues or camera stores can inform you about this electronic equipment.) Play the show through, marking changes with the sync. The slides will then change automatically.

Variations and Additions

Have students consider the following possibilities in creating their media project:

- Use two slide projectors, placing the odd-numbered slides in one tray and the even-numbered slides in another. Project two different images on two screens at the same time. Or alternate images on one screen, using a dissolve unit which allows images to fade in and out of one another. This creates a smooth series of images rather than the black space you get using one projector.

► Find a short movie that expresses the theme of your project. Play it simultaneously with your slides. If it's shorter than the show, decide at what point it would be most effective, and turn on the movie projector at that point. If it's longer, decide what scene is most effective and wind the film to that point when you are setting up your equipment. Mark on your written script where you want it to begin. You probably won't want to use the sound track, so remember to turn that down.

► Create a handmade film that uses colors, images, shapes, and words that reflect or reinforce the mood or feeling you are trying to portray, or that add contrast to your major mood.

► Videotape a soap opera, commercial, or news program from television and juxtapose it with your slides and/or film; or create a pantomime or improvisation that you videotape for your show.

Of course, it is not necessary to begin with the sound track and proceed through pictures and films. A student may have some nature pictures that he wishes to use, and he may look for music or literature to go with that. He may want to simply work with moods and feelings using handmade film and music. What's most important is to be imaginative and flexible, allowing ideas to grow and conceptions to change as a result of the interaction between the ideas and the materials.

SUMMARY AND TROUBLESHOOTING

Get with It Teacher

Perhaps the most difficult aspect of using media in the classroom is not what to do with it, but managing the technical aspects—the reels, plugs, cassettes, wiring. Trouble regularly crops up, and as far as we can see, there are only two major ways of solving problems:

1. Know how to handle the equipment skillfully, so you don't make errors due to lack of familiarity with it. (Alternatively, you or the school's AV department can make certain you have a technician available to help at all times).

2. Make certain the equipment is kept in good repair and not misused by those who either don't know how or don't care about using it correctly.

Media use can be frustrating. Bettie M. Kelley, an English teacher in Port Allegany, Pennsylvania, has written of some of her experiences, and we'd like to close this section by sharing them with you:

> I was born fifty years too late. In the good old days of blackboards, chalk, and textbooks, there were no temperamental tape recorders, provoking projectors, and reluctant record players to plague schoolmarms—only difficult students, balky school boards, and whimsical administrators. Times were easier. If the chalk crumbled in your hand, you merely reached for another piece; if you were two textbooks short, you could count on eager volunteers to share; if the pen ran dry, you simply made more ink from available lampblack. But now—all has changed.
>
> The methods people say, "Your students are living in a machine age; they expect to visualize some of their lessons, not merely to hear them. We are living in an electronic time; people will have to learn to interpret the spoken word more often than the

written word. They will become bored with traditional methods. You must be current. You must get with it."

So you try. You order films the required five weeks in advance and hope your human lesson plans have kept pace with the central computer. If not, you'll find that on the day you begin your study of John Steinbeck, your film on Mark Twain finally arrives. But even if your timing is good, your problems are still many.

You must prepare yourself by previewing the "film" (under no circumstances is this audiovisual device to be called a movie) and compiling questions to ask the class. You must arrive at the storage room early enough to make sure a fellow teacher hasn't "mislaid" your assigned machine. These "bandits of the A-V department" have been known to hide projectors in broom closets and record players in file cabinets. They are an elusive breed, difficult to trap. If this is your lucky day, though, you are able to find a machine not labeled "bulb broken" or "to be sent for repairs" or "cord frayed" (in a real pinch, you can use scotch tape here). Assuming you can also find a cart, you begin to wheel your prize down the hall, clearing a path through throngs of students headed for the cafeteria.

Arriving at your room, you must wait for the cheers of "Oh boy, no class today; we're havin' a movie" to die down. Then you appoint a student in charge of the screen, and amidst much fussing and a few pinched fingers, he manages to assemble the tripod and raise the white sheet. You already feel that raising a white cloth might be appropriate, too.

Then, the focal point of sixty eager and challenging eyes, you step to center stage, which happens to be at the back of the hall. You remove the film from the can, rip off the seal and place the round hole of the reel onto the square peg of the machine. Then you reverse the procedure, this time noting that "This Side Out" on the reel actually means something. Pressing the automatic loading device (without which you would never have contemplated this madness) you insert the well-chewed end of the film into the slot. If your luck is still holding, the machine will grasp the film in its hungry teeth and begin the unwinding operation. Stop machine, attach film to take-up reel, restart machine and wait. Nothing happens? Remember that the volume knob is separate.

You have forgotten to warm up the audio. Another pause while your charges scrape desks on the floor and write on their hands with felt tip pens. Use this moment to remind them that today is not a day off; they are expected to take notes on the film. "Notes? We can't see in the dark."

Start machine again; turn down volume (someone from the next room is banging on the wall); settle back in the small desk, carefully poised to head off the next catastrophe. A hush settles, a few eager students are writing down the producer's name; all are listening intently. You have finally overcome the odds—you have beaten the machine.

What's that noise? A fire drill? It can't be; the principal didn't know this was Film Day. And the film has to be returned tomorrow. Back to the books and blackboard. Next month, the video tape player; after that, Skylab, here I come.*

* Bettie M. Kelley, "Get with It, Teacher," *The English Journal* 63 (October 1974): 61–62.

PART THREE

Resources for Teaching English

APPENDIX A

English-Related Magazines and Journals

Arizona English Bulletin
Subscriptions: Arizona English Teachers Assocation*
Publishing Schedule: Three issues yearly
Focus: Both practical and theoretical articles related to all levels of language arts education.

California English
Subscriptions: California Assocation of Teachers of English*
Publishing Schedule: Six issues yearly
Focus: Practical articles, reviews, and resources for classroom English teachers at all levels.

College Composition and Communication
Subscriptions: National Council of Teachers of English
1111 Kenyon Road
Urbana, Ill. 61801
Publishing Schedule: Four issues yearly
Focus: Theoretical and practical articles on the teaching of college composition; many articles appropriate for secondary writing teachers.

College English
Subscriptions: National Council of Teachers of English
1111 Kenyon Road
Urbana, Ill. 61801
Publishing Schedule: Monthly, September through April
Focus: Theory, pedagogy, curriculum, and political issues related to the teaching of college level literature, language, and composition.

English Education
Subscriptions: National Council of Teachers of English
1111 Kenyon Road
Urbana, Ill. 61801
Publishing Schedule: Four issues yearly
Focus: Directed toward instructors and supervisors involved in teacher preparation and in-service education with articles describing successful teacher-education programs and curriculum and program design.

The English Journal
Subscriptions: National Council of Teachers of English
1111 Kenyon Road
Urbana, Ill. 61801
Publishing Schedule: Monthly, September through May
Focus: Articles on all aspects of the teaching of English language, literature, and composition in middle, junior, or senior high school; also general pieces in the field of English and education.

The English Record
Subscriptions: New York State English Council*
Publishing Schedule: Four issues yearly
Focus: Articles on pedagogy, literary criticism, book reviews, and research reports relevant to the teaching of English on all levels.

English in Texas
Subscriptions: Texas Council of Teachers of English*
Publishing Schedule: Quarterly
Focus: K–college; diversity of topics related to language arts teaching.

Florida English Journal
Subscriptions: Florida Council of Teachers of English*
Publishing Schedule: Two issues yearly
Focus: For classroom teachers of English and language arts at all levels.

Focus
Subscriptions: New Jersey Council of Teachers of English*
Publishing Schedule: Quarterly
Focus: Local news and short articles of interest to secondary English teachers.

Georgia English Counselor
Subscriptions: Georgia Council of Teachers of English*
Publishing Schedule: Quarterly
Focus: News of regional interest and articles for teaching English at all levels.

Illinois English Bulletin
Subscriptions: Illinois Association of Teachers of English*
Publishing Schedule: Quarterly
Focus: Articles for English teachers at all levels; emphasis on practical ideas.

Indiana English Journal
Subscriptions: Indiana Council of Teachers of English*
Publishing Schedule: Quarterly
Focus: Articles for English and language arts teachers at all levels.

Iowa English Bulletin
Subscriptions: Iowa Council of Teachers of English*
Publishing Schedule: Two issues yearly
Focus: Stresses composition, but includes articles on theory, pedagogy, and literary criticism.

Journal of Popular Culture
Subscriptions: Popular Culture Association
University Hall
Bowling Green University
Bowling Green, Ohio 43403
Publishing Schedule: Four issues yearly
Focus: Articles analyzing all aspects and trends in current and historical popular culture.

Journal of Reading
Subscriptions: International Reading Association
800 Barksdale Road
Newark, Del. 19711
Publication Schedule: Eight issues yearly
Focus: Theoretical and practical articles, program descriptions, research reports, and reviews for teachers involved in secondary reading instruction.

Kansas English
Subscriptions: Kansas Association of Teachers of English*
Publishing Schedule: Three issues yearly
Focus: Devoted to the teaching of composition and literature with one issue featuring the writing of Kansas students.

Language Arts
Subscriptions: National Council of Teachers of English
1111 Kenyon Road
Urbana, Ill. 61801
Publishing Schedule: Eight issues yearly
Focus: Major journal of NCTE for elementary language arts teachers, with wide diversity of articles on theory, classroom teaching ideas, book reviews, and research reports.

The Leaflet
Subscriptions: New England Association of Teachers of English*
Publishing Schedule: Quarterly
Focus: Articles covering the range of language arts teaching at all levels.

Learning
Subscriptions: *Learning*
1255 Portland Place
Boulder, Col. 80302
Publishing Schedule: Nine issues yearly
Focus: Directed primarily toward elementary/middle-school education with many teaching ideas and resources.

Louisiana English Journal
Subscriptions: Louisiana Council of Teachers of English*
Publishing Schedule: Two issues yearly
Focus: Emphasis on practical teaching ideas for composition, in particular.

Maryland English Journal
Subscriptions: Maryland Council of Teachers of English*
Publishing Schedule: Two issues yearly
Focus: Articles on classroom teaching ideas for reading, language, and writing.

Media and Methods
Subscriptions: Media and Methods
134 N. 13th St.
Philadelphia, Pa. 19107
Publishing Schedule: Nine times yearly
Focus: Classroom ideas and resources for teaching language, literature, and composition, as well as for using electronic media.

The Michigan English Teacher
Subscriptions: Michigan Council of Teachers of English*
Publishing Schedule: Monthly, September through May
Focus: Newsletter format with information on regional events, as well as teaching ideas for composition, language, and literature; directed primarily toward elementary and secondary teachers.

The Nebraska English Counselor
Subscriptions: Nebraska Council of Teachers of English*
Publication Schedule: Quarterly
Focus: Practical classroom ideas for teaching English at all levels.

North Carolina English Teacher
Subscriptions: North Carolina English Teachers Association*
Publishing Schedule: Three issues yearly
Focus: Language arts pedagogy for secondary and elementary school.

North Dakota English
Subscriptions: North Dakota Council of Teachers of English*
Publishing Schedule: Quarterly
Focus: Directed primarily toward the teaching of composition at all levels, but also contains articles on language, literature, and educational issues.

Ohio English Bulletin
Subscriptions: English Association of Ohio
Publishing Schedule: Quarterly
Focus: Diversity of articles for English and language arts teachers, K–college.

Reading Horizons
Subscriptions: Reading Center and Clinic
Western Michigan University
Kalamazoo, Mich. 49008

Publishing Schedule: Quarterly
Focus: Book reviews and articles appropriate to the teaching of reading at all levels.

Reading Improvement
Subscriptions: Project Innovation
P. O. Box 566
Chula Vista, Calif. 95109
Publishing Schedule: Quarterly
Focus: Articles on a diversity of topics in reading for all levels.

The Reading Teacher
Subscriptions: International Reading Association
800 Barksdale Road
Newark, Del. 19711
Publishing Schedule: Eight issues yearly
Focus: IRA's elementary level journal with a wide variety of articles, reviews, research reports, program descriptions, and teaching ideas.

Reading World
Subscriptions: Dr. George McNinch
Publications Business Manager
University of Southern Mississippi
Southern Station Box 26
Hattiesburg, Miss. 39401
Publishing Schedule: Quarterly
Focus: Emphasis on college reading and reading research

Research in the Teaching of English
Subscriptions: National Council of Teachers of English
1111 Kenyon Road
Urbana, Ill. 61801
Publishing Schedule: Three issues yearly
Focus: Reports of research done at various levels in composition, language, and literature.

Teachers and Writers Magazine
Subscriptions: Teachers and Writers
186 West 4th Street
New York, N.Y. 10014

Publishing Schedule: Three issues yearly
Focus: Teaching ideas and student writings developed and collected by writers and artists involved in T & W workshops in schools and communities.

Virginia English Bulletin
Subscriptions: Virginia Association of Teachers of English*
Publication Schedule: Two issues yearly
Focus: Current issues and problems in the teaching of English at all levels.

SOURCES

Bowden, Nancy Butler, and Lee Mountain. "How to Get Published: A Directory of English Language Arts Journals." *The English Journal,* January 1978, pp. 74–78.

Buehler, Carl J., ed., *Directory of Learning Resources for Reading.* Gales Ferry, Conn.: Education Systems, Inc., 1978.

* Denotes an affiliate of the National Council of Teachers of English. For current address, write NCTE, 1111 Kenyon Road, Urbana, Illinois 61801.

APPENDIX B

Directory of Professional Organizations

American Library Association
50 E. Huron
Chicago, Ill. 60611
Executive Director: Robert Wedgeworth

A professional association for people involved in library services.

Association for Supervision and Curriculum Development
1701 K Street, N.W., Suite 1100
Washington, D.C. 20006
Executive Director: Gordon Cawelti

Publishes *Educational Leadership;* professional organization for supervisors, curriculum coordinators, and school administrators.

International Reading Association
800 Barksdale Road
Newark, Del. 19711
Executive Director: Ralph C. Staiger

Publishes *The Reading Teacher, Journal of Reading,* and *Reading Research Quarterly;* national professional organization for teachers and specialists concerned with reading; also has many local affiliates.

National Association of Secondary School Principals
1904 Association Drive
Reston, Va. 22091
Executive Secretary: Owen B. Kiernan

Publishes the *NASSP Bulletin* for junior-high, middle-school, and senior-high administrators.

National Council of Teachers of English
1111 Kenyon Road
Urbana, Ill. 61801
Executive Secretary: Robert F. Hogan

Publishes three major journals: *Language Arts* (elementary), *The English Journal* (secondary), and *College English* (college); also publishes *College Composition and Communication, English Education, Research in the Teaching of English,* and *Councilgrams,* a summary of news items of interest to teachers.

National Education Association
1201 16th Street, N.W.
Washington, D.C. 20036
Executive Secretary: Terry Herndon

Publishes *Today's Education;* professional organization for teachers and educators focusing on a broad range of issues and concerns in education.

State and local English teachers' associations are too numerous to list, but the odds are there is one in your area. Write to the National Council of Teachers of English for a list of organizations. If there isn't one near you, consider starting one; you can affiliate with NCTE for $25 per year, and affiliation gives you access to national services and an inexpensive speaker's bureau.

Many organizations offer an inexpensive membership rate for students enrolled in teacher preparation programs. The NCTE rate, for example, is about 25 percent of the cost of full membership.

APPENDIX C

Publishers of Professional and Instructional Materials

This list includes publishers and distributors of materials for both students and teachers. Materials include paperbacks; media; films; recordings; texts, handbooks, and series for literature, reading, and composition. Write to the publishers for specific information about materials and prices.

Abingdon Press
201 Eighth Avenue S.
Nashville, Tennessee 37202

Acropolis Books Ltd.
2400 Seventeenth Street, N.W.
Washington, D.C. 20009

Addison-Wesley Publishing Co.
Reading, Massachusetts 01867

Allyn & Bacon, Inc.
470 Atlantic Ave.
Boston, Massachusetts 02210

American Book Company
450 W. 33rd Street
New York, New York 10001

AMSCO School Publications, Inc.
315 Hudson Street
New York, New York 10013

American Guidance Service, Inc. (AGS)
Publishing Building
Circle Pines, Minnesota 55014

Paul S. Amidon & Associates, Inc.
5408 Chicago Avenue S.
Minneapolis, Minnesota 55417

Appleton-Century-Crofts
292 Madison Avenue
New York, New York 10017

Atlantic-Little, Brown and Company
34 Beacon Street
Boston, Massachusetts 02106

Avon Books
Education Department
959 Eighth Avenue
New York, New York 10019

Ballantine Books
Education Department
201 East 50th Street
New York, New York 10022

Bantam Books, Inc.
666 Fifth Avenue
New York, New York 10019

Barnell Loft, LTD.
111 South Centre Avenue
Rockville Centre, New York 11570

Barron's Educational Series, Inc.
113 Crossways Park Drive
Woodbury, New York 11797

Behavioral Research Laboratories
P.O. Box 577
Palo Alto, California 94302

Bell and Howell Company
Audio Visual Products Division
7100 McCormick Road
Chicago, Illinois 60645

Benefic Press
10300 W. Roosevelt Road
Westchester, Illinois 60153

Berkley Publishing Corporation
200 Madison Avenue
New York, New York 10016

BFA Educational Media
2211 Michigan Avenue
P.O. Box 1795
Santa Monica, California 90406

Bobbs-Merrill Company, Inc.
430 West 62nd Street
Indianapolis, Indiana 46206

Book Lab Inc.
1449 37th Street
Brooklyn, New York 11218

Bosustow Productions
1649 11th Street
Santa Monica, California 90404

R. R. Bowker Company
1180 Avenue of the Americas
New York, New York 10036

Bowmar
Box 3623
Glendale, California 91201

William C. Brown Company
2460 Kerper Boulevard
Dubuque, Iowa 52001

Caedmon Records, Inc.
505 8th Avenue
New York, New York 10018

Cambridge Book Company
488 Madison Avenue
New York, New York 10022

The Center for Humanities, Inc.
Two Holland Avenue
White Plains, New York 10603

Centron Films
1621 West Ninth Street
Box 687
Lawrence, Kansas 66044

Chicorel Library Publishing Corp.
275 Central Park West
New York, New York 10024

Children's Press, Inc.
1224 W. Van Buren Street
Chicago, Illinois 60607

Chilton Book Company
201 King of Prussia Road
Radnor, Pennsylvania 19089

Communacad
Box 541
Wilton, Connecticut 06897

The Continental Press, Inc.
Elizabeth, Pennsylvania 17022

Coronet Films, Inc.
65 E. South Water Street
Chicago, Illinois 60601

Creative Playthings, Inc.
Edinburg Road
Cranbury, New Jersey 08540

Croft, Inc.
283 Greenwich Avenue
Greenwich, Connecticut 06830

Croft-NEI Publications
24 Rope Ferry Road
Waterford, Connecticut 06386

T. Y. Crowell Co., Inc.
666 Fifth Avenue
New York, New York 10019

The John Day Company, Inc.
666 Fifth Avenue
New York, New York 10019

Delacorte Press
750 Third Avenue
New York, New York 10017

Dell Publishing Company
1 Dag Hammarskjold Plaza
New York, New York 10017

T. S. Denison and Co., Inc.
5100 W. 82nd Street
Minneapolis, Minnesota 55437

Dexter and Westbrook, LTD.
958 Church Street
Baldwin, New York 11510

The Dial Press
750 Third Avenue
New York, New York 10017

Dover Publications, Inc.
180 Varick Street
New York, New York 10014

Dreier Educational Systems, Inc.
320 Raritan Avenue
Highland Park, New Jersey 08904

Dufour Editions, Inc.
Chester Springs, Pennsylvania 19425

Economy Company
1901 N. Walnut
Oklahoma City, Oklahoma 73105

Education House, Inc.
2619 Ryan Drive
Indianapolis, Indiana 46220

Educational Activities, Inc.
P.O. Box 392
Freeport, New York 11520

Educational Audio Visual Inc.
Pleasantville, New York 10570

Educators Publishing Service, Inc.
75 Moulton Street
Cambridge, Massachusetts 02138

Educulture
3184 "J" Airway Avenue
Costa Mesa, California 92626

Encyclopaedia Britannica, Inc.
425 N. Michigan Avenue
Chicago, Illinois 60611

E. P. Dutton & Company, Inc.
201 Park Avenue S.
New York, New York 10003

Everett/Edwards, Inc.
P.O. Box 1060
Deland, Florida 32720

Fearon Publishers
6 Davis Drive
Belmont, California 94002

The Feminist Press
Box 334R
Old Westbury, New York 11568

Field Enterprises Educational Corporation
510 Merchandise Mart Plaza
Chicago, Illinois 60654

Filmfair Communications
10900 Ventura Boulevard
Studio City, California 91604

Films for the Humanities, Inc.
P.O. Box 2053
Princeton, New Jersey 08540

Follett Corporation
1010 W. Washington Boulevard
Chicago, Illinois 60607

Gale Research Company
Book Tower
Detroit, Michigan 48226

Garrard Publishing Company
1607 N. Market Street
Champaign, Illinois 61820

Ginn and Company
191 Spring Street
Lexington, Massachusetts 02173

Glencoe Publishing Company, Inc.
17337 Ventura Boulevard
Encino, California 91316

Globe Book Company, Inc.
175 Fifth Avenue
New York, New York 10010

Grolier Educational Corporation
845 Third Avenue
New York, New York 10022

G. K. Hall & Company
70 Lincoln Street
Boston, Massachusetts 02111

Harcourt Brace Jovanovich
757 Third Avenue
New York, New York 10017

Harper & Row Publishers, Inc.
10 E. 53rd Street
New York, New York 10022

Hart Publishing Company
15 West 4th Street
New York, New York 10012

Hayden Book Company
50 Essex Street
Rochelle Park, New Jersey 07662

D. C. Heath and Company
125 Spring Street
Lexington, Massachusetts 02173

Holt, Rinehart and Winston, Inc.
383 Madison Avenue
New York, New York 10017

Houghton Mifflin Company
1 Beacon Street
Boston, Massachusetts 02107

Institute of Modern Languages, Inc.
2622 Pittman Drive
Silver Spring, Maryland 20910

Interact
Box 262
Lakeside, California 92040

International Film Bureau, Inc.
322 S. Michigan Avenue
Chicago, Illinois 60604

Jabberwocky
2143 Lombard Street
San Francisco, California 94123

Jamestown Press
P.O. Box 6743
Providence, Rhode Island 02904

Jenn Publications
Box 1155
Louisville, Kentucky 40201

Kennikat Press
90 South Bayles Ave.
Port Washington, New York 11050

King Features
235 East 45th Street
New York, New York 10017

Laidlaw Brothers
Thatcher and Madison Streets
River Forest, Illinois 60305

Learning Corporation of America
1350 Avenue of the Americas
New York, New York 10019

Learning Ventures
A Multimedia Division of Bantam Books
666 Fifth Avenue
New York, New York 10019

Lerner Publication Company
241 First Avenue, N.
Minneapolis, Minnesota 55401

J. B. Lippincott Company
E. Washington Square
Philadelphia, Pennsylvania 19105

Little, Brown and Company
34 Beacon Street
Boston, Massachusetts 02106

Litton Educational Publishing, Inc.
450 W. 33rd Street
New York, New York 10001

Lyons & Carnahan Division
Rand McNally & Company
8255 Central Park Avenue
Skokie, Illinois 60076

McGraw-Hill Book and Education
Services Group
1221 Avenue of the Americas
New York, New York 10020

Macmillan, Inc.
866 Third Avenue
New York, New York 10022

Mass Media Associates, Inc.
1720 Chouteau Ave.
St. Louis, Missouri 63103

Charles E. Merrill Publishing Co.
1300 Alum Creek Drive
Columbus, Ohio 43216

Midwest Publications Company, Inc.
P.O. Box 129
Troy, Michigan 48084

Miller-Brody Productions
342 Madison Avenue
New York, New York 10017

Modern Curriculum Press
13900 Prospect Road
Cleveland, Ohio 44136

William Morrow and Company, Inc.
105 Madison Avenue
New York, New York 10016

National Educational Film Center
Route Two
Finksburg, Maryland 21048

National Gallery of Art
Washington, D.C. 20565

National Textbook Company
8259 Niles Center Road
Skokie, Illinois 60076

National Union of Christian Schools
865 28th Street, S.E.
Grand Rapids, Michigan 49508

Thomas Nelson, Inc.
30 East 42nd Street
New York, New York 10017

New American Library
1301 Avenue of the Americas
New York, New York 10019

New Reader's Press
Box 131
Syracuse, New York 13210

Newbury House Publishers, Inc.
5 Warehouse Lane
Rowley, Massachusetts 01969

Noble and Noble Publishers, Inc.
1 Dag Hammarskjold Plaza
New York, New York 10017

Open Court Publishing Company
1058 Eighth Street
La Salle, Illinois 61301

Oxford University Press
200 Madison Avenue
New York, New York 10016

Parents' Magazine Press
52 Vanderbilt Avenue
New York, New York 10017

Pelican Publishing Company
630 Burmaster Street
Gretna, Louisiana 70053

Pendulum Press, Inc.
The Academic Building
Saw Mill Road
West Haven, Connecticut 06516

Penguin Books
625 Madison Avenue
New York, New York 10022

The Perfection Form Company
1000 North Second Avenue
Logan, Iowa 51546

Perspective Films
369 West Erie Street
Chicago, Illinois 60610

S. G. Phillips, Inc.
305 West 86th Street
New York, New York 10024

Pocket Books
Education Department
1230 Avenue of the Americas
New York, New York 10020

Prentice-Hall, Inc.
Englewood Cliffs, New Jersey 07632

G. P. Putnam's Sons
200 Madison Avenue
New York, New York 10016

Pyramid Films
Box 1048
Santa Monica, California 90406

Random House
201 E. 50th Street
New York, New York 10022

Reader's Digest Educational Division
Pleasantville, New York 10570

The Reading Laboratory
55 Day Street
South Norwalk, Connecticut 06854

Alan Sands Productions
565 Fifth Avenue
New York, New York 10017

Scarecrow Press, Inc.
52 Liberty St.
Metuchen, New Jersey 08840

Schocken Books
200 Madison Avenue
New York, New York 10016

Scholastic Magazines, Inc.
50 West 44th Street
New York, New York 10036

Science Research Associates, Inc.
259 E. Erie Street
Chicago, Illinois 60611

Scott, Foresman and Company
1900 E. Lake Avenue
Glenview, Illinois 60025

Silver Burdett Company
250 James Street
Morristown, New Jersey 07960

Simon and Schuster
630 Fifth Avenue
New York, New York 10020

Society for Visual Education
1345 Diversey Parkway
Chicago, Illinois 60614

Spectrum Educational Media
P.O. Box 611
Mattoon, Illinois 61938

Steck-Vaughn Company
P.O. Box 2028
Austin, Texas 78767

Teachers College Press
Columbia University
1234 Amsterdam Avenue
New York, New York 10027

Teleketics
1229 South Santee Street
Los Angeles, California 90015

Time-Life Multimedia
Time & Life Building
Room 32–48
New York, New York 10020

Troll Associates
320 Route 17
Mahwah, New Jersey 07430

The Viking Press
625 Madison Avenue
New York, New York 10022

Franklin Watts, Inc.
845 Third Avenue
New York, New York 10022

Westinghouse Learning Corporation
100 Park Avenue
New York, New York 10022

Weston Woods
Weston, Connecticut 06880

Albert Whitman & Company
560 West Lake Street
Chicago, Illinois 60606

John Wiley and Sons, Inc.
605 Third Avenue
New York, New York 10016

Winston Press
Department RG–1
25 Groveland Terrace
Minneapolis, Minnesota 55403

Winthrop Publishers, Inc.
17 Dunster Street
Cambridge, Massachusetts 02138

Wombat Productions
Little Lake
Glendale Road
Box 70
Ossining, New York 10562

Xerox Education Division
1200 High Ridge Road
Stamford, Connecticut 06902

Young Reader's Press, Inc.
A Simon and Schuster Company
1 West 39th Street
New York, New York 10018

Youth Education Systems
49 Gleason Avenue
Stamford, Connecticut 06902

Zweig Associates
20800 Beach Boulevard
Huntington Beach, California 92648

APPENDIX D

Government Resources

The United States Government has myriad resources in printed materials, as well as speakers and films, available free or at a minimal fee. Contact the various departments directly or write to the Superintendent of Documents, U.S. Government Printing Office, Washington, D.C. 20402 for information about particular areas of interest. The list of government departments below will provide you with a starting point for locating government resources.

Department of Agriculture
Fourteenth Street and Independence Ave. S.W.
Washington, D.C. 20250

Concerned with quality in food supply, rural development, and maintenance of farm income; the Forest Service and soil conservation are also among the interests of this Department; request a free copy of List 5 of current available publications and prices through the Office of Communication.

Department of Commerce
Fourteenth Street between Constitution Ave. and East Street N.W.
Washington, D.C. 20230

This department can provide information on a wide diversity of activities—the census, patents and trademarks, telecommunications systems, the Bureau of Standards, tourism, science and technology, and the ocean and atmosphere, in addition to its better-known work in international and domestic economic development and technological interests. Ask for the *Business Service Checklist* through the Superintendent of Documents.

Department of Defense
The Pentagon
Washington, D.C. 20301

Write to the Staff Assistant for Public Correspondence, Office of the Assistant Secretary of Defense (Public Affairs) for information about the various branches of the military, in addition to the Defense Advanced Research Projects Agency, which conducts research for defense security, intelligence, investigation, communication, and logistics for private industry as well as government use.

Department of Health, Education and Welfare
330 Independence Ave. S.W.
Washington, D.C. 20201

The above address will get you in touch with the Office of Human Development, concerned with the welfare of children and youth, aging adults, the handicapped, and mentally retarded. For information on education, write: Education Division, 400 Maryland S.W., Washington, D.C. 20202; information on drug and alcohol abuse, mental health, and disease control is available through Public Health Service, 5600 Fishers Lane, Rockville, Md. 20852. Publications on prenatal care, child care, smoking, drinking, child development, and many more are available through the Superintendent of Documents.

Department of Housing and Urban Development
451 Seventh Street S.W.
Washington, D.C. 20410

Write to the Publications Service Center, Room B-258, for publications on the improvement of communities and neighborhood rehabilitation for home owners and renters; also responsible for disaster assistance and insurance.

Department of the Interior
C Street between 18th and 19th Streets N.W.
Washington, D.C. 20240

Concerned with conservation, wildlife, energy, American Indians, fish and parks, land and water, reclamation.

Department of Justice
Constitution Ave and 10th Street N.W.
Washington, D.C. 20530

The Attorney General's Office with interest in criminal and civil law, civil rights, immigration and citizenship, prisons and parole, law enforcement and the FBI.

Department of Labor
200 Constitution Ave. N.W.
Washington, D.C. 20210

Concerned with the welfare, working conditions, and employment opportunities of the American wage earner.

Department of State
2201 C Street N.W.
Washington, D.C. 20520

For information about foreign policy, relationships with other countries, foreign service, embassies and ambassadors, write to the Office of Media Services, Public Correspondence Division, Room 5821, Bureau of Public Affairs, Department of State.

Department of Transportation
400 Seventh Street S.W.
Washington, D.C. 20590

Oversees federal aviation, as well as highways, railroads, traffic concerns, and urban mass transportation.

Department of Treasury
Fifteenth Street and Pennsylvania Ave. N.W.
Washington, D.C. 20220

Manufactures coins and currency and sets tax and fiscal policies.

SOURCE

1978/79 United States Government Manual
Office of the Federal Register
National Archives and Records Service
Washington, D.C. 20408

The *U.S. Government Manual* is available for $6.50 through the Superintendent of Documents, U.S. Government Printing Office, Washington, D.C.

20402. It's a 902-page document that describes the departments listed here in much greater detail, in addition to providing the names and functions of fifty-nine government agencies and some information on quasi-official agencies and a few international organizations. Addresses and telephone numbers of top personnel within these agencies and Departments are also provided. Finally, more specific information about speakers, films, publications, and other resources are given.

APPENDIX E

Contests

Like most things in this world, contests have a tendency to be transient. Although we've chosen from among the more stable and well established for this section, be sure to write well in advance of when you would like to enter students in a contest to obtain information about requirements, deadlines, and awards.

CREATIVE WRITING CONTESTS

Atlantic Monthly
"Creative Writing Contest"
8 Arlington Street
Boston, Mass. 02116

English Journal
"Spring Poetry Festival"
1111 Kenyon Road
Urbana, Ill. 61801

Guideposts Magazine
"Youth Writing Contest"
747 Third Avenue
New York, N.Y. 10017

National Council of Teachers of English Achievement in Writing Program
1111 Kenyon Road
Urbana, Ill. 61801

Poetry Society of America
Lieberman Award
15 Gramercy Park
New York, N.Y. 10003

Redbook's Young Writers' Contest
Box F-2
230 Park Avenue
New York, N.Y. 10017

Scholastic Magazines
"Creative Writing Awards"
50 West 44th Street
New York, N.Y. 10036

Seventeen Magazine
"Short Story Contest"
850 Third Avenue
New York, N.Y. 10022

Youth Magazine
"Creative Arts Awards"
1505 Race St.
Room 1203
Philadelphia, Pa. 19102

NEWSPAPER AND YEARBOOK CONTESTS

American Newspaper Publishers Association
"Most Valuable Staffer Award"
P.O. Box 17407
Dulles International Airport
Washington, D.C. 20041

National Scholastic Press Association
"Critical Evaluation"
720 Washington Ave., S.E.
University of Minnesota
Minneapolis, Minn. 55414

Columbia Scholastic Press Association
"Annual Newspaper Contest"
"Annual Yearbook-Magazine Contest"
Box 11, Central Mail Room
Columbia University
New York, N.Y. 10027

ORATORICAL CONTESTS

Improved BPO Elks of the World
"Elks Oratorical Contest"
1522 N. 16th St.
Philadelphia, Pa. 19121

Knights of Pythias
"Public Speaking Contest"
47 N. Grant St.
Stockton, Calif. 95202

National Forensic League
"National Tournament"
114 Watson St.
Ripon, Wis. 54971

MEDIA CONTESTS

"Young People's Radio Festival"
"National Young Filmmakers Festival"
Center for Understanding Media
75 Horatio Street
New York, N.Y. 10014

"The Scout Photo Scholarship Awards"
Scouting Division
Boy Scouts of America
New Brunswick, N.J. 08902

"Kodak Teenage Movie Awards" (Department 841F)
"Community Service Photography Awards" (Department 842)
Eastman Kodak Company
343 State Street
Rochester, N.Y. 14650

"Scholastic Photography Award"
50 West 44th Street
New York, N.Y. 10036

"New England Student Film Festival"
University Film Study Center
Box 275
Cambridge, Mass. 02138

"Chicago International Film Festival"
235 West Eugenie Street
Chicago, Ill. 60614

"Washington National Student Film Festival"
Gene F. Weiss, Festival Director
University of Maryland
Radio-TV-Film Division
College Park, Md. 20742

"Ann Arbor Film Festival"
George Manupelli
Box 283
Ann Arbor, Mich. 48107

"Bellevue Film Festival"
376 Bellevue Square
Bellevue, Wash. 98004

"New England Film Festival"
Larry Silverman
Boston University
Boston, Mass. 02115

"Independent Filmmakers Exposition"
Brooklyn Academy of Music
30 Lafayette Street
Brooklyn, N.Y. 11217

"International Film and TV Festival"
251 West 57th Street
New York, N.Y. 10019

"Student/Educational Film Festival"
Dr. Michael F. Stramaglia
302 State Office Building
Springfield, Ill. 62706

"Long Island International Film
Festival"
J. Arcuri Film Productions, Inc.
124 Brown Street
Mineola, N.Y. 11501

SOURCES

Bennett, John H. "A Directory of Writing Contests." *The English Journal* 64 (January 1975): 98–100.

Cromer, Nancy. "Media Award Contests for Students." *The English Journal* 64 (January 1975): 102–4.

"NAASP Advisory List of National Contests and Activities: 1977-78." *NAASP Bulletin,* September 1977, pp. 119–24.

"Prize Offers," a monthly column in *The Writer.*

APPENDIX F

It's Free

Teachers can literally inundate their classrooms with free and inexpensive materials—print and nonprint—on all manner of subjects of interest to both teachers and students. Materials available can be used for interdisciplinary units, individualized research projects, stimuli for writing projects, or just for free-time browsing for pleasure or information. The titles listed below represent only a small percentage of the hundreds of resources listed in three very good books describing free and inexpensive materials. You might want to include these in your own library.

Free and Inexpensive Learning Materials, edited by Norman R. Moore. Nashville: Division of Surveys and Field Services, George Peabody College for Teachers, 1974.

This book focuses primarily on materials to supplement information found in school textbooks which could be used as teaching aids or references. Even so, there is a wide diversity in the materials classified under nearly 100 topical headings, including family life and problems, social and political concerns, art, music, literature, and a variety of foreign countries.

1001 Valuable Things You Can Get Free, by Mort Weisinger. New York: Bantam Books, 1977.

The twenty-four categories of things you can get free listed in this book include charts, posters, maps, films, and calendars, as well as printed booklets and pamphlets on everything from gardening and building to travel and career guides.

The Catalog of Free Things, by Jeffrey Feinman and Mark Weiss. New York: William Morrow and Company, Inc., 1976.

In addition to the kinds of materials found in *1001 Valuable Things*—home, health, beauty, work, and pleasure—this book contains sections on "Plays," and "Students and Teachers." The book is also the most attractive and clearest in format and layout.

The English Journal is another source of materials through its column "Sources of Free and Inexpensive Materials." This list includes samplings from "More Sources of Free and Inexpensive Materials," by Travis Ball, *The English Journal* 65 (January 1976): 83–86.

A sampling of materials found in "free" catalogues:

CAREERS

The New Architect
American Institute of Architects
1735 New York Ave. N.W.
Washington, D.C. 20006

A Career in Astronomy
American Astronomical Society
Princeton, N.J. 08540

Realistic Counseling of High School Girls
NOW, Inc.
P.O. Box 86031
Pittsburgh, Pa. 15221

Summer Employment in Federal Agencies
U.S. Civil Service Commission
Washington, D.C. 20415

200 Ways to Put Your Talent to Work in the Health Field
National Health Council
Radio City Station
New York, N.Y. 10019

Jobs and Opportunities for Writers
Writer's Digest
Dept. WBJ
9933 Alliance Rd.
Cincinnati, Ohio 46242

Geophysics: The Earth in Space
American Geophysical Union
1707 L St. N.W.
Washington, D.C. 20036

PARENTS AND CHILDREN

Guide for the First-Time Babysitter
Johnson & Johnson
501 George St.
New Brunswick, N.J. 08903

Discipline
Involvement Circulation Dept.
41 Madison Ave.
Toronto, Ontario, Canada
M5R 2S2
25¢ for postage and handling

How Children Develop Intellectually
Publications
National Association for Retarded Citizens
P.O. Box 6109
Arlington, Tex. 76011
25¢ for postage and handling

Teens—Are Your Parents . . . Widowed? Divorced? Separated? Never Married?
Parents Without Partners, Inc.
Suite 1000
7910 Woodmont Ave.
Washington, D.C. 20014

Children and Television: An ACT Bibliography
Action for Children's Television
46 Austin St.
Newtonville, Mass. 02160
25¢ for postage and handling

Mothers at Work
Metropolitan Life
Health and Welfare Division
1 Madison Ave.
New York, N.Y. 10010

Questions and Answers
National Clearinghouse for Drug Abuse Information
Box 1080
Washington, D.C. 20013

Publications Catalog
Planned Parenthood-World Population
810 7th Ave.
New York, N.Y. 10019

TRAVEL AND FOREIGN COUNTRIES

Art Museums in America
The American Assembly
Columbia University
New York, N.Y. 10027

The Battle of Gettysburg
Great Smoky Mountains National Park
Rocky Mountain National Park
Grand Teton National Park
Banff and Jasper National Parks
Glacier National Park
California

Comprehensive Communications
P.O. Box 385
Scarsdale, N.Y. 10583
auto tape tours and pamphlets

Armenia
Kiev
Leningrad
Intourist Office
45 East 49 St.
New York, N.Y. 10017

Indians of New Mexico
Tourist Division
New Mexico Department of Development
113 Washington
Sante Fe, N.M. 87503

Getting Around Overseas: Europe and the Mediterranean
Getting Around Overseas: Caribbean, Mexico, Central and South America
A T & T Long Lines
Room 843
5 World Trade Center
New York, N.Y. 10048
Include SASE

United States Customs and You
Department of Treasury
Bureau of Customs
Washington, D.C. 20226

Your Vacation Checklist
Kemper Insurance Co.
Advertising and Public Affairs Dept.
Long Grove, Ill. 60049

Kit on Denmark
Danish Information Office
Consulate General of Denmark
280 Park Ave.
New York, N.Y. 10017

Facts About Germany
Lufthansa German Airlines
1640 Hempstead Tpke.
East Meadow, N.Y. 11554

All You Have to Know About American Youth Hostels
American Youth Hostels, Inc.
National Headquarters
Delaplane, Va. 22025

Pilgrims' Map of the Holy Land
Israel Government Tourist Office
488 Madison Ave.
New York, N.Y. 10022

Summer Jobs in Europe
Council on International Educational Exchange
777 United Nations Plaza
New York, N.Y. 10017

Au Pair Jobs Abroad
European Job Chart
Leads on Jobs Abroad
Mademoiselle Magazine
Box 3389
Grand Central Station
New York, N.Y. 10017
35¢ each

WOMEN

Affirmative Action Resources #1
Project on the Status and Education of Women
Association of American Colleges
1818 R Street N.W.
Washington, D.C. 20009

The Feminist Press Catalog
The Feminist Press
SUNY/College at Old Westbury
P.O. Box 334
Old Westbury, N.Y. 11568
Include large SASE

The Independent Years
The Life Cycle Center
Kimberly-Clark Corp.
Neenah, Wis. 54956

National Network of Local Resource Centers for Women
Catalyst
5 East 82 Street
New York, N.Y. 10025

FILMS

Extension Service Catalog of Free Films and Slide Sets
National Gallery of Art
Extension Service
Washington, D.C. 20565

Free-Loan Film Catalog
Modern Talking Picture Service, Inc.
2323 New Hyde Park Rd.
New Hyde Park, N.Y. 10040

Motion Pictures from Union Carbide
Union Carbide Corporation
270 Park Ave.
New York, N.Y. 10017

Catalog of Free Films
Association-Sterling Films
600 Grand Ave.
Ridgefield, N.J. 07657

PICTURES AND POSTERS

Documents from America's Past
Consumer Information Center
Pueblo, Colo. 81009
Catalog of reproductions of documents available through the National Achieves.

United States Map
Advertising Manager
Union Pacific Railroad Co.
1416 Dodge St.
Omaha, Neb. 68179

Holy Land Map
Israel Ministry of Tourism
488 Madison Ave.
New York, N.Y. 10022

The Teaching of Shakespeare 4-Color Literary Posters
Cliffs Notes
Mr. James L. McKee
Faculty Coordinator
P.O. Box 80728
Lincoln. Neb. 68501
free requested on school letterhead

Empire State Building Map
Empire State Bldg. Company
350 Fifth Ave.
New York, N.Y. 10001

Plant Hardiness Zone Map, #M814
Publications
Office of Communication
U.S. Department of Agriculture
Washington, D.C. 20250

Think Orange Poster
Sunkist
P.O. Box 7888
Van Nuys, Calif. 91409

A Hero Ain't Nothing But a Sandwich
Mary Dove
Working
Alive
All God's Dangers: The Life of Nate Shaw
Avon Books
Educational Department
959 Eighth Avenue
New York, N.Y. 10019
posters

LANGUAGE AND LITERATURE

Appalbrochure
Appalshop, Inc.
P.O. Box 743
Whitesburg, Ken. 41858

Handbook of Debate Rules
Argo Community High School
7329 West 63rd Street
Summit, Ill. 60501
25¢ for postage

Guide to College Writing Programs
Associated Writing Programs
Washington College
Chestertown, Md. 21620

Educator's Guide to Creative Audio Tape Techniques
Audio Magnetics Corporation
P.O. Box 140
Cardena, Calif. 90248

Teacher's Guides:
Alive
Working
Watership Down
A Hero Ain't Nothing But a Sandwich
A Minicourse on Death
Avon Books
Educational Department
959 Eighth Avenue
New York, N.Y. 10019

Media Survival Kit: An AV Selection Guide
Baker and Taylor Company
Audio-Visual Services Division
P.O. Box 230
Momence, Ill. 60954

Developing Awareness Through Poetry
Cultural Diversity and Ethnic Alienation
Perspectives on Criminal Justice
Center for Twentieth Century Studies
The University of Wisconsin at Milwaukee
Milwaukee, Wis. 53201

Catalog of Plays and Stage Crew Guide
I. E. Clark
P.O. Box 246
Schulenburg, Tex. 78956

Starting Early: Books on Ecology-Related Themes for Children
Ecology Center
2179 Allston Way
Berkeley, Calif. 94704
SASE—legal size

From Cover to Cover: Publishing in Your Classroom
Encyclopaedia Britannica Educational Corporation
Instructional Services Department
425 North Michigan Avenue
Chicago, Ill. 60611

Instructors Guides:
The Best Short Stories of Jack London
Counterparts: Classic and Contemporary American Short Stories
Death Wish
Eight Short Novels
Isaac Asimov's Short Science Fiction
Fawcett Publications, Inc.
Education Department
Greenwich, Conn. 06830

Making a Dictionary
Macmillan Publishing Company
School Division
100 Front and Brown Streets
Riverside, N.J. 08075

Easy-to-Read Books for Teenagers
New York Public Library
Young Adult Services
8 East 40th Street
New York, N.Y. 10016
25¢

How to Produce a High School Magazine
Scholastic Publications
Eve Sennett
50 West 44th Street
New York, N.Y. 10036
SASE–#10

Creative Teaching: A Guide to Making Your Own Instructional Materials
Seal, Inc.
Derby, Conn. 06418

What's New in Video Equipment
H. Wilson Corporation
55 West Taft Drive
South Holland, Ill. 60473

When ordering materials, expect some delay in getting a response (sometimes six to ten weeks), and expect some responses to be that the item is no longer available.

For additional sources of free and inexpensive materials, contact state and local government agencies, educational divisions of businesses and industries, and college and university extension services.

APPENDIX G

A Selected Bibliography in the Teaching of English

ISSUES AND APPROACHES

Brown, George I. *Human Teaching for Human Learning.* New York: Viking Press, 1971.

Bruner, Jerome. *On Knowing: Essays for the Left Hand.* Cambridge, Mass.: Harvard University Press, 1962.

Dennison, George. *The Lives of Children.* New York: Vintage Books, 1969.

Dixon, John. *Growth through English: Set in the Perspective of the Seventies.* Urbana, Ill.: National Council of Teachers of English, 1975.

Farrell, Edmund. *Deciding the Future: A Forecast of Responsibilities of Secondary Teachers of English, 1970–2000 A.D.* Urbana, Ill.: NCTE, 1971.

Gartner, Alan, Mary Kohler, and Frank Riessman. *Children Teach Children.* New York: Harper & Row, 1971.

Ginott, Haim. *Between Parent and Teenager.* New York: Avon, 1971.

Ginsburg, Herbert. *Myth of the Deprived Child: Poor, Children's Intellect and Education.* Englewood Cliffs, N.J.: Prentice-Hall, 1972.

Greer, Mary, and Bonnie Rubenstein. *Will the Real Teacher Please Stand Up?* Pacific Palisades, Calif.: Goodyear, 1972.

Harvey, Robert C., and Carole Kirkton. *Annotated Index to the English Journal 1964–1970.* Urbana, Ill.: NCTE, 1971.

Hawley, Robert C., and Isabel L. Hawley. *Human Values in the Classroom: A Handbook for Teachers.* New York: Hart, 1975.

Hillocks, George Jr. *Alternatives in English: A Critical Appraisal of Elective Programs.* Urbana, Ill.: ERIC/RCS, 1972.

Hipple, Theodore, ed. *The Future of Education: 1970–2000.* Pacific Palisades, Calif.: Goodyear, 1974.

Hipple, Theodore. *Teaching English in the Secondary Schools.* New York: Macmillan, 1973.

Illich, Ivan. *Deschooling Society.* New York: Harper & Row, 1971.

Insel, Deborah. "Foxfire in the City," *The English Journal,* September 1975, pp. 36–38.

Judy, Stephen N. *Explorations in the Teaching of Secondary English.* New York: Dodd, Mead/Harper & Row, 1974, 1980.

Kozol, Jonathan. *Free Schools.* Boston: Houghton Mifflin, 1972.

Marshall, Sybil. *An Experiment in Education.* Cambridge: Cambridge University Press, 1963.

Moffett, James. *A Student-Centered Language Arts Curriculum: Grades K–13.* Boston: Houghton Mifflin, 1968.

Moffett, James. *Teaching the Universe of Discourse.* Boston: Houghton Mifflin, 1968.

Moore, Eva. "How to, Not What: A Course in Choosing." *The English Journal,* November 1975, pp. 40–45.

Muller, Herbert. *The Uses of English.* New York: Holt, Rinehart and Winston, 1967.

Postman, Neil, and Charles Weingartner. *The School Book.* New York: Dell, 1973.

Postman, Neil, and Charles Weingartner. *Teaching as a Subversive Activity.* New York: Delacorte Press, 1969.

Raths, Louis E., Merrill Harmin, and Sidney B. Simon. *Values and Teaching.* Columbus: Charles E. Merrill, 1966.

Repo, Satu, ed. *This Book Is About Schools.* New York: Vintage, 1970.

Rinkel, Margaret. "A Kaleidoscopic View of Individualization." *The English Journal,* October 1975, pp. 27–39.

Rogers, Carl. *Freedom to Learn.* Columbus: Charles E. Merrill, 1969.

Shuman, R. Baird, ed. *Creative Approaches to the Teaching of English: Secondary.* Itasca, Ill.: Peacock Publishers, 1974.

Simon, Sidney. *Values Clarification: A Handbook of Practical Strategies for Teachers and Students.* New York: Hart, 1972.

Styles, Ken, and Gray Cavanagh. "How to Design a Multilevel Course of Study to Bring About Quality Learning." *The English Journal,* February 1975, pp. 73–75.

Summerfield, Geoffrey. *English for the Secondary School.* London: Batsford, 1965.

Summerfield, Geoffrey. *Topics in English.* London: Batsford, 1965.

Sweet, Johanna. "An Experience Portfolio." *The English Journal,* September 1976, pp. 50–51.

Whitehead, Frank. *The Disappearing Dais.* London: Chatto and Windus, 1966.

Wigginton, Eliot. *The Foxfire Book.* Garden City: Anchor Books, 1972.

EVALUATION

Doggett, Maran. "The ABC Affair." *The English Journal,* March 1975, pp. 72–73.

Hoffman, Banesh. *The Tyranny of Testing.* New York: Collier Books, 1962.

Kirschenbaum, Howard, Sidney B. Simon, and Rodney W. Napier. *Wad 'Ja Get?* New York: Hart, 1971.

Lewis, Kenneth. "Putting the Hidden Curriculum of Grading to Work." *The English Journal,* March 1975, pp. 82–84.

Mager, Robert. *Preparing Instructional Objectives.* Palo Alto, Calif.: Fearon, 1962.

National Council of Teachers of English. *The Use and Abuse of Standardized Tests—A First Aid Kit for the Walking Wounded.* Urbana, Ill.: NCTE, 1973.

Nystrand, Martin. "The Politics of Rank Ordering." *The English Journal,* March 1975, pp. 42–45.

Wright, John L. "Learning Objectives and the Teaching of English," *The English Journal,* April 1976, pp. 32–36.

COMPOSITION

Britton, James, et al. *The Development of Writing Abilities 11–18.* London: Macmillan Education, 1975.

Britton, James, ed. *Talking and Writing.* London: Methuen, 1967.

Brown, J. et al. *Free Writing! A Group Approach.* Rochelle Park, N.J.: Hayden Book Co., 1977.

Brown, Rosellen, et al. *The Whole Word Catalog.* New York: Virgil Books, 1972.

Christensen, Francis. *Notes Toward a New Rhetoric.* New York: Harper, 1967.

Cooper, Charles R., and Lee Odell. *Evaluating Writing: Describing, Measuring, Judging.* Urbana, Ill.: NCTE, 1977.

Elbow, Peter. *Writing Without Teachers.* New York: Oxford University Press, 1973.

Emig, Janet. *The Composing Process of Twelfth Graders.* Urbana, Ill.: NCTE, 1971.

Evertts, Eldonna L., ed. *Explorations in Children's Writing.* Urbana, Ill.: NCTE, 1970.

Gibson, Walker. *Tough, Sweet, and Stuffy.* Bloomington: Indiana University Press, 1966.

Hawley, Robert C., Sidney B. Simon, and D. D. Britton. *Composition for Personal Growth.* New York: Hart, 1973.

Holbrook, David. *Children's Writing.* Cambridge: Cambridge University Press, 1967.

Koch, Carl, and James M. Brazil. *Strategies for Teaching the Composition Process.* Urbana, Ill.: NCTE, 1978.

Koch, Kenneth. *Wishes, Lies, and Dreams.* New York: Vintage Books, 1970.

Macrorie, Ken. *Telling Writing.* New York: Hayden, 1970.

Macrorie, Ken. *Uptaught.* New York: Hayden, 1970.

Macrorie, Ken. *Writing to Be Read.* New York: Hayden, 1968.

Martin, Nancy, et al. *Writing and Learning Across the Curriculum 11–16.* London: Schools Council Publications, 1976.

Norton, James H., and Francis Gretton. *Writing Incredibly Short Plays, Poems, Stories.* New York: Harcourt Brace Jovanovich, Inc., 1972.

O'Hare, Frank. *Sentence Combining: Improving Student Writing without Formal Grammar Instruction.* Urbana, Ill.: NCTE, 1971.

Strunk, William, and E. B. White. *The Elements of Style.* New York: Macmillan, 1973.

Turabian, Kate. *Guide to the Writing of Term and Research Papers.* Chicago: Phoenix, 1974.

Weiss, Harvey. *How to Make Your Own Books.* New York: Crowell, 1974.

Young, Richard, Alton Becker, and Kenneth Pike. *Rhetoric: Discovery and Change.* New York: Harcourt, 1970.

LANGUAGE

Barnes, Douglas, James Britton, and Harold Rosen. *Language, the Learner, and the School.* London: Penguin, 1970.

Bernard, J. R. *A Short Guide to Traditional Grammar.* Sydney University Press (International Scholarly Book Services, Forest Grove, Oregon), 1975.

Braddock, Richard, Richard Lloyd-Jones, and Lowell Schoer. *Research in Written Composition.* Urbana, Ill.: NCTE, 1963.

Britton, James. *Language and Learning.* Urbana, Ill.: NCTE, 1970.

Chomsky, Noam. *Language and Mind.* New York: Harcourt, 1968.

Committee on the Students' Right to Their Own Language. *Students' Right to Their Own Language: A Selected, Annotated Bibliography.* Urbana, Ill.: NCTE, 1973.

Dillard, J. L. *Black English.* New York: Random House, 1972.

Doughty, Peter, John Pearce, and Geoffrey Thornton. *Language in Use.* Lexington, Mass.: Ginn, 1972.

Elgin, Suzette Haden. *Primer of Transformational Grammar for Rank Beginners.* Urbana, Ill.: NCTE, 1975.

Elgin, Suzette Haden. *What Is Linguistics?* Englewood Cliffs, N.J.: Prentice-Hall, 1973.

Farb, Peter. *Word Play: What Happens When People Talk.* New York: Bantam Books, 1973.

Fowler, H. W. *A Dictionary of Modern English Usage* (2nd ed.). London and New York: Oxford University Press, 1965.

Friend, Beverly. "Strange Bedfellows: Science Fiction, Linguistics, and Education." *The English Journal,* October 1973, pp. 998–1003.

Hall, Edward. *The Silent Language.* New York: Doubleday, 1959.

Hayakawa, S. I. *Language in Thought and Action.* New York: Harcourt Brace Jovanovich, 1972.

Haynes, Elizabeth. "Using Research in Preparing to Teach Writing." *The English Journal,* January 1978, pp. 82–88.

Joos, Martin. *The Five Clocks.* New York: Harcourt Brace and World, 1947.

Labov, William. *Language of the Inner City.* Philadelphia: University of Pennsylvania Press, 1972.

Labov, William. *The Study of Non-Standard English.* Urbana, Ill.: NCTE, 1970.

Lester, Mark. *Constructing an English Grammar.* New York: Random House, 1973.

Lester, Mark. *Words and Sentences.* New York: Random House, 1973.

Malmstrom, Jean. *Grammar Basics: A Reading/Writing Approach.* Rochelle Park, N.J.: Hayden Books, 1977.

Malmstrom, Jean, and Janice Lee. *Teaching Linguistically, Principles and Practices for High Schools.* New York: Appleton-Century-Crofts, 1971.

Mitchell, Diana. "Children's Literature in the Junior High? Of Course!" *The English Journal,* April 1977, 62–64.

Mueller, Lavonne. "The Word Museum." *The English Journal,* May 1974, pp. 75–78.

Reynolds, William. *Dialects in America.* New York: Random House, 1973.

Sherwin, Stephen. *Four Problems in Teaching English: A Critique of Research.* Urbana, Ill.: NCTE, 1969.

Shipley, Joseph. *Wordplay.* New York: Hawthorne Books, 1972.

Shuy, Roger W. *Discovering American Dialects.* Urbana, Ill.: NCTE, 1967.

Smitherman, Geneva. *Talkin' and Testifyin': The Language of Black America.* Boston: Houghton Mifflin, 1977.

Taylor, Ruth. "Linguistic Experiment in the English Class: Easy, Interesting Exercises to Do." *The English Journal,* December 1976, pp. 45–51.

LITERATURE

Bleich, David. *Readings and Feelings: An Introduction to Subjective Criticism.* Urbana, Ill: NCTE, 1975.

Booth, Wayne. *The Rhetoric of Fiction.* Chicago: University of Chicago Press, 1961.

Burton, Dwight. *Literature Study in the High School* (3d ed.). New York: Holt, Rinehart and Winston, 1970.

Ciardi, John. *How Does a Poem Mean?* Boston: Houghton Mifflin, 1960.

Donelson, Ken, ed. *Books for You: A Booklist for Senior High Students.* Urbana, Ill.: NCTE, 1976.

Duke, Charles. *Creative Dramatics and English Teaching.* Urbana, Ill.: NCTE, 1974.

Dunning, Stephen. *Teaching Literature to Adolescents.* Glenview, Ill.: Scott, Foresman, 1974.

Fader, Daniel, and Elton McNeil. *Hooked on Books: Program and Proof.* New York: Berkeley Medallion, 1966, 1968, 1975.

Forster, E. M. *Aspects of the Novel.* New York: Harcourt, Brace and World, 1947.

Harding, W. D. *Response to Literature.* Urbana, Ill.: NCTE, 1968.

Holland, Norman. *The Dynamics of Literary Response.* New York: Norton, 1975.

Klonsky, Milton. *Speaking Pictures: A Gallery of Pictorial Poetry from the Sixteenth Century to the Present.* New York: Harmony Books, 1975.

Meade, Richard, and Robert Small, eds. *Literature for Adolescents: Selection and Use.* Columbus: Charles E. Merrill, 1973.

Peck, Richard. *Transitions: A Literary Casebook.* New York: Random House, 1974.

Purves, Alan, ed. *How Porcupines Make Love: Notes on a Response-Centered Curriculum.* Boston: Ginn, 1973.

Purves, Alan, and Richard Beach. *Literature and the Reader: Research in Response to Literature, Reading Interests and the Teaching of Literature.* Urbana, Ill.: NCTE, 1972.

Reid, Virginia M., ed. *Reading Ladders for Human Relations* (5th ed.). Washington, D.C.: American Council on Education, 1972.

Rosenblatt, Louise. *Literature as Exploration* (revised edition). New York: Noble and Noble, 1967.

MEDIA

Allen, Don. *The Electric Humanities.* Dayton, Ohio: Pflaum, 1971.

Clarke, John H. "One Minute of Hate: Multimedia Misuse Pre-1984." *The English Journal,* October 1974, pp. 50–51.

Giblin, Thomas. *Popular Media and the Teaching of English.* Pacific Palisades, Calif.: Goodyear, 1972.

Laybourn, Kit, ed. *Doing the Media.* New York: Barnes and Noble, 1972.

McLuhan, Marshall, Kathryn Hutchon, and Eric McLuhan. *City as Classroom.* Agincourt, Ontario: The Book Society of Canada Limited, 1977.

Maynard, Richard A. *The Celluloid Curriculum.* New York: Hayden, 1971.

Postman, Neil. *Television and the Teaching of English.* Urbana, Ill.: NCTE, 1961.

Valdes, Joan, and Jeanne Crow. *The Media Works.* Dayton, Ohio: Pflaum, 1973.

READING

Committee on the Right to Read. *Students' Right to Read.* Urbana, Ill.: NCTE, 1962.

Fader, Daniel. *The Naked Children.* New York: Macmillan, 1971.

Goodman, Kenneth, and Olive Niles. *Reading: Process and Program.* Urbana, Ill.: NCTE, 1972.

Herber, Harold. *Teacher Reading in the Content Areas.* Englewood Cliffs, N.J.: Prentice-Hall, 1970.

Kohl, Herbert. *Reading, How To.* New York: Dutton, 1973.

Lamberg, Walter. "Helping Reluctant Readers Help Themselves: Interest Inventories." *The English Journal,* November 1977, pp. 42–43.

Ruddell, Robert. *Accountability and Reading Instruction.* Urbana, Ill.: NCTE, 1973.

Shepherd, David. *Comprehensive High School Reading Methods.* New York: Charles E. Merrill, 1973.

Smith, Frank, ed. *Psycholinguistics and Reading.* New York: Holt, Rinehart and Winston, 1973.

Smith, Frank. *Understanding Reading.* New York: Holt, Rinehart and Winston, 1971.

Wardhaugh, Ronald. *Reading: A Linguistic Perspective.* New York: Harcourt, 1969.

Winkeljohann, Sister Rosemary, ed. *The Politics of Reading: Point-Counterpoint.* Urbana, Ill.: IRA and ERIC, 1973.

INDEX

Note that each chapter's content also is indexed under the title of the chapter; the chapter titles are italicized.